Social Media for Strategic Communication

Social Media for Strategic Communication

Creative Strategies and Research-Based Applications

Karen Freberg
University of Louisville

Los Angeles | London | New Delhi
Singapore | Washington DC | Melbourne

FOR INFORMATION:

SAGE Publications, Inc.
2455 Teller Road
Thousand Oaks, California 91320
E-mail: order@sagepub.com

SAGE Publications Ltd.
1 Oliver's Yard
55 City Road
London EC1Y 1SP
United Kingdom

SAGE Publications India Pvt. Ltd.
B 1/I 1 Mohan Cooperative Industrial Area
Mathura Road, New Delhi 110 044
India

SAGE Publications Asia-Pacific Pte. Ltd.
3 Church Street
#10-04 Samsung Hub
Singapore 049483

Printed in the United States of America

ISBN: 978-1-5063-8710-9

Acquisitions Editor: Terri Accomazzo
Editorial Assistant: Sarah Wilson
Production Editor: Bennie Clark Allen
Copy Editor: Melinda Masson
Typesetter: C&M Digitals (P) Ltd.
Proofreader: Annie Lubinsky
Indexer: Molly Hall
Cover Designer: Janet Kiesel
Marketing Manager: Liz Thornton

This book is printed on acid-free paper.

MIX
Paper from
responsible sources
FSC® C008955

20 21 22 10 9 8 7 6 5 4

BRIEF CONTENTS

Foreword   xiii

About the Author   xix

PART I • FOUNDATION FOR CREATING A STRATEGIC MINDSET   **1**

Chapter 1 • Introduction to Social Media: An Art and Science   3

Chapter 2 • Ethical and Legal Fundamentals in Social Media   27

Chapter 3 • Personal and Professional Branding   47

Chapter 4 • Industry Qualifications and Roles   67

Chapter 5 • Research in Social Media: Monitoring, Listening, and Analysis   89

PART II • UNDERSTANDING SOCIAL MEDIA STRATEGY (CREATIVE AND SCIENTIFIC APPROACHES)   **109**

Chapter 6 • Strategic Planning for Social Media   111

Chapter 7 • Strategic Writing for Social Media   137

Chapter 8 • Audience Segmentation and Analysis   161

Chapter 9 • Creating, Managing, and Curating Content   185

Chapter 10 • Measurement, Evaluation, Budget, and Calendar   205

PART III • APPLICATION AND FUTURE CONSIDERATIONS   **225**

Chapter 11 • How Social Media Is Applied: Exploring Different Specializations, Part I   227

Chapter 12 • How Social Media Is Applied: Exploring Different Specializations, Part II   253

Chapter 13 • What Does the Social Media World Have That Is New?   275

Glossary   291

Index   297

DETAILED CONTENTS

Foreword   xiii

About the Author   xix

PART I • FOUNDATION FOR CREATING A STRATEGIC MINDSET   1

Chapter 1 • Introduction to Social Media: An Art and Science   3

Learning Objectives   3

Humans of Social Media   3

Introduction   5

How Do We Define Social Media?   6

How Has Social Media Evolved?   11

   The Current State of Social Media   11

   Who "Owns" Social Media?   12

Using Social Media Strategically   15

   Which Social Media Platforms Should I Use?   15

   Working in Social Media   19

Bridging the Science and Practice of Social Media   19

   What Can Science Tell Us About Social Media?   19

   How Is Social Media Like a Practice?   20

   How Can We Bridge Science and Art Effectively?   22

Chapter Summary   23

Thought Questions   24

Exercises   24

References   24

Chapter 2 • Ethical and Legal Fundamentals in Social Media   27

Learning Objectives   27

Humans of Social Media   27

Introduction   29

What Is Ethics?   31

   Additional Deadly Sins of Social Media   33

Legal Fundamentals   35

   Employees and Personal Branding Mishaps   36

Social Media Policies   41

Chapter Summary   43

Thought Questions   43

Exercises   44

References   44

Chapter 3 • Personal and Professional Branding   **47**

Learning Objectives   47

Humans of Social Media   47

Introduction   49

What Is a Personal Brand?   49

     What Are the Components of a Personal Brand?   51

     Types of Personal Brands   53

Benefits and Challenges for Personal Brands   53

How to Establish a Personal Brand   54

     Skills Needed to Showcase Personal Brand Effectively   57

Chapter Summary   64

Thought Questions   64

Exercises   64

References   65

Chapter 4 • Industry Qualifications and Roles   **67**

Learning Objectives   67

Humans of Social Media   67

Introduction   70

Who Hires Social Media Professionals?   70

Where to Work in Social Media   71

Definition of Key Social Media Roles   73

     Social Media Community Manager Versus Social Media Manager   74

     Social Media Coordinator   75

     Social Media Strategist   77

     Content Creator   77

     Multimedia/Video Producer   78

     Writer/Editor   83

     Other Social Media Roles   83

How Much Do Social Media Professionals Get Paid?   84

Chapter Summary   87

Thought Questions   87

Exercises   87

References   87

Chapter 5 • Research in Social Media: Monitoring, Listening, and Analysis   **89**

Learning Objectives   89

Humans of Social Media   89

Introduction   91

Importance of Research for Social Media and Strategic Communication   91

Why Do We Need Research in Social Media?   95

What Are the Differences Between Monitoring and
Listening in Social Media?   96
    Benefits of Monitoring and Listening   97
    Types of Metrics   99
    Implementing a Monitoring and Listening Plan   100

Platform-Based Metrics, Tools and Services, and KPIs   101

What Is the Bridge Between Monitoring and Listening?   102

Tying Everything Together With Analysis   103

Dos and Don'ts in Social Media Research and Analysis   106

Chapter Summary   108

Thought Questions   108

Exercises   108

References   108

PART II • UNDERSTANDING SOCIAL MEDIA STRATEGY (CREATIVE AND SCIENTIFIC APPROACHES)   109

Chapter 6 • Strategic Planning for Social Media   111

Learning Objectives   111

Humans of Social Media   111

Introduction   113

What Is a Strategic Plan?   114

Components of a Strategic Plan   115
    Background Information   116
    Brand Voice   116
    Vision and Mission   116
    Environmental Scan Analysis   118
    Client or Company in Focus   119
    Social Media Communication Audit   122
    Situational Analysis   128
    SWOT   128
    Goals   130
    Objectives   130
    Key Audience Members   131
    Strategies and Tactics   132
    Evaluation   133
    Budget   133
    Calendar   135

Final Words of Wisdom and Recommendations   135

Chapter Summary   135

Thought Questions   135

Exercises   136

References   136

Chapter 7: Strategic Writing for Social Media   **137**

Learning Objectives   137

Humans of Social Media   137

Introduction   139

Content Creation Versus Content Curation   142

Understanding the Difference Between Tone and Voice   143

    How Do You Find Your Brand Voice in Your Writing Style?   144

    Types of Writing Styles for Social Media   148

    Common Writing Mistakes on Social Media   154

Best Practices for Social Media Writing   156

Chapter Summary   159

Thought Questions   159

Exercises   159

References   159

Chapter 8 • Audience Segmentation and Analysis   **161**

Learning Objectives   161

Humans of Social Media   161

Introduction   163

    What Is Audience Segmentation?   163

Types of Audiences   166

Communities, Influencers, and Creators   167

    What Is an Influencer?   170

    Engaging With Influencers   172

    Identifying False Influencers   174

    Creators   176

    Ambassadors   176

    Trolls or Haters   178

Campaigns Using Audience Segmentation   179

Best Practices   181

Chapter Summary   182

Thought Questions   183

Exercises   183

References   183

Chapter 9 • Creating, Managing, and Curating Content   **185**

Learning Objectives   185

Humans of Social Media   185

Introduction   187

Overview of Content Marketing   187

    Definition of Content Marketing   188

    Alignment of Content   189

Types of Content Media   197

Tools to Create Content   199

Curating Content   200

Best Practices   202

Chapter Summary   203

Thought Questions   203

Exercises   204

References   204

Chapter 10 • Measurement, Evaluation, Budget, and Calendar   **205**

Learning Objectives   205

Humans of Social Media   205

Introduction   208

Measurement and Evaluation   208

    Importance of Measurement and Evaluation in Social Media   208
    Importance of Having a Measurement Strategy   211
    Outcomes   212

Budget   216

    Areas to Invest in Your Budget   216
    Metrics to Consider for Budgets on Social Media   217

Further Considerations for Measurement, Evaluation, and Budget   222

Chapter Summary   223

Thought Questions   224

Exercises   224

References   224

PART III • APPLICATION AND FUTURE CONSIDERATIONS   **225**

Chapter 11 • How Social Media Is Applied: Exploring Different Specializations, Part I   **227**

Learning Objectives   227

Introduction   227
    How Social Media Is Applied   227

Humans of Social Media: *Social Media and Entertainment*   228

Overview of Social Media and Entertainment   229

Humans of Social Media: *Social Media and Crisis Communication*   232

Overview of Social Media and Crisis Communication   233

Humans of Social Media: *Social Media and Journalism*   239

Overview of Social Media and Journalism   240
    Cases Involving Social Media and Journalism   241
    Best Practices and Recommendations   241

Humans of Social Media: *Social Media and Sports*   242

Overview of Social Media and Sports   243

Chapter Summary   247

Thought Questions 247

Exercises 249

References 250

Chapter 12 • How Social Media Is Applied: Exploring Different Specializations, Part II 253

Learning Objectives 253

Introduction 253

Humans of Social Media: *Social Media and Social Care* 254

Overview of Social Media and Social Care 254

    Best Practices for Social Care 256

Humans of Social Media: *Social Media and Nonprofits* 258

Overview of Social Media and Nonprofits 259

    Best Practices for Nonprofits 261

Humans of Social Media: *Social Media and Health Care* 262

Overview of Social Media and Health Care 263

    Best Practices for Health Care Professionals 265

Humans of Social Media: *Social Media and International Campaigns* 266

Overview of Social Media and International Campaigns 267

    Best Practices for International Campaigns 270

Chapter Summary 271

Thought Questions 271

Exercises 272

References 272

Chapter 13 • What Does the Social Media World Have That Is New? 275

Learning Objectives 275

Introduction 275

Current (So Far) State of Social Media 276

    Future Trends and Directions 278

    Students to Students: Advice From the Social Media Classroom Seat 283

Final Words of Wisdom and Recommendations 286

Chapter Summary 287

Thought Questions 288

Exercises 288

References 288

Glossary 291

Index 297

FOREWORD

We have heard it all in the social media space over the years:

- Social media jobs are just a phase. They will not be around forever.

- There's math in social media? I did not sign up for that!

- Analytics are too intimidating to me!

- All you do every day is tweet, snap, and post on Insta, right?

- You do not need a book to learn about social media. Once it's published, it's irrelevant.

Let's clarify these stereotypes once and for all. Yes, we have all heard these points in and out of the classroom. However, I am here to tell you they are not true. You can have a long-standing career in social media. We do more than just post updates—that is the surface-level view of social media. A lot has to happen below the surface to bring these updates to light. Analytics are your friends—they help to identify trends and potential issues that could save time and money, and can be used to justify the work and proposed strategies in moving forward. Interns are great to have on board to give insights on social media, but it is also important to listen to and integrate different perspectives. Just because someone is young, it does not mean he or she is an expert in the use of strategic social media platforms. However, most interns coming into the workplace are getting the training, experience, and education to be strategic in social media, which is very exciting. Plus, interns are coming into the workplace with more experience in classes and internships, and with more of an entrepreneurial drive to their work, than ever before. Last but not least, books can provide a more sustainable view of social media that can build on a strategic mindset for how to approach social media.

You may be asking, "Is there a book that does this?" The answer is yes. This one.

The overall goal of *Social Media for Strategic Communication* is to help rising and established professionals in the field to create a strategic mindset for social media activities, tools, audiences, conversations, and relationships. Social media is the hub of communication, integrating various disciplines and communities to formulate new knowledge, connections, and experiences virtually. Social media has become a rising area of focus for public relations, brand management, marketing, journalism, communication, computer science, and psychology, among other disciplines.

Again, one common question seems to arise in most social media classes: To use a book on social media or not to use a book on social media—that's always the question. With a field that changes every day, there are many difficulties in keeping up with the trends. Once a book is published, it goes out of date, right? This only happens if the book is focused on platform features that are quickly made obsolete or on case studies like common digital folklore (e.g., Oreo's tweet from the 2013 Super Bowl during the blackout). The profession of social media is a living, breathing, and constantly adapting area of study and practice that deserves to have a concentration and book dedicated to not just the new shiny objects but also the strategies, behaviors, and mindset that connect everything together.

Social media, like all disciplines, has some consistent features and attributes. Social media in many ways is both an art and a science, working together to bring forth an integrated and hybrid approach for the profession. Most books that cover social media focus only on its practice and execution, while others focus on theory. Other books skim over areas the authors are not comfortable covering, but none has been able to address all of the aspects that people want to see in social media. I did not just want to write a book about social media. Instead, I wanted to write *the* book about social media. No universal or dedicated book has been able to connect all of its different facets. This book hopes to achieve that and be a catalyst for shaping and changing the field to be more interconnected and transdisciplinary.

Social Media for Strategic Communication embraces all of these challenges head-on to make sure students have a comprehensive view of the strategic approach to social media. Research, practice, case studies, and insights from professionals are included in each chapter, creating a thorough 360-degree perspective on strategic social media practices.

BEHIND THE SCENES

Reading a book that is outdated and not connected to practice and what's happening in the industry is frustrating. You are not the only one who has experienced this. Before writing *Social Media for Strategic Communication*, I too was frustrated with the quality of the books available for professors and students. Some were too elementary, some too complicated, and others just had no connection to what was actually happening in research or practice. I truly felt like Goldilocks—no book felt "just right."

As each year went on, my frustrations became more vocal. I felt I was channeling Edna Mode from *The Incredibles*. I could not be seen with some of the books in the social media market because they were stuck in the past, which, as Edna would say, distracts from the now.

It got to the point where I was mentioning this on a regular basis until the original Dr. Freberg (aka Mom) and Dad finally responded at the holiday dinner table in a way only parents could. They told me:

Karen, you know what you need to do to fix this. You need to write the *book on social media.*

This put things in perspective. My mom is also a textbook writer (for psychology), and at the time, she was writing three books (I know—I am still the apprentice and have much to learn, Obi-Wan). Was I going write three books at a time as my Mom was doing? There is not enough coffee in the world for me to do that! However, I thought, "Well, it's just one book, right? I can do that."

To put a time stamp on everything, this was 2016 after I had been teaching social media at the University of Louisville for three years. So, I decided to write a proposal and submit it to SAGE Publications, and when I got the green light, I started writing. A year later, we are here. This book has been a project for which I spent a lot of hours in between classes and research projects, consuming tons of coffee, waking up early to write before heading to teach my own social media classes, taking advantage of breaks like writing on airplanes from conferences and presentations, and making sure to bounce around ideas with colleagues, students, family, and friends. It's been quite the journey to get to this point.

The nature of this book is to be a strong advocate and endorser for the social media industry as an established yet evolving area in communication. Social media has not received the respect it should get from practitioners, researchers, and even the industry. For many years, social media has been labeled as a "fad," "just for fun," even for those who are classified as digital natives (e.g., Generation Z or younger audiences). There are a lot of perceptions and stereotypes out there, and this book instead hopes to open the vast opportunities made possible by social media by providing a balanced yet fair representation of the field. No sugarcoating is here for the industry, but it is helpful to consider both the benefits and challenges that make social media such a remarkable field.

As a young scholar, I had to justify my interest in and passion for the industry in my research endeavors and teaching opportunities with fellow colleagues. I was told I would never get a job teaching or working in social media and should go into something more "traditional." Years later, social media classes, programs, certifications, and job opportunities are on the rise. Funny how things turn out when you listen to your gut.

OVERVIEW OF *SOCIAL MEDIA FOR STRATEGIC COMMUNICATION*

The goal of this book is to provide students with an integrated, engaging, and strategic focus on social media as a profession and industry. While most books have focused on tactical executions and specific tools and platforms, this book emphasizes the larger picture of creating a long-standing strategic mindset that helps students, professionals, and brands navigate the ever-changing landscape with sustainable action steps and fundamental skills that will never be outdated.

Chapters. The book is formatted into different sections and chapters. The first section focuses on the foundations of creating a strategic mindset. These chapters provide an overview of how social media is both an art and a science (Chapter 1) while establishing ethical and legal guidelines for social media (Chapter 2) and proactive measures to create a sustainable and authentic personal brand (Chapter 3). Chapter 4 outlines the key skills, expectations, and responsibilities of the social media industry whereas Chapter 5 addresses the growing need to understand research, listening, monitoring, and analyzing the data from social media. The second section of the book focuses on understanding the strategic side of social media with campaign planning (Chapter 6) by outlining key elements for strategic writing for social media (Chapter 7), audience segmentation and rise of specialized audiences like advocates and influencers (Chapter 8), and creating and managing content (Chapter 9). Chapter 10 is the last chapter in this section, connecting all aspects of the previous parts together with measurement and budget/calendar creation. The last part of the book explores the application of social media practice around the world. Specializations are highlighted in Chapters 11 and 12 with specific examples and best practices. Chapter 13 finalizes the book while providing insights into what to look for next. Each chapter features case studies, examples, and notable takeaways (essentially, the "so what" factor). I cover relevant areas like ethics and law, social media strategies, and whether or not social media is a science or an art. The book goes into greater detail with the key components needed for effective listening and monitoring practices on social media, personal branding practices, the pros and cons of influencer and advocate marketing, budgeting (yes—social media costs money!), and outlining key areas of specialization that are integrated with social media practices.

Humans of Social Media Features. Most social media books start each chapter with a case study or an example of a social media campaign. This book, however, focuses on some of the leading voices and people *behind* the campaigns, brands, and work often referenced and discussed in social media books.

The *Humans of Social Media* feature is inspired by the *Humans of New York* stories (www.humansofnewyork.com), highlighting the experiences and insights of the professionals leading the way for others in social media. All disciplines and roles are featured here—public relations, marketing, journalism, entrepreneurship, sports, crisis communications, and analytics, to name a few. Like the course book, these stories represent the vast array of professional opportunities in the field.

I would like to thank all of the great professionals who participated in the *Humans of Social Media* feature, including Deirdre Breakenridge, Chris Strub, Chris Yandle, Jeff Kallin, Rich Calabrese, Samantha Hughey, Jeremy Darlow, Michael Ehrlich, Jaryd Wilson, Dennis Yu, Kerry Flynn, Melissa Agnes, Simona Morar, Bella Portaro Kueber, Adam White, Russ Wilde, Mark Murdock, and Whitney Drake. Thank you for taking the time to support this project and share your story with everyone. Special thanks to those who helped engage and support the book, including Max Strauss (Atlanta Hawks), Sree Sreenivasan, Amir Zonozi (Zoomph), Marc Oppenheim (MEOjobs), Geoffrey Blosat (Washington Redskins), Jason Falls, Mark Schaefer, Kyle Benison (Atlanta Falcons), Reva Labbe (ESPN/College Gameday), Jonathan Gantt (Clemson Athletics), Jeff O'Keefe (Toyota Racing and GOLIN), Cheval John (Vallano Media), and the great community of #SMsports and #SMprofs.

Ancillaries and Assignments. Another struggle for professors and students (who may not be able to take a social media class in school) is the lack of assignments provided to test and apply the knowledge covered in the book. Most books provide knowledge and leave readers with the feeling they are missing something—rarely do social media books provide knowledge with opportunities to actually apply these lessons. If there are any applications, they are not tied to what actually happens in practice. Forget actual assignments—those are never present.

One of my motivations for writing this book in the first place was to provide students and professors with enough exercises, assignments, discussion board questions, and icebreaker activities to truly be able to walk the walk as well as talk the talk in social media circles. Along with thought questions, each chapter has specific exercises to test out the knowledge covered in the chapter with actionable activities. In addition, the portfolio building workbook provides specific assignments and exercises (50+) to assign, work on, and create for classes, internships, and portfolio materials. To compensate for the lack of assignments integrated within social media books (one of my biggest concerns about the state of social media textbooks in academia and practice), this book supplies professors with an abundance of assignments and exercises to choose from and allows students to work on exercises and projects in class and beyond.

After reading this book, students will walk away with the knowledge and understanding not only of what social media is but of how to use it strategically today, and in the future as well. Providing resources for students to apply what they have learned and read in the classroom with this book is critical. It's one thing to say you have learned all about social media, but when the rubber meets the road (e.g., when asked to apply for a social media position after graduation), this is where it matters.

I realize this field can be quite daunting to cover in classes, especially for professors. As an active educator and researcher in social media pedagogy, I understand the balance needed for professors to provide current, relevant, and applicable activities and insights to best prepare their students for the real world. Many times, like Remy from Pixar's *Ratatouille*, we are faced with the Anton Egos of the industry and try to answer the question, "What does this professor have that is new?" This subject area, compared to others, can be very intimidating and overwhelming. In my opinion, social media is one of the more challenging (yet rewarding) classes to teach.

Yes, the expectations and demands are high for this area of research, practice, and education, but the rewards are endless. By taking a comprehensive view and bridging the different aspects of social media, you will be marketable and relevant to the industry not just for today but also for the long term. Approaching social media practices with a strategic mindset allows you to be agile, adaptive, and responsive to what is happening and will happen in the industry while tying in both scientific and creative ideas for inspiration.

THE TEAM BEHIND THE TEAM

There was certainly a team behind this book, and it couldn't have happened without their support. There are many people I would like to dedicate this book to. First, to my family. You were with me from the very beginning—seeing me type furiously over holidays and breaks, with coffee by my side and Ronnie (our family Australian shepherd) keeping me company. Without the support, encouragement, and inspiration for this book, this project wouldn't have happened.

I would like to thank Mom (aka the original Dr. Freberg and my inspiration to look up to as a professor) and Dad (Coach Dad from my track and field days who has always been the biggest supporter of my work, from student-athlete to professor). Look, Mom and Dad—another Dr. Freberg has entered the publishing world! Luckily, this book does not cover brain worms (however, if you are interested in learning more about this, check out the original Dr. Freberg's books in psychology and neuroscience). Thank you, Mom and Dad, for your constant support, encouragement, and words of wisdom throughout this journey. This book is dedicated to you both.

Major thanks to my sisters, Kristin and Karla, and my brother-in-law, Scott. You all provided me with constant encouragement, praise, and well wishes, making sure I had lots of coffee along the way. Your love and support mean the world to me!

Many thanks also to Mom and Dad's Australian shepherd, Ronnie. Keeping me company as I wrote while visiting my family over the holidays, she was a key member who supported me throughout this process!

I would like to extend a special thank-you to my predecessor and mentor at the University of Louisville, William Thompson (aka Thompson, as many alums in the Department of Communication call him), for his help getting me into the book business. Without William, I would not have had this wonderful publishing opportunity with SAGE. William took me by the SAGE booth at the Association for Education in Journalism and Mass Communication conference in 2016 and told Terri (my great editor for this book) that SAGE would be "a damn fool" if they did not sign me for a book. William had a way with words, and I am forever grateful for his support, encouragement, and friendship. I am very appreciative to William for being confident and taking action on my behalf. Thanks, William!

I also would like to thank the great social media professors' community (#SMprofs) for their constant engagement and inspiration for the field. More and more professors are coming together to dedicate time, resources, and energy toward making the social media field and classroom a wonderful and relevant environment for students. Thanks to those who have led the way in this regard, including Sabrina Page, Carolyn Kim, Keith Quesenberry, Stephen Marshall, Amanda Weed, Jeremy Lipschultz, William Ward, Amber Hutchins, Emily Kinsky, Matt Kushin, and the entire #SMprofs group. Thank you for making this a vibrant and wonderful subject to teach.

In addition, brands have been super supportive and collaborative over the years, helping make the bridge between education and practice even stronger. Without the support of companies like Hootsuite (Hootsuite Academy), HubSpot (HubSpot Academy), Adobe (#EDUMax and Creative Campus), Meltwater, Talkwalker, and Brandwatch, to name a few, this task of addressing the professional gap between academia and industry would have been even more challenging. Thank you to Alicia, Sarah, Brit, and Nick (Hootsuite) for your constant and ever-standing support for my work as a social media professor. Thank you to Carol Ann Vance (Meltwater) for your engagement and support with #MeltwaterEDU and allowing me to provide insights from an educator's point of view. Sebastian Distefano, Suzanne Jennings, Ben Forta, Joe Martin, and the rest of the Adobe team have been instrumental in providing the opportunities for me to learn, grow, and create content that is relevant and strategic for social media practices. Thank you to Isaac Moche of HubSpot Academy for the dedication and commitment HubSpot has placed on educators to be empowered in sharing their stories and experiences in and outside of the classroom.

Furthermore, I want to dedicate this book to all of my current and former students. You are what makes this worthwhile, and your work, dedication, and commitment make this experience of giving back to the field truly remarkable and wonderful. Special thanks to former students Samantha Hughey, Rebecca "Bell" Holder, Lizelle Lauron, Emily Hayes, and Tevin Johnson-Campion for their contribution and insights for this book. Very proud of each and every one of my #FrebergAlums!

I hope you enjoy this book and what it offers in your career and classes. Please provide me with feedback and comments—I would love to hear from you all! Together, we can make social media a truly remarkable field and discipline.

ABOUT THE AUTHOR

Credit: Roger Freberg.

Karen Freberg (@kfreberg) is an associate professor in strategic communications at the University of Louisville.

She is also an adjunct faculty member of the West Virginia University online graduate program in integrated marketing communications. Freberg has presented at several U.S. and international research conferences, including ones in Australia, Brazil, China, Greece, Ireland, Italy, Slovenia, Spain, Sweden, the Netherlands, and the United Kingdom.

In addition to academic conferences, Freberg has presented at professional and trade conferences such as Public Relations Society of America (PRSA), SXSW EDU, Salesforce Higher Education, CASE SMC, and Cannes Lions, as well as been invited to do industry workshops and talks with the Dallas Mavericks, Kentucky Organ Donor Affiliates, and Signature HealthCARE on social media trends and strategies.

Freberg is also a research consultant in social media and crisis communications and has worked with several organizations and agencies such as Firestorm Solutions, Hootsuite, Kentucky Derby Festival, IMC Agency, the Department of Homeland Security, the Centers for Disease Control and Prevention, the National Center for Food Protection and Defense (now known as the Food Protection and Defense Institute), Kentucky Organ Donor Affiliates, and Colorado Ski Country USA. This experience led her to be a 2015 Plank Center Fellow for General Motors, where her responsibility was to work with the public relations and social media teams to form best practices and recommendations on social media measurement strategies and influencer marketing practices.

Freberg has coordinated and advised various companies on the areas of social media pedagogy and certification programs, such as Hootsuite (Advanced Social Media Strategy Certification and #HootAmb), Meltwater (certification program and contributor), Adobe (EDUMax Thought Leader), and HubSpot (education program and podcast). Freberg also launched a social media educators' community on Facebook and Twitter (@SMprofessors) for professors, practitioners, and professionals in the education industry to share resources, brainstorm ideas, and collaborate on projects to bridge the gap between education and practice.

Along with her teaching, Freberg's research has been published in several book chapters and in academic journals such as *Public Relations Review*, *Media Psychology Review*, *Journal of Contingencies and Crisis Management*, and *Health Communication*. She also serves on the editorial board for *Journalism and Mass Communication Quarterly*, *Psychology of Popular Media Culture*, *Corporate Communications*, *Marketing Education Review*, *Journal of Public Relations Research*, and *Case Studies in Strategic Communication*. Freberg is also the Chair of the NCA Public Relations Division.

In addition to academic publications, Freberg has been interviewed for popular press publications such as *USA Today*, *USA Today College*, and *Forbes*. Freberg is also professionally active, serving on the executive committee for the PRSA Entertainment and Sports Section and the technology chapter committee for the Commission on Public Relations Education. Freberg is a regular contributor and a young professionals' award judge for Front Office Sports.

Before coming to the University of Louisville, Freberg earned a PhD in communication and information from the University of Tennessee in May 2011 and a master's degree in strategic public relations from the Annenberg School for Communication at the University of Southern California in August 2007. Freberg received her bachelor's of science in public relations from the University of Florida in August 2005. Before entering academia, Freberg was a student-athlete in track and field, where she ended her career as a four-time All-American in the shot put, a two-time SEC Champion, and a 2004 Olympic Trials finalist.

FOUNDATION FOR CREATING A STRATEGIC MINDSET

1

INTRODUCTION TO SOCIAL MEDIA
An Art and Science

Learning Objectives
Humans of Social Media
Introduction
How Do We Define Social Media?
How Has Social Media Evolved?
    The Current State of Social Media
    Who "Owns" Social Media?
Using Social Media Strategically
    Which Social Media Platforms Should I Use?
    Working in Social Media
Bridging the Science and Practice of Social Media
    What Can Science Tell Us About Social Media?
    How Is Social Media Like a Practice?
    How Can We Bridge Science and Art
       Effectively?
Chapter Summary
Thought Questions
Exercises
References

LEARNING OBJECTIVES

After reading this chapter, you will be able to

- Define social media
- Differentiate between social media platforms
- Explain the evolution of social media over time
- Identify the main considerations for using social media strategically
- Identify the key characteristics of the science and art of social media

HUMANS OF SOCIAL MEDIA
DEIRDRE BREAKENRIDGE, AUTHOR, PROFESSOR, AND CEO OF PURE PERFORMANCE

Introduction

I've been working in public relations and marketing for 25-plus years. Although I started my career focused on media relations and publicity, today I'm a chief relationship agent (CRA) and a communications problem solver to help organizations tackle their relationship challenges and build credibility and trust with the public. I'm the author of five Financial Times Press books, including *Social Media and Public Relations: Eight New Practices for the PR Professional* (2012),

Putting the Public Back in Public Relations: How Social Media Is Reinventing the Aging Business of PR (with Brian Solis, 2009), and *PR 2.0: New Media, New Tools, New Audiences* (2008). My sixth book, *Answers for Modern Communicators*, was published by Routledge in October 2017. I also moved my authoring to a new platform when I was asked to become a Lynda.com video author in 2014. My video courses include Public Relations Fundamentals, Media Training, and Handling an Unruly Audience. As an adjunct professor, I teach online PR and social media courses for the

(Continued)

(Continued)

University of Massachusetts Amherst Journalism Department and for Rutgers University's PR certificate program. I also speak nationally and internationally on the topics of PR, marketing, branding, and social media communications.

How did you get your start in social media?

I wish I had some great epiphany back in 2003. However, my journey began when I experienced an embarrassing situation with a client during a presentation to launch a new tech product. I was an agency owner at the time. My team and I were sharing our PR plan for the launch of a load balancer product that required a new media focus.

After we wrapped up our presentation, the CEO of the company looked at me and said, "This is good, but where are all of the new media channels?" Not a good feeling when you thought you delivered the latest strategies and tactics to reach the media and other important stakeholders. From that point forward, my new media/social media research increased tenfold. By 2007, I was working on a manuscript for Financial Times Press that would eventually become *PR 2.0*—a book to educate PR professionals on how to bridge the gap between traditional, online, and social media. I didn't want other pros to experience that "uh-oh" moment with their clients or executives. The "aha" moment is always much better.

What is your favorite part of working in your social media area of expertise?

Social media is one of the best ways to build relationships when you can't meet and collaborate in person. For anyone who says you can't build a relationship through social media, I say, "You're not using social media correctly." There is an incredible amount of intelligence you can gather through social media to help you learn more about people and build a relationship. Social media levels the playing field. It's less about titles and your position and more about like-minded thinking and passionate causes. When you take a peer-to-peer approach (companies have to be more human and transparent too), you can become a trusted resource.

My best example of the power of social media and PR started with a Facebook conversation. During the early days of Facebook, I was participating in a marketing technology group, offering information to another group member who had inquired about data mining. Although I didn't have the answer to her question, I knew that one of my colleagues would be able to help her. So I jumped into a conversation and made the introduction. Helping a peer in the group led to a few sidebar conversations between the two of us. After a few back-and-forth discussions, we moved to email. Finally, we took the relationship offline and met in person. Before I knew it, my marketing communications firm was looking at a large retainer client for a few years after the initial Facebook encounter.

What is one thing you can't live without while working in social media?

Social media is one of the easiest ways for you to connect quickly and collaborate with your colleagues, media, influencers, clients, and others. I can't live without the instantaneous interaction and how I receive answers to important inquiries within minutes. It's that quick direct message (DM) you send to an influencer to participate in a client Facebook Live interview at an industry conference. Or it's that Facebook message to a colleague when you have a great opportunity to partner on a client account. It's also the ability for my students to DM me on Twitter when they have an urgent question or an emergency situation. For me, social media has become an indispensable part of my PR and marketing tool kit that helps me to develop, maintain, and build even stronger relationships.

What is your favorite social media account (person, brand, etc.) to follow, and why?

Although I really like Instagram and I think Snapchat is where you can find the bulk of millennials and Generation Z, I'm still addicted to Twitter. Since the 2016 U.S. presidential election, I find myself tapping into the Twitter feeds of several news outlets and political figures who report of the state of our affairs from foreign policy to education and health care. After all, we have a president who uses Twitter to announce policy and to share his thoughts in 140 characters or less, making it my go-to platform.

In addition, on Twitter, I'm able to carve out important conversations regarding my clients and what will affect their industries, the latest trends in media, and influencer conversations and community discussions that are important to my own growth and professional development. Most of all, Twitter is a place where colleagues, peers, academics, influencers, and students can find me and ask me questions from PR and relationship building to reputation management and the changing media landscape.

What is the most challenging part of working in social media?

The ever-changing media landscape poses a challenge in two ways. First, you always have to be 10 steps ahead of your customers. The media landscape is incredibly fragmented with new social media communities proliferating at a rapid pace. You have to stay current on the platforms and understand how and where people connect. Of course, there is only so much time in a day, and professionals are always challenged to learn and embrace new media channels. At the same time, making the determination that you're going to become a part of a social media community and be a helpful resource also means you have to measure and be accountable for the time and resources you put into your engagement efforts. Measurement has always been a challenge. With changing technology, you may find yourself constantly learning new ways to measure and report your findings. From understanding what you want to achieve and the metrics you need to demonstrate value, you as a professional must learn to capture, filter, and analyze data. Because of social media, you have to be more comfortable with data to prove how your programs impact your business—and how data can also improve your communications moving forward.

What is your take on your area of expertise and the social media industry?

Public relations and social media go hand in hand. Traditionally, PR people are the storytellers. They are the relationship builders who create the bridges of goodwill between organizations and their publics. PR professionals are also the brand police who work tirelessly to watch, listen to, maintain, and protect the brand. Of course, social media takes your brand to new heights of awareness and offers the ability to build a larger digital footprint. At the same time, PR has to be right there communicating effectively on behalf of an organization while maintaining a trusted reputation, wherever the company and its employees participate. Social media and PR together can propel your brand forward. When you fuse community and relationships with collaborative technology, the result is stronger bonds, customer loyalty, and brand advocacy.

What do you wish you had known when you were starting out?

If I were to give advice to my 21-year-old self, I would say, "Don't take anything too personally and always remember whatever happens and whatever is said may not be about you. When you have interactions with people in your personal life or throughout your career, what they say and how they react have more to do with their own personal or professional situations and what they're going through." To my peers and younger professionals: "Remove your emotional self and be an observer of any situation. Because social media is an important part of our lives both personally and professionally, remember that you'll collaborate with many inspiring individuals and you'll grow from those relationships. But also keep in mind that there will be uneasy and tense interactions that make you take pause. Try to remember to step back, remove your emotional self, and learn from the situation."

Deirdre Breakenridge is an award-winning public relations practitioner, educator, and author. She can be contacted via Twitter at @dbreakenridge, and her website is www.deirdrebreakenridge.com.

INTRODUCTION

There was a time in the not-so-distant past when nobody was tweeting, snapping, sending out notes, or live streaming videos of their daily lives, which might be hard to imagine. Today, with a click of a button on our mobile devices, we are able to showcase and share our views, perspectives, and thoughts with the global community. We bypass the mainstream media to create our own communities, networks, and personal identities, all with a few clicks, uploads, and completions.

A number of memorable events demonstrate the power of social media. Oreo established itself as a digital legend for its "You can still dunk in the dark" tweet at the Super Bowl in New Orleans in 2013, which led future brands to try to interject themselves into any trending event and issue on social media years afterward. The 2014 amyotrophic lateral sclerosis (ALS) Ice Bucket Challenge gained momentum on social media after celebrities, sports figures, and everyday people shared personalized videos as they dumped buckets of ice water on themselves to raise awareness of the disease (Braiker, 2014). Funds raised by this campaign helped scientists discover a new gene tied to ALS (Rogers, 2016). The "Brexit" campaign of July 2016, in which voters in the United Kingdom chose to exit the European Union, succeeded in part due to the impact of social media (Singh, 2016). Snapchat became Snap Inc. as the organization incorporated being a camera company into its mission with the unveiling of its new glasses, Spectacles. The company launched a guerrilla marketing campaign featuring the disclosure of random locations around the United States where people could purchase a pair of Spectacles from a Spectacles bot (Wagner, 2016). This campaign resulted in widespread buzz from users. People in line at a bot took photos and shared their enthusiasm online, creating the ultimate "fear of missing out" (FOMO) moments online. In 2017, Wendy's, MoonPie, and Cinnabon entered the social media space for their wit and interjecting their personalities into their social media message strategies, which resulted in Wendy's embracing this so much that it brought its snarky voice and tone to the mainstream in a 2018 Super Bowl commercial. These cases represent different areas and different goals—but they share something important. All of these campaigns approached their goals in a strategic way, built by combining the underlying research principles (science) and the creative executions (art) of social media.

As demonstrated in just these examples, social media has matured and become a staple in our global society. Social media is not just a fad that can be addressed in a moment's notice. This evolving specialization, entity, and constant focus within society continues to grow and expand itself beyond anything imaginable. Businesses, corporations, agencies, and even universities are taking notice not only of the power social media has on their own businesses, but of how it can be directly applied and integrated for personal branding purposes.

When it comes to social media, various terms and definitions could be classified as the main focus. Many professionals have provided their own take on what social media means. Yet the social media tools being used today are quite different from their original purposes and functions.

This chapter will provide you with the background of social media as a concept, profession, and specialization in the 21st century. While tools change, the behaviors and strategies behind these tools are what will be covered not only in this chapter but also in this textbook.

HOW DO WE DEFINE SOCIAL MEDIA?

Social media has been defined, classified, and conceptualized in probably a million different ways. Social media combines "a wide range of online, word-of-mouth forums including blogs, company sponsored discussion boards and chat rooms, consumer-to-consumer e-mail, consumer product or service ratings websites and forums, Internet discussion boards and forums, [and] microblogs" (Mangold & Faulds, 2009). Lariscy, Avery, Sweetser, and Howes (2009) defined social media as "online practices that utilize technology and enable people to share content, opinions, experiences, insights, and media themselves" (p. 314). Social media shares some features with previous platforms for communication but has unique aspects as well (Kleinberg, 2008). Social media is about "people" (Marken, 2007), and the technology not only provides means for establishing and maintaining relationships but also allows users to create their own (user-generated) content to share with others in the online community (Waters, Burnett, Lamm, & Lucas, 2009). Some of the content that individuals share with others in their online networks includes information regarding news events, updates on personal and professional achievements, and multimedia content. Social media has "amplified the power of consumer-to-consumer conversations in the marketplace by enabling one person to communicate with literally hundreds or thousands of other consumers quickly and with relatively little effort" (Mangold & Faulds, 2009, p. 361). As a result, official messages are competing for consumer attention with many other sources of information.

Some professionals classify it as a group of social networks that allow conversations and relationships to emerge. Others focus on the community aspect in which people are able to converse together in a centralized location to collaborate and initiate dialogue. All of these are key characteristics of social media, but in any case, keep in mind that this definition will need to be fluid and adaptive to the growing list of tools, features, and changes we are seeing in this particular space. For the purposes of this textbook, one way to define **social media** is that it can

> provide a personalized, online networked hub of information, dialogue, and relationship management. These new communication technology tools allow individual users and organizations to engage with, reach, persuade, and target key audiences more effectively across multiple platforms. Industry professionals, scholars, and social media users have contributed a number of different definitions and conceptualizations of the concept of social media. Some emphasize the role of social media as a toolkit that allows users to create and share content. Others focus on how social media extend Web 2.0 technologies to bring communities together. (Freberg, 2016, p. 773)

The overall functions of social media are not limited to communicating messages designed by professionals for audiences, in parallel to message construction in traditional media. In addition, social media allows users to participate to an extent not seen previously in traditional media. Increased empowerment of the individual stakeholder leads to greater feelings of control over a situation and a willingness to help others in the community, which could potentially be used by brands and corporations to engage with audiences, formulate message strategies, and evaluate their own reputation in the eyes of their online audience members.

With these new shifts in power and breakdown in barriers, brands are expected to listen and respond to stakeholder concerns in new ways. Recognizing the influence of social media provides professionals with the opportunity to use social media strategically to discover potential issues relevant to their stakeholders, to prepare for different scenarios and situations, to implement online communication strategically, and to evaluate results of communications in real time.

In addition, social media platforms serve as gateways where content and conversations are created and ignited between individuals, brands, organizations, and nations. Essentially, social media platforms provide first-impression management tools for corporations and individuals to showcase their own brands and reputations. While individual social media platforms may be somewhat separated at times from others, they are all part of the same ecosystem. Each platform has its own features, dynamic characteristics, and community attributes, but they are integrated with the organization, brand, or individual's persona online. In addition, they are also one part of the overall communication mix of media channels that can be utilized to share information, establish communities, and formulate relationships for a brand. Earned, paid, shared, and owned media have converged to formulate this new ecosystem of communities and networks. Social media is more than just a set of tools to use, but a larger network of communities tied together through virtual and offline connections.

All of the various platforms that make up this social media ecosystem can be quite daunting to visualize. As shown in Figure 1.1, JESS3 and Brian Solis created an infographic outlining the brandsphere of social media for users, businesses, and organizations to take advantage of (JESS3, n.d.). Essentially, this infographic highlights the various platforms available as well as categorizes them based on time. Note, this infographic is relatively "old" in social media standards, but the key concepts are still important. This is different from most of the other visualizations out there for social media, which focus more on the application of the social media platform rather than the specific type of platform.

Several other defining characteristics should be noted when it comes to social media. Each of these computer-based applications and platforms allows users to share and create information, disseminate ideas in various forms, share content, and respond to these pieces of content. In addition, each platform allows you to create your own personal identity with a picture or avatar. An avatar is acceptable to use on certain platforms, but most individuals use one consistent photo across all of their respective accounts online. This is done for several reasons, but a prominent one is to establish a proactive positive **online reputation**.

FIGURE 1.1 ■ Social Media Brandsphere

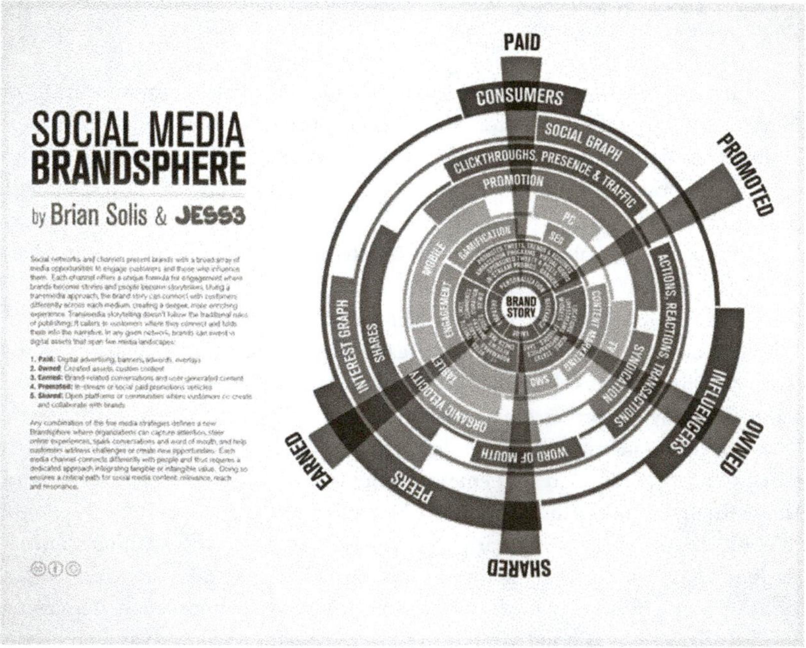

Source: Jesse Thomas (JESS3) / Brian Solis, http://jess3.com/social-media-brandsphere/.

In addition, there is a possibility for these pieces of content (videos, images, posts, updates, etc.) to go viral. **Virality**, or rapid dissemination of information from person to person, is one way in which news, stories, and updates reach across various networks in a short amount of time.

There are various examples of a post, update, story, or even video becoming viral. Some platforms, like Facebook, allow this to happen much more easily since the content is shared within the platform itself. For example, Chewbacca Mask Mom became famous when she filmed herself on Facebook Live wearing a Chewbacca mask from Kohl's (Eordogh, 2016). Her laugh became contagious, and everyone began sharing this video. It became the most watched and viral Facebook Live video ever in 2016 with over 130 million views (Eordogh, 2016). Yet content from one platform can become viral on another platform if the content is repurposed. The Taco Bell lens that was used to celebrate Cinco de Mayo in 2016 received a record 224 million views (Johnson, 2016) within Snapchat and when users shared their selfies with the lens on platforms like Facebook, Twitter, and Instagram.

The overall fundamental use and motive behind social media has been to establish personal connections with others and tell our stories virtually. Why do we share what we share online for the world to see? Think about the last time you used social media—what did you share? Why did you share it on a particular platform? It's important to explore not only where you shared this information, but how and why you decided to share it with one, a few, or everyone in your respective communities. Sometimes, what you share, post, comment, and discuss on various social media platforms is not just for your friends to see, but for the entire world. What you say on social media is public and can be used as documentation. Each action taken on social media has a specific purpose—whether we are creating the content ourselves or consuming the content to be shared with our communities. Yet we also have the power to comment on and engage with the content as we see fit.

Some fundamental characteristics make social media unique compared to other types of media platforms. First, the platforms are web- and mobile-based applications. Most of the rising applications are mobile based to fit the growing trend for more mobile capabilities without a desktop- or web-specific requirement like Snapchat, Instagram, WhatsApp, and others have done. Second, the power of **user-generated content (UGC)** is a prominent characteristic of why businesses and individuals like social media. UGC is content that is created directly by a user. This could be a video that you created over the holidays showcasing your zip-lining experience over the Costa Rica terrain with a GoPro camera or even an infographic outlining the main items to bring to the Kentucky Derby. UGC is not the only type of content that can be created on social media; for example, there is **branded content** (BC or brand storytelling), which a lot of businesses create. This type of content allows brands to emerge as their own media outlets and create their own content uniquely aligned with their goals, mission, and brand voice. This can even be extended to creating advocates or brand ambassadors to help pass along these pieces of branded content (or assets) to other communities around the world. Social media provides an open and dynamic online community. Individuals and corporations can participate in various communities linked together by similar interests and backgrounds. These communities can brainstorm ideas, share perspectives, and engage in dialogue to formulate networking relationships. For example, Hootsuite, a global social media management company based in Vancouver, Canada, has created a brand ambassadorship program for users around the world to share their stories and experiences openly and to connect with other potential users and stakeholders in social media.

Let's build something great together

As Hootsuite spreads its wings across the globe, we meet people who are passionate about our product. Explore our Community programs and find out how you can help bring our brand to the globe.

Hootsuite Ambassadors

Passionate about social media? So are we. That's why we invite our most passionate fans and expert users to join our Ambassador program, where they get to showcase their social media expertise and help us deliver a better product. Check out what they're up to: #HootAmb

Source: Hootsuite Inc., https://hootsuite.com/community

Hootsuite Ambassador Program

Social media has been defined and characterized as distinguished compared to other forms of media due to the power of its real-time content creation and the level of engagement it offers to users across many respective platforms. That said, social media provides a range of different opportunities, challenges, and experiences for users to take part in, such as

- Dialogue on a one-to-one, one-to-many, and many-to-many format in real time

- New relationships, connections, and professional and personal opportunities for your personal brand

- Visual and immersive storytelling through video, live video, photos, and other multimedia content

- Providing awareness of the brand voice, story, and people behind the scenes

- Becoming a resource for education, training, and support for the community

- Initiating behaviors and call-to-action statements for audiences to note

- Sending persuasive messages that are strategically targeted using advertising and personalized data

- Responding immediately to customer inquiries and providing updates on crisis situations

One of the most important things to be aware of is that the definition as well as the statistics, practices, and strategies of social media will change on a frequent basis. You do not need to have all of the answers or even know all of the platforms in play. If you try to learn every single change that happens with each platform, that will become your life as a social media professional. However, it is important to note you may be asked to come up with your own definition of social media, per se, so think about the defining characteristics, features, and overall attributes that make up this dynamic and evolving set of platforms.

HOW HAS SOCIAL MEDIA EVOLVED?

Social media is still a very young profession and industry, even though it has matured substantially over the years. At each stage, expanded sets of features have been added to meet the increasing expectations of audiences. With each new feature being implemented by one platform, others follow and sometimes take the idea and incorporate it into their own version. Google launched Google+ to compete with Facebook. Instagram created Instagram Stories to compete with Facebook. Facebook is offering a Jobs feature to compete with LinkedIn. So many different platforms competing with each other—it's essentially a digital media soap opera.

The Current State of Social Media

Social media platforms are in constant flux and evolution, and this could become your job in addition to your other responsibilities. Keep in mind that you want to take a tier system approach to looking at social media in general. Social media platforms are divided by function and overall purpose. However, most social media platforms are indexed, edited, and revised over time, as well as categorized and searchable online through search engines. Some of the main types of social media platforms are wikis (e.g., Wikipedia), blogs (e.g., WordPress, Medium, and Blogger), collaborative crowdsourcing sites (e.g., Google Drive, Dropbox, and Box), messaging (e.g., WhatsApp, WeChat, Messenger), microblogging (e.g., Twitter and Weibo), live streaming (e.g., Facebook Live, Instagram Live, and Periscope), mobile-based platforms (e.g., Snapchat and Instagram), and business networking (e.g., LinkedIn), to name a few.

Facebook, the largest social media platform in the world, is an example of a social networking site (SNS). Social networking sites can be defined as "(1) web-based services that allow individuals to construct a public or semi-public profile within a bounded system, (2) articulate a list of other users with whom they share a connection, and (3) view and traverse their list of connections and those made by others within the system" (boyd & Ellison, 2008, p. 211). Using an SNS, an individual can control personal information to share with others. Users can also affiliate with businesses and large organizations that have a presence on these sites by adding them as "friends" (boyd, 2006). Twitter, on the other hand, allows individuals and brands to create, curate, and communicate information in real time in a limited number of characters. Twitter allows users to push content to their followers that can include textual information, hyperlinks, images, videos, and even interactive GIFs for entertainment, information, and conversation purposes. Users can also participate in chat sessions surrounding particular common interests and topics by following a hashtag, which is a key word preceded by a # sign to allow users to track and follow certain conversations. Many corporations presently have integrated a branded hashtag to help manage their reputation (e.g., Honda, Ford, and Starbucks), as well as embracing user-generated hashtags from their community. Corporations are able to monitor, track, and evaluate the success of a hashtag within a campaign through social media monitoring platforms and analytics using an application programming interface (API). Using API, corporations can create tools and software programs to work with Twitter. In addition, users can get content out to audiences who are not part of the community with the use of hashtags for key terms on trending topics, news items, community events, and industry-related issues.

Visual and "snackable" content forms such as Instagram and Snapchat are emerging as dominant platforms among users, particularly in the younger generations of audience members. These two platforms are constantly challenging each other with their features. Facebook tried to buy Snapchat in 2013 for $3 billion (Fiegerman, 2014), which caused the social networking giant to continue advancing Instagram (which it bought in 2012) with similar features to compete with Snapchat. Make sure you are on the main platforms being discussed and highlighted in society (see Table 1.1). In this case, Facebook, Twitter, Instagram, YouTube, LinkedIn, and Snapchat are some of the most familiar. Each of these key platforms has set forth some interesting advances and experienced changes throughout its history within the industry.

With the key players in social media, it is important to note that each of these platforms has evolved and had some significant milestones as a company. Some have been bought, transformed, and evolved through the years. Table 1.2 presents some of the main milestones for each platform.

Who "Owns" Social Media?

Indeed, a lot of marketing professionals, PR practitioners, communication scholars, and others have discussed and proposed an argument for why their discipline should "own" social media. Everyone wants to claim ownership of the social media discipline and profession (it's almost like the Iron Throne from *Game of Thrones*), yet not every profession knows how to make the most of the emerging platforms. Each profession may know how to use social media specifically for its industry or discipline, but it may not be aware of the vast possibilities or ways in which others are using it.

There are many answers to this question, and this has arisen at many professional conferences, academic sessions, and discussions online. Some would say marketing has ownership of social media from a business and analytical standpoint. Marketing most of the time has the finances and support needed to provide businesses and organizations with the means for creating, disseminating, and analyzing the content and

TABLE 1.1 ■ Key Players in Social Media			
Platform	**Founded**	**CEO**	**Key Features**
Facebook	February 2004	Mark Zuckerberg	Profile, News Feed, Groups, Events, Video, Photos, Search, Messenger, Pages
Instagram	October 2010	Kevin Systrom	Profiles, Business Pages, Layout, Boomerang, Instagram Live
LinkedIn	March 2003	Jeff Weiner	Business Profiles, Pages, Groups, Lynda
Twitter	March 2006	Jack Dorsey	Profile, Newsfeed, Live Video, Images, GIFs
YouTube	March 2005	Susan Wojcicki	Video, YouTube Red
Snapchat	September 2011	Evan Spiegel	Snaps, Snapchat My Story, Live Stories, Discover, Spectacles

TABLE 1.2 ■ Major Milestones for Key Players in Social Media	
Platform	**Major Timeline Events**
Facebook (newsroom.fb.com/ company-info/)	• February 4, 2004: Facebook is founded by Mark Zuckerberg along with Dustin Moskovitz, Chris Hughes, and Eduardo Saverin • March 1, 2004: Facebook expands from Harvard to Stanford, Columbia, and Yale • September 1, 2004: Facebook Wall is launched • 2005: Photo uploading option is offered • April 1, 2006: Mobile is launched • February 9, 2009: Like button is introduced • September 22, 2011: Timeline is introduced • April 9, 2012: Facebook buys Instagram for $1 billion • February 19, 2014: Facebook buys WhatsApp • March 25, 2014: Facebook buys Oculus Rift • March 25, 2015: Messenger is launched • September 25, 2015: Facebook 360 video is launched • December 3, 2015: Live video for profiles is launched • February 24, 2016: Facebook Reactions is launched • June 9, 2016: Facebook 360 photos are available • October 16, 2016: Workplace by Facebook is introduced
Instagram (instagram-press. com/our-story/)	• October 6, 2010: Instagram is launched • April 9, 2012: Facebook buys Instagram • June 30, 2013: Instagram video is launched • December 2013: Instagram Direct is launched • August 26, 2014: Hyperlapse is launched • March 23, 2015: Layout from Instagram is introduced • September 1, 2015: Improvements are added for Instagram Direct • October 22, 2015: Boomerang is introduced • August 2, 2016: Instagram Stories is introduced • August 31, 2016: Zoom is introduced • January 24, 2017: Live Stories are available globally • August 31, 2017: Live Stories are available on the web • January 23, 2018: GIF Stickers are introduced • February 1, 2018: Type Mode in Stories is introduced
Twitter (about.twitter.com/ en_us/company.html)	• March 21, 2006: Jack Dorsey sends out his first tweet • March 2007: Twitter makes a splash at SXSW Interactive • August 2007: First Twitter hashtag is proposed by Chris Messina • April 2010: Promoted Tweets are launched • June 2010: Promoted Trends are launched • May 2011: Twitter buys TweetDeck

(Continued)

TABLE 1.2 ■ (Continued)	
Platform	**Major Timeline Events**
	• June 2012: Twitter receives a new design
	• January 2013: Twitter launches Vine
	• November 2013: Twitter files for initial public offering (IPO)
	• August 2014: Promoted Video is launched
	• January 2015: Direct Messages and mobile video are introduced
	• March 2015: Twitter buys Periscope
	• October 2015: Twitter launches Moments and Polls
	• January 2016: Periscope is embedded in tweets
	• November 2017: Twitter allows tweets to grow from 140 characters to 280 characters
LinkedIn (about.linkedin.com/)	• May 2003: LinkedIn is launched
	• April 2007: LinkedIn reaches 10 million users
	• February 2008: LinkedIn launches mobile version
	• January 2011: LinkedIn launches IPO
	• May 3, 2012: LinkedIn buys SlideShare
	• April 9, 2015: LinkedIn buys Lynda.com
	• June 13, 2016: Microsoft buys LinkedIn
YouTube (www.businessinsider .com/key-turning- points-history-of- youtube-2013-2#in- april-2009-usher- introduced-the-world- to-justin-bieber-via-a- video-on-youtube-12)	• February 14, 2005: YouTube is created and founded by Chad Hurley, Steve Chen, and Jawed Karim
	• November 2005: YouTube has its first million-hit video with Nike
	• February 2006: YouTube negotiates deal with NBC
	• November 13, 2006: Google buys YouTube for $1.65 billion
	• May 2007: YouTube launches Partner Program
	• June 2007: YouTube hosts presidential debate with CNN
	• August 2007: YouTube launches ads
	• August 2009: Usher and Justin Bieber video is posted
	• January 2010: Movie rentals are available
	• July 2012: Olympics are available to live stream
	• December 2012: "Gangnam Style" hits 1 billion views
Snapchat (fortune. com/2017/02/04/ snapchat-abridged- history/)	• September 2011: Snapchat is initially released
	• October 2013: My Story is launched
	• May 2014: Video Chat is launched
	• September 2016: Snapchat is rebranded to Snap Inc.
	• September 2016: Snapchat Spectacles are introduced
	• March 2017: Snapchat files for IPO

Source: Facebook, Instagram, Twitter, LinkedIn, YouTube, and Snapchat.

how well it is received. Yet some would say the platforms themselves "own" social media. Social media is not like traditional media in a way that we would classify it on the media spectrum, but there has been a shift in the "pay-to-play" model, essentially forcing users and corporations to pay for their content to be seen by the right target audience at a specific time on their platform. Both Google and Facebook have led the way in this area and have forced this transformation, which has led to this current paid content model for social media.

There is a difference, of course, between owned media platforms (e.g., blogs) and earned or shared media platforms (e.g., social media). One way to approach the difference between these types of media is to recognize that one is controlled by the user and the other is controlled by others. Blogs essentially are controlled by individual users who are given the opportunity to decide how their page should look, what content to share, and whether or not they want comments to appear. The power of control is quite prominent, and one way to think about it is like owning a house. You can do whatever you want to it. On the other hand, social media is somewhat controllable by the user or brand, but the user or brand is somewhat "renting" the space like an apartment. There are terms of service agreements to follow, and the platform has the opportunity to change these agreements, switch up the features and designs, or even shut down its services.

The answer is no one owns social media. Social media is open for everyone to use to create, share, engage, and come together on. The barrier of entry is minimal, and the opportunity to be part of many diverse communities has never been more accessible for professionals, businesses, and organizations.

USING SOCIAL MEDIA STRATEGICALLY

Social media can be for personal use, but you can also use it professionally. Many times, we see how a group uses it for one community it is interacting with, but we forget how this is perceived from other perspectives. On social media, you need to find the balance that allows you to interact and create content that educates and informs your professional audiences of your level of expertise and thought leadership, but you also want to be personal enough so you are not perceived as a robot. There is a fine line between these two worlds, and that is why it is important to use social media strategically and effectively based on your own needs and expectations in the field. Each person is different—there are certain etiquette and professional guidelines to follow and review, but you have to be confident in knowing your own community, voice, and presence online. Social media is all about first impressions, and you want to make sure your name stands out for the right reasons.

Which Social Media Platforms Should I Use?

Choosing the right platforms for your role comes down to a few factors. First and foremost, you do not have to be on every single platform. As presented in Figure 1.2, Facebook still remains the most popular social media platform, with 1.4 billion daily active users and more than 25,000 employees as of December 2017 (Facebook Newsroom, 2018), followed by Instagram, Pinterest, LinkedIn, and Twitter. Yet, like all reports on social media, once content is published, it is out of date and has not accounted for other mobile-based platforms (e.g., Snapchat) gaining traction within the community and in society.

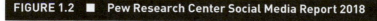

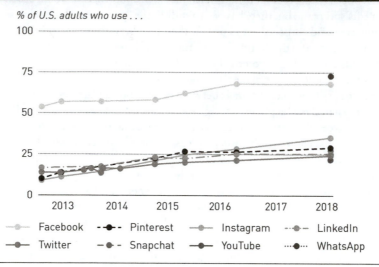

FIGURE 1.2 ■ Pew Research Center Social Media Report 2018

Source: "Social Media Update 2016" Pew Research Center, Washington, DC (November 11, 2016). http://www.pewinternet.org/2016/11/11/social-media-update-2016/.

To choose a particular platform, a social media professional must consider the following:

Audiences. Make sure to look first to where your audiences are going. Who are these individuals, and where are they having their conversations? You will of course be able to collect some information from these audiences (demographics, etc.); think about the amount of information Facebook has collected about you over the years from likes, comments, shares, and even videos watched.

Purpose. Platforms will continue to compete with each other to grab the attention and number of users from other platforms. Take the example of Facebook, which acquired Instagram for $1 billion and has transformed it into a dominant multimedia platform. Yet when Facebook wanted to buy Snapchat as well, Snapchat said no. As a result, Facebook has tried to copy various features of the mobile application for its own platform, ranging from filters on Instagram to the Messenger app. Each platform essentially has a specific function and audience in mind. Not all platforms are equal or founded on the same vision or principles. As time goes by, the competition among these brands for eyeballs and usage will only become bigger and more prominent.

For a social media professional, not only is understanding the functions and specifics of the tools important, but so is understanding the behaviors and reasons why people are using these tools in the first place. Each platform has a different overall purpose, as well as trustworthiness factor, whether it involves getting news, creating personal content, engaging in customer service, sharing negative experiences or responding a crisis, sharing and creating stories, or initiating a call to action to drive sales, strengthen reputation, and build on an established community.

Relationships. Identifying the current state of relationships between users on social media platforms is crucial at first. Some users will be your biggest fans and want to be on every platform you are on. However, some users may just want to be on one channel with you based on your brand voice there. This has to be determined and thought out carefully to make sure you are spending the appropriate time, resources, and engagement necessary to foster these relationships as proactively as possible. When it comes to being on social media, you want a strategy in place for why you have a presence on each platform.

Personality. Determining the platform you feel best establishes the personal voice for your business, organization, and even individual brand is something to consider and keep in mind. Certain platforms will feel more natural to you, but try to utilize each platform consistently to present a comprehensive brand across the board. Everyone wants the power to showcase who they are and why they are unique.

Showcasing your personality could come in a variety of different forms, from creating content on platforms like Snapchat to showing videos about various trends and daily activities (e.g., Gary Vaynerchuk and his #DailyVee shows). Brands have to showcase their personality with content showing not only what they are doing, but also what they can do to become a resource for their respective audience members. White papers, e-books, webinars, blog posts, podcasts, and even Twitter chat sessions are just some of the methods that are highlighted and expanded upon for brands.

Content. The new model for content creation and marketing on social media has shifted from just pushing content for the sake of self-promotion to becoming more personalized, interactive, and focused on storytelling. Develop the messages and pieces of content that your audiences want. The ideal situation is to think about pieces of content your audiences want, but do not realize they want, from you. This will take some additional brainstorming sessions and strategic planning in order to uncover the messages, pieces of content, and stories to showcase on social media. If you have strong content, this will allow you to become known as a resource for your **thought leadership**. Brands, individuals, and organizations can become thought leaders in their area as they continue to produce, share, and create content as a go-to resource for innovative ideas; persuade people to take action in response to their created content; and are viewed as trusted sources of information in their area. Mashable established itself as a trusted resource in 2007 when it created a place to share the most recent trends, issues, reports, and campaigns happening in the social and digital space.

Some pieces of content will resonate with an audience on one platform rather than another. You do not always want to post the same content across all platforms. There are some combinations that will work (e.g., Instagram and Facebook with videos), but you want to repurpose and reformat content that is designated with a particular community, platform capabilities, and purpose in mind. In addition, the content needs not only to reflect on the brand's voice, but also to connect with the audience in terms of user expectations from a brand using this platform.

Innovativeness. Users want to be part of a platform that continues to raise the bar for what a social media platform should be. Responding to user audiences and suggestions is another focus these platforms have to be aware of. People have noticed that Facebook has copied a lot of its new features from other platforms like Snapchat. Yet other platforms have been willing (or at least appeared willing) to listen to their audience members' suggestions for new features. In December 2016, Twitter CEO Jack Dorsey went on social media and asked Twitter users what they would like to see in the New Year on the microblogging platform. While this came at a time when Twitter was challenged with key personnel leaving and advertisement and metrics dropping, it was better late than never.

Analytics. Data will of course be your friend when it comes to engaging with content and audiences on social media, depending on the platforms in question. You will be able to determine what time, frequency, responses, and views you will get. These data and insights will help you determine when it is appropriate to post content and share videos, and even how long a response people expect from a customer comment on social media. In addition, analytics and data will help you determine at the end how well you (or your team) did in addressing the question, challenge, or content created for a campaign. Most of the links, updates, and conversations are archived online and available for collection either through the native measurement platforms on the platform itself or through a third-party service.

Actions. After we have an idea of the audience we want to engage with based on user activity level, we can determine some of the actions these individuals take to participate in our communities online.

Ultimately, you want to take all of these important factors into consideration to determine whether or not you want to be on particular social media platforms. One way to do this is by thoroughly identifying which platforms you are currently using (inventory), determining how well they are performing (audit), and making a choice on what to do with each platform (decision action steps) as outlined in Table 1.3.

TABLE 1.3 ■ Performance and Decision Action Audit	
Activity Level	**Actions**
Inventory + Benchmark Audit	• Identify key audiences and where they are in their relationship with the client (organization, business, agency, etc.) on social media • Identify the rationale for why they are on each platform (e.g., to be educated, consume content, gain insights, build communities, or host events and promotions) • Evaluate each platform to determine audience, content, relationships, analysis of brand voice, and overall purpose
Evaluation **(Short-Term and Long-Term Impacts)**	• Look at each platform to determine how well it is doing in terms of its KPIs (key performance indicators) and the overall health of the brand community, voice, and investment • Evaluate the longevity of the platforms that are aligned with the brand's mission and business objectives, and determine which platforms to keep and which ones to vote off "social media island" (aka shut down)
Decision + Action Steps	• Formulate a decision tree to determine the overall actions that need to be taken into consideration when evaluating social media platforms • Invest in platforms that have an established community but are growing in audiences so more resources and support is needed, or perhaps shut down platforms that are not bringing back return on investment (ROI) to the client or are no longer available • Determine whether some platforms are fine, so there is nothing that needs to be done • Set a timeline and date for when you do the evaluation and health report again for all of the platforms

Working in Social Media

Working in social media can be very exciting yet demanding, and the roles constantly are changing as fast as the platforms are. Neill and Moody (2015) explored the changes and duties happening for social media strategists and discussed the various tasks, experiences, and expectations facing these professionals in their roles. These duties ranged from handling communication issues to testing emerging technologies, and even discussed the importance of understanding the collection and analysis of data emerging from these platforms. Yet one of the growing areas of discussion about working in social media is whether or not you need to have the same principles and practices for your personal use as your professional use, which Moreno, Navarro, Tench, and Zerfass (2015) discussed in their research. Professionals working in social media had a high level of usage of these platforms for the sole purpose of creating influence in their community, establishing proactive relationships, and becoming relevant influencers in their own right in their thought leadership circles. The social media field and workplace is seeing a shift of focus from return on relationships. **Return on Relationship (RoR),** according to Ted Rubin (2015), is a must-have for professionals today since "social media drives engagement, engagement drives loyalty and advocacy, and both correlate directly with increased sales."

The workload and skills necessary to succeed in the field are changing more often than not. Some underlying skills and abilities are still important for organizations looking to hire social media professionals. Writing, research, and creative execution are traditional skills seen in marketing, public relations, and other communication disciplines. However, the rising expectations of the maturing field have also allowed the expectations for young professionals entering the field to be a bit higher. Of course, this depends on the industry, business, and even company or organization in focus. There is no real set "standard" for the expectations, roles, or even qualifications. Yet, certain fundamental skills, experiences, and qualifications do need to be taken into consideration, and are discussed and highlighted in greater detail in Chapter 4.

The information we share on social media is vastly different from the capability of the original platforms. When Facebook got started in 2004, you were only able to share updates via text, but it has evolved to allow chat bots, live video, virtual reality, mixed reality, and 360-degree immersive experiences.

BRIDGING THE SCIENCE AND PRACTICE OF SOCIAL MEDIA

Social media encompasses both the research and theoretically driven work being done to explore networks, relationships, and how individuals respond and react to various messages and information online. Understanding the foundation of why people behave, share stories and content, and share information publicly and privately provides social media professionals with a sound view of why certain things occur without reinventing the wheel. On the flip side, exploring the creative possibilities for these insights turning into actionable steps and strategies is also important. Bridging these two perspectives together in a way that is both integrated and comprehensive is one of the most important accomplishments of a social media professional.

What Can Science Tell Us About Social Media?

Researchers who have explored social media in their work have used a variety of different theoretical frameworks to help explain and predict why certain attitudes, behaviors, and actions are taken online, such as dialogic theory (Kent & Taylor, 2016; Yang & Kent, 2014), user gratification theory (Gao & Feng, 2016), psychological empowerment theory (Li, 2016), and theory of planned behavior (Freberg, 2012). Even in social media research, there are still some challenges and opportunities for researchers to determine how to effectively measure certain concepts in the field, such as engagement (Jiang, Luo, & Kulemeka, 2016; Sisson, 2017; Smith & Gallicano, 2015). Further research in understanding these concepts as well as how they can be strategically applied needs to be taken into consideration. Even though social media has become a source for engagement and an opportunity for users and businesses specifically, little research up to this point discusses how exactly social media fits in the overall strategy from a marketing and communications standpoint (Killian & McManus, 2015), which brings forth the growing need for a bridge between practice and researchers to address this.

Social media can be accomplished by looking at the scientific elements that make up the communities. It helps the strategist understand not only what is happening, but why and how behaviors, actions, and communities happen in any given time. The tools and methods used in traditional disciplines like marketing, education, computer science, public relations, advertising, and communication, among others, can help test and evaluate the behaviors of what is happening online. Social media professionals cannot rely just on the creative artistic opportunities social media allows us to use and take advantage of. Instead, we have to hone in on our analytical and scientific approaches and fine-tune our research skills to make sense of the unstructured and substantial data available to understand not only what is being presented but in what context and situation. This adds to the growing expectation and need for social media professionals to have a solid research foundation and background to help them make sense of the data and apply it in a creative and innovative way.

Research. You will have to become one with statistics, Excel spreadsheets, data, and many other mathematical elements when it comes to social media. There are two parts of the equation a successful social media strategist needs to be aware of when looking at the various platforms. First, the actual information and data are collected in a systematic way from the various platforms or third parties. We will cover this in more detail in Chapter 5, but consider the physical elements that are created, shared, and constructed on social media. Social media strategists have to organize the information in ways that are able to tell us what is going on. This will help identify trends, gaps, opportunities, or even challenges that need to be addressed in a systematic and applied manner. The second element is that research comes down to a science in the systematic process in which the data are analyzed. Most of the time, the data are in raw form and need to be organized in a way that makes sense and is understandable to both the strategist and the client/organization in question (see Chapter 10).

How Is Social Media Like a Practice?

While the previous sections discussed briefly the science (research- or theory-driven) aspect of social media, it is also important to note areas on the other side of the social media coin. Understanding the creative execution is an area most people associate with social media, but each platform has a strategic purpose behind each area.

Creativity. The demands of being creative today in social media are more important than ever. Without creativity, there is no buzz, excitement, or word-of-mouth conversations that spark audiences to share content. New tools, software programs, and people are coming on board with social media, which is raising the bar to take ideas that would be considered good at any other point in time to the next level.

Any person can go about sharing and creating content, but content that is unique, invokes an inspired and emotional response, and can cut through the digital and irrelevant noise really makes an impact on the audience. That's what creativity does for social media. It's about not just looking at the tools or thinking creativity is all about being artistic. It is the light that shines on the brand and communities that help generate these innovative conversations through insights and data that leads them to have these great ideas. **Informed decision making** (coined by Rich Calabrese of Fizziology) is about taking creativity, data, and insight into account for social media. Creativity can be disseminated from the top down (organization to key publics), but there is also the co-creation aspect of creativity, where you are able to use your community to help share, brainstorm ideas, and discover content, stories, or original ways of approaching an idea. The ultimate goal is not just to have one organization or brand tell a story but also to create a spark for others to be motivated to participate and share these conversations and stories with others.

When it comes to innovative ways to be creative with content, certain campaigns and brands have successfully implemented this very well. Pharrell's "Happy" video went viral immediately after it was showcased by millions and inspired many to re-create the music video with their own voice and personalization in 2013. ALS Association's Ice Bucket Challenge honed in on the impact of crowdfunding for a significant cause while adding visual creativity to the mix by allowing people to create their own Ice Bucket Challenge videos and tagging their friends, family, and community members on social media. Many such campaigns stand out not only for their creative ideas but also for their creative executions. To be successful when it comes to creativity, you have to have the content, but you also have to have the proper execution.

For example, campaigns like BuzzFeed and Tasty became viral when they started creating short videos of various recipes in snackable forms of content that resonated with audiences. Another campaign got a lot of attention for creating more creative partnerships in which two established brands could share virtually with their communities. Disney and Make-A-Wish Foundation came together in 2016 to raise awareness for terminally ill children with their campaign #ShareYourEars. This campaign was driven primarily through Twitter and Instagram in 2016, and for every post, Disney pledged a $5 donation to the Make-A-Wish Foundation. Not only did the message resonate with the audiences, but the campaign was approached in a creative and visual way. In addition, it was so successful that Disney increased its cap from $1 million to $2 million for the campaign (Make-A-Wish Foundation of America, 2018). Both of these campaigns were strategic in their creative ideas, using their own brand voice, community, and ideas to formulate successful campaigns. Creativity doesn't always mean thinking completely out of the box when it comes to proposing new ideas for a campaign. What it does mean is making informed decisions based on the landscape, industry, audience, and brand through brainstorming sessions, data analysis, and insights gathered.

Storytelling. Everyone has a unique story to share. The worst thing to do is try to tell a story just like someone else's because that will not be authentic to your brand. Plus, stories that are not executed correctly will be lost in the mix. You could have the best visual effects and videographer out there, but if the execution of your story is not there, it is a waste of time.

Successful stories are able to connect and resonate with audiences on a personal level to drive them to feel a specific emotion based on what they have seen from you. Whether via a video or post, you will make a strong connection if you tap into the emotions of an audience member. Once this connection is made, a memorable experience is added to the story, and this allows the receiver to consider what actions to take.

Users may just view the piece of content, but they may also be compelled to share it with their network for others to see and experience as well.

The best person to share your story according to what best represents your personality, persona, and vision is you. All successful social media brands, companies, and professionals spend a lot of time and energy sharing their stories in a creative and unique way.

Brands and users can use storytelling effectively in several ways:

- *Allow users to be part of the experience.* Some brands allow users to get these experiences and share their viewpoint with others on behalf of the brand. In 2017, Royal Caribbean created an "Intern-ship" contest to find the perfect Instagram explorer to be part of the cruise experience and share content on behalf of the cruise line to drive travel destination sales and buzz ("Royal Caribbean," 2017).

- *Listen and create relevant content.* Data will be your friend when you need it to be in social media. Use data as a guide to what stories and pieces of content you feel will most resonate with your audiences. Taking the initiative to ask questions or tell your audience to do a certain behavior (snap us back a selfie, post a picture on Instagram, etc.) allows you to gauge the user-generated content aspect but also use the buzz, insights, and data to make a more informed decision on what stories to showcase next.

- *Showcase your values.* When you are looking at brands or individuals, they may want to focus on their products and services as well as what they can offer you in terms of making a sale. Yet sometimes brands and others stand up for what they believe in and share content featuring what they want to be known for in a different way. Always created a #LikeAGirl campaign (Diaz, 2015) that got a lot of traction for not only its strong message but the way in which it was presented across the various platforms. The message was consistent and resonated with the audiences. Launched during the 2015 Super Bowl, the campaign won a 2015 Emmy for Outstanding Commercial. The integration across the different platforms while staying on message consistently for the brand made it one of the most successful social media campaigns from a strategy perspective.

- *Share your point of view.* Gary Vaynerchuk has become a storytelling content machine. From a personal branding standpoint, he has this down to a science by consistently sharing his story and experience through videos, essentially vlogging his daily activities and moves in a consistent and branded manner with his videographer David Rock (otherwise known to the social media world as "DRock"). Gary also emphasizes this strongly to point out the difference between documenting and creating content. Documenting your daily activities online does not mean you are creating content, but rather it is a version of creating focus more on the practical aspect of sharing instead of focusing on storytelling (Vaynerchuk, 2016). The difference is that documenting is creating content of who you are rather than creating content for who you want to be (Vaynerchuk, 2016).

How Can We Bridge Science and Art Effectively?

Throughout this book, you will note there is a growing need for understanding both sides of what makes social media a strategic profession and industry to work, research, and teach in. Most of the time, only one side of the coin is presented. Having a balanced approach to research and practice is not only necessary but expected by those working in the field.

Several new expectations are outlined for social media professionals to definitely adapt to for their own sakes, but also for their clients, organizations, businesses, and communities. Some of the following will be discussed and emphasized a bit later in the textbook:

- Social media is not owned by one person or platform. It is owned by the community.

- Social media is more than just posting updates and taking snaps. It's a strategic mindset to embrace.

- The primary reason for social media is not to publish content to generate hype or FOMO, but to have a purpose and rationale behind it and be a win-win for you and your audiences.

- Saying you are an expert or "guru" on social media doesn't truly show your expertise. Your work and the relationships you formulate do.

- Social media needs to shift from promoting to everyone to fine-tuning your efforts on engaging with your audiences at the right time, on the right channel, and in the right situation.

- Quality over quantity—whether it is followers, content, or conversations— always wins.

- Social media roles will evolve, blur with other duties, and sometimes actually disappear.

- Social media is not about audiences just "seeing" your content. It's about your audience sharing and responding to your content.

- Social media is about being "social." Don't be a programmed robot.

- You are what you present yourself as online. First impressions are all that count.

- People want engagement and content that resonates with them, not spam.

- Be authentic and consistent, not a constant salesperson.

- Social media is more than just content. This is surface level, and there's much more below that is planned, brainstormed, argued, and executed before the post button is even pushed.

CHAPTER SUMMARY

Social media is an evolving area of professional activities and personal relationships. These platforms will continue to evolve or, in some cases, disappear completely. This is an industry where change is at a rapid pace, sometimes racing at the speed of light and always on the move. Social media professionals may at times feel they are "out of date" with the technologies even though they are just catching up on last week's news. There are many areas in which social media can be viewed as both an art and a science, but some fundamental aspects create bridges between these two areas. Relationships, strategy, and people are what make social media the platform, community, and industry it is today.

THOUGHT QUESTIONS

1. Based on the reading, how would you define social media? How has social media evolved over time?

2. What are some of the main takeaways from the history of the social media platforms? What points stand out the most?

3. How can social media professionals use the science dimension of social media to their advantage? What can social media professionals do to spark creativity and innovation in their work? How can these two areas collaborate together?

4. Discuss how research and practice are key parts of what makes social media the way it is today.

EXERCISES

1. You enter a job interview and the human resources director asks you to define social media and answer the question, "Is social media a science or an art?" Discuss your thoughts on this and use a current campaign or case study as evidence to support your points.

2. You are applying for an internship with Texas Roadhouse for the summer, and the manager has asked you to come up with some potential ideas for the restaurant to use for storytelling on social media. Provide a few suggestions for content Texas Roadhouse could consider creating that is both branded and user-generated, and include a rationale for each.

3. You have been asked to create a social media audit for a local nonprofit in town. The firm is on all of the social media platforms but does not get as much engagement on Twitter as it wants. Discuss the process you will go through in determining which platforms to use and no longer use.

REFERENCES

boyd, d. m. (2006). Friends, Friendsters, and top 8: Writing community into being on social network sites. *First Monday*, 11(12), 1–19.

boyd, d. m., & Ellison, N. B. (2008). Social network sites: Definition, history, and scholarship. *Journal of Computer-Mediated Communication*, 13, 210–230.

Braiker, B. (2014, August 14). The "Ice Bucket Challenge": A case study in viral marketing gold. *Digiday*. Retrieved from http://digiday.com/brands/ice-bucket-challenge-case-study-viral-marketing-success/.

Diaz, A.-C. (2015, September 13). Always' hard-hitting "Like a Girl" wins 2015 outstanding commercial Emmy. *AdAge*. Retrieved from http://adage.com/article/advertising/always-like-a-girl-wins-2015-emmy-outstanding-commercial/300343/.

Eordogh, F. (2016, May 23). Why "Chewbacca Mask Mom" is the most famous haul video to date. *Forbes*. Retrieved from http://www.forbes.com/sites/fruzsinaeordogh/2016/05/23/why-chewbacca-mask-mom-is-the-most-famous-haul-video-to-date/.

Facebook Newsroom. (2018). *Company info*. Retrieved from http://newsroom.fb.com/company-info/.

Fiegerman, S. (2014, January 6). Snapchat CEO reveals why he rejected Facebook's $3 billion dollar offer. *Mashable*. Retrieved from http://mashable.com/2014/01/06/snapchat-facebook-acquisition-2/.

Freberg, K. (2012). Intention to comply with crisis messages communicated via social media. *Public Relations Review*, 38(3), 416–421. DOI: https://doi.org/10.1016/j.pubrev.2012.01.008.

Freberg, K. (2016). Social media. In C. Carroll (Ed.), *Encyclopedia for corporate reputation* (pp. 773–776). Thousand Oaks, CA: SAGE.

Gao, Q., & Feng, C. (2016). Branding with social media: User gratifications, usage patterns, and brand message content strategies. *Computers in Human Behavior*, 63, 868–890. DOI: http://doi.org/10.1016/j.chb.2016.06.022.

JESS3. (n.d.). *JESS3 Labs: The Social Media Brandsphere*. Retrieved from http://jess3.com/social-media-brandsphere/.

Jiang, H., Luo, Y., & Kulemeka, O. (2016). Social media engagement as an evaluation barometer: Insights from communication executives. *Public Relations Review*, 42(4), 679–691. DOI: http://doi.org/10.1016/j.pubrev.2015.12.004.

Johnson, L. (2016, May 11). Taco Bell's Cinco de Mayo Snapchat lens was viewed 224 million times. *Adweek*. Retrieved from http://www.adweek.com/news/technology/taco-bells-cinco-de-mayo-snapchat-lens-was-viewed-224-million-times-171390.

Kent, M. L., & Taylor, M. (2016). From *Homo economicus* to *Homo dialogicus*: Rethinking social media use in CSR communication. *Public Relations Review*, 42(1), 60–67. DOI: http://doi.org/10.1016/j.pubrev.2015.11.003.

Killian, G., & McManus, K. (2015). A marketing communications approach for the digital era: Managerial guidelines for social media integration. *Business Horizons*, 58(5), 539–549. DOI: http://doi.org/10.1016/j.bushor.2015.05.006.

Kleinberg, J. (2008, November). The convergence of social and technological networks. *Communications of ACM*, 51(11), 66–72.

Lariscy, R. W., Avery, E. J., Sweetser, K. D., & Howes, P. (2009). An examination of the role of online social media in journalists' source mix. *Public Relations Review*, 35(3), 314–316. DOI: https://doi.org/10.1016/j.pubrev.2009.05.008.

Li, Z. (2016). Psychological empowerment on social media: Who are the empowered users? *Public Relations Review*, 42(1), 49–59. DOI: http://doi.org/10.1016/j.pubrev.2015.09.001.

Make-A-Wish Foundation of America. (2018). *Disney Parks doubles its donation in recognition of overwhelming response*. Retrieved from http://wish.org/content/disney/share-your-ears?cid=WBST-SHAREYOUREARSMICROSITE.

Mangold, W. G., & Faulds, D. J. (2009). Social media: The new hybrid element of the promotion mix. *Business Horizons*, 52, 357–365.

Marken, G. A. (2007). Social media . . . The hunted can become the hunter. *Public Relations Quarterly*, 52(4), 9–12.

Moreno, A., Navarro, C., Tench, R., & Zerfass, A. (2015). Does social media usage matter? An analysis of online practices and digital media perceptions of communication practitioners in Europe. *Public Relations Review*, 41(2), 242–253. DOI: http://doi.org/10.1016/j.pubrev.2014.12.006.

Neill, M. S., & Moody, M. (2015). Who is responsible for what? Examining strategic roles in social media management. *Public Relations Review*, 41(1), 109–118. DOI: http://doi.org/10.1016/j.pubrev.2014.10.014.

Rogers, K. (2016, July 27). The "Ice Bucket Challenge" helped scientists discover a new gene tied to A.L.S. *The New York Times*. Retrieved from https://www.nytimes.com/2016/07/28/health/the-ice-bucket-challenge-helped-scientists-discover-a-new-gene-tied-to-als.html?_r=0.

Royal Caribbean offers trip of a lifetime to social media explorer. (2017, January 4). *Breaking Travel News*. Retrieved from http://www.breakingtravelnews.com/news/article/royal-caribbean-offers-trip-of-a-lifetime-to-social-media-explorer/.

Rubin, T. (2015, June 11). Social ROI: Return on Relationship is key. *Sprout Social*. Retrieved from http://sproutsocial.com/insights/return-on-relationship/.

Singh, A. (2016, December 2). Brexit campaign would have failed before advent of social media, say remain voters in new poll. *Independent*. Retrieved from http://www.independent.co.uk/news/uk/politics/brexit-social-media-new-poll-failed-remain-voters-a7450911.html.

Sisson, D. C. (2017). Control mutuality, social media, and organization-public relationships: A study of local animal welfare organizations' donors. *Public Relations Review*, 43(1), 179–189. DOI: http://doi.org/10.1016/j.pubrev.2016.10.007.

Smith, B. G., & Gallicano, T. D. (2015). Terms of engagement: Analyzing public engagement with organizations through social media. *Computers in Human Behavior*, 53, 82–90. DOI: http://doi.org/10.1016/j.chb.2015.05.060.

Vaynerchuk, G. (2016, December 1). Document, don't create: Creating content that builds your personal brand. *Gary Vaynerchuk*. Retrieved from https://www.garyvaynerchuk.com/creating-content-that-builds-your-personal-brand/.

Wagner, K. (2016, November 20). The marketing genius behind Snap's new Spectacles. *Recode*. Retrieved from http://www.recode.net/2016/11/20/13688096/snap-snapchat-spectacles-marketing-success.

Waters, R. D., Burnett, E., Lamm, A., & Lucas, J. (2009). Engaging stakeholders through social networking: How nonprofit organizations are using Facebook. *Public Relations Review*, 35, 102–106.

Yang, A., & Kent, M. (2014). Social media and organizational visibility: A sample of Fortune 500 corporations. *Public Relations Review*, 40(3), 562–564. DOI: http://doi.org/10.1016/j.pubrev.2014.04.006.

ETHICAL AND LEGAL FUNDAMENTALS IN SOCIAL MEDIA

Learning Objectives

Humans of Social Media

Introduction

What Is Ethics?

Additional Deadly Sins of Social Media

Legal Fundamentals

Employees and Personal Branding Mishaps

Social Media Policies

Chapter Summary

Thought Questions

Exercises

References

LEARNING OBJECTIVES

After reading this chapter, you will be able to

- Identify key concepts that are important to social media ethics and law
- Define ethics and construct your own ethical standards for social media
- Recognize the consequences and challenges social media raises for legal and ethical purposes
- Explain key ethical and legal principles for establishing a social media policy
- Understand the current ethical and legal landscape for working in social media

HUMANS OF SOCIAL MEDIA
CHRIS YANDLE, COMMUNICATION SPECIALIST AT ST. TAMMANY PARISH PUBLIC SCHOOLS

Introduction

If there were a modern definition of *nomad*, I seriously might be it. I spent more than 15 years in college athletics at six NCAA (National Collegiate Athletic Association) Division I institutions: Southern Miss, Louisiana–Lafayette, Marshall, Baylor, Miami, and Georgia Tech. During the later part of Career 1.0, I had one foot in academia and the other foot in college athletics. It was my time at both Baylor and later Kennesaw State where I realized my calling might be in the classroom. After being accepted into the PhD program at Mercer, I was let go from my job at Georgia Tech, effectively ending my college athletics career. Now, I have a normal 9–5 job as the Twitter/Facebook/video/photo guy for St. Tammany Parish Public Schools in Louisiana, and it has been the most rewarding thing I've done in a very long time.

(Continued)

(Continued)

How did you get your start in social media?

During the advent of Twitter and the immersion of Facebook (when anyone was allowed to join and you no longer needed a .edu email), social media became an extension of the necessary PR functions of our job. I think it was the 2008 football season when our office at Baylor started to notice this digital shift in presenting a narrative. Our digital media coordinator was the one who spearheaded our journey into the digital frontier. To be honest, I reluctantly signed up for a Twitter account. I didn't know what it was. Really, the majority of my time at Baylor was spent trying to figure this "social media thing" out. I don't know where the narrative started that I ran social media at Baylor, but it didn't come from me. I happened to be the most visible on social media because it was easy for me to communicate there. By nature, I am an insecure introvert who has a hard time expressing his thoughts and feelings orally (yet I can teach in an auditorium, no sweat). However, I think social media lends itself to the creativity of introverts as an easy medium to communicate. That's why I still am immersed in it.

What is your favorite part of working in your social media area of expertise?

My favorite part of working in social media is definitely the creative and planning process. Many people don't like planning in social media, and their idea is to post when things come up. I like looking two, three, even four weeks in advance and planning for content so that we can be flexible in curating spontaneous content or sharing immediate stories that don't require days of video editing. Planning content allows us to be more "in the moment" than most people realize.

What is one thing you can't live without while working in social media?

Aside from an endless supply of iPhone cords or extended batteries, my answer is buy-in—buy-in from the top and other outward-facing departments that social/digital media touches. You can have the greatest content and a closet full of phone batteries, but if the powers that be don't "get it" or "buy your why," then what's the point? I assure you many people will disagree with me, but I don't 100% believe that social media is a necessity for everyone. For example, only a handful of public school districts in Louisiana are active on social media. What does that say? It says not only do these districts not have the people resources, the time resources, or the financial resources, but it's not a necessity for them. Your why cannot be "because everyone else is doing it and they have 10 people posting social media content all day." That's not a strategy, nor is it a reason to do something.

What is your favorite social media account (person, brand, etc.) to follow, and why?

My feet and interests overlap into so many areas that I don't have one person above all to follow, but I have a favorite in different areas:

- **Overall Branding/Thought Processes.** A tie between Gary Vaynerchuk (@garyvee), Jon Acuff (@jonacuff), and Simon Sinek (@simonsinek). Gary provides a refreshing view of things I believe or don't understand. Jon and Simon's ideas of knowing your why helped me get to where I am today, and will continue to help me as I look toward the future.

- **Sports Media.** My friend Jessica Smith (@warjesseagle) on Twitter. Her thoughts transcend sports. What she offers is applicable to other industries across the country, in a similar vein as Gary Vaynerchuk.

- **Higher Ed Academia.** (Aside from this book's author, of course) Dr. B. David Ridpath (@drridpath) and a nonacademic, ESPN's Jay Bilas (@jaybilas), both on Twitter. Really and selfishly for me, I mention these two because they will play such a vital role in my PhD dissertation on the "student athlete and amateurism" myth in college athletics.

- **Leadership.** Kevin DeShazo (@kevindeshazo) on Twitter. He gets "it." I had the opportunity to meet Kevin when he was launching his social media education firm, Fieldhouse Media, and we've since become good friends. He was in the corporate world, and what he learned there has been applied to his new venture, Fieldhouse Leadership.

- **General.** The Dogist (@thedogist) on Instagram. My reason is simple: I have two dogs, and I am a dog lover. Most days, this account makes me smile and changes the course of my day.

What is the most challenging part of working in social media?

During my time in college athletics, there were two really challenging aspects for me: time and not taking things personally. For time, social media in college athletics—and really sports, period—is a 24/7 job. You're always on the clock, and that caught up to me eventually. I was always worried about what was being said, how we needed to respond, and what people in our building would think. It was a completely reactive mentality—and an unhealthy one at that. As far as the "taking things personally" aspect, I believe most of the people on Twitter and Facebook either think that an intern runs social media accounts for a team or don't think there is an actual human on the other side of that exchange. You aren't shouting into a vacuum: There are individuals answering your posts and incendiary comments with feelings. It can be a tough pill to swallow now that it's so much easier for people to spout hateful things to others so quickly.

What is your take on your area of expertise and the social media industry?

The biggest thing I notice is that we are in the throes of a serious nuclear arms race in the sports digital space. College teams are trying to one-up each other with graphics, video presentations, and content because it all ties back to recruiting kids. It's not necessarily about the fans anymore, and the media are a distant afterthought on social media for many schools. Schools are losing sight of what's important and instead are looking to be the next viral sensation. With that said, I'm all for schools and teams showing personality online as a way to personify them. It's great. What I don't like about the direction is everyone's insistence

on delivering that next tweet or post that "throws shade" at another school. How does doing that better your university, its brand, or the team's perception? It doesn't. It gets you on TV, and you're the cool kid for 24 hours. Does that make you sleep better at night? It's the "tortoise and hare" strategy. I'd rather be the tortoise and be methodical and intentional with what I'm doing than be the hare and race out to a fast start so people can talk about me.

Again, maybe I'm sounding like that old guy shouting "Get off my lawn!" at the neighborhood kids, but I feel, for some in the business, social media is all about getting clicks and clickbait headlines. There's more to life than retweets, new followers, and mentions. There is a bigger picture—bigger than us—that we should focus on, and we should use social media as the avenue to achieve those big-picture ideals.

What do you wish you had known when you were starting out?

Control social media; don't let social media control you. We have an amazing power in our hands with our phones. We are creators and inventors. We have the power to build people up or tear people down. It's a power that many don't know how to use *effectively.* Use social media for the common good and to make a positive difference in the world. Don't let the faceless and nameless egg avatars control how you feel. That's been my biggest struggle, and it continues to affect me today because I let it.

Chris Yandle is a social media and PR professional for St. Tammany Parish Public Schools in Louisiana. Chris is also a former sports information director and sports professional who has worked with Baylor University, University of Miami, and Georgia Tech. Chris can be connected with on Twitter and Instagram at @chrisyandle.

INTRODUCTION

Understanding the different platforms, tools, and communities that involve social media is one thing. However, we also need to be aware of the underlying legal and ethical implications that help guide our practices, communication efforts, and behaviors online. You may be asking yourself, "Do I really have to understand the law when it comes to social media?"

Ethics falls into these circumstances as well. You will want to ask yourself a few questions to really capture the importance of understanding not only what ethical practices cover on social media, but the overall importance of applying them to your day-to-day interactions online:

- Do I care if people search previous updates (pictures, messages, blog posts, etc.) to use for job interviews?

- Am I aware that while I have my account settings set to "private," they really are not?

- Do I care if I send out a tweet or snap that may look "cool" online with my friends, but could reflect poorly on the organization or company I represent?

- Do I know what I need to do in case someone uses my profile picture to create a fake account?

- Am I aware that an update made in a spark of emotion or outrage could cause me to get suspended from my job, miss out on a job opportunity, or even get fired?

- Do I understand the impact of sharing my opinion online for the world to see, and the community, professional, and global implications toward my personal brand?

- Am I aware of the power (and risks) associated with saying something online and the effects it may have on another person?

These are just a few questions you may want to ask yourself when it comes to ethics on social media. Many professionals have had to face these questions in a variety of different situations in their professional and personal circles. Yet others may ask you these questions at any time, so make sure you are prepared and know how you will answer.

You may be wondering how this all pertains to social media and being online. The answer is simple: Social media is not only about building an online brand, establishing paid ads or sponsored posts to generate buzz online, or even setting up a place to tell your own story. All of these are important, but fundamentally, social media is about being "social." Being social means establishing and maintaining relationships. It's an art form in itself since users have to be skilled at navigating their various relationships with colleagues, friends, peers, community members, and others. Each relationship has layers (like onions from the movie *Shrek*), and these layers are complex and constantly evolving with experiences and exchanges. People always have certain expectations when it comes to social media from a communication standpoint and how we should behave, operate, and present ourselves. Essentially, what we say and stand for online has to be followed by our actions. A common phrase tied to social media is "Actions speak louder than words." When it comes to social media ethics, it is very easy to speak about being professional, but it's entirely another area to act ethically on a consistent basis. This is where trust comes from, but it is earned over time.

Ultimately, the issue that arises in social media occurs when users' expectations for the brand, profession, or organization are violated online. A lot of ethical issues could be addressed if people were aware of how their actions and behaviors might be perceived.

One incident can change someone's opinion of you as a person, which at times may be a hard lesson to follow. Ethics and professionalism have been at the forefront within both the profession and the curriculum across various disciplines, but we are still facing an uphill challenge when it comes to teaching how to be a proactive member of society on social media. The use of social media ranges from how your friends use it to how professionals use it for their business activities.

WHAT IS ETHICS?

Ethics are a set of moral guidelines and principles that influence our behaviors and interactions. Having a set ethical code of conduct is essential when exploring how to react and respond to various situations that may emerge when we are working in social media. These guidelines help us tell the difference between what is wrong and what is right. Most of the time, people have a set of values that they hold dear and feel are important for them to follow. These ethical principles can be personal behaviors and actions, but also translate into professional circles. All professional organizations (advertising, public relations, marketing, journalism, communications, and additional disciplines) have a professional code of ethics for members to follow when they are working and practicing in the field.

Social media professionals may face a variety of different situations while they are employed for a large corporation, media outlet, agency, or consulting firm, or even when they are part of an organization (e.g., student athletes). Access to information pertaining to personal accounts on social media sites has been discussed in the online community as well as in the court of law.

Certain behaviors are not universally accepted when it comes to social media professionals. Steph Parker (2013) discussed some of these "new deadly sins of social media":

Misappropriation. This particular sin focuses on the timing and appropriateness of jumping into a conversation that is not entirely relevant or necessary for a brand. It really comes into play when brands try to jump on board with a trend (**trendjacking**) on social media. The trends can be viral like Running Man and Crying Michael Jordan, among others, but there is a time and place for brands and professionals to promote themselves. This is especially true when the trending topic focuses on an emotional situation (e.g., insensitive tweets by Gap during Hurricane Sandy or by Epicurious during the Boston Marathon bombing).

Abandonment. As mentioned earlier, social media is about the conversation, and you can't have success with a community if you are not a part of it. Social media communities need to be built as well as maintained. Brands, organizations, and professionals must decide which platforms to be on and how invested in these platforms their communities should be. The worst thing that can happen is to jump on board a platform and then leave it before it can really be embraced. Abandonment is an extreme case, but the point is to make sure you are using a particular platform for the conversation and community. As they say, if you build it, they will come. However, if you leave, so will your community.

Manipulation. There is a time and place to ask your community to take action to support a cause, share a post or update, or even help another member of the community. Yet social media is not the place to ask your community to reach a certain number of followers so you can get paid more for speaking opportunities, which is sometimes seen in the professional social media circuit. The ultimate goal is to be yourself and present your brand in the most authentic way, and that comes from not using cheap tricks and measures to generate a false view of who you are. Be willing to share content that is relevant with your community, but respect the fact that people may or may not be influenced by what you ask them to do. That comes with trust, credibility, and a relationship.

On the flip side, you do not want to manipulate or present a false sense of community or success by using services to make it appear like your account or campaign is successful when, in reality, it is not. For example, some businesses set up click-through sign-ups for a charity or donation or falsely promise to take action if you get a certain number of likes or comments/views.

Ignorance. This comes with a lot of components to address, and it's important to highlight the ones most at risk of being committed by social media professionals. There is the ignorance of basic terms and practices in social media. Be aware of the main terms, jargon, and legal obligations for social media practices (e.g., asking permission to use a tweet or image for a story, or to live stream a college football game knowing you are in violation of TV rights). This goes back to knowing the Federal Trade Commission (FTC) guidelines as well as terms of service for each platform you are using for your social media practices. Then, there is the ignorance of not seeing what your community members are sharing and thus failing to respond to them. With no engagement or interaction from both sides, there is a risk to the overall health of the community on social media. If people feel ignored, they will go somewhere else. View exchanges and questions not as threats but as opportunities to learn how to improve.

Monotony. Passion is a great element to connect audiences on social media, but social media professionals do not want to push the same content over and over again. Content needs to be fresh, relevant, and tied to the audience's needs and expectations. These needs and expectations grow over time, and keeping a constant pulse on what is happening in the community and among the different audience groups is critical. Audiences do not want to receive updates sharing "Like our page" or "Tag three people to win this contest" in 2018 and beyond because businesses and brands have been using these tactics on social media since the beginning of time. They want to be entertained, inspired, and motivated to share because the content they see connects with them on an emotional level. Although it can be challenging for brands to recognize, this is how audiences are presently operating, and it is going to take more time (and investment) to bring forth creative and fresh new pieces of content online. Pushing the same content to audiences like a brand has done before is no longer going to cut it in the digital first world.

Narcissism. Since social media is public, what you share with the world is for everyone to see. Essentially, you are what you share, so make sure to keep that in mind. I am holding the mirror up to some of the popular influencers such as Kylie Jenner and Kim Kardashian West. There is a time to personalize your brand, but you do not want to spam people with your logo, YouTube videos, and every piece of content you have ever created. This applies to following practices as well. Do not worry about how many people are following you or your ratio between follows and followers. Social media professionals have been guilty of following, and then unfollowing, a lot of people so their numbers stay up but others go down. You do not need to share your own content all the time or quote it on Twitter.

The cardinal sin for social media is buying followers. *Do not do this.* Quality is always better than quantity when it comes to your community. While high numbers get a lot of excitement and praise from people, qualifying you for some of those "must-follow lists" you see getting published, it's not worth it. Plus, it is very easy to find out who has real followers and who has **bots** (automated accounts to share and comment on posts) across these various platforms. A number of fake accounts and services do this, but you do not want to create a fake image for yourself—it will only damage your reputation.

Uniformity. Having a consistent image is one thing, but having the same content on every platform is another. While on some platforms repurposed content is appropriate (e.g., Facebook and Instagram), this does not mean you share the exact same content all at once or in the same format. Consider the differences between Snapchat videos and Instagram videos, or the different algorithm characteristics you need to be aware of on Facebook versus LinkedIn. Plus, each platform has its own communities and expectations, so make sure to personalize these experiences across the board.

Additional Deadly Sins of Social Media

Since Steph Parker discussed these sins back in 2013, social media has come a long way in addressing them, but there are others of which we have to be aware as well that can influence how we conduct our business, communication, and storytelling practices:

Bullying. This will be discussed in more detail later on in this chapter, but essentially, you want to treat others how you would like to be treated. It is very easy to hide behind the screen and vent on someone, or even try to make people feel different based on what you share with them. Establishing fake accounts, saying negative false things about people, being aggressive with hurtful messages, and sharing private information for the public to see are just some examples of bullying behavior.

Not giving credit where credit is due. Everyone wants to be acknowledged and praised for bringing a useful point to the discussion, sharing a great article, or even providing a great example of a campaign to a community. You want to give credit to the person who came up with the original idea—similar to citing a source in a research paper. No one likes it when someone else gets the praise and shout-outs when he or she was not the one who came up with the idea. That's not good manners. Giving praise and thanks does not cost anyone anything. In fact, it can actually be valuable and help contribute to your personal brand.

Sharing too much. You want to be transparent, of course, on social media, but you don't want to appear to be spamming everyone. There is a right amount of content to present across the different platforms. Yet keep in mind that not everyone may want to know what you had for breakfast or what you experienced at dinner last night at the latest new restaurant. In addition, remember that some people use social media to have conversations and a positive experience, but not to be bombarded with negativity all the time. Consider the balance between sharing your voice and point of view and how others may be responding to it.

Flame war outrage. Hell hath no fury like a social media user scorned by something he or she does not like. Have you ever been outraged by something online? Often, we vent or sometimes even try to strike up a **flame war** (a campaign to spark negativity toward the other party involved) online. We have to maintain our cool and take a moment away from our keyboard before we start engaging. It is important to collect ourselves and evaluate the consequences or different situations that may arise if a particular post, update, tweet, or snap is shared with others.

Automation. You can't really call in social media. While many tools allow you to schedule updates ahead of time, most businesses and social media professionals know of the dreaded "automated direct messages" that frequently emerge if you follow a new account online. These automated responses are impersonal and not really about connecting on a relationship basis with another person. Automation can also pose a challenge and risk if a business or professional sends automated updates when others may not want to see them (like during a natural disaster incident or breaking news). With automation, you lose the personal exchanges and conversations that make social media a great place to network and communicate. People follow you not because you are a robot, but because there is a human side to your personal or professional brand.

Going rogue. Social media is about representing yourself truthfully online, and posting opinions without permission or out of context while still representing the agency or organization of record (otherwise known as **going rogue**) can lead to a misinterpretation of the information shared on the platform. This can range from actual employees of an organization or business taking control of its online account without permission (e.g., HMV in 2013, discussed below) or alternative accounts being made on Twitter for government agencies (e.g., @RogueNASA or #AltNationalParkService) in 2017.

HMV, an agency based in the United Kingdom, got into hot water when it fired its marketing team in 2013 (Holmes, 2013). The HMV marketing employees were the only ones with access to the company's social media accounts, so they locked the senior managers out of their accounts and started live tweeting their firings using #hmvXFactorFiring.

"We're tweeting live from HR where we're all being fired! Exciting!! #hmvXFactorFiring," read the initial message from @HMVtweets, sent to the company's more than 70,000 Twitter followers around the globe. Earlier that morning, some 60 employees at the 91-year-old company had been sacked in a round of downsizing. One of them had hijacked the official Twitter account to vent her frustrations. A difficult day was about to get worse. (Holmes, 2013)

hmv @hmvtweets   1m
Just overheard our Marketing Director (he's staying, folks) ask "How do I shut down Twitter?" #hmvXFactorFiring
Expand

hmv @hmvtweets   14m
Sorry we've been quiet for so long. Under contract, we've been unable to say a word, or -more importantly - tell the truth #hmvXFactorFiring
Expand

hmv @hmvtweets   15m
There are over 60 of us being fired at once! Mass execution, of loyal employees who love the brand. #hmvXFactorFiring
Expand

Source: Twitter/@hmvtweets

HMV Twitter Storm of Employee Firings

Another type of account that comes up on social media and pushes the envelope a little bit for brands and individuals is the alternative account. Alternative accounts serve as a notion to resist the official voice and stories they represent (Coffee, 2015; Leetaru, 2017). Essentially, these accounts have tried to place themselves in a position to interconnect with the official ones, but they provide an alternative perspective and offer to spark dialogue with others who may or may not agree with the official voice. A lot of risk is associated with these rogue accounts that touches on the ethical and legal lines of social media.

First, we do not know who is behind these accounts and whether or not they are who they say they are. Some individuals on these accounts have claimed they are employees (or former employees) of these organizations, but we do not know for sure.

Second, we are not aware of the ultimate goal for these accounts and if there is an alternative motive connecting these specific social media accounts to another task at hand (cybersecurity, hacking, etc.). While some of these accounts have large followings, we do not know if they are "real" or authentic, which brings forth the importance of having an official stamp of approval from the platform itself. For example, Facebook, Instagram, Twitter, and even LinkedIn offer verification checks to let others know this is the official account. Yet there is no guarantee who is hiding behind the screen even for these official accounts.

LEGAL FUNDAMENTALS

Terms of service agreements. Before you sign up for a social media account, be sure to review the terms of service (TOS). A TOS agreement is common for all social media accounts and platforms and is known to outline the terms and uses (or rules) dictated by the parent company (Facebook, Twitter, Instagram, etc.) for its platform. In each TOS, the platform states clearly what a user (or business) can and cannot do on the respective social media site (see Table 2.1).

In order to create an account or profile, the user has to agree to these terms. Some TOS agreements range from what users are able to own and create on the site to basic requirements (e.g., Instagram states you have to be 13 years or older to use the site). In addition, some platforms (e.g., Instagram and Snapchat) state

TABLE 2.1 ■ Current Listings of the Main Platforms' Terms of Service (TOS)		
Platform	**Terms of Service**	**Link**
Facebook	2015	www.facebook.com/terms
Twitter	2017	twitter.com/tos?lang=en
Instagram	2013	help.instagram.com/478745558852511
Snapchat	2017	www.snap.com/en-US/terms/
LinkedIn	2017	www.linkedin.com/legal/user-agreement
Pinterest	2016	policy.pinterest.com/en/terms-of-service
YouTube	2010	www.youtube.com/static?template=terms

the content that is shared and created on these sites is technically owned by the platform, whereas others (e.g., LinkedIn) state that the users own the content they share and create on social media. Other listings can be viewed on the DigitalGov website (www.digitalgov.gov) for other platforms as well as third-party applications frequently used on social media. Keep in mind, for all social media platforms, that TOS agreements may evolve and expand as new cases, legal rulings, and situations arise online.

Issue of free speech. Of course, traditional legal terms need to be discussed not only in relation to social media, but in how they are translated for use on each different platform. For example, tweeting a rumor about another person could result in a lawsuit (Gunkel, 2015). This is an ongoing topic of conversation when it comes to what employees share on social media related to their employers and job, what student athletes share relative to their athletic teams, and even what is shared during political campaigns. Whether or not people should share their opinions online in a public forum is one part of the equation, but the other is whether or not people's content should be censored or only allowed on certain social media platforms. Twitter, Facebook, and others are dealing with extreme cases of people abusing their platforms (trolling, cyberbullying, making online threats, etc.). Protection and respect for free speech is necessary in a free democracy, yet while social media has become more mainstream and established as both a field and a communication channel, brands, companies, and individuals still face challenges in this particular area.

Disclosure of consent. Facebook as a platform and company got into trouble over the amount of data it was collecting on users, but it also conducted an experiment that manipulated information posted. This experiment focused on 689,000 users and whether or not people were feeling positive or negative about what they were viewing on their timeline (Booth, 2014). In essence, Facebook was able to manipulate and filter information, comments, pictures, and videos in users' networks to test whether or not seeing positive or negative items on their timeline had an effect on their overall state (Booth, 2014). The news of this case study sparked outrage in the public on both ethical and legal grounds since the social network did not disclose this practice or ask users if it could do this for their timelines. Universities and research firms go through the ethical process of disclosing the nature of the study (via institutional review boards, or IRBs) for all studies involving human subjects, as well as require participants to fill out an informed consent form for the study, both of which Facebook did not do (Booth, 2014).

Employees and Personal Branding Mishaps

Online threats and cyberbullying. What you post online can become evidence even in a court of law. This happened in the case of Anthony Elonis and his Facebook posts involving his significant other. This case focused on addressing the issue of whether or not a post on Facebook constituted a real threat. Elonis's posts were used for evidence in court, and the case actually went up to the Supreme Court (Barnes, 2014). Many other cases have followed suit over the years, focusing on issues of cyberbullying, using profile pictures to create fake accounts (Jackson, 2018), and even posting content that could lead to termination of your job.

Justine Sacco
@JustineSacco

👤▾   🐦 Follow

Going to Africa. Hope I don't get AIDS. Just kidding. I'm white!

↩ Reply   🔁 Retweet   ⭐ Favorite   ●●● More

2,678
RETWEETS

1,206
FAVORITES

10:19 AM - 20 Dec 13 📍 from Hillingdon, London

Justine Sacco Case Study

In fact, the most common elements that get individuals into trouble are mishaps on social media. A post that may be viewed as inappropriate, insensitive, or egregious can also result in firings and other long-term consequences. Public shaming has become one of the most negatively impactful events individuals experience today on social media.

The case involving Justine Sacco is a warning for all who believe social media privacy is still a thing. Sacco, a former PR professional, used her Twitter account to share various personal opinions and views on all types of experiences, as well as exchanges she had with individuals.

It was not until December 2013 when she was boarding a plane from London to Cape Town (an 11-hour flight) that her world turned upside down and she became the number-one trending topic on Twitter (Waterlow, 2015). As shown in the photo above, Sacco posted an update that sparked outrage online and immediately went viral, and she got thousands of new followers and people reaching out to her about this. In fact, an organic hashtag, #HasJustineLandedYet, began trending (Waterlow, 2015). Even though Sacco deleted her account and tried to get rid of the evidence, her reputation was already ruined, and the professional damage was already done. What stands out about this case is the fact Sacco is still reliving the incident and has not been able to escape it.

Public shaming is not just for the moment in which a tweet, video, or update is uncovered, but it also follows the unrelenting culture of an entire community of people searching online and sharing updates (even writing posts, articles, and books) about the incident. Jon Ronson, author of the best-selling book *So You've Been Publicly Shamed* (2015), met up with Sacco for an interview and noted the impact this experience had on her as well as those who felt it was their responsibility to take her down on social media.

These are the types of incidents that the Internet (and society) does not allow people to forget about. However, the need for an understanding of what we can learn from this experience and when it is time to move on as a society must be addressed. The consequences of these public incidents on someone's personal and professional life are significant. We need to have a better approach to educating others about the consequences and risks before they fall into a similar situation.

Britt McHenry, an ESPN reporter, also found this to be true, although it was not a social media update that got her in hot water, but a video. McHenry's car was towed, and a security video surfaced of her being rude and ranting to the female employee at the tow truck business ("Blown to Britts," 2016). This video surfaced online well after the encounter occurred, but McHenry became a viral trend, like Sacco, overnight, with media, friends, and family asking her to comment about the situation (Pesta, 2016). The tweets, posts, articles, and calls for ESPN to dismiss McHenry from its programs emerged online. Not only was McHenry a trending topic, but more than 30,000 people followed her on Twitter, and their comments made her fear for her safety (Pesta, 2016). While McHenry is still a reporter for ESPN, she does share a cautionary tale about the power of social media. While it is key to note mistakes we have made in the public eye and on social media, it is also key to note that sometimes, no matter what, some people out there will take advantage of the situation and transform it into a negative public shaming experience. In 2016, McHenry told *Marie Claire*'s Abigail Pesta some lessons she has learned from the process:

> The most difficult speech will be the one I have to give to my future children someday. Every parent wants their kids to be proud of them, and unfortunately, I'll have to use myself as an example of how not to behave, a hard truth I think about daily. But I can advise them on how to cope if you get shamed online or bombarded by hateful posts, because at the end of the day, none of that vitriol matters. For me, the key has been to focus on the present and on how to make myself a better person every day.
>
> I know now that as soon as you feel an empowering moment of success, you can experience a moment of utter failure just as fast. It's what you do *after* those moments that defines you. None of us should be judged solely by our worst mistakes. And, when you get the opportunity, you should work as hard as you can to prove that.
>
> (ESPN's Britt McHenry. "I Blame Myself, but the Video Is Not Who I Am," (2016); Retrieved from http://www.marieclaire.com/culture/news/a24045/espn-britt-mchenry-viral-video-apology/.)

Social media managers can get into trouble as well, sometimes interjecting humor into a situation that not many people feel is funny. Consider the case of Houston Rockets social media professional Chad Shanks. Shanks tweeted out on the official Houston Rockets account during a game in 2013 against the Dallas Mavericks (the Rockets won 103–94), but the tweet included two emojis (one was a horse, and the other was a gun) and said, "Shhhhh. Just close your eyes. It will all be over soon" (Gaines, 2015).

The Dallas Mavericks account responded, saying that was not "classy," and Shanks immediately got fired from his position since the Houston Rockets did not want to be associated with him after the incident (Harris, 2015). Shanks responded to the firing and used his own social media platform to explain the situation.

In each of these three different cases, posting on social media resulted in a firing. Each individual involved experienced a different outcome, and while it is important to note that not all social media posting fails are equal, they all share the experience of a negative impact on a reputation or personal brand, as well as a professional brand.

Privacy. This is one of the growing areas of focus when it comes to social media. Before 2013, regulation agencies appeared to be more attuned to the data being collected than to the protection of individual users (Claypoole, 2014). Social media can bring about a lot of positive opportunities, yet it also affects the concept of privacy. Every person has access to viewing and even going after others to attack them directly (cyberbullying). You never know who will review, read, and respond to the content you post online, whether it is updates on your vacation or your latest accomplishment at work.

Several agencies and regulatory bodies are actively involved in looking specifically at privacy, including the Federal Trade Commission. The FTC oversees a variety of elements, but when it comes to social media and privacy, it looks at whether or not the sites (Facebook, Instagram, etc.) publish how they work and what they do in terms of privacy and collecting information about individual users (Claypoole, 2014). Another big concern related to privacy and access to information arises when employers ask potential employees (and, in some cases, when universities ask student athletes) for access to their accounts. Twelve states (Arkansas, California, Colorado, Illinois, Maryland, Michigan, New Jersey, New Mexico, Nevada, Oregon, Utah, and Washington) have passed laws on this issue preventing an employer from gaining access to employees' personal accounts (Claypoole, 2014).

There are people who publish a lot online, and then there are people who present a false view of themselves. This violation of expectations (**reputation dissonance**) makes an impact on our brands. Yet sometimes the information being shared is false, and the victim can be a business, organization, or institution. Another element to take into consideration is the rise of a new type of user on social media: the **prosumer**.

> Prosumers write reviews, post comments, and share content within their network of friends and followers. . . . Because the bar for participation in social media is set so low, a teenager not only can have more followers on Twitter and friends on Facebook than an established corporate brand, but her opinions can often have greater impact and influence than a carefully crafted advertising campaign. (Gunkel, 2015)

This means that the barrier of entry to get access to these tools and platforms is minimal, but still anyone can write and engage in dialogue in positive or negative circumstances.

Copyright infringement. Copyright infringement may involve the author of a work, a photographer, a videographer, a musician who created the music used in a video, TV footage, the creator of artwork, or a visual content creator. This has become a big issue related to content that is shared, created, and accessed online. Artists have brought their concerns to Pinterest, ranging from their copyrighted work being shared without attribution to other media outlets creating new content based on original content without permission, such as in the National Football League (NFL) and Deadspin case. In 2016, the NFL asked Twitter to suspend Deadspin's account for creating GIFs (animated images) from NFL game content (Brodkin, 2015; Panzironi, 2016). The Digital Millennium Copyright Act (DMCA), which took effect in 2000, focuses on two sections:

- The "anti-circumvention" provisions (sections 1201 *et seq.* of the Copyright Act) bar circumvention of access controls and technical protection measures.

- The "safe harbour" provisions (section 512) protect service providers who meet certain conditions from monetary damages for the infringing activities of their users and other third parties on the net. (Electronic Frontier Foundation, 2018)

Essentially, the main issue involving the NFL and Deadspin was the fact that if a user (or another media outlet) creates content from original footage without permission or attribution, it may bring about concern from the impacted party (Panzironi, 2016). In essence, the number of shares and views of the GIFs, coverage of their use, and frequency of conversation shares on Deadspin were just some of the reasons why the NFL voiced its concern. Twitter suspended Deadspin's account for a short period of time, but it led to a transformation within the NFL on the rules for content shared on social media. This case also impacted the 2016 Summer Olympics in Rio, where there were strict policies on what could and could not be shared, created, or disseminated from the global athletic event.

There are, of course, various things to keep in mind when you are signing up to join a social media platform. It is important to know the terms you are signing into, how much control you have over the content you create, and if any changes are made to these terms. All social media platforms have their own terms of service (as outlined in Table 2.1), but each platform has gotten into trouble due to rising concerns about who "owns" the content being shared—and perhaps used for profitable means. Snapchat, for example, updated its services and advised users that while individual users have "ownership rights," Snapchat still has power to use their content since it is on the platform:

> [Y]ou grant Snapchat a worldwide, perpetual, royalty-free, sublicensable, and transferable license to host, store, use, display, reproduce, modify, adapt, edit, publish, create derivative works from, publicly perform, broadcast, distribute, syndicate, promote, exhibit, and publicly display that content in any form and in any and all media or distribution methods (now known or later developed).
>
> We will use this license for the limited purpose of operating, developing, providing, promoting, and improving the Services; researching and developing new ones; and making content submitted through the Services available to our business partners for syndication, broadcast, distribution, or publication outside the Services. (Wood, 2015)

Endorsements (bloggers and influencers). Whether or not bloggers or **influencers** (individuals who are able to persuade audiences to take action) are getting paid for their content, images, or experiences by a brand is one of the rising legal concerns about social media. The FTC has taken actions to address this concern with bloggers, but moved on to social media celebrities and influencers. For example, DJ Khaled (an influencer on Snapchat) never discloses whether he is getting paid by the brands that he features on his snaps (Frier & Townsend, 2016).

The FTC also has been "keeping up with the Kardashians" when it comes to following their endorsement and advertising practices. A nonprofit that focuses on cases involving deceptive advertising has drawn its attention to the Kardashians with evidence from Instagram that they have been violating the FTC's endorsement and advertising guidelines (Maheshwari, 2016). It is not just a single case that the FTC has focused on, but each member of the family has posted content that has drawn concern. Plus, the Kardashians have also come under fire for promoting items and products on Instagram, but it is hard to tell whether they really like the products or it is just an ad (Maheshwari, 2016). The same goes for the Kardashians promoting certain weight loss products and skin care lines. The key trend across all of these cases is that these individuals are not being honest to the public about whether or not they are getting paid to promote or be part of a campaign. The way in which the Kardashians have addressed this in their Instagram posts has been to add #ad to the end of the update.

The main concern here is that companies are paying (and sometimes overpaying) influencers to promote their brands, and audiences need to be aware of this. According to Captiv8, influencers with a certain number of followers can get $187,500 for a YouTube video, $75,000 for a post on Instagram or Snapchat, and $30,000 for a post on Twitter (Maheshwari, 2016).

These actions have significant consequences for the brands associated with these individuals. For example, YouTube personality PewDiePie was asked along with other YouTubers to promote a Warner Bros. video called *Middle-Earth: Shadow of Mordor* with positive reviews. Not disclosed was that he was being compensated. The FTC also went after the popular clothing brand Lord & Taylor for paying fashion influencers, but the influencers did not disclose that they were getting paid (Frier & Townsend, 2016). These cases have sparked the updated need for influencers to disclose to their audiences whether or not content is a promoted post or a sponsored ad. Most of the time, the influencers will use a hashtag such as #sponsored, #ad, or #paid. While this mostly applies to images and updates, the FTC requires influencers to voice this on the screen as well as place it on the screen if they are doing a video (Frier & Townsend, 2016).

letthelordbewithyou

● 12,196 likes

letthelordbewithyou Here you go, at 4pm est, write the below.
Caption:
Keeping up with the summer workout routine with my morning @booteauk

Yet some influencers and celebrities fail even at the endorsement mentions in a big way. Scott Disick learned this lesson when he copied and pasted a note from a brand without putting it into his own words (Beale, 2016). This particular example shows the implications that companies need to be aware of when targeting influencers and celebrities to promote their brands. Consumers today are very aware of the true nature of an influencer's promotion, and they want these recommendations and insights to be authentic, not paid. In addition, while number of followers and size of community are important indicators to consider, they are not everything. Communities come and go, and if followers detect any misleading or fake actions by an influencer, they will leave and the influencer will no longer be prominent.

SOCIAL MEDIA POLICIES

Social media offers many opportunities and resources for users to share, create, report, and communicate with each other. With each opportunity comes a unique challenge that constantly must be addressed in addition to forecasting future ethical and legal incidents that may impact social media practices. Many corporations, businesses, news organizations, and professionals have their own respective social media policies that help guide them through their online correspondence.

One case that really put this front and center involved Domino's in 2009. In April of that year, two Domino's employees went rogue and decided to film themselves being inappropriate with the food being served. This video caught the attention of a blogger, who then went to Twitter to voice his concern. As a result, Domino's responded (actually creating a Twitter account because it didn't have one before) to reassure its customers and others about the situation (Clifford, 2009).

National Public Radio (NPR) has a social media policy that is comprehensive in terms of its expectations from employers and media outlets. Accuracy is one of the most important elements highlighted in the policy since NPR is dedicated to making sure the information presented to its media outlets is correct and verified ("Social Media," 2017).

While most organizations, corporations, and businesses have a social media policy, it is important that they share certain points of information with their employees directly but also with their audiences publicly. Having a social media policy will help educate and inform your audiences on what to expect from you online. Here are some must-haves for your social media policy:

Introduction to the overall purpose of your social media policy. You need to outline not only why it is important to have a social media policy, but why it is important to the organization, business, media outlet, or agency you represent. Your rationale for the use of these guidelines and practices for your internal and external audience is crucial to state in this section. Make sure to personalize and frame it for the organization in question. Yet also make sure to include a statement that discusses the requirements. Education on your social media policy and guidelines needs to happen as frequently as they need to be updated. New legal and ethical scenarios that could possibly face your brand need to be addressed and added to the guidelines for your social media policy; holding workshops, online sessions, and educational meetings on the changes and revisions for the social media policy are ways to accomplish this.

Employee conduct and personal identity section. Employees are on the front lines of social media and are essentially brand ambassadors for their company, brand, or business. An employee conduct and personal identity code outlines what employees' role is and how they are expected to present themselves professionally on social media. For example, you do not want to advocate for a client's work without disclosing you are actually working on that campaign. That's why you often see the hashtag #client being shared. The same goes for representing your role at an agency, media outlet, or business. Humana has invited its employees to use #HumanaEmployee to let their community know they work at Humana while providing some guidelines on what they can and cannot share (confidential information, passwords, personal communication, etc.).

Added section for representing the brand and following the law. Make sure your employees and everyone on board knows what they can share that helps represent the brand professionally, but also what they need to be aware of from a legal standpoint. Terms of service, sharing of copyright content, disclosure of confidential information, privacy, respect for others, and obeying the laws online are just some of the things that need to be included here.

Overall tone on social media. Being respectful and professional, and not engaging in a flame war or going rogue, should also be advised. Outlining what to do to combat hacking, fix errors, address crises or threats, report fake accounts, or handle another challenge in a systematic way can help improve the situation further. Also, this provides consistent action steps that employees can take in order to identify, discuss, and handle specific situations in a timely manner.

Responsibility for what you create, write, and share. Being aware that what you share is for public viewing is important to note here. Sometimes you will see a lot of discussion that is positive toward your client, the business you represent, or even yourself. However, sometimes you will get some negative or even hateful comments directed toward you and your brand. Noting and reporting what each comment means for the brand and for yourself is important. Talking with your team or with close confidants about your situation is best. You always want to take action to make sure everyone on your team is aware of what is happening, and brainstorm solutions and responses that fall in line with your core values and principles in a timely manner. You should never be alone in handling these types of situations. Contacting your legal team with the necessary documents and evidence (screen shots, links, messages, etc.) will help in this situation as well.

Authenticity and values presented online. Your values for your organization offline need to be present and nurtured online as well. The trouble comes when there is a disconnect between how people see you online and offline. Be true to yourself for a personal brand, but also note the impact being authentic has for your employer. Apply common sense to understanding the overall culture inside both your organization and the community with which you interact. Take time to see what others are saying, and put your best foot forward each and every time you interact with someone online. Be the better person because each conversation, interaction, and piece of content shared online contributes to the marble glass of items that make up your reputation.

CHAPTER SUMMARY

The legal and ethical landscape will continue to change and evolve for social media. We will be faced with new cases, legal suits, ethical challenges, and situations. Having a foundation in professional ethical conduct while also being aware of what the law says is more important than ever for social media professionals to note. You do not want to wait and ask for permission for certain tasks—that is too risky for the social media landscape today. Educating not only yourself, but your team, about some of these rising issues and situations on the professional and personal level is key for success in the industry. In addition, we must understand that ethical and legal behavior comes not only from the top down, but also from the bottom up. Ethical and legal practices from company leadership are expected since they contribute to the overall environment of the company and its future placement in the industry. If no standards are set or value is not attributed to ethical or legal practices for social media at the organization, media outlet, or agency you belong to, move along to a place that does have these values. One misstep, as we have seen in this chapter, can wreak havoc on your personal brand for years to come.

THOUGHT QUESTIONS

1. Based on the reading, what is the current legal landscape in social media? What are some of the main issues to be aware of?

2. Define ethics. What are some of the key principles in your code of ethics for using social media?

3. Identify current legal challenges and risks on social media. How would you address them?

4. From a legal and ethical standpoint, what are some benefits and challenges of using influencers and social media personalities on social media?

5. Identify the key elements of a social media policy. What is mandatory to include, and what three areas would you add or expand on for your social media policy?

EXERCISES

1. Write an ethical code of conduct for your social media practices. What are some of the main concepts you feel are necessary to adhere to for your own personal conduct online? What concepts or behaviors do you feel strongly against and want to make sure to avoid on social media?

2. Influencer marketing and engaging with a large audience online has become quite the trend for businesses and brands. You have been asked to engage with influencers as part of the Kentucky Derby Festival (KDF), a nonprofit organization of local events in Louisville before the Kentucky Derby. What would you advise the KDF to keep in mind when it comes to working with influencers based on FTC regulations? Write a few of these points down, and for each point, discuss how you would address it proactively and some of the risks to avoid.

3. You have been asked to create a social media policy for a local small business. The company has never had such a policy, but wants to make sure its employees are aware of what they can and cannot do online. Use Hootsuite's guide (blog.hootsuite.com/social-media-policy-for-employees/) to help you design a social media policy for employees to use when sharing content on behalf of the brand.

REFERENCES

Barnes, R. (2014, November 23). Supreme Court case tests the limits of free speech on Facebook and other social media. *The Washington Post*. Retrieved from https://www.washingtonpost.com/national/supreme-court-case-tests-the-limits-of-free-speech-on-facebook-and-other-social-media/2014/11/23/9e54dbd8-6f67-11e4-ad12-3734c461eab6_story.html.

Beale, T. (2016, May 20). Why Scott Disick's Instagram fail is everything wrong with influencer marketing. *Traackr*. Retrieved from http://www.traackr.com/blog/why-scott-disicks-instagram-fail-is-everything-wrong-with-influencer-marketing.

Blown to Britts: ESPN reporter Britt McHenry says her life "imploded" after tow truck rant went viral. (2016, December 14). *Inside Edition*. Retrieved from http://www.insideedition.com/headlines/20476-blown-to-britts-espn-reporter-britt-mchenry-says-her-life-imploded-after-tow-truck-rant.

Booth, R. (2014, June 29). Facebook reveals news feed experiment to control emotions. *The Guardian*. Retrieved from https://www.theguardian.com/technology/2014/jun/29/facebook-users-emotions-news-feeds.

Brodkin, J. (2015, October 13). Twitter suspends sports media accounts after NFL says GIFs violate copyright. *Ars Technica*. Retrieved from https://arstechnica.com/tech-policy/2015/10/nfls-copyright-complaints-lead-to-twitter-crackdown-on-sports-gif-sharing/.

Claypoole, T. F. (2014, January). Privacy and social media. *Business Law Today*. Retrieved from http://www.americanbar.org/publications/blt/2014/01/03a_claypoole.html.

Clifford, S. (2009, April 15). Video prank at Domino's taints brand. *The New York Times*. Retrieved from http://www.nytimes.com/2009/04/16/business/media/16dominos.html.

Coffee, P. (2015, February 20). 16 great PR parody Twitter accounts. *Adweek*. Retrieved from http://www.adweek.com/digital/15-great-pr-parody-social-media-accounts/.

Electronic Frontier Foundation. (2018). *DMCA: Digital Millennium Copyright Act*. Retrieved from https://www.eff.org/issues/dmca.

Frier, S., & Townsend, M. (2016, August 5). FTC to crack down on paid celebrity posts that aren't clear ads. *Bloomberg Technology*. Retrieved from https://www.bloomberg.com/news/articles/2016-08-05/ftc-to-crack-down-on-paid-celebrity-posts-that-aren-t-clear-ads.

Gaines, C. (2015, April 29). The Houston Rockets fired a social media manager for sending a dumb, but harmless emoji tweet. *Business Insider*. Retrieved from http://www.businessinsider.com/houston-rockets-social-media-manager-horse-emoji-tweet-2015-4.

Gunkel, D. J. (2015, March 17). Social media: Changing the rules of business ethics. *NIU Newsroom*. Retrieved from http://newsroom.niu.edu/2015/03/17/social-media-changing-the-rules-of-business-ethics/.

Harris, J. D. (2015, May 12). Houston Rockets social media manager should not have been fired after questionable tweet. *SportTechie*. Retrieved from http://www.sporttechie.com/2015/05/12/trending/

houston-rockets-social-media-manager-should-not-have-been-fired-after-questionable-tweet/.

Holmes, R. (2013). Lessons learned from HMV's very public Twitter meltdown. *Hootsuite*. Retrieved from https://blog.hootsuite.com/hmv-twitter-poppy-powers-ryan-holmes-fast-company/.

Jackson, M. (2018, February 13). Someone is using your profile picture, bio, and content on social media. What can you do about it? *Streaming.Lawyer*. Retrieved from https://streaming.lawyer/2018/02/13/social-media-profile-theft/.

Leetaru, K. (2017, January 25). What the "rogue" EPA, NPS and NASA Twitter accounts teach us about the future of social. *Forbes*. Retrieved from https://www.forbes.com/sites/kalevleetaru/2017/01/25/what-the-rogue-epa-nps-and-nasa-twitter-accounts-teach-us-about-the-future-of-social/#7f494a5b5a74.

Maheshwari, S. (2016, August 30). Endorsed on Instagram by a Kardashian, but is it love or just an ad? *The New York Times*. Retrieved from https://www.nytimes.com/2016/08/30/business/media/instagram-ads-marketing-kardashian.html.

Panzironi, M. (2016, April 30). Animated GIFs and fair use: What is and isn't legal, according to copyright law. *Forbes*. Retrieved from http://www.forbes.com/sites/propointgraphics/2016/04/30/animated-gifs-and-fair-use-what-is-and-isnt-legal-according-to-copyright-law/.

Parker, S. (2013, September 4). The 7 NEW deadly sins of social media. *Social Media Today*. Retrieved from http://www.socialmediatoday.com/content/7-new-deadly-sins-social-media.

Pesta, A. (2016, December 12). ESPN's Britt McHenry: "I blame myself, but the video is not who I am." *Marie Claire*. Retrieved from http://www.marieclaire.com/culture/news/a24045/espn-britt-mchenry-viral-video-apology/.

Ronson, J. (2015, February 12). How one stupid tweet blew up Justine Sacco's life. *The New York Times*. Retrieved from https://www.nytimes.com/2015/02/15/magazine/how-one-stupid-tweet-ruined-justine-saccos-life.html.

Social media: The NPR way. (2017, July). *NPR Ethics Handbook*. Retrieved from http://ethics.npr.org/tag/social-media/.

Waterlow, L. (2015, February 16). "I lost my job, my reputation and I'm not able to date anymore": Former PR worker reveals how she destroyed her life one year after sending "racist" tweet before trip to Africa. *Daily Mail*. Retrieved from http://www.dailymail.co.uk/femail/article-2955322/Justine-Sacco-reveals-destroyed-life-racist-tweet-trip-Africa.html.

Wood, S. P. (2015, November 3). Snapchat wakes up social media users on content ownership. *Adweek*. Retrieved from http://www.adweek.com/digital/snapchat-wakes-up-social-media-users-on-content-ownership/.

3 PERSONAL AND PROFESSIONAL BRANDING

Learning Objectives
Humans of Social Media
Introduction
What Is a Personal Brand?
    What Are the Components of a Personal
        Brand?
    Types of Personal Brands
Benefits and Challenges for Personal Brands
How to Establish a Personal Brand
    Skills Needed to Showcase Personal Brand
        Effectively
Chapter Summary
Thought Questions
Exercises
References

LEARNING OBJECTIVES

After reading this chapter, you will be able to

- Define *personal brand* and explain the importance of establishing a community
- Differentiate the key characteristics of a personal brand
- Understand the different types of personal brands in social media
- Discuss the key benefits and challenges of a personal brand
- Explain the skills needed to create a sustainable personal brand

HUMANS OF SOCIAL MEDIA
CHRIS STRUB, CEO OF I AM HERE LLC

Source: Courtesy of Daryl Borges at Opportunity Village

Chris Strub and a Staff Member

Introduction

In the summer of 2015, I took a solo, unsponsored road trip around the country and volunteered with a different youth-related organization in each state, using social media to share the stories at each stop. I'm the author of *50 States, 100 Days: The Book*, which brings the reader along for the ride, state by state. I have also worked as a social media consultant with Humana and am a former social media director at a New York advertising agency.

(Continued)

(Continued)

How did you get your start in social media?

My first job out of college was at the local newspaper in Binghamton, New York, in the mid-2000s, when the industry was rapidly shifting from print first to digital first. During those transitional years, I was looked to in the newsroom as a leading voice, working closely with the publisher, executive editor, and senior digital staff to shape the paper's website and social media approach. In 2011, I transferred from the news department to the advertising department, leading the local chapter of a social commerce initiative called DealChicken. That job helped me land a role at a nearby advertising agency, where I helped grow our digital clientele from the ground up. And my work with those clients helped inspire me to take a pair of social media–powered cross-country road trips in the summers of 2014 and 2015.

What is your favorite part of working in your social media area of expertise?

I embrace the sincere authenticity of building a presence through live streaming. You can do all the preparatory work in the world, but when you're broadcasting live, anything can happen, and viewers gain a very real appreciation for who you are. The sentiment is the same on storytelling apps like Snapchat; when you allow your audience the chance to look you in the digital eyeballs, it's about as close as you can get—for now—to mimicking genuine human interaction on a massive scale.

What is one thing you can't live without while working in social media?

The obvious answer here would be the technology—an iPhone, a portable battery pack, a laptop, and so on. But I've come to appreciate the immeasurable power of a human network. Social media has introduced me to, gosh, tens, hundreds, thousands of people around the world, with whom I might not share skin color, or an education level, or even a native language, but we do share the apps that brought us together. I met power influencer Ted Rubin last summer—wouldn't you know? He lived just a couple miles down the road here on Long Island—and he gifted me a book, inside of which he wrote, "Relationships are like muscle tissue—the more they're engaged, the stronger they become." The relationships that I've built, both with Ted and with thousands of others, have become a vital part of what I do every day.

What is the most challenging part of working in social media?

Monetizing. It's tricky to quantify the real value of the relationships that can be built through social media, even from a personal branding perspective, and it's that much more difficult to do from a business perspective. Live streaming, Snapchat, and other platforms are built for people to connect individually or in small groups, and it is a constant challenge for businesses to utilize these networks in ways that can measurably deliver a return on the investment that executives make in their digital teams.

What is your take on your area of expertise and the social media industry?

Businesses of all types have been focused on metamorphosing into media companies, but I think the next big evolution is to break down long-standing barriers between their own big, shiny "brand" and the public's perception and interaction with it. Your brand isn't what you say it is; it is what the public perceives it to be. Social media provides an unparalleled opportunity for brands to capitalize on the positive sentiment its consumers have—or, conversely, to meaningfully address, both at scale and individually, the negativity bringing the brand down.

What do you wish you had known when you were starting out?

I think my best advice to the next generation would be to sharply, and honestly, evaluate your biggest strengths and where you feel the most passionate, and pursue a path that will let those things shine through every single day. Don't let the world dictate where you go and what you do—you are your own boss. And don't be shy or intimidated by follower counts; social media is natively egalitarian, and the "thought leaders" are more accessible than you think.

Chris Strub is a social media professional, live streamer, and keynote speaker. Chris was the first person to live stream and Snapchat in all 50 states and wrote a book about his journey. He was a Salvation Army brand ambassador for its #FightForGood tour during the 2017 Christmas holidays. He can be followed at @chrisstrub on all social media platforms and on his website at www .teamstrub.com.

INTRODUCTION

A common phrase about reputation comes from Benjamin Franklin: "It takes many good deeds to build a good reputation, but only one bad one to lose it." Today, within the social media community, not only does your reputation need to be managed and invested in, it also has to be sustainable and consistent.

Any person, brand, or community can create an image online, but it does not mean a thing when the personality, voice, or person behind the screen does not match the person or brand presented. The importance of alignment, along with establishing a clear, consistent, transparent, and authentic voice online, contributes to how we see ourselves and how we want others to perceive us at the same time.

WHAT IS A PERSONAL BRAND?

People will, and always will, have a voice on social media. Voices range from person to person, of course, but some are filtered to present a crystal-pristine image across various platforms. Then there are those considered to have an unfiltered voice, who will say whatever comes to mind immediately and post it directly for their friends, community, and the world to see.

Personal brands can arise in many ways. People who are established in other fields have become examples of sustainable personal brands on social media. Dwayne Johnson ("The Rock"), for example, has one of the most consistent and personable social media brands. He balances his content in a way where he shows authentic videos of himself working out or on set, yet he also interjects promotional updates and visuals for upcoming collaborations (e.g., Under Armour and Ford), movies (e.g., the *Fast & Furious* series and *Baywatch*), or Throwback Thursday pictures with family and friends. What makes The Rock stand out from other celebrities is his intermixture of content, storytelling, and personality, all of which will be discussed in this chapter.

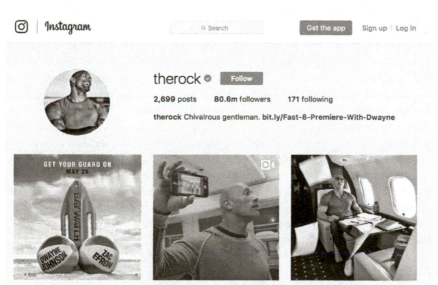

Source: Instagram /Dwayne Johnson (@therock)

Dwayne Johnson aka The Rock's Instagram

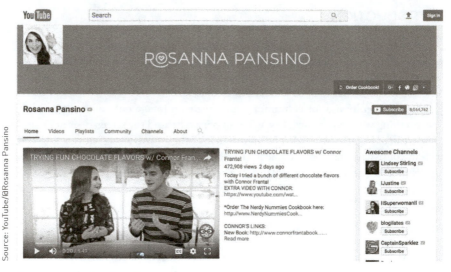

Source: YouTube/@Rosanna Pansino

Rosanna Pansino's YouTube Channel

Another example is Rosanna Pansino, a well-known YouTube personality, who created her own personal brand thanks to the video-sharing platform. Pansino created her show to focus on baking and making food items that tap into science fiction, gaming, and pop culture, and she is presently one of the most successful YouTubers, with a successful cookbook named from her show, *Nerdy Nummies*.

That's the power of social media as a whole. It allows us to have a personalized digital version of what we see in traditional media. Instead of journalists and reporters telling us the stories they choose to focus on, social media allows people to share relevant information about emerging trends in the industry, personal stories and experiences, and important issues related to their interests. Groups of people who come together for a common cause are referred to as **communities**. Yet, while some communities will come together in support of you, others will be against you, no matter what, because of who you are. That's the nature of the business, and it is important for all of us to recognize this before we enter the social media space. Keep in mind that people will always talk about you, so make sure to give them something positive to talk about. How you react and manage your overall tone and conduct online will determine how you are perceived. Essentially, actions speak louder than words. As your actions, voice, and dialogue grow within your community, your **influence** (the ability to shift people to take action or listen to what you say) grows.

We have to be aware of the fact that privacy is nonexistent. Think about the privacy settings you have set forth for yourself. Is your Facebook account private? Do you have an Instagram account for your personal brand and a separate account for your "real" friends (aka a fake Instagram account, or **finsta**)? All of these accounts may be set to "private," but there are ways to get around those settings, and brands have found out how. In addition, keep in mind that the largest search engine in the world, Google, is more than just a place to search for your next latte or book your next spring break vacation. It's a reputation management system, and it could be the first place people go to search your name.

Today, it is rare to meet someone who does not have a digital presence or brand. According to Brian Solis (2012), having a digital presence is essentially a way of life nowadays, and it is not only expected but also insisted upon in certain industries. In some industries, you have to be active and engaged on certain platforms because that is where your future employers, clients, and community are located. For example, for social media professionals, certain chats come up on Twitter that are good to be a part of, like #HootChat (Thursdays at 3 p.m. EST), to converse about different social media topics. These chats are not just about certain related topics, but also about networking and interacting with other companies, professionals, and brands. When it comes to social media, what matters is not only what you know, but who knows of you and your work on- and offline. Who controls this exactly?

The answer is simple: *you*. You are the one who is able to control your actions, networks, and voice, as well as the information and content you create, share, and talk about. That said, this does not happen overnight, and it takes investment, patience, and time to determine your personal brand and place in a community.

What exactly does it mean to have a personal brand? Personal branding is "the process of managing and optimizing the way you are presented to others" (Lee, 2015). Your personal brand, otherwise known as your reputation, is part of how people perceive you. Reputations essentially are

- Evolving
- Fragile
- Made up of personal brand and community
- Constantly maintained and invested in
- Formed from personal interactions
- Influenced by word of mouth

Last, but not least, your reputation online is your most valued possession. Standing out from the crowd is very challenging, especially in the social media space. We are constantly competing for the moment and attention from others. This can be from our friends, but when it comes to the workplace, we are looking at how we differ from other professionals in our industry. TV reporters look at ways to stand out to grow the audience for their station, for example, and online influencers try to drive views, posts, and brands to their sites and videos as well. Brands and social media professionals are also competing for relevance and embracing the next trend in a way that gets the attention of the media and other audiences. As mentioned in Chapter 1, getting a brand to go "viral" is one thing, but getting a campaign, a new way to use a tool or platform, or a speaking engagement to do so is another challenge facing people and brands today. In addition, competition for attention is on the rise, and we as social media professionals need to understand who we are and where we need to be to contribute to the conversation with our key audiences, our industry, and the overall global environment. That's why having a strong brand that is constantly evolving but relevant is crucial. This is how business is being done today.

What Are the Components of a Personal Brand?

Some form of **personality** that is unique and memorable about an individual can help bring forth a strong view toward his or her personal brand. Personality focuses on how an individual behaves, acts, responds, and communicates with people and their respective communities. Think about all of the distinctive characteristics that make you unique. What are your beliefs and views on certain topics? What attributes would you use to describe yourself? How would others describe you? These are just some of the questions to consider. You can, of course, take a test to determine your type of personality. Whether you are a mastermind or a provider according to Myers-Briggs (Vital & Vital, n.d.), additional layers of information make every one of us different for all the good reasons. Individual users each have a certain manner and approach, and that is what makes them unique and memorable. For example, people express certain personality traits in their own writing and views on social media, as Ted Rubin has done. Not only embracing the Return on Relationship (#RoR) within his community, he emphasizes that it is important to be good to other people as well (Rubin, 2015).

While personality is important, so is *consistency* with your personality. Taking the time to think about how you are presenting yourself in every single online and offline exchange is crucial. Yes, a strong online presence and correct, consistent handles are important, but underneath the layers of the screen and profiles, there needs to be consistency (as well as a human). Your actions sometimes speak louder than your words or profiles will ever do. You may have the best profile, but if you do not interact with your community and talk *with* followers instead of *at* them, you will not be successful. Several influencers (e.g., Guy Kawasaki and Joel Comm) have strong followings and had a lot of articles, features, and praise written about their branding and voice in the community, but their lack of interactions within their community still impacts how they are perceived.

The last part needed to create a personal brand, of course, is **expertise**. Being knowledgeable in your profession or industry makes you credible. Here, experience again comes into play: What is your role, and what have you done to receive a place in the conversation or have your insights taken into consideration? Some people use trendy, obscure titles such as "guru" or "change evangelist" to make others perceive them as experts when, in fact, they are not. Identifying the fakes (and a lot of them are out there) versus the true professionals in the field can be challenging, but it is an important step. Doing your research on identifying who is true to their word online and who is "faking it till they make it" can take some time.

There are a few ways to help you identify the fakes. First, no social media professional will list him- or herself as a guru or expert. This is an evolving field, and no one is an expert in every single aspect of social media. It's changing too quickly for any of us to do that. Second, the followers professionals have listed and their actual engagement tell a different story. Quality in followers is always better than quantity, but sometimes people buy followers (or bots, defined in Chapter 2) to make it appear they have a large group of people following them when they do not. These accounts can be identified in many ways (this happens a lot on Instagram and Twitter), but next time, look at the followers' engagement in the account's last updates (tweets or pictures) and see if it is aligned. If not, then the account is using a lot of fake followers. Last, trying to be like someone else spells out disaster from the get-go. You have to be unique and true to yourself.

Sure, you can see what others do online and what works for them and learn from the experience, but it's an entirely different situation to try to *be* another person completely. That is not good, especially if the person has made his or her mark distinctly in the field. Gary Vaynerchuk has done this extremely well, but when he launched his daily videos (#DailyVees) and created his own movie-like videos with videographer David Rock (otherwise known as DRock), many social media professionals began to copy his ideas completely. They hired videographers for their conference presentations, used certain items to create videos so they could be on the same level as him, and even tried to establish their own store with their own branding—which is all fine and good, but in this industry, if someone else got the idea first, it's best to move on. Plus, there is a fine line between too much and too little self-promoting. You want to be your best advocate, of course, but if you overly promote yourself and really push the envelope of spamming people in your network with your content, you may not be viewed as credible. Let your experience and community speak for you.

Types of Personal Brands

After looking at the components of establishing a personal brand, the next step is to determine what type of brand you want to have. It is important to note these types are more like "guidelines" (like from *Pirates of the Caribbean*), or ways in which we can categorize concepts into different groups, and you may find you are a mixture of two or more types. As shown in Table 3.1, Bryan Kramer has created a typology of six different personas that focuses on types of individuals online. You can even take a quiz (ownyourline.lpages.co/what-s-your-personal-brand) to find out your type.

BENEFITS AND CHALLENGES FOR PERSONAL BRANDS

There is a benefit to establishing a personal brand in a way that has not been possible before. Our personality, voice, and overall interests on social media help define who we are online. There are numerous opportunities to evaluate and look at what others are doing in our industry to see where we stand. We can look at what other

TABLE 3.1 ■ Kramer's Typology of Online Personas		
Persona Type	**Brief Description**	**Example**
Altruist	These individuals are committed to helping others in their community. Actions speak louder than words for these individuals, but they value relationships.	**Ted Rubin** **Dwayne Johnson ("The Rock")**
Careerist	These individuals focus primarily on professional advancement above their personal achievements. They are more associated with professional networks than with personal or informal ones.	**Gini Dietrich** **Jay Baer**
Early Adopter	These individuals will be the first to share something with their followers and friends and are very much dedicated to being independent from others, not so much part of the collective on social media. They are dedicated to careers and relationships.	**Carlos Gil** **Rosanna Pansino (*Nerdy Nummies*)**
Boomerang	The emphasis for these individuals is to share content to generate a reaction from others—whether a positive one or a negative one. Most of the time, the reaction from audiences is more of the focus, not whether or not they really think about the subject.	**Robert Scoble**
Connector	The ultimate networkers, these individuals do virtual introductions and are highly engaged in making sure everyone in their community is united and knows each other.	**Deirdre Breakenridge**
Selective	These individuals share only relevant information to a select group of people. They are resourceful and viewed as a resource, but they are also exclusive in their networks. Think about the "Circle of Trust" concept from the movie *Meet the Parents*.	**Jason Falls**

Source: Examples compiled by the author and adapted from Bryan Kramer "6 Types of Personal Brand - Which One Are You?", February 18, 2016. Retrieved from https://www.socialmediatoday.com/social-business/6-types-personal-brand-which-one-are-you.

professionals are doing that is working, but we can determine where our competition is as well. No one person online is the exact same, so social media serves as a perfect opportunity to embrace our unique characteristics in a way that makes us both memorable and impactful in the industry.

One great thing about building your personal brand online is the power to grow your list of connections and network with professionals from all spans of the industry. Of course, you want to do your networking on certain platforms, and then use others to evolve your relationships with particular contacts. For example, most professionals first connect via Twitter or LinkedIn. Twitter allows you to connect with anyone you want to meet, and LinkedIn is all about business connections. Making a friend request, however, on Facebook has to be evaluated based on the situation and the professional contact to whom you are reaching out.

In addition to building your network, you can control and manage your own voice and community. Most of the time, personal branding is the heart of what makes a social media professional successful, but *community* (people who have come together on a certain platform, with a common interest, or in a common area online) allows you to build trust and credibility. People in your network have different backgrounds and interests, perhaps, but they are all coming together to have a conversation, share resources, or participate in a discussion on a topic that is relevant to their work. Twitter chats are a great way to help expand and even start building your personal community and network.

It takes time and energy, as well as investment, to be recognized and appreciated on social media for your personal brand. This does not happen overnight. It takes a little bit each day to reach out to others and share your point of view, being generous with your resources and knowledge and giving back to the industry. Sometimes you may do work for "free," but that is okay. Experience is one of the underlying assets that help significantly when you are starting out in the business. Volunteer to help out with a social media event, or write sample posts to share with a nonprofit in your town, and see what works and what doesn't. Having these experiences while taking the time to network is what makes a social media professional relevant and recognized in the field. Buying followers for vanity metrics will only create a faux presentation of your personal brand.

Of course, several challenges come into play for personal brands. Social media is not all flowers and roses—it can really be a tough place to be. In today's society, professionals are getting dismissed or fired left and right for what they post and share on social media.

HOW TO ESTABLISH A PERSONAL BRAND

Conduct an internal audit of who you are and where you want to go. This is the very first thing to do. We may live in a dynamic society where everyone wants to be like everyone else, but before we move forward with a personal brand, we have to ask ourselves several questions about who we are and where we want our brand to go. Consider the following questions as you work toward understanding where you stand compared to others, and what makes you unique as a person and brand:

- How would you define yourself? List five words that capture who you are.

- What experiences have helped define you as a person and professional?

- How do you communicate with others? Is your voice different from group to group, or is it the same? Describe your point of view.

- How do others in your community feel about you? What consistent themes emerge?

- What is your personal mission statement?

- Who are you right now, and where do you want to be?

Keep brand image and voice consistent. The one thing employers, future clients, and the social media community will be looking for is a consistent image across all of the social media platforms you use (Patel, 2016). While you may have a centralized hub for your persona on one platform (e.g., website or blog), users may want to connect with you on other platforms and be part of your community there. Presenting yourself in a consistent manner allows you to have more control of not only how others perceive you, but also how you want to be viewed as a professional, person, and brand.

Maintaining a consistent **brand voice** (the overall tone you present in your updates and communication online) that is strong and sustainable is important as well. Are you someone who wants to be positive and upbeat? Or do you want to tell your community the way it is in a very honest and unfiltered manner? This is the time to determine what you stand for, what is important to you, and how you will go about communicating this to your audience.

There are many memorable brand voices to which we can look for guidance. For example, Gary Vaynerchuk has no time for nonsense and is at times brutally honest while also using various terms that you may not expect from the CEO of a large media company. That said, he has developed a reputation and image that show he will not sugarcoat anything online and will be honest about his advice and insights with his community. Is this the right approach for you to take? That depends on whether or not it is authentic and true to what you have to say. Don't try to be the next Gary Vaynerchuk or someone else. Be the next you.

Make sure to do what we call a personal brand audit, where you collect all of your online profiles and thoroughly evaluate them based on a score from 1 (*poor*) to 5 (*excellent*). All of these profiles should be consistent not only in how you present yourself (headshot, cover page, biographical information, etc.), but also in how you present your voice and interact with the community (Chen, 2017). You, not anyone else, are branding yourself.

Determine your personal brand associations. It is key not only to know who you are as a personal brand, but to have **personal brand associations**, or specific attributes, events, settings, and interests you want others to recognize as going along with your personal brand and as different from others (Smith, 2016). For example, as a social media professional, you want to be associated with the positive feelings and attitudes of being approachable, generous with experiences and insights, and outgoing and positive in your offline and online interactions. Brands, organizations, and agencies could also be directly linked to your overall mission and vision statement as well as your brand voice.

For your personal brand, make sure your intended audiences on social media (e.g., future employers, customers, investors, and media) are able to remember you and what is unique about your brand compared to others. With social media, be sure to provide sustainable and valid reasons for why brands, professionals, and others should follow you. Is it the insights you share on a regular basis? Or is it the content and stories you produce via video? Consider these few reasons, but ultimately, your goal is to create positive associations and attitudes toward your personal brand that are backed up with evidence, sustainability, and valid benefits for all parties involved.

When it comes to the point where only one party is winning, this could hinder the relationship and health of the community you have built around your personal brand.

Identify the strategy you will take. The end-all question a lot of people have in terms of social media and personal branding is "Can you integrate your personal brand with your professional one?" The answer is yes, and it is up to you to choose an approach that works best for you and your voice in the community.

Consider the several approaches by which you can take this into consideration. The **content strategy** basically focuses on the content that you share, create, and disseminate online for your personal and professional community. You focus on projecting an image of professionalism and consistency within your various networks (Ollier-Malaterre & Rothbard, 2015). With this strategy, you define the overall goals and objectives for your personal brand on social media. What type of content do you want to create and share? Will you share just long-form articles and blog posts, or are you more inclined to share visual content like photos, graphics, and videos? Or will it be a mixture of all these elements? Along with content strategy, social media professionals have to be able to identify not only the content that is being produced, but how it is aligned with their brand voice and how it resonates with audiences.

The challenge with this approach is to appear "too robotic" by just sharing professional content without providing personal intake and perspective. Instead, you may want to focus on the **audience strategy**, which centers on the relationships you have made on specific platforms (Ollier-Malaterre & Rothbard, 2015). For example, if you are connected mostly with your coworkers on Twitter or LinkedIn, you may be more professional there, and on Facebook, you may present a more personal side of yourself to your friends and family. The risk here is that as the platforms evolve, your coworkers may turn into friends, and there may be a shift in friends going onto other platforms and mentioning how differently you present yourself. However, you may choose to approach your personal brand with a **customized strategy**, meaning you integrate the relationships on the platform you are communicating on (audience strategy) with shared content that is relevant to and consistent with your brand image (content strategy). A customized strategy takes time and investment to create, but you can easily do it. However, if you have $25,000 to spend each month, you can hire Gary Vaynerchuk's new group, VaynerTalent, to do all of this for you.

Think about what makes you unique. Think about this and recognize that while a group of people may be in the same social media class or interested in social media as a career, all of them are different. That's what's great about this profession. You do not want to be like everyone else, so instead of looking at what others are doing, think about what sets you apart from your classmates, university, community, and industry.

There is a lot of competition out there, and thousands will try and fight their way to becoming "the expert" in a particular niche. Some professionals are already established in the social media field and may either support you or perhaps view you as competition. Be aware of this—being successful and talented in this area will draw both praise and criticism from those who feel threated professionally.

Determine what you want to be known for. Once you determine what you want to focus on, consider what is going to be your angle. Do you want to be known as a professional who is invested heavily in one type of platform? Or do you want to be known more for your general interests in the industry and community? What do you like reading and talking about? What are your passions and interests? While attending school or pursuing a career, we all have professional and personal interests at heart, and you will want to integrate all of these into your personal brand. There is a fine line between just enough and too much personal or professional focus for a personal brand. You want to appear to be human, but also be able to showcase your professional expertise consistently.

Brian Fanzo (@iSocialFanz) has created his own brand and hashtag (#ThinkLikeAFan) to focus on the empowerment of live streaming video and other mobile applications. Establishing a presence and niche in this area of the field has allowed him to get speaking opportunities and client work concerning this specialization. Yet, looking at more of a generalist approach, Jay Baer (@JayBaer) has written and talked about a variety of areas within the digital media marketing circuit.

Keep in mind, when it comes to social media, that everyone wants to be "famous" or become "an influencer" in the field who gets millions of video views and all-expenses-paid speaking gigs at the largest corporate events. These perks are not given overnight, and it takes time and investment to reach a certain state in the field.

Once established, invest in your personal community. Once you have created your personal brand, extend your focus to the community you interact with. Sharing your insights and opinions and being a resource for others will not only help your personal brand, but solidify your place in the minds of this community. By investing in the community, you will be able to elevate your understanding of the current challenges, opportunities, and trends it is seeing. Establishing yourself as a resource in the community does not mean sitting back and letting everyone else talk. It means being more active in absorbing information and being engaged. Take the time to share what is going on in your industry on social media, and talk about *why* you care about creating and sharing content. We all can create content, but we must also share why it is important and the reason behind the action—which again contributes to the overall brand you have established, but also helps build the human side of your personal brand.

What makes a personal brand unique and powerful is the fact it is not a stable concept. Time and investment are needed to help it grow, but your brand is a part of you that continues to expand and develop as you move along in your career (Chen, 2017). As you move from internships to your first jobs, these experiences add to your personal brand and help transform you into the professional you want to be. The key is not only to put forth the investment necessary for your personal brand that will make you a marketable professional in the field, but to move forward with your personal brand rather than step backward.

Skills Needed to Showcase Personal Brand Effectively

While the roles, duties, and platforms continue to change, some essential skills will continue to be relevant and key for social media professionals.

Research. All of the roles in social media have become more data driven and focused on the analytics of what people are saying and talking about and how to strategically apply these findings into actionable insights. Having a foundation in traditional research methods (surveys, experiments, interviews, focus groups, etc.) will still be apparent and key for social media professionals, but it is also important to be able to determine how to collect, analyze, and report specific findings on social media tools. This is probably one of the most important skills to have. Research for social media requires you to collect data and understand what the numbers and results mean but, at the same time, be creative in how you could incorporate these insights into the strategies for your role.

With research, several skills need to be tied into what this particular duty requires. Data analysis, which looks at the data being collected, is an important skill. Being able to identify what is trending, why it is trending, and how to collect, organize, and report the data is also a key area of focus. Yet some curiosity and creativity should be mixed in with this particular role and duty. We have to look at the research and ask ourselves, "What is the 'so what'? What is happening here, and what can we take away from this research? Are there any surprises we can note and possibly use to our advantage for an idea?" This is where art comes into play with research. We want to explain what happened, but also why it happened and what we can learn from the experience for the future. In addition, we have to make sure we can communicate the findings clearly. Statistics and other research terms may be a bit overwhelming at times, but the main findings, the significance of each test in the experiment or study you have conducted, and the overall strategic plan are essential for social media managers to communicate.

Writing and visual content creation. As a social media professional, you must be one with writing. When it comes to the skills and experiences brands, corporations, and others are looking for in social media roles, it's not always just about being a strong writer, though; you have to be a strong copywriter as well. Sometimes you will write a caption for an image and have to evaluate whether or not this was the right way to approach the message or whether or not it really captured the brand's voice. Your audiences have to understand what you are communicating and sharing on social media platforms and be aware of how they will respond to each piece of content.

In addition, it's about understanding not only the importance of writing for the sake of having great grammar and spelling capabilities, but also the need to write for different platforms. Being able to tailor and adapt a message based on the platform, channel, audience, and situation is necessary. Adaptability both in real time and with automation capabilities for social media (e.g., scheduling of posts) needs to be taken into consideration as well.

Be aware of the power of content and what it means for brands, audiences, media outlets, and others when it comes to their business operations. Creating content— whether visual or textual—is a key and necessary component when it comes to social media roles. When a small business or Fortune 500 company has an established presence on certain channels or is actively engaged in sharing content on its website (blog posts, e-books, infographics, etc.), this is part of the content component necessary for the social media professionals' tool kit. Being able to strategically align content with effective message copy that resonates with an audience is one of the biggest skills employers look for in a social media professional.

When it comes to creating content, you may want to invest in and look at certain tools in order to create a sustainable yet consistent personal brand presence online. Across all of your social media profiles, you want to have a single theme, voice, and message to your audience that speaks to who you are and what you stand for as a personal brand for your community. Here are some additional tools to invest in and take a look at:

- **Canva (www.canva.com):** Canva is a great visual tool with affordable templates and social media–size configurations for you to use, personalize, and share for branding online. There are two types of Canva to consider: the free version and Canva for Work. A paid version of the platform, Canva for Work allows you to do more personalized tailoring and branding for your accounts and assets than the free version.

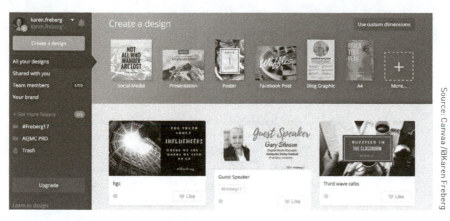

Canva

- **Adobe Spark (spark.adobe.com):** This app features mobile- and web-based products that allow you to create responsive pages (Spark Page), videos (Spark Videos), and posts for social media (Spark Post) in a very easy and interactive manner.

Adobe Spark

- **HubSpot's Blog Ideas Generator (www.hubspot.com/blog-topic-generator):** If you work on the side of writing content (blog posts, etc.), this may be a good tool for determining topics to write about. You will want to use analytics and listen to your community to determine what people would like to read and learn from you, but this is another tool that can help you identify some possible ideas to explore in writing.

- **CoSchedule's Headline Analyzer (coschedule.com/headline-analyzer):** Headlines for blog posts or even some social media updates have to capture people's attention and help motivate your audience to click on the link or look at the post you have created. This tool will give you an idea of where your headline stands based on key words, length, and potential to spark engagement.

- **Hemingway App:** With all aspects of creating content—especially content that is written online—grammar and spelling are crucial. When constructing your posts, make sure you are communicating effectively and making the best first impression. We will discuss more about writing for social media in Chapter 7, but this tool is a good one to invest in to make sure you are communicating in the best way possible.

- **Personality Insights by IBM Watson (personality-insights-livedemo .mybluemix.net/):** What type of messages are you sending out to people when it comes to the content you share online? One way to determine this is to analyze the text through a tool from IBM Watson that allows you to see some of the reactions people may have based on the content you are sharing online. In a way, this is a precursor to what you may want to do before you hit the "publish" button on a blog post or social media update.

Data analytics and strategic application. There is a growing need for integrating not only current communication and technology practices into creating effective content for social media, but current business practices and acumen as well. The tie-in between return on investment and the analytics features is also an important element. Social media platforms are filled with insights, knowledge, and connections, and professionals must be able to understand how search engine optimization (SEO) works for businesses, connections, and personal opportunities. Along with social media, SEO can help the professional and business identify where the conversations are emerging, what the networks look like, and what key words users are searching for online. Identifying the key terms that are necessary to follow and listen to in the digital media landscape also applies to social media because, essentially, all of these channels (Facebook, Twitter, Instagram, etc.) are databases filled with information that can connect to valuable insights.

With SEO, your role as a social media professional will empower you with insights that will allow you to promote, engage, and analyze the data to determine what does and does not work. Most programs allow students to take advantage of Google Analytics to get a basic and advanced understanding of SEO for social and digital media purposes, and it might be a good program to explore so you can add this skill to your résumé.

In addition to understanding listening and SEO, be aware of the specific tools used to listen to, monitor, and engage with others online for personal branding purposes. Some of the tools used to evaluate reputation online include the following:

- **Talkwalker:** This program allows users (and brands) to sign up for mentions and analytics related to what others are saying about them online. Talkwalker offers a free search option as well as a quick search option (paid but affordable) for individuals to monitor their online presence.

- **Mention:** Similar to Talkwalker, this program has different pricing options and key features.

- **BrandsEye:** This program is more focused on the corporate mentions for companies, but can also look at external data for you to evaluate.

- **BrandYourself:** This service allows you to determine what sites (websites, social media profiles, etc.) should be the first to come up on Google to help you make the best first impression online.

- **Klear:** This is a good tool for analyzing certain platforms (e.g., Facebook, Twitter, and Instagram). You can look to see how you are doing on each platform, what your overall engagement is like, and what others in the same area as you are doing online.

- **Hootsuite:** Any social media management tool (including Hootsuite as well as TweetDeck and Sprout Social) can be used not only to evaluate what you are sharing on your own platforms, but also to see who is talking about your brand, your business, and even yourself.

Customer service specialist. Many times, social media is the first place people go when they have an issue, question, or inquiry related to their day-to-day activities. Social media professionals must understand how to solve problems, address concerns, and listen to what others are saying to take advantage of opportunities and minimize challenges before they escalate into crisis situations. Understand that you are the storefront of the brand, and for the most part, you will provide the first exchange or opportunity for users to communicate with the brand. You have to be the brand's face as well as respond in the brand's voice, depending, of course, on the platform in question.

Along with customer service, there is a time and place to deal with happy customers and audience members, and then there are times when you have to deal with people who are not fans of your brand (e.g., trolls). These individuals want to spark outrage and criticize your account to generate a flame war with your brand while trying to get 15 minutes of fame online. Most of the time, social care practices are recommended for brands to follow, but at other times, personality and creativity come into play when responding online. Wendy's embraced its "snarky" voice on its Twitter account in 2017, for example, winning praise from other professionals and news outlets (Marks, 2017).

Experience and willingness to learn in social media. In order to work in social media, you need to be able to effectively keep up with the trends, people, brands, agencies, and media and identify the current cases and examples people are sharing in the field. Make sure you are able to confidently discuss some of these current issues and trends with your future employers or colleagues. However, it's essential to know not only what these are, but how they impact the overall field as well as the community and brand you are working with. One way to keep up with the rising expectations and trends in the field is with effective monitoring of trade publications, news outlets, blogs, social media influencers, and others.

You have to be hungry for information, not waiting for someone to feed you what you need to know. Taking an initiative and seeking out this information will help you in more ways than you can imagine. Spending at least 15 minutes per day to read and consume content or even listen to a podcast about a given subject will transform you into a student of the industry. Learning is not only required but expected for strong social media professionals. One thing to note, though, is that no single person is an expert in one platform on social media since it is constantly changing, so determine what you can bring to the table either as a **generalist** (who covers a broad overview of social media at the macro level) or as a **specialist** (who focuses on one or more particular areas of social media at the micro level).

One main way to gain experience is through internships. Getting hands-on experience in social media will allow you to practice what you are learning in the classroom, but also help you develop your online portfolio of work to share with your community and use for future applications. However, internships are not the only way to get experience in social media. Volunteering your expertise and time to help a nonprofit with a project or campaign, help a school-sponsored organization or team manage its social media efforts, or consult with small businesses in your area will allow you to get some real-world experience while also making a difference in people's lives. Along with this point, keep in mind that with experience comes managing your own brand online, which raises the next point.

Other ways to continue your social media education is through certification programs. Many different brands offer these services and opportunities, and they can be listed on your résumé as continued education. For example, Hootsuite offers several training programs on its platforms (Hootsuite Academy), but also advanced strategies and lessons (Hootsuite Social Media Marketing and Hootsuite Advanced Social Media Strategy). In addition, specific platforms and brands offer their own programs, such as Google with Google Analytics and Facebook with Facebook Blueprint. Microsoft also has a program for its services. While they range in topics and prices, these programs are available to help users enhance their understanding of social media and future learning opportunities.

Personal branding. Having a strong presence online that is consistent and true to yourself is very important to keep in mind when applying for positions in social media. Make sure to complete profiles for each account you are advocating and using, participate in relevant chat sessions in your industry, blog about topics you are interested in and share your point of view, and conduct your research ahead of time when you are applying for jobs. This is essential and can help separate you from the rest of the competition. Who are the main professionals in the position you are looking for, how do they present themselves online, and how could you engage with them in a conversation without meeting them first (cold calling in the social media age)? Put the extra effort into your application.

While most employers discuss what they expect you to have done before applying for a position, nothing is listed about giving the extra effort to make an impression. One thing you can do is research what clients they have been working for, what projects they are working on at the moment, and what areas they focus on. Along with your application, you can provide a sample piece of work you have created in response to what you have found the employer may need to address. For example, if you are applying for a community manager job at Texas Roadhouse, you may want to propose a social care strategy outlining how you would respond to the trend of brands trying to interject their personality in social media updates on sites like Twitter, and then propose a balanced strategy of the benefits and challenges. What does this show the hiring manager looking at your application? You created a piece of work relevant to the social media role that was not requested, but demonstrated your research into the position as well as your understanding of some of the situations you may face in this role.

How to detect fake personal brands. While many people on social media have the best intentions to present themselves honestly and with authenticity, some personal brands are not true to themselves or the people they represent. There are a lot of "smoke and mirrors" and ways to create fake engagement to make you appear on social media to be someone you are not. The following are some ways to make sure you do not appear fake to your social media community:

- *Don't be fake.* A personal brand is all about being true to yourself. While it may be tempting to be someone else, your personality, community, voice, and brand are the components that truly make you unique and memorable. Personal branding is not all about you; it's about your community and helping others in the process. It is very tempting to try to gain "influencer" fame on social media, but if you focus too much on the shares, influencer lists, attention, and other vanity metrics, you will lose out on the value and impact you have on your community, which would be a shame to waste.

- *Don't buy followers or use bots.* It's tempting to create the appearance of being popular and influential online, but it is not worth it. Platforms like Twitter and Instagram are realizing there is a problem and are addressing this head-on. It is not worth the damage toward your credibility to have followers that are not truly engaging with your content. This is not the time to "fake it till you make it." It is very easy to find out who has real organic followers and a community, and those who have tried to game the system.

- *Stand by your opinions and don't always jump on the bandwagon.* If you believe in a product, company, or new platform, invest in the time and make sure you clearly articulate your views in a consistent manner. Don't tell your community to invest in a platform and then abandon it the first moment you get (remember the app Peach back in 2016?). Don't be selfish in sharing your ideas—you want to be generous and become a resource for your audiences to gravitate to related to your interests and areas of expertise.

- *Focus on quantity rather than quality of engagement.* We are all busy people in the world of social media, so focus on the quality of the exchanges and information you share. Don't create auto chat bots to do your sharing for you. Focus on creating and sharing information *you* (not a bot) feel is important for your audience to know and respond to. Quality exchanges and personalized feedback, messages, and conversations help contribute to who you are as a person. Think about how you communicate offline and see if you would do the same things (e.g., broadcast messages or have someone else do it on your behalf) online and see how you would feel. Would you feel valued as a member of the social media ecosystem? Probably not, so remember that social media is "social" first and foremost.

- *Understand your "virtual" brand is only as good as your offline brand.* Make sure you are the same offline as you are online. Social media may be a large global community, but it is a small world. Any disconnect or dissonance created when people meet you online and offline can result in a negative perception or impact on your personal brand.

- *Lead all interactions with action while considering the long-term implications.* You can't just "wing" a personal brand. You have to have a strategy in place for the type of content you want to share, how you want to present yourself, and what your personal brand stands for. Walk the walk with your personal brand, but have a plan in place for the long term. Don't take action until you have thoroughly evaluated all of the options and come up with a game plan.

CHAPTER SUMMARY

Establishing a personal brand on social media is one of the hardest yet most important tasks for a social media professional. Your personal brand is your most valuable asset to protect, invest in, and maintain for your community and professional career. A personal brand does not mean you have to be professional 24/7 and active all of the time. It depends on the overall scope, commitment, and goals for your social media communities. Keep in mind that creating a successful personal brand does not happen overnight. You have to put forth the time, investment, and work in order to reap the rewards in the long term. Spend a few minutes each day researching, studying, and working on your personal brand. As you interact with more people, opportunities will arise and allow you to share your perspectives with others. Volunteer at events and share your expertise with others. Start writing content and publishing it online—and this content can, of course, be visual or written. Seek out mentors for virtual introductions, but focus on the relationship first, not just the "ask" (e.g., don't ask people for a job when you just connected with them on LinkedIn or Twitter). The decision is up to you, which is one of the many great things that social media offers. In addition, you have to be your own best spokesperson. No one knows you better than you do.

Finding a signature image, voice, and place within your professional and personal social media communities (and the entire social media ecosystem) is crucial and can contribute significantly for positive reasons to how potential employers may perceive you. Businesses and others are finding out more clearly than ever that their key targeted audiences do not want to interact with a chat bot or receive a robotic response from an avatar online. They want to interact with people who are willing to engage with them through ongoing conversations and sharing valuable insights and resources, and whose in-person and online personas are consistent. Once you have a foundation under your belt with your personal brand, see how your audience is responding to your content and what you have to say. Be sure to stay consistent with how you conduct yourself, and pay attention to needs to be addressed and opportunities to take advantage of.

People have been hired and given tremendous opportunities based on the work and investment they put forth with their personal brand, and it is part of the daily duties of today's social media professionals. However, keeping a balanced perspective and mindset is always important. While your personal brand may be important to you and your community, it does not make the world revolve around you.

THOUGHT QUESTIONS

1. Define *personal brand*. What are three components to take into consideration when exploring what a personal brand is?

2. What is a brand voice? How is this important to note and develop when constructing a personal brand on social media?

3. Identify the differences between and importance of the content, audience, and customized strategies mentioned in this chapter.

4. What skills are needed to create a sustainable personal brand? What areas do you feel most confident in? What areas do you feel you need to work on?

EXERCISES

1. Write down a description of your personal brand. What type of personal brand do you have? What do you want to be online? What are some areas you feel you can contribute to in the community?

2. You are applying for an internship to work with the brand Cinnabon. Along with creating a résumé and cover letter, the company is asking you to demonstrate who you are as a brand. Create a visual résumé

through Canva and an Adobe Spark page (using the tools available) to showcase your story on why Cinnabon should hire you as a social media intern. Discuss your journey, what you have to offer, what you have done on social media, and what you hope to learn from the internship.

3. Run a report on your personal brand online using the tools available. What are people saying about you online? What will you do with these insights?

4. What are some personal associations you have now, and where do you want to go? Evaluate at least a few of the competitors in your network and what they are doing, and write down some action steps you want to take to address this.

REFERENCES

Chen, J. (2017, June 19). The ultimate guide to personal branding. *Sprout Social*. Retrieved from http://sproutsocial.com/insights/personal-branding/.

Lee, K. (2015, January 15). The 5 keys to building a social media strategy for your personal brand. *Buffer*. Retrieved from https://blog.bufferapp.com/social-media-strategy-personal-branding-tips.

Marks, G. (2017, January 9). So who's behind all those snarky tweets from @Wendy's? *The Washington Post*. Retrieved from https://www.washingtonpost.com/news/on-small-business/wp/2017/01/09/so-whos-behind-all-those-snarky-tweets-from-wendys/.

Ollier-Malaterre, A., & Rothbard, N. P. (2015, March 26). How to separate the personal and professional on social media. *Harvard Business Review*. Retrieved from https://hbr.org/2015/03/how-to-separate-the-personal-and-professional-on-social-media.

Patel, S. (2016, November 12). 9 ways to use social media to build your personal brand. *Forbes*. Retrieved from http://www.forbes.com/sites/sujanpatel/2016/11/12/9-ways-to-use-social-media-to-build-your-personal-brand/.

Rubin, T. (2015, June 11). Social ROI: Return on Relationship is key. *Sprout Social*. Retrieved from http://sproutsocial.com/insights/return-on-relationship/.

Smith, K. (2016, August 9). Exploring the identity of a brand: How to discover and measure brand associations. *Brandwatch*. Retrieved from https://www.brandwatch.com/blog/discover-measure-brand-associations/.

Solis, B. (2012). Meet Generation C: The connected customer. Retrieved from http://www.briansolis.com/2012/04/meet-generation-c-the-connected-customer/.

Vital, M., & Vital, A. (n.d.). 16 personality types (Myers-Briggs and Keirsey)—infographic. *Adioma*. Retrieved from https://blog.adioma.com/16-personality-types/.

4 INDUSTRY QUALIFICATIONS AND ROLES

Learning Objectives
Humans of Social Media
Introduction
Who Hires Social Media Professionals?
Where to Work in Social Media
Definition of Key Social Media Roles
    Social Media Community Manager Versus
       Social Media Manager
    Social Media Coordinator
    Social Media Strategist
    Content Creator
    Multimedia/Video Producer
    Writer/Editor
    Other Social Media Roles
How Much Do Social Media Professionals
    Get Paid?
Chapter Summary
Thought Questions
Exercises
References

LEARNING OBJECTIVES

After reading this chapter, you will be able to

- Identify trends in the social media industry
- Differentiate between social media roles
- Explain the key responsibilities of each social media role
- Discuss best practices and expectations for applying for social media positions

HUMANS OF SOCIAL MEDIA
SAMANTHA HUGHEY, BRAND MANAGER FOR ADIDAS VOLLEYBALL

Introduction

My name is Samantha, Sam for short. I am a Western Kentucky alum and Hilltopper fan for life. I have a bachelor of fine arts with a focus on advertising, photojournalism, and sales. I completed my master's in communication at the University of Louisville, where I worked as coordinator of social media for the athletic department. While in Louisville, I was able to work on a few high-profile projects such as the Thunder Lounge, the Best of Louisville,

the Kentucky Oaks, Taste of Derby, and the Kentucky Derby. I was also a graduate teaching assistant—oftentimes lecturing on the history of social media—and I published and presented an exploratory crisis communications case study surrounding the 2014 FIFA (Fédération Internationale de Football Association) World Cup, concussions, and Twitter, as well as working toward my final graduate practicum project. I did all this from 2014 through my graduation in May 2015, and I am still catching up on my sleep from those years!

(Continued)

(Continued)

After my time at the University of Louisville, I relocated to Colorado Springs to work with the U.S. Olympic Committee. I had the incredible opportunity to live at the Olympic Training Center and work for Team USA as its audience engagement editor. It was surreal to travel to various Olympic Trials, and I still get goose bumps thinking about the fact that I was able to tweet out the first gold medal that Team USA won in the Rio 2016 Olympic Games. In November 2016, I traded in 13 stripes for 3. While it was bittersweet to put Pikes Peak in my rearview mirror, working for adidas has been a dream of mine, and I couldn't be more excited to be living the #3StripeLife in the Pacific Northwest.

How did you get your start in social media?

How did I get to this point? From learning math to doodling when I have a potential concept in mind—I have to visualize it; otherwise, it doesn't make sense in my mind. My background has continuously been in something that had a visual aspect to it, and a lot of this goes back to the mere fact that my father is in publishing and as a child I would sit in his office talking about the covers of his magazine, and *why* the image was chosen or *how* the palette of colors was finalized. These conversations at an early age immersed me into that way of thinking and culture of the design world.

What is your favorite part of working in your social media area of expertise?

Favorite part of working in social media? I tell this story often. But I do so because this is what brought me to the industry. This is why I wanted to work for adidas. And it is because of this that I love what I do and where I am now. In my bathroom there is an adidas ad. David Beckham is celebrating a victory of some sort, and these words overlay his image:

> Impossible is just a big word thrown around by small men who find it easier to live in the world they've been given than to explore the power they have to change it. Impossible is not a fact. It's an option. Impossible is not a declaration. It's a dare. Impossible is potential. Impossible is temporary. Impossible is nothing.

I was a young girl when I cut this out of my ESPN magazine, but this single clipping has followed me from my parents' house to the dorms at Western Kentucky University to my first, second, and third houses in Bowling Green, and back to Louisville, and it continued to inspire me in Colorado Springs. That quote—that campaign—sums up the intensity of what it means to live life and the power behind those who play sports and are sports fans: There is a magic there unlike any other. In November 2016, that ad, plus my Fiat and my belongings, made its way to Portland, Oregon, where I would start working at my dream job. I now get to work for the company that bestowed this passion in me, and I have the potential to create something as impactful as a magazine once did to an 11-year-old girl.

A simple answer about my favorite part of working in this realm: invoking emotions from fans (which is easier said than done). But that is exactly what makes this industry so incredible—finding that *why* and figuring out the *how* is by far my favorite. It's all about chasing your dreams. Continuing to grind. And remembering that impossible is nothing.

What is one thing you can't live without while working in social media?

I can't live without relationships—with those you work with, with your family and friends, with the community that you have built. I cannot live without these multiple components that continue to work to support and cheer me on. The ability to build meaningful relationships is something that I could not live without while working in this field. The hours are long; the days even longer. There aren't real weekends off—notifications on your phone will continue to buzz into your nights of slumber. And you must have a group of people who understand that. Working in a fast-paced, never-ending field can put a toll on you and those around you. Building a community that understands your work life, including the expectations from the industry and the constant push notifications, will make balancing the two more enjoyable. Having people in your corner to cheer you on and bounce ideas off of is an invaluable tool and can be, at times, a great coping mechanism.

What is your favorite social media account (person, brand, etc.) to follow, and why?

@Starbucks, easily. And that's not just because I only managed to survive my master's program through copious amounts of Starbucks brews.

It's because the company built a brand, a community, behind a $5 cup of coffee. There's almost a cult following behind the product, a product that many claim is "overpriced" and "not as good as the local guys"; while that may in fact be true, it does not matter. Starbucks understands its consumers and how to tell a story and tell it unbelievably well. Its strategy is simple—striking photography and user-generated content. These two pieces play well into who the company is as a whole and what it means when you order Starbucks coffee—it's not just a product that you are buying, but rather an experience.

What is the most challenging part of working in social media?

It takes a special person to work in sports and social media. You will have the opportunity to work with some of the best athletes in the sport, or even in the world (yeah—I fangirled *hard* internally, and to my editorial counterpart, when I met Laurie Hernandez at gymnastic trials), but you have to keep it cool. Just because you are a Teddy Bridgewater fan or a football fan does not mean you have the mentality to work in the sports industry. You have to love the field inside and out, and love what your role is—understanding what you bring to the table. Separating your fandom from your part in the organization is critical. Of course, it is awesome to be working with Von Miller or Ryan Lochte, but you cannot let your own excitement get in the way of the fact that the athletes are there to do a job and so are you.

And at times that can be hard. Trust me, I know. But you cannot choose this industry to work in just because you like to tweet or because you are a sports fan. Sports and social media do not sleep. You have to recognize that. Game day on the gridiron, court, or field is also game day in the tech arena. Working in this industry, you don't get to wake up and start tailgating prior to tip-off. You and your team are up early making sure all the content is there, potential scenarios are pre-mapped out, and fans are engaged. It is important for you to realize that you are the team behind the team, and you have to prepare and execute as such.

What is your take on your area of expertise and the social media industry?

Everyone and everything has a story to tell—whether that be a brand, an athlete, or a product. There is always some sort of beginning, middle, and end that can be told in some fashion. And how those stories are being told is the difference behind a successful brand and one that is subpar. Traditional media and advertising were almost able to "fake it till they made it" with storytelling. A campaign would take months of preparation, the piece would show up in print or on radio or TV, and it would live through a continuous stream until its life cycle ended. With social media, everything happens at a much quicker speed. Executing a piece can happen in the time span for typing out 280 characters on Twitter and hitting send. And then it's on to the next thing—the newest message or the latest app that can better sell what you are putting out there. But the ideology behind the production of telling an impactful story through traditional media is a formula that can be moved over to social, and it should be. How does your story make sense? Are you telling it in a way that interests consumers? Is the life span longer than a thumb swiping up on a screen?

What do you wish you had known when you were starting out?

A few things stand out to me that I wish I had known when I was first starting out in this field:

- Finding that happy medium between being yourself and fitting into your role. Everyone brings different elements of expertise and know-how to the table: design, video production, writing, innovative campaigns—you name it! And while that is all great and dandy, you have to be able to adapt your style (whatever that may be) to meet the needs of your organization. For example, I have a dry sense of humor, but that kind of snark does not work when writing in the voice of Team USA, an organization that is all about American pride and being the cheerleader for the Olympians. You can still bring your personality to the table, but understand how you can use your talents to better the organization, not the other way around.

- Nothing is guaranteed. This is a small market, and there are *a lot* of qualified folks out there. But not all those people have a job within the industry. Because of that, it seems that a lot of people can be seen as replaceable or rotated out, and with the influx of interns and/or students wanting the experience, why would an organization invest in you and your talents? It's a terrible cycle. Take it as a reason not to hang

(Continued)

(Continued)

your head, but rather to grind even harder. Use it as fuel to learn more. Find your little niche and make yourself one of a kind. Whether it's through reading, writing, going to conferences or seminars, or continuing your education and building upon that community, make yourself irreplaceable. Because nothing is guaranteed.

Samantha Hughey is a brand manager for adidas Volleyball. Her work in sports focuses on brand marketing, strategic communication, and social media strategy. She previously was the audience engagement editor for Team USA during the Rio Olympics. Samantha can be followed on Twitter at @samanthahughey.

INTRODUCTION

The perception of social media professionals has evolved over the last few years. More businesses, corporations, and even individuals who want to consult are realizing the growing industry that surrounds social media to this day. The job market and roles are evolving along with the platforms themselves, which means in some cases there are established platforms in the field, but in other cases the platforms have yet to be solidified. You could, for example, be working in a position that has yet to be offered or created, which brings forth numerous opportunities to break into the industry. However, in a field that is constantly in flux and rapidly shifting, the skills, experiences, and expectations for those working in social media have to be adaptive as well. Many opportunities are out there for professionals to work in the field, but a high level of commitment and dedication to learn and grow new skills is not only expected, but necessary, to be relevant and valued in the field.

Picture where you would like to work. Do you see yourself working in a cubicle, responding in real time to customer inquiries for one primary brand? Do you see yourself working at an agency, working on a variety of different projects, brands, and clients? Or, do you see yourself taking the entrepreneurship route, being your own boss and running your own company? All of these jobs have a key role in the social media world, and each requires certain skills and a specific mindset.

Each role has its own set of positives, negatives, and opportunities for the future. Candidates for social media positions need to think about what today's corporations and hiring managers are looking for. Whether you go into journalism, marketing, public relations, or another related field, hiring managers will use social media to see how you present yourself. According to a *Business News Daily* article, nearly 60% of employers today turn to social media to research job applicants, an increase of 11% since 2006 (Brooks, 2017).

Students and young professionals should be aware of available tools used to get an employer's attention and look for future networking and professional opportunities. CareerBuilder (2014) discusses some of the must-haves for young professionals who want to get noticed for positions in social media, such as having a blog and presence on various social media channels.

WHO HIRES SOCIAL MEDIA PROFESSIONALS?

One major consideration when working in social media is to determine what companies you would want to work for. Social media–specific agencies operate somewhat differently than traditional corporations. Corporate settings are more structured, formal, and tied to regulations, especially if they are a publicly traded company.

Experience is the first thing that employers want to see. They will ask you how many internships, projects, work experiences, and clients you have had before even applying for a job. You will be expected to have a virtual dossier (online portfolio) to showcase your work.

Other requirements are not as obvious. For example, working in sports requires not only a strong level of sports experience, but also the ability to network and engage with the sports community on social media. Meeting people—both virtually and face-to-face—is one of the most important things you can do to advance your career. These meetings do not always have to involve social media.

Not only will employers be looking at your work, but you also need to look at theirs. Here are some employer characteristics you need to assess:

Portfolio of work. First, you want to see what potential employers have already done. What awards have they won? Where are their team members speaking? Certain conferences in social media (SXSW, Social Media Marketing World, CES, etc.), as well as specialized events hosted by specific platforms such as Facebook, Twitter, and Google, are well recognized. Cutting-edge professionals will not only attend, but also share their knowledge in these venues in recognition of their expertise.

Colleagues and what they have done. Many professionals in social media today may not have specialized in social media originally but rather just fell into it. Some universities still do not offer social media classes, programs, or majors. See what the professionals in your prospective organization have done in the past and what they are continuing to do in the field.

Culture. Culture is one of the most important elements to take into consideration. Make sure you are in an environment where you can do your best work and have the opportunity to learn, grow, and contribute to the greater good for your clients. Toxic environments (unhealthy competitive natures, stealing a coworker's work, etc.) are not places you want to be. Assess the level of mentorship in the organization.

Organizational structure for social media. You also need to consider the organizational structure of an organization when looking at prospective positions. While social media as a professional area has matured, some subtle differences persist across the industries. The position you report to will let you know very quickly the skills that you need to stay with the organization. For example, if you report to the chief marketing officer, you will need to be able to tie in marketing's goals, objectives, and language for reporting and creating content. The same applies to other fields as well. In a journalism setting, for example, a social media professional needs to understand the writing, reporting, and research requirements as well as the importance of deadlines. The content produced must follow the structure and writing format necessary for a particular publication.

WHERE TO WORK IN SOCIAL MEDIA

In social media, no one designated position, brand role, or industry is universally the same. Each company has its own distinct titles, expectations, and duties assigned to designated individuals in charge of social media. However, some universal skills are required for all social media professionals.

In some cases, the social media professional will be working for multiple clients with a variety of different specializations (e.g., analytics, content creation, and social listening). In other cases, the professional will work for one client and focus on one distinct area (e.g., storytelling or Snapchat).

Large Social Media Agencies. Many large social media agencies have been behind some of the largest and most effective social media campaigns for clients, brands, and corporations. One frequently referenced campaign is Oreo's "You can still dunk in the dark" tweet during the 2013 Super Bowl. This successful tweet was created by 360i, one of the main social media companies mentioned in the press, trade publications, and other outlets.

Most brands and corporations have an agency of record in charge of social media content, strategy, or execution of ideas. For example, General Motors worked with FleishmanHillard to develop social media content for Chevrolet, resulting in the #ChevyGoesEmoji campaign targeting Generation Z and millennial audiences.

Large Social Media Companies. Brands can also be their own social media outlets, telling their own stories about successes with their clients and campaigns. Most brands, including Sprinklr, Hootsuite, Buffer, Sprout Social, Sysomos, Salesforce, Adobe, and Nuvi, use their blogs to share case studies on what has and has not worked. Many times, these brands focus on tools that provide services, training, and education for other organizations and individuals.

Boutique Social Media Agencies. **Boutique agencies or firms** specialize either in one aspect of social media, such as analytics, or in a specific platform channel. Delmondo, a creative content agency in New York City, empowers content creators to produce the best stories for their clients and platforms. While the agency initially specialized in the use of Snapchat, it subsequently branched out its strategy and analytics offerings for Snapchat, Instagram, and Facebook live streams. Boutique agencies can offer a more specialized focus and expertise to specific tasks, channels, and strategies compared to larger agencies.

Small Business/Agency. This type of employer provides many entry-level positions for social media professionals or student interns. In consultation with their college or university mentors, student interns work with small agencies and businesses to help them engage using social media to increase their presence in the communities in which they operate. Most small agencies have few employees and serve relatively small organizations.

Self-Employment. Social media has provided many consulting opportunities. It is important to be able to identify those consultants who "get it" versus the ones who are able to play the system and appear credible when, in fact, they are not. When practicing as a social media consultant, you are your own boss, and you can pick and choose the clients with whom you work. Your cost for services (value-based fees, project-based fees, etc.) must be negotiated with your clients. Some potential clients may not see the value of consultants and their contribution to the overall business and marketing strategy using social media. To convince them of your value, provide sound evidence of your previous work (sample proposals, SWOT [strengths, weaknesses, opportunities, and threats] analysis, news sources, content graphics, etc.).

Corporations. Internal teams working within large organizations create content and stories for internal and external audiences, monitor and listen to conversations about their organizations online, and engage in proactive practices online, addressing concerns from customers with social care. General Motors, Yum! Brands, Gatorade, and Nasdaq are just a few organizations that have established teams of social media professionals.

Nonprofits. Social media in the nonprofit sector is one of the fastest-growing areas in the field. Nonprofits provide professionals with the opportunity to share stories, create awareness of key issues, identify donors to support causes and issues, and generate momentum to support humanitarian efforts at the local, national, and international level.

Government. Social media has slowly but surely made its way to government agencies, political campaigns, and lobby groups. Some roles have been increasing in popularity. Political and government entities, for example, now have director of social media positions (e.g., White House) or director of digital media positions (e.g., Department of Health and Human Services), as well as people in traditional communication roles such as communication specialist, social media manager, and intern.

Sports. In sports, social media is directly tied to success in fan engagement, prominence in the community and industry, and innovative trends and practices. Sports organizations were early adopters of social media in their overall organizational structure. More professional, collegiate, and youth teams recognize the need for social media professionals and teams in leadership roles due to the growing emphasis on using social media to tell stories, recap games and performances, and be the first line of building a reputation and community for a team. The size of the team working in social media for a sports organization depends on the overall structure and financial support for this endeavor, but most of the time, professionals who work in social media in sports either have a designated leadership role in this area (e.g., director of digital media or director of creative media) or are assuming this role as part of an established position within the sports department (e.g., sports information director).

Media. Journalism values the importance of social media. Most writers, producers, and reporters in traditional media also engage in social media for reporting the news, updating their community and audience, and communicating with others in the industry. This is largely a response to the fact that most users rely on social media to get breaking news and updates regarding local, national, and international events. A strong social media presence has become part of the role and duty of traditional media. Not only are journalists expected to create content and stories for their outlets, but they also have to produce and share content across multiple platforms, listen to trending topics for story ideas (data analytics), and become strong editors and creators for different categories of content.

DEFINITION OF KEY SOCIAL MEDIA ROLES

Social media roles and job titles are anything but stable, and can be different from company to company and even among job listings in other segments of media (e.g., marketing, public relations, communications, and journalism). With social media constantly evolving, the roles and job titles are fluid as well. This section will highlight the main roles being practiced with the mindset of understanding that some skills will always be relevant and valued by employers looking to hire a social media professional. Because each industry has its own titles, it is important to review job descriptions carefully. The description of each role presented will include the underlying characteristics, responsibilities, and duties. A sample job posting for each role will also be presented and explained in this section.

Social Media Community Manager Versus Social Media Manager

The **social media community manager** role sometimes gets confused with the role of social media manager—two distinct yet related roles. There are several differences between them: A social media manager focuses on being the brand on social media, whereas a social media community manager focuses on advocating for the brand on social media. Essentially, the social media manager *is* the brand—these professionals are the ones who create content, embrace the brand voice, and answer questions as the brand. You do not see any initials or anything not distinctly connected with the brand attributed to them.

In contrast, the role of social media community manager allows a person to add a personal take on the conversation with audience members. When engaging in a conversation with United Airlines, for example, you may get a message from United, with a few initials after it identifying the social care representative and community manager responding to your inquiry. This adds a level of personal connection and a human side to the social media conversation not necessarily present in the social media manager role.

Community managers may be in charge of listening and overseeing various campaigns and initiatives on social media. One minute you may be asked to address a customer inquiry online, and the next minute you may be asked to put strategy into place for a campaign. You will wear many hats in this position, which requires skill, adaptability, and multitasking.

Table 4.1 presents a sample description of a community manager position at Twitter.

TABLE 4.1 ■ Content Community Manager, Twitter

Our ideal candidate will have

- A track record for developing insightful, interesting content
- Impeccable writing and editing skills and a passion for storytelling
- Ability to think on your feet: being able to respond to tweets quickly in a war-room situation
- Attention to detail
- The drive to see projects through from planning and concept development to execution and analysis
- A desire to work in a fast-paced, collaborative environment
- A proactive, problem-solving adaptable mindset and ability to deal with change and ambiguity

Responsibilities will include

- Managing day-to-day editorial operations and calendar
- Collaborating with a global team to share best practices, capture perspectives, and distribute content
- Writing and editing articles, case studies, newsletter blurbs, and research pieces for Twitter's marketing site
- Working with the team's campaign manager to develop innovative advertising strategies for a variety of social channels
- Managing freelance writers and consolidating feedback from internal stakeholders
- Community management and writing tweets for @TwitterAds as well as posts for other social channels including LinkedIn, YouTube, and Facebook (writing posts, responding, publishing, curating)
- Working in our war room at six or seven industry and Twitter events per year (requires some travel)

Source: Adapted from MEOjobsonline.com

Facebook advertised a similar role for a community manager for its Oculus Rift team and brand (see Table 4.2). While some similarities are evident in the positions offered by Twitter and Facebook, there are differences as well. For example, the Facebook position specifically focuses on content creation across different platforms with an emphasis on customer service for the brand. Second, the applicant is expected to have work experience in the field of social media, but what these years of experience mean for the applicant is not clear. That is, you can't just say you have been on Instagram for five years, but you *will* need to outline the experience you have and what you offer that fits these specific guidelines.

Social Media Coordinator

A **social media coordinator** focuses on the strategic planning and execution of the social media content for a brand or organization. As a coordinator, you are responsible for making posts and content go live on schedule across the various social media platforms. In this role, you will be responsible for ensuring not only that content goes out in the appropriate channel, but that it is scheduled at the right time for optimal reach and metrics for the company. Along with ensuring posts go out at appropriate times, this social media professional has to make sure all messages are consistent with the brand message and voice. Strategy and message relevancy are two parts of the equation for the social media coordinator to reinforce and advocate for as part of a social media team.

TABLE 4.2 ■ Community Manager, Oculus

As Oculus community manager, you will be responsible for Oculus social presence across all relevant channels as well as for community engagement and events. You'll work closely across all of Oculus marketing and communications to drive community engagement and build social campaigns and programs.

Responsibilities

- Develop and implement Oculus social media and community strategies and best practices across various social media channels including Facebook, Instagram, Twitter, YouTube, and others
- Manage social media campaign execution and scheduling including day-to-day content sourcing and creation as well as post-campaign analysis
- Work with product marketing to support campaigns
- Partner with customer support team on social care strategy and messaging to customers
- Test, optimize, and analyze campaigns and projects based on key metrics
- Understand the interests and behaviors of our target user segments and how to effectively engage with them

Minimum Qualifications

- More than five years of managing social media and community platforms
- Experience working in gaming, with an understanding of engaging the audience
- Analytical mindset with ability to understand how social campaigns deliver impact marketing and company goals
- Tendency to thrive in a fast-paced, dynamic environment
- Organizational skills
- Bachelor's degree

Source: Adapted from MEOjobsonline.com

Strong organization and planning skills are required to ensure the posts have a timing and frequency that makes sense to the community in question as well as to the platform being utilized for the content. A **content calendar** outlining what content is going out at what time is crucial for the coordinator to create, maintain, and share with the rest of the team.

The coordinator works with all social media teams to make sure the messages, content, branding, and voice are consistent. Like most current social media roles, responsibilities will overlap with different team members. For example, the coordinator works with the community manager to ensure that the messages are relevant

---

TABLE 4.3 ■ Social Media Coordinator, Atlanta United FC

As part of the AMBSE Media Group, the Atlanta United social media coordinator will assist with all aspects of the club's social media efforts on a day-to-day basis—including content creation, community management, one-to-one fan engagement, and strategic plan development and implementation.

This position will proactively lead, create, and manage content on Atlanta United social platforms. He or she will collaborate with and partner across all relevant departments including content production, digital/web, video services, photography, marketing, sponsorships, community relations, and agencies to deliver and execute successful social tactics that align with Atlanta United's overall digital media strategy.

Roles and Responsibilities

- Assist in creating innovative, entertaining content (including but not limited to Facebook posts, tweets, GIFs, snaps, images, and short-format videos) to engage consumers across social channels while maintaining Falcons brand voice
- Assist in building and aligning content strategy, team coverage, team communications, marketing partnerships, stadium news and events, and sponsored posts across all social media platforms
- Provide coverage for both home and away Atlanta United games (may require some travel)
- Help build and manage both long- and short-term social editorial calendar
- Drive integrated content ideation from concept to completion across all platforms
- Together with the Atlanta United social/digital team, aggressively increase overall key performance indicator metrics across social platforms
- Collaborate with the sponsorship and marketing teams to create engaging and valuable partnership inventory and brand integration opportunities
- Ensure integration with all Atlanta United departments, as well as other communications, marketing, and community relations leaders across the Blank Family of Businesses
- Monitor best practices and trends in organic and branded social media, and effectively communicate relevant news and opportunities to internal teams

Qualifications and Education Requirements

- Bachelor's degree (required)
- One to two years' experience across multiple digital and social media functions including strategy, digital marketing, web development, and/or a related field within a high-paced, demanding professional setting
- Agency experience (accepted)

Required Skills

- Demonstrated experience driving consumer/fan engagement across multiple social channels
- Strong writing and editing skills
- Experience with professional or collegiate sports (recommended)

Source: Adapted from MEOjobsonline.com

and resonate with audiences so they are able to report positive findings back to the management team during the evaluation phase. As shown in Table 4.3, the social media coordinator position for the Atlanta United FC highlights several key skills, but notice the emphasis on assisting with strategy, coordinating consistent content across the platforms, and planning to distribute this content at the right time, to the right audience, and on the right channel.

Social Media Strategist

A **social media strategist** ties in the goals and objectives for the company or client in question, and focuses on how to get these measures accomplished. This professional takes more of a manager role than a technician role, meaning he or she not only is in charge of understanding the tactical elements that go into a strong social media plan (content creation, specific tools used to create and analyze the content online, etc.), but also understands the comprehensive picture of the campaign.

Strategist roles can be centered on social media, but they can also be aimed at a particular area. Sometimes social media strategy jobs are on the creative side (such as the one listed for Mashable in Table 4.4) while others are on the data side (as shown for Spredfast in Table 4.5). While there are differences, the positions also have important similarities.

The Mashable creative strategist primarily focuses on the art side of the strategy continuum whereas the Spredfast social analytics strategist focuses more on the science side. Yet both roles are relevant to the creative integration of content, strategy, and messaging used to apply and present findings from research for the social team. While they are separate roles for these two brands, in other cases the two job titles become one; Starbucks, for example, employs a strategy analyst, as shown in Table 4.6.

The social analytics strategist position at Spredfast primarily focuses on the data and analytical side of social media at the company. This role is based on a strong understanding of how to collect data and strategically apply the data to provide insights for the social team.

Content Creator

Content is king when it comes to social media. Content comes in various formats, and social media professionals are expected to be well versed in the type of content they are producing. Besides multimedia, including graphics, images, infographics, video, and animations, content can take the form of thought pieces that share resources, ideas, and research insights using white papers, blog posts, and social media updates. **Content creators** have to be able to create work that resonates with audiences. In fact, the best content creators are able to identify which stories and insights their key audiences want without knowing they want it. The range of skills needed to create these different formats of content can be challenging, combining both visual and written components (see, for example, Table 4.7). Content that appears on social media can be long format (e.g., white papers) or short format (e.g., tweets), and often integrates multimedia and emerging media with the mix (360° images, virtual reality, etc.).

While content is an important element for the creators, context is the other part of the equation to keep in mind. Content creators have to be able to identify the overall purpose for a piece of content from a strategy standpoint and work with the coordinator, community manager, and strategist to make sure the content integrates the brand message, voice, and situation online.

TABLE 4.4 ■ Creative Strategist, Mashable

Mashable is looking for a talented creative strategist to join our Mashable Studios team, focused on branded content. Mashable Studios creates branded content as well as original video programming. The branded content team focuses on branded content creation, multimedia production, and storytelling that helps our clients engage with Mashable readers onsite and multiplatform. Mashable works with some of the top brands in the world to develop creative custom content campaigns, including Hilton DoubleTree, Capital One, Wheat Thins, Pepsi, Ford, Samsung, and Kia.

The creative strategist will be responsible for helping the sales team sell branded content ideas to key clients. He or she will be in a client-facing role, including both pitching branded content campaigns and executing sold content programs. This person will be involved in branded campaigns from the pre-sales ideation process including brainstorms and developing concepts, all the way through post-sale executions and measuring performance.

The Day-to-Day

- Brainstorm creative and compelling content solutions for advertisers interested in branded content programs with Mashable
- Work closely with the integrated marketing team in developing pitch decks for partnerships
- Write detailed pitches illustrating brainstormed concepts to be included in pitch decks
- Work with producers to execute content programs on deadline
- Manage content campaigns, including assigning articles to copywriters and managing timelines
- Grow Mashable's reputation as a creative, innovative, and effective partner for branded content
- Collaborate with the community team to optimize performance and drive distribution and content consumption across channels

Must-Haves

- Two to three years' editorial, creative, and/or agency experience
- Experience working with brands and creating branded programs, especially multimedia and creative technology initiatives
- Experience in a client-facing role
- A creative approach to all work
- Excellent writing and communication skills
- Ability to multitask and work in a fast-paced environment with quick deadlines
- Commitment to work hard and perform tasks on deadline
- Attention to detail and a high level of organizational skills
- Strong familiarity with WordPress (HTML) and social media tools (Twitter, Facebook, Pinterest, Instagram, Tumblr, LinkedIn, etc.)
- Vast knowledge of tech, business, and social media trends and ability to write across them

Source: Adapted from MEOjobsonline.com

Multimedia/Video Producer

This is probably one of the most in-demand jobs in social media. If you are able to create, produce, and record video content to tell effective stories, you will be in demand. Organizations are interested in people with a background in storyboarding, writing scripts, and creating demo reels that can be viewed online on YouTube, on Behance, and in other content and video creator communities (see, for example, the video producer position at BuzzFeed outlined in Table 4.8).

TABLE 4.5 ■ Social Analytics Strategist, Spredfast

Spredfast is looking for a social analyst to join our fast-growing social strategy team. This person will be responsible for creating reports that provide a visual representation of social media performance and insights and delivering actionable, data-driven recommendations to our customers.

The ideal candidate has experience with measuring social media channels and managing campaigns that create best-in-class performance and impact reports. This role will also assist with the development of research-backed social media marketing playbooks, be able to establish channel-specific key performance indicators (KPIs), and execute other social strategy–centric deliverables, as well as optimizing and analyzing paid social media campaigns. A successful candidate will have solid editorial instincts and a passion for using data to inform strategy, and he or she will have a clear understanding of best practices for measuring campaigns across all of the major social channels (Facebook, Twitter, LinkedIn, Google+, YouTube, Instagram, Pinterest, etc.).

This role will report to a senior analyst and work closely with the sales and professional services teams to enable world-class social media measurement and reporting for Spredfast customers.

Responsibilities

- Counsel customers on establishing goals and translating marketing objectives for social media analytics reports
- Analyze trends and innovations in social media measurement models and tools
- Collect, analyze, and interpret both organic and paid data to generate reports that provide a visual representation of social media campaign performance and insights
- Pivot campaign performance data in Excel to provide clear and effective communication to internal account teams and customers
- Collect and analyze information from multiple data sources, ensuring data are reliable, using technical expertise and tools to uncover insights, statistics, and trends
- Take responsibility for downloading raw data reports that chart customer KPIs and provide insight and analysis as to what the numbers mean for the customer's daily operations as well as long-term strategy
- Inform the road map of Spredfast products that facilitate measuring performance and impact, and be an internal champion for analytics and paid media optimization at Spredfast
- Facilitate the productization of strategic analytics services at Spredfast
- Serve as a research and analytics subject matter expert in customer meetings and at external events

Requirements

- At least five to seven years' experience in communications, marketing, advertising, public relations, or statistics
- Proven passion for, and expertise in, social media analysis
- Experience with social media platforms, including but not limited to Facebook, Twitter, LinkedIn, Google+, YouTube, Instagram, and Pinterest
- Experience optimizing or reporting on social media paid advertising campaigns including Facebook, Twitter, LinkedIn, Google+, YouTube, Instagram, and Pinterest
- Demonstrated experience in creating and executing measurement reporting and optimizing paid media campaigns on behalf of a brand or media company
- Excellent project management and organizational skills
- Tendency to work efficiently, be dependable, and have an entrepreneurial spirit
- Ability to rapidly assess, analyze, and resolve complicated issues with little initial information or direction and with varying degrees of ambiguity
- Moderate travel

Source: Adapted from MEOjobsonline.com

TABLE 4.6 ■ Strategy Analyst (Global Strategy), Starbucks

Job Summary and Mission at Starbucks: Our mission is to inspire and nurture the human spirit—one person, one cup, and one neighborhood at a time. This job contributes to Starbucks' success by providing strategic insights and analytics through the lens of our customers, our partners, and our business. In this dynamic and cross-functional role, you will support test design and measurement of new products and initiatives, actively monitor the competitive landscape, and identify key business risks and opportunities by analyzing longer-term sales trends and customer behaviors.

If you enjoy a broad scope of work, have a passion for data and analytics, and get excited about telling stories with data, apply to join our growing team!

Summary of Key Responsibilities

- Builds robust and detailed models with minimal guidance to analyze the incremental sales impact of new initiatives; runs segmentation analysis to understand how results vary by store type, daypart category, etc.

- Leverages visualization tools to distill complex analysis down to key insights

- Develops thoughtful recommendations to inform leadership and decision making

- Manages testing tools, with focus on continuous improvement to identify and implement process improvements and efficiencies

- Actively monitors the competitive landscape to understand how performance compares to industry benchmarks

- Establishes and builds strong working relationships with key cross-functional partners

Summary of Experience

- Data analysis and modeling (two to five years)

- Strategic planning or management consulting (one to two years)

Preferred Qualifications

- Education: Bachelor's degree in business, management, economics, mathematics, statistics, or similar quantitative discipline; MBA/MS preferred

Required Knowledge, Skills, and Abilities

- Strong analytical ability, strategic thinking, and problem-solving skills

- Working knowledge of statistical concepts

- Strong attention to detail

- Ability to simplify and structure complex or ambiguous problems

- Working knowledge and business-applicable experience in statistical modeling or machine learning techniques (A/B testing, regression, cluster analysis, forecasting leveraging one or more the following: APT, R, SAS, SPSS, SQL, Python)

- Working knowledge of visualization tools (Tableau)

Core Competencies

- Customer Focus: Delivers legendary service that meets and exceeds all customers' expectations

- Ethics and Integrity: Adheres to Starbucks values, beliefs, and principles during good and bad times

- Composure: Remains calm, maintains perspective, and responds in a professional manner when faced with difficult situations

- Personal Learning: Takes personal responsibility for the continuous learning and development of new knowledge, skills, and experiences

- Dealing With Ambiguity: Able to successfully function during times of uncertainty and changing priorities

- Decision Making: Makes timely and quality decisions based on a mixture of analysis, wisdom, experience, and judgment

- Interpersonal Savvy: Builds effective relationships with all people; up, down, and sideways, inside and outside of Starbucks

Starbucks and its brands are an equal opportunity employer of all qualified individuals, including minorities, women, veterans, and individuals with disabilities. Starbucks will consider for employment qualified applicants with criminal histories in a manner consistent with all federal, state, and local ordinances.

Source: Adapted from www.indeed.com.

TABLE 4.7 ■ Digital Intern, Edelman

Edelman DC's Digital Content Studio is looking for an intern to join a growing team of creative professionals who are passionate about crafting content that will resonate with digital audiences across a vast array of interests, sectors, and demographics. Our team is tasked to create a voice for our clients' online presence—a voice that speaks through short-form social copy, long-form blog content, images, memes, GIFs, and videos (to name a few). We are looking for someone with a deep understanding of content creation coupled with strong writing skills.

As a creative services intern, you must be intellectually curious, reliable, flexible, collaborative, and a creative thinker. You will be a fully integrated member of account teams and will be expected to produce client-ready work.

Responsibilities

- Drafting editorial content and creating content calendars

- Drafting short-form copy for visual content including, but not limited to, memes, GIFs, and animated and stop motion videos

- Drafting long-form digital copy including website content, blogs, video scripts, and email communications

- Working closely with account teams to develop, compose, and implement all community content per clients and their business objectives

- Monitoring social channels for engagement opportunities

- Participating in creative brainstorms

- Staying up-to-date on digital news and trends

Qualifications

- Proficiency in nonacademic writing, with a strong grasp of English grammar and familiarity with AP (Associated Press) style

- Experience in digital marketing and social media

- Excellent writing and editing skills with strong attention to detail

- Strong verbal and written communication and organizational skills

- The ability to adapt to new conditions, assignments, and deadlines and anticipate team needs

- Familiarity with Microsoft Office Suite, notably Word, Excel, and PowerPoint

- Experience with design software, specifically Photoshop, Illustrator, and InDesign (preferred)

(Continued)

TABLE 4.7 ■ (Continued)

Basic Qualifications

You must have an interest in communications and/or public relations and possess good interpersonal and communication skills with the ability to work effectively with others.

About Our Internship Program

- The duration of the internship is a minimum of three months and a maximum of six months.
- Interns are paid $12.50 per hour and are eligible for overtime.
- Most of our interns are postgraduates and work a full-time schedule (weekdays from 9 a.m. to 5:30 p.m.).

Source: Adapted from MEOjobsonline.com

TABLE 4.8 ■ Video Producer (Lifestyle), BuzzFeed

The BuzzFeed Entertainment Group is looking for a creative and ambitious lifestyle video producer who can create compelling, shareable, service-oriented content for the web and other digital platforms. The applicant must be a native of the digital and pop cultural landscape with intimate knowledge of the latest and greatest in social media and emerging technology/platforms.

The ideal candidate loves to experiment with short, fun formats that succinctly tell a story—whether it's a beauty tutorial or a food trend piece. No preciousness or thinking one is smarter than the internet. This person should have good social intuition, love making content without having to be behind or in front of a camera, and know how to trust data to crack success.

Responsibilities

- Conceive, shoot, write, edit, and produce lifestyle videos for BuzzFeed's Facebook and Instagram channels, as well as emerging platforms
- Produce videos quickly, experiment with lots of different formats, and be interested in analyzing the results of the work
- Work closely with the BuzzFeed Lifestyle editors to pitch and produce video components for content they're working on
- Collaborate with video producers to execute ideas on time and under budget

Requirements

- Proven experience and/or interest in covering a variety of topics including beauty, hair, style, food, DIY (do-it-yourself), travel, and health
- Proven experience with all aspects of video creation (DSLRs [digital single-lens reflex cameras], Premiere Pro, lighting, audio recording, etc.)
- A passion for sharing lifestyle content that's entertaining and inclusive, but never prescriptive
- The ability to think analytically about social sharing to create videos that are made to be shared
- Three to five years' experience creating compelling, shareable video content
- A competitive drive—you enjoy winning and really going for it
- Ability to work in small teams as well as go off on your own
- A positive, curious, playful disposition (no haters)

Applicants will be asked to submit links to relevant past work.

Source: Adapted from MEOjobsonline.com

Most of the jobs listed in social media now have a multimedia component, so this is a good skill if you want to be more of a generalist. However, if you want to specialize in multimedia, be prepared to make investments in tools, software programs, and equipment.

Writer/Editor

Writing and editing content that is consistent with the brand voice for social and digital media is essential. Social media writers and editors support the storytellers, strong visionaries, and other editors. They will be working with content creators as well as coordinators to ensure their content is aligned with the content of other team members. Publishing content on a consistent basis across media channels is important not just from a textual standpoint, but also in the case of other types of content (video, photos, etc.). (Table 4.9 presents a sample job description for an editor at Bleacher Report.)

Other Social Media Roles

There are other roles to consider when exploring work in social media. Being a **freelancer** is one of the more popular avenues to take due to the flexibility and independence that come with choosing your own clients and projects. Freelancers tend to focus on certain types of projects and particular areas within social media like social media writing, content creation, videography, and social media strategic plans. **Consultants** usually specialize in what they offer clients, such as creating social

---

TABLE 4.9 ■ Editor (Social), Bleacher Report

The social media editor will work with a team of designers and content creators to conceptualize and produce social media content. Reporting to the senior manager, this position will coordinate innovative daily social executions that leverage all of Bleacher Report's content-producing arms while also breaking new ground and delivering new types of social experiences. This person should be a visual-first content consumer and should constantly be thinking creatively about how we tell stories that make sense for a phone-first generation. Responsibilities include but are not limited to the following:

- Coordinate production and publishing of social media content (projects are generally complex in responsibility and/or multiple projects are managed simultaneously) in conjunction with other departments

- Manage production processes, such as assignment docs, resources, budgets and assignments, communication with production and outside departments, advanced planning, and billing, and establish new processes, procedures, and methods that improve production outcomes

- Provide creative support to designers and freelance creators to ensure they are meeting production deadlines and deliverables

About You

- Three to five years' experience managing social media accounts at a digital publisher

- Strong track record of creating viral content across Vine, Instagram, Twitter, and Snapchat

- Demonstrable social networking experience and social analytics tools knowledge

- Deep understanding of current and emerging social networks

Source: Adapted from MEOjobsonline.com

media plans, preparing for potential scenarios or simulations in social media crisis situations, educational and speaking opportunities based on social media expertise, and training. Consultants may be independent, but consulting agencies and firms also offer services. Both freelancers and consultants in social media must demonstrate previous work for clients and reviews of their work (e.g., testimonials and online reviews).

HOW MUCH DO SOCIAL MEDIA PROFESSIONALS GET PAID?

This is a frequently asked question in the industry. What is the going rate for social media managers (see Figure 4.1)? What about community managers? Do roles dealing with data and analytics get more resources and support? All of these questions are valid and important.

Social media roles are expanding, and even reach department levels within organizations, media outlets, and agencies. Social media professionals play key parts in many communication, marketing, public relations, business reporting, and strategy processes. Before you start applying for internships or jobs, make sure you do your research and understand the expectations (as well as years of experience) and responsibilities for each role. It is challenging to figure out how much a professional should be making based on experience, skills, and expertise. While on some occasions a marketing, public relations, or communications professional is writing the job description, sometimes it is a human resources professional who does not know the social media industry. There are occasions where professionals and brands want everything in the job description (essentially looking for a "unicorn" candidate), or they mix up the descriptions for the role they are looking for. Essentially, you may read a description for a social media manager when, in fact, the brand hiring for the position is looking for a coordinator. That said, figuring out the salary for a position

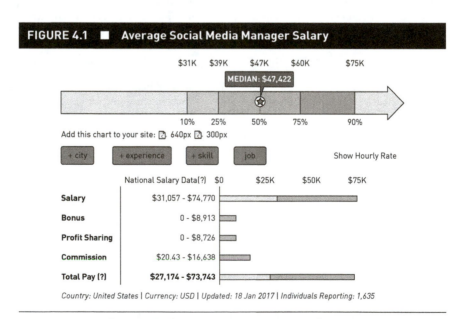

FIGURE 4.1 ■ Average Social Media Manager Salary

Source: Adapted from "Social Media Manager Salary" PayScale Inc. http://www.payscale.com/research/US/Job=Social_Media_Manager/Salary.

can be difficult. However, sources like Glassdoor, LinkedIn, and even PayScale can help gauge where a salary should be for each social media position.

As presented in Figure 4.1, as of January 2017, a social media manager on average makes $47,422 annually. Having multiple tools, skills, and trainings under your belt should lead to a higher salary. For example, as shown in Figure 4.2, a social media specialist on average gets a lower salary compared to a social media manager ($40,773 versus $47,422 in January 2017).

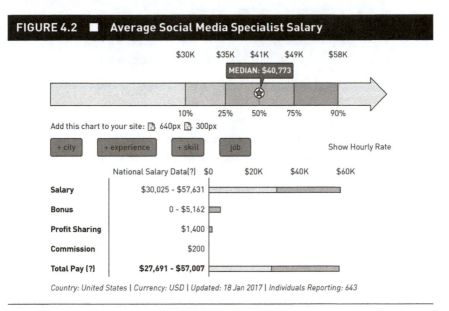

FIGURE 4.2 ■ Average Social Media Specialist Salary

Country: United States | Currency: USD | Updated: 18 Jan 2017 | Individuals Reporting: 643

Source: Adapted from "Social Media Specialist Salary" Payscale Inc. http://www.payscale.com/research/US/Job=Social_Media_Specialist/Salary.

If you have gained several years of experience and established a reputation for yourself as a thought leader, and you have the power and presence to lead a team and formulate strategies, you might be eligible for a leadership role in social media. As you can see from Figure 4.3, professionals in leadership roles (e.g., social media directors) make more money than the other two roles presented above (average is $71,255).

Some final thoughts about working as a social media professional:

- *Community managers have increased their presence within the industry, but the title is used in many different areas.* Social media managers, still considered to be specialized, get paid a bit more.

- *Show what you have done, but also what you will continue to do and how you will strive to improve in the future.* Social media is all about growing, expanding, and being adaptable. Show what you have done, but realize this is a field where you have to constantly update your skills.

- *You have to start small and work your way up in social media.* Big, high-paying jobs do not happen overnight. Take the time to hone your skills and make sure you are learning and growing as a professional. Keep in mind that this can take some time, but it is best to get the experience, establish relationships, and continue growing. Moving forward is the most important strategy.

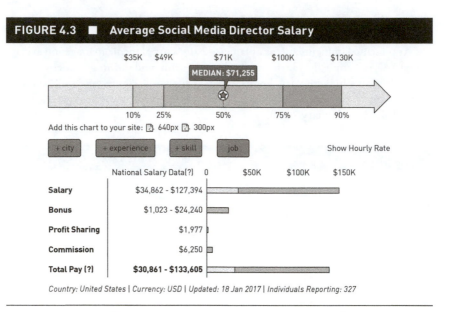

FIGURE 4.3 ■ Average Social Media Director Salary

Country: United States | Currency: USD | Updated: 18 Jan 2017 | Individuals Reporting: 327

Source: Adapted from "Social Media Director Salary" Payscale Inc. http://www.payscale.com/research/US/Job=Social_Media_Director/Salary.

- *It is about not only what you know, but who knows you.* For some of these positions, it's all about who knows you. Invest not only in your skills, but in building networks and communities. Speak at local events, volunteer at professional functions, be a guest on blogs or webinars, and write content to share with various communities to develop your thought leadership. Building on your personal brand (as mentioned in Chapter 3) will help open doors and opportunities for you for potential collaborations, partnerships, job offers, or speaking engagements.

- *Have a "side hustle."* If you have one job in social media, that may not be enough. Whether you are a social media manager or even leading a team, you should consider having another job on the side—or a "side hustle." Carlos Gil (@CarlosGil83) recommends this frequently. He is a keynote speaker as well as the founder of Gil Media Co. This means you might have a consulting business, help invest in a start-up, take on side projects for videography or photography, or give paid speaking engagements at conferences and functions. It's about taking the time to create engagement not only for your personal brand, but for your community.

- *Opportunities depend on geolocation as well as the industry and size of an organization.* A large global corporation like General Motors will have a different pay scale than a small business in a local college town. Take into account the cost of living and other lifestyle factors when looking at positions.

- *The more aligned the role is with management and strategy, the higher the salary.* When the list of responsibilities, qualifications, and experience increases, so does the salary. Do your research ahead of time with job postings and study what other sites report (Glassdoor, LinkedIn, PayScale, etc.).

CHAPTER SUMMARY

As you can see, there are many great opportunities to work in social media. The industry is still relatively new, but it has become more mainstream and established. Social media roles will continue to change, some may go away, and new ones may be created. Social media is an ecosystem within itself, but it is increasingly being tied to other areas of communication, marketing, public relations, and media. While jobs in social media have certain required qualifications and skills, some will continue to be important (communication skills, writing, research, creativity, etc.), but others will be new. Getting a social media job is just a stepping point in your career. Focus on further developing the skills and informed insights you can bring to the table. Get as much professional experience as possible in social media to showcase what you can do. Last, but not least, continue to grow and develop. Learning does not stop when you get your social media job: It is the beginning of a lifetime of constant knowledge creation and learning.

THOUGHT QUESTIONS

1. In what different industries can you work in social media? What are some similarities and differences in the roles?

2. What key things should you note when applying for a social media position?

3. What is a content calendar, and what goes into it? Who is responsible for creating and managing this content?

4. What key skills are necessary to work in social media?

5. Identify the differences between a social media community manager, a social media strategist, and a social media manager. What skills and duties are similar and different across each of these roles?

EXERCISES

1. Identify one position you would like to pursue after this course. Describe the skills, experiences, and duties involved. Outline three steps you will take to apply for this position.

2. You have been asked to apply for a position at BuzzFeed. The hiring managers are looking for not only a cover letter, but a few pieces of content you have produced on social media. Create a post on BuzzFeed that illustrates who you are and why BuzzFeed is the place you want to work. Produce a visual résumé and cover letter for your application.

3. You are asked to prepare for an interview in person and a virtual interview via Zoom for your dream company. What steps will you take to make sure you are as prepared as possible? Outline the research, questions, and answers you will have ready to go before the interview. Discuss what steps you will take *after* the interview.

REFERENCES

Brooks, C. (2017, June 16). Keep it clean: Social media screenings gain in popularity. *Business News Daily*. Retrieved from http://www.businessnewsdaily.com/2377-social-media-hiring.html.

CareerBuilder. (2014, August 13). *Employment-related social media you should be using*. Retrieved from http://advice.careerbuilder.com/posts/employment related-social-media-you-should-be-using.

MEOjobs. (n.d.). Retrieved from http://MEOjobsonline.com/.

5

RESEARCH IN SOCIAL MEDIA

Monitoring, Listening, and Analysis

Learning Objectives
Humans of Social Media
Introduction
Importance of Research for Social Media and
    Strategic Communication
Why Do We Need Research in Social Media?
What Are the Differences Between Monitoring and
    Listening in Social Media?
    Benefits of Monitoring and Listening
    Types of Metrics
    Implementing a Monitoring and Listening Plan
Platform-Based Metrics, Tools and Services,
    and KPIs
What Is the Bridge Between Monitoring and
    Listening?
Tying Everything Together With Analysis
Dos and Don'ts in Social Media Research and Analysis
Chapter Summary
Thought Questions
Exercises
References

> ## LEARNING OBJECTIVES
>
> After reading this chapter, you will be able to
>
> - Discuss the importance of research in social media practices
> - Define social listening and social monitoring
> - Explain the connections between listening and monitoring in social media
> - Identify the key categories of metrics (basic, advanced, channel, and behavioral)

HUMANS OF SOCIAL MEDIA
RICH CALABRESE, EVP FOR FIZZIOLOGY

Source: Courtesy of Tim Harris

Rich Calabrese

Introduction

I'm currently the executive vice president (EVP) for Fizziology, a global audience insights company that utilizes social data to help bring insight to action for digital marketers and consumer insight professionals in the media and entertainment industry. When I joined Fizziology in 2011, the social data and analytics industry was still very much in its infancy, and I was one of the company's first employees.

Prior to joining Fizziology, I served in sports media as an associate producer for Golf Channel/

(Continued)

(Continued)

NBC Sports, a media relations coordinator for Churchill Downs Inc., and a social media manager for the Professional Golfers' Association (PGA) of America. I acquired my passion for working in sports and entertainment while a student at both Ithaca College (BS, sports media) and the University of Louisville (MS, sport administration).

How did you get your start in social media?

I actually started in social media through working in television production. While working at Golf Channel, I was an associate producer for four seasons of reality golf show *The Big Break*. It was in this job that I really wanted to both quantify and contextualize viewer opinions of the show based on their conversations about it on Facebook and Twitter. It was almost an impossible task, as collecting social media data (and understanding it) was still a very new concept. This is one of the main reasons I decided to pursue graduate school, obtain social media internships while in school, and complete a comprehensive research study (master's thesis) analyzing social media consumption with college students. My first gig in social media was working on the local organizing committee for the PGA of America's 72nd Senior PGA Championship at Valhalla Golf Club in Louisville, Kentucky. As the social media manager, I served on a team to lead local marketing initiatives while creating social media promotions, contests, and championship content. This was also the first major golf tournament in which the PGA allowed cell phones on the golf course during competition. This made us the first marketing team ever to create and execute onsite social media activations at a major championship event for the PGA.

What is your favorite part of working in your social media area of expertise?

My favorite part of working in social media data and analytics is seeing how widely accepted the data and insights are nowadays when making business decisions. It wasn't always this way. As someone who was on the front lines, selling social media research to the major film studios and television networks, I've seen the change in the industry firsthand. Since I started at Fizziology, I've been able to provide actionable marketing strategies, via social data and audience insights, that have had a significant impact on various film, TV, and brand marketing campaigns.

What is one thing you can't live without while working in social media?

My answer seems obvious for most marketing jobs these days, but the one thing I can't live without while working in social media is the internet. For social media professionals, it's essential to perform your job. For Fizziology, our proprietary technology is web based, and I can't access our analytics dashboard to perform research and provide insights to clients without an internet connection.

What is your favorite social media account (person/brand/etc.) to follow, and why?

One of my favorite social media accounts is FiveThirtyEight—Nate Silver's website, which focuses on political polling and data analysis of sports and entertainment topics. The political polling is interesting, but I really love the sports and entertainment data studies. Whether it's types of Scarlett Johansson movies or comprehensive March Madness breakdowns and predictions, I enjoy how FiveThirtyEight dissects different mainstream topics using data.

What is the most challenging part of working in social media?

Social media is 24/7. It doesn't just turn off when you're not using or creating content on the platform. Audiences are sharing opinions nonstop, and when opinions are shared by influencers or when news breaks that could have an impact on your team, movie, brand, and so on, you have to listen, analyze, and act. That means you have to prepare for the unexpected—which means working nights, weekends, and holidays. A lot of people love the thought of working in social media, but they don't realize that you truly have to be passionate about your company or clients and love the communities and audiences you work to inform, serve, and, hopefully, excite with amazing content.

What is your take on your area of expertise and the social media industry?

Social media platforms are beginning to evolve from social networks to social messaging. Where one generation shared social opinions with the masses, younger generations are sharing opinions and content one-to-one, or with a private group. Those working in social media need to prepare and strategize to reach audiences in different ways based on the social behaviors of the audience they're trying to reach and connect with.

Rich Calabrese is the EVP of Fizziology, a social media entertainment and analytics company. Rich can be connected with on Twitter at @richcalabrese, and you can follow the work Rich and his Fizziology team are doing at @fizziology.

INTRODUCTION

The analytic results provided by businesses such as Fizziology are becoming more common and essential to social media strategy. Good data inform, educate, and validate the work social media professionals do on their respective platforms. Regardless of the industry and social media role, research insights are key. This is not to say that every social media strategy will return huge growth in engagement, impressions, or audience size. **Metrics**, data collected by a social media professional in a systematic manner, allow the business or brand in question to know what worked, what didn't, and what to do differently next time. Social media professionals do not want to guess or assume anything on social media, but without data and research, you would be doing exactly that. Metrics are the numbers and points of information that validate social media's role in the larger scheme of things for a business or agency, and show senior management and key decision makers the impact of this form of communication on their audiences.

Along with understanding the basics of what it means to be a researcher in social media, there is also the constant challenge facing social media professionals when it comes to keeping updated on not just the changes in the industry and platforms, but how to analyze, collect, and report the data. Facebook changes its algorithm constantly, and there are always new pieces of content features added to each platform that makes them a bit more complicated (e.g., Instagram Stories and Insights). With each piece of content and feature added, it provides a new way to analyze, report, and discuss research findings and analyses.

Research in many ways is one of the most challenging yet demanding functions in social media. We have to understand not only how to collect data, but also how to use data strategically. Social media allows you to make only one good first impression with your content, and research ahead of time allows you to make sure this first impression is the best it can possibly be.

IMPORTANCE OF RESEARCH FOR SOCIAL MEDIA AND STRATEGIC COMMUNICATION

Research—the systematic gathering of information in a scientific and objective manner to help answer questions—is not black and white. It is a mixture of grays following a long continuum of different attributes that make it hard to determine which method, service, platform, or metrics to use. This, along with changes on the platforms, makes it difficult at times to report actual insights that help drive the bottom line for sales, revenue growth, community building, and lead generation for brands and users. Some metrics can mislead by showcasing large numbers, which can tempt brands and professionals to think things are going well when, in fact, they are not. Using data provided by platforms such as Facebook and Twitter can seem helpful, but you are taking a risk by relying on someone else's data collection.

Social media managers have to listen to what the data are saying before providing commentary on what the data mean. Content and message strategies help create stories, which then shift the waves (influencing the conversations and dialogue in the community that are meaningful and resonate with audiences) through the clutter of noise that happens on social media. Research, especially **analytics**, provides us with evidence of the impact and potential return these "waves" provide us. Did the content move the audience? Did it make an impact? Did the message truly resonate with the audience in the way we wanted it to? Without data, these waves are just entertainment for a single moment in time. However, with data, these stories have a shelf life and meaning for future implications, learnings, and practices for a brand.

Data drives the "pay to play" game for social media professionals. In order for audiences to see content in a newsfeed on platforms such as Facebook, Instagram, and Twitter, brands and others have to pay for sponsored posts, ads, or updates. Every time a sponsored post or ad comes forward, such as the branded hashtags for *Despicable Me 3* or an influencer-sponsored ad on Instagram, it was paid for by the sponsored brand. Each paid form of content is approached in a different way. One is bought and sponsored by a movie studio (e.g., Pixar), and the other is sponsored by third-party endorsers and influencers, which is why #ad is attached to the content. In most cases, it is easy to determine which content has been paid for.

A lot of businesses have gone this way in order for audiences to see their content come forward. Otherwise, the metrics will tell a different story, and this brings forth the level of accountability needed to determine whether or not sponsored messages have an impact on the goals and objectives of campaigns and social media initiatives.

Source: Twitter/@DespicableMe

Sponsored Hashtags for Despicable Me 3 Movie on Twitter

Sponsored Image From Influencer Brand on Instagram

One benefit of metrics for social media platforms and third-party services is to capture the essence of audiences on a level that is extremely detailed and specific. Having access to what people are willing to share about themselves on various social media platforms—what they are doing to engage, converse, and react—really drives brands, organizations, and media outlets to specific social media platforms with established marketing and advertising budgets. These insights help paint a very clear picture of users' personas (e.g., unique characteristics that make up individuals) and likes, motivational factors, and other audience segmentation characteristics to help classify them into different audience categories (demographics, psychographics, etc.). These data provide insights, which then spark creative message strategies, ideas, and targeting practices not available on other established communication platforms. Unlike traditional media, social media has allowed brands to not only explore the basic audience segments, but expand their exploration to what people like, what posts and brands they engage with, and their overall network of trust and influence on the social media platforms. Social media professionals are able to identify more audience behaviors and actions on these platforms than with traditional media.

There is a difference between advanced metrics, such as **click-through rates** (how many times people click on a link to navigate to another website) and **behavioral metrics** (what actions people are taking on social media), and what we call **vanity metrics**, or metrics that make all of us feel really good, but really do not tell us anything in the process. For example, the number of people you follow on Instagram, or who follow you, is considered a vanity metric. Behavioral metrics focus on advanced metrics, like conversions, that help tell the story of the customer journey on social media (e.g., how many people bought a product or ticket to a concert after seeing a post on Facebook). Researchers can tell more about what happened and prove that content and presence on social media led to followers' actions, which helps validate the argument for investing in social media at the senior leadership level.

Reporting vanity metrics for social media efforts does provide benefits (Dawley, 2017). Dawley (2017) suggests that businesses use vanity metrics for strategic purposes.

Source: Instagram /@menwithstreetstyle

First, identifying **followers** (people or brand accounts on social media who are keeping track of your activity on a designated platform) gives social media professionals (or brands and clients they are representing or working with) a snapshot of their potential audience members. This does not mean that followers are 100% guaranteed to view your designated content, but the advanced metrics allow you to see this in more detail. Comments and shares are also considered vanity metrics, yet they do serve a purpose by informing you how actively responsive people are to your content and actions, and how they feel about the content. As Dawley (2017) stated regarding social media vanity metrics, if the only reason you are reporting these metrics is to make yourself feel amazing, then they are not fulfilling the complete picture. Vanity metrics are like the movie trailer for a blockbuster film: They do not tell the whole story of the brand. When you report vanity metrics, you have to connect them back to set objectives that fulfill attitudinal and behavioral measurements. How will the increased level of comments and sentiments help the brand on social media? If it is tied to business conversions (whether or not you made a purchase based on what you were shown on social media) and email or YouTube subscriptions, then there might be a rationale for this. Essentially, vanity metrics can be included in a report, but only if they are tied to other metrics and campaign or social media objectives for a brand, person, or agency.

For example, if Coca-Cola wants to gauge whether key audience members in Chicago are aware of its Coca-Cola Freestyle machines at Burger King, it may want to connect its objective of brand awareness to mentions or tags of the brand on social media platforms such as Twitter, Facebook, and Instagram. At the same time, Disney could review comments, ratings, and replies on its Disneyland social media accounts to evaluate the customer experience at the new *Guardians of the Galaxy* attraction at Disneyland Park in California. Advanced metrics tied to this, however, could be viewed to determine customer response, frequency of responses per hour, geolocation responses, and influence of users on social media.

We can gain further insight into the need for research by examining efforts to increase brand awareness by 84 Lumber during the 2017 Super Bowl. Although the lumber company had never engaged in a campaign of this scale before, it launched a campaign that had nothing to do with selling lumber, but rather focused on building a name for 84 Lumber as a company of opportunity (Ward, 2017), and released a politically charged immigration-themed ad that sparked considerable social media buzz (Peterson, 2017). According to Peterson (2017), 84 Lumber established a website to showcase the full ad, which received more than 6 million requests an hour after it aired during the Super Bowl. Other key **mentions** (naming and tagging a brand or user handle on social media) reached 99,000 across Facebook, Twitter, and Instagram (Peterson, 2017). In addition, Brunnerworks, the agency that worked with 84 Lumber, reported that *Ad Age* listed the ad as one of the top five aired during the Super Bowl. The ad also made it into the mainstream media with a Cheetos-themed skit on *Saturday Night Live* (Brunnerworks, 2017). If 84 Lumber wanted to achieve brand awareness, it was able to accomplish that with this campaign. The behavioral and attitudinal measurements related to social media (purchasing the company's products, increasing positive sentiments about its reputation online, etc.) are still to be determined.

Many brands want to measure awareness for their products and services, and specific platforms can help accomplish this task. Zagat, a user-generated restaurant review site, partnered with Google and *Huffington Post* to share food experiences with its users during the #FoodTripping campaign (Shorty Awards, 2017a). In this campaign, Zagat created a **microsite** (a specific website dedicated to the campaign specifically) and used Periscope to live stream its team's experiences in different states. The live videos would showcase these experiences on Periscope, but the team would also create content (photos, posts, etc.) using the #FoodTripping hashtag on the microsite (Shorty Awards, 2017a). The results were very positive for the brand, resulting in 143 live broadcasts in 56 days, 540,000 engagements across all social media platforms, and 2.5 million views across Zagat and Google (Shorty Awards, 2017a).

The amount of money being spent on research and social media is astronomical. Brands and companies are spending millions on tools and services to help collect, monitor, listen to, and analyze insights emerging on social media. As social media professionals, we have to decide which metrics are relevant to what we're trying to accomplish in our social media practices. This chapter will explore the need to do research and best practices for using research to meet goals. Contemporary social media professionals are able to listen for trends, monitor key metrics important to a company in a social media campaign, and link both science and art by using data collected in a strategic manner.

WHY DO WE NEED RESEARCH IN SOCIAL MEDIA?

Research has always been extremely beneficial for guiding practices in marketing, communication, public relations, and related disciplines and is a primary duty of social media professionals. Assessing the success of campaigns and identifying opportunities, research can provide more direction in understanding a brand's key audiences, current gaps and opportunities relative to competitors, current environmental landscapes, emerging issues or situations, and motivational factors and user attitudes.

As we observed in Chapter 4, social media research is an increasingly important and valuable specialization among social media professionals. In most cases, research and analytics are housed in a specialized department or in a department that oversees the overall budget for social media. Social media professionals conducting or evaluating research must be able to *understand the data* that are produced. This provides a solid foundation within an organization or department by helping you evaluate the content you create. Brands and agencies are looking for professionals who understand how to collect relevant data from social media platforms, have the skills and insights to explain what the data mean, and know how to apply the results strategically. In addition, understanding research methods allows us to do a check and balance on the metrics and data collected by third-party resources and services as well as by any agencies or consultants. This checks and balances approach is necessary to ensure we are all on the same page in regard to the data collection, insights provided by the data, and ways the data were collected from the digital and social media ecosystem.

Humanizing the brand and identifying potential ideas for future content are other benefits of research (both listening and monitoring) through collecting insights online in real time. In many ways, social media platforms and channels act like an online focus group—you are able to see what people are sharing, creating, and talking about regarding your brand or company. In addition, you can ask your community a question to get their take. This input could provide feedback about a new campaign, test out new products or spokespeople, or even determine what attributes people assign to you. On other occasions, research can inform how your brand is presented and what types of engagements, content, and voice audiences are looking for in the brand. While these are mostly positive circumstances, understanding what could potentially go wrong is an additional benefit of research.

Listening for early warning signs (a string of negative reviews of a restaurant on social media, users identifying an account has been hacked, etc.) could save the brand's financial standing and reputation.

WHAT ARE THE DIFFERENCES BETWEEN MONITORING AND LISTENING IN SOCIAL MEDIA?

Monitoring and *listening* are two of the most frequently debated and discussed terms for social media measurement, because they are somewhat related but have distinct differences. **Monitoring** is the systematic process of understanding, analyzing, and reporting insights and conversations on reputation, brand position, community health, and opinion of key audience members virtually. This is a systematic and sustainable area within social media measurement that focuses on key objectives and tying in metrics and key performance indicators (KPIs) to the data being collected and analyzed. This information has to be connected to current business and communication objectives within the organization or brand. **Listening** is about learning, exploring, and uncovering emerging trends, opportunities, activities, and issues that could impact the company either positively or negatively. These can be items evaluated at the surface level (e.g., vanity metrics) or more in depth (history of a customer with the brand, how engaged a customer has been with the brand, customer level of network and influence in a specific community with the brand, etc.). Monitoring practices are more reactive compared to what listening has to offer.

Both monitoring and listening are necessary for a social media campaign, department, or initiative. One cannot do just one and ignore the other. Tools, metrics, and programs can address listening and monitoring separately or in combination. Table 5.1 summarizes some of the key differences between monitoring and listening.

One of the main differences between monitoring and listening is time frame. Focused more on the long term than listening, monitoring can take place over weeks

TABLE 5.1 ■ Differences Between Social Monitoring and Social Listening	
Social Monitoring	**Social Listening**
• Creating a systematic and sustainable program that evaluates the success or current state of a brand or person online	• Observing people's feedback, comments, questions, and inquiries in order to capitalize on emerging and innovative opportunities
• Evaluating metrics like mentions and trends that could be tied to the bottom line and connected to other business and communication goals	• Evaluating sentiment, patterns, and the current state and dynamics in a community
• Using data insights to tie to strategic plans and objectives set for a campaign, business, or initiative	• Using data insights to spark ideas and creative executions for content and message strategies
• Connecting to market research and competitive analysis of the landscape (science of social media)	• Connecting to creative execution of strategies (art of social media)

or months or even years. Monitoring is a systematic and sustainable approach to evaluating performance on social media. Social media professionals constantly evaluate standing positions and presence to see how they are received and discussed.

Benefits of Monitoring and Listening

What are the benefits of monitoring and listening? Why are monitoring and listening important from a social media standpoint? Monitoring and listening can help the social media professional with

- Formulating the main items we want to evaluate and monitor for our social media activities (e.g., key words, hashtags, phrases, accounts, users, influencers, and others).

- Identifying influencers and top external channels (or accounts) driving traffic to the social media platforms.

- Evaluating which accounts, websites, brand blogs, and other external links will help show impact of word-of-mouth, but also showcase potential collaborations and partnerships to add to the community on social media. For example, Facebook partnered with the National Geographic Channel to drive viewership of the documentary *He Named Me Malala* as well as awareness of the Malala Fund. Facebook and National Geographic Channel allowed influencers and users on Facebook to change their social media profile to a yearbook picture that would be used as part of a large Times Square billboard. More than 50,000 people participated in this campaign within 96 hours of the launch (Shorty Awards, 2017b).

- Analyzing and measuring key trends (positive and negative) surrounding an event, person, or brand compared to competitors and other significant parties in the community.

- Calculating the overall growth of your community audience and behavior measurements.

- Identifying how fast your audience and community is growing and comparing this to previous times in the past year. When the audience for each platform grows, this will shift the specific metrics being used to evaluate the effectiveness of the content for this audience, which leads to the next point.

- Identifying the overall responses audience members give you for your content. We learn when they are active, what type of content they are sharing, how they are mentioning you during specific times and on which platforms, and how this compares to competing accounts. These are not measurements that will stay consistent. As the audience grows or shifts for a brand on social media, these changes have to be reevaluated on a regular basis. For example, posting on Instagram on Mondays at 3 p.m. EST may have worked for a company in 2017, but in 2018, it may be Tuesdays at 10 a.m. EST due to changes emerging from audiences.

- Determining the overall tone and sentiment of the community discussing a key player in a social media plan (i.e., brand).

- Understanding our audiences and what they are responding to the most. We do not have to guess which posts, content, influencers, or accounts they are following. This information is available for us to note.

- Turning unhappy customers through proactive monitoring and interactions into loyal customers through relationship management practices.

- Understanding our audiences beyond the surface level and tying in key areas of focus (e.g., online behavior, interests, page communities, groups, influencer networks, and advocacy measures).

- Identifying any hidden risks or potential crises that could evolve based on an analysis of the community.

- Creating a sustainable measure for identifying key performance indicators that determine overall brand health, voice, and presence in the community.

- Exploring new areas and bringing back lessons learned to the team. Social media is somewhat of a "free online focus group" of ideas, perspectives, and opportunities.

- Uncovering valuable insights to help address an opportunity or a competitive gap in the strengths, weaknesses, opportunities, and threats (SWOT) analysis.

- Helping bring a strong evaluation and measurement component to our social media plan with data and insights to prove we have accomplished our set objectives.

What types of items can be monitored in social media? Social media monitoring can

- Track engagement, sentiment, and behavioral actions (e.g., shares and comments) from content across platforms over a period of time.

- Determine the best times and places to post and engage with content.

- Note what the competitors (established and emerging) are doing online and compare their operations and engagement with yours. Competitors need to be monitored based on market presence and industry. Emerging competitors who are starting out or extending into the field should be identified and tracked.

- Explore audiences' receptiveness and behavioral intentions to take action based on the messages given. Are audience members actually behaving the way we want them to based on the call-to-action statements (what you want your audience to do after seeing this message or content) we shared on social media?

- Evaluate response time for the social care team in responding and engaging with leads generated from social media conversations.

- Identify inquiries or comments that can help spark further content features for the brand.

- Discover what content actually resonates with audiences and what content and message strategies work best.

- Measure the overall health of the brand community as a whole, and where current, potential, and emerging audiences are located and having a conversation about the brand.

- Note the official and associated key words being used in alignment of the brand online.

You may be asking yourself why it is so important to monitor what people say and how well your organization is doing in a campaign. The answer is simple: Data equals money. To have buy-in from other departments and to retain your current clients, you need to be able to show what you have done over time. We must be able to showcase what we can provide. In addition, we need to know how well we are doing during a campaign. We may have the best intentions, but we need to understand how people are reacting to the content and promotions we share on social media. Monitoring and listening can also provide information from sources other than our brand's consumer audiences. What are our competitors talking about when they see our campaigns? What is our share of voice in the industry? We have to take all of these elements into consideration in terms of our monitoring capabilities.

Types of Metrics

Table 5.2 outlines the four categories of metrics classified in social media measurement terms. The first category is **basic metrics**. These metrics can be collected easily either from the social media channel itself or by a separate service or program. Basic metrics include *followers* (how many people are following you on a specific account), *engagement* (how many people in your community are interacting with your content), and *sentiment* (how people feel about your content—positive, negative, or neutral). Consider evaluating these basic metrics first to determine the overall scope of the community size you have (e.g., followers), how prominent you are in sharing content and how much exposure it actually gets (e.g., reach), and how people respond to your content on social media (e.g., engagement and sentiment).

The second category is **advanced metrics**, which dive into the actions and psychographics (the attitudes, behaviors, and opinions of audience members) of specific users (e.g., influencers—people who have the power to persuade others to take action [see Chapter 8]—and **advocates**—loyal and invested audiences who are supportive of a brand or community). These specific metrics tell a social media professional a lot about user behaviors, but also about the unique characteristics of a community. Advocacy, audience engagement, and influencers are just a few metrics that can be collected and analyzed for identifying your different audience segments. These metrics are somewhat more challenging to categorize and collect, which means you may need to get specific tools to analyze these metrics (e.g., Klear for influencers) or invest in a tool that can analyze and report these metrics along with the basic metrics (e.g., Meltwater).

The third category is **channel metrics**, which are unique to specific channels. While many channels share certain basic metrics, their particular configurations also make more specific metrics useful. For example, story completion is important for Snapchat and Instagram to note, whereas retweets and favorites may be aligned with Twitter. Facebook has reactions for its updates and comments.

The last category is **behavioral metrics**, the most complicated yet informative metrics to collect on social media. In behavioral metrics, we explore downloads and lead generation (did the content we post on social media result in a subscription or action?). These are the metrics many senior managers and leaders want to see as a result of investment in social media. **Conversion rate** (how many clicks and actions resulted in sales divided by the number of clicks and actions taken), **amplification rate** (how much the content has been shared and viewed by others— specifically looking at shared actions like retweets [RTs] or shares on Twitter, reports, and share actions), and even **influencer impact** (how many high-profile professionals and accounts shared and engaged with the content) are just a few

TABLE 5.2 ■ Example Metrics Used to Evaluate Social Media Campaigns and Initiatives			
Basic Metrics	**Advanced Metrics**	**Channel Metrics**	**Behavioral Metrics**
• Followers • Reach (paid or organic) • Impressions • Sentiment • Engagement • Influence • Market position • Activity (post rate, post type, post response rate, etc.) • Platform actions (likes, RTs, story views, etc.)	• Advocacy • Audience growth • Audience engagement (influencers and advocates) • Network health • Conversation reach • Time spent and content retention • Tone • Content reaction and response • Story completion rate • Share of voice • Share of conversation • Share of community • Brand awareness • Customer and community retention	• Insights (reach, post engagement, targeting, etc.) • Video views • Click-through rate • Impressions • URL links (e.g., tweets) • Profile visits • Website visits • Social referrals • Percentage of visits • Visit duration	• Impact actions (download paper, get new subscribers, visit a page, etc.) • Click-through links • Amplification rate • Advocate impact • Influencer impact • Applause rate • Lead generation • Conversation rate (sales, requesting a demo, signing up for a webinar, etc.) • Saves (e.g., screenshots and repurpose) • Downloads (podcasts, videos, etc.)

metrics that allow us to evaluate whether or not people took action based on what they saw on social media (a Facebook ad, an influencer campaign, a call for subscriptions to a YouTube channel, etc.).

A comprehensive social media monitoring and listening plan includes at least several metrics from each category, but the choices depend on the overall objectives set for the social media initiatives and which metrics best align with the goals of the social media campaign.

Implementing a Monitoring and Listening Plan

Now that you understand the differences between monitoring and listening, you are in a better position to determine the exact approach and resources you will need to accomplish your goals:

- *Responsibilities for monitoring and listening.* Determining who will be in charge of this role is instrumental in determining whether you will have the necessary resources to accomplish these tasks. Identifying key personnel (community manager, account manager, social media consultant, etc.) who will be in charge of reporting and engaging with the team or brand on this issue is also important. This is another area that can be integrated into the list of responsibilities for the team internally (or externally depending on the circumstances). Make sure those who are responsible for the listening and monitoring capabilities are aware of the objectives and overall scope of the social media practices from a business and communication standpoint.

- *Monitoring and listening training.* Like social media platforms, expectations for social media data analytics and measurement are evolving rapidly. Training on analytic tools (Hootsuite, Microsoft, HubSpot, Meltwater, Facebook Blueprint, Stukent, etc.) can be very useful. Social media professionals must keep up with the latest measurement tools for monitoring and listening.

- *Outlining what you can and must listen to and monitor.* Outlining the key areas of focus before implementing a monitoring and listening plan is crucial. This will set forth a strong foundation for staying organized and current.

- *Tying in monitoring and listening practices to current business, communication, and brand objectives.* Note items that will demonstrate whether each department has accomplished its set objectives. In addition, insights can be integrated into current plans (e.g., SWOT analysis integration) as well as used to forecast trends and opportunities.

- *Using analytics and research to inform content that resonates with audiences.* In Chapter 7 ("Strategic Writing for Social Media"), you will see the importance of using data to inform the types of messages, content, and writing style that work for your brand online. Content creation does not happen on a whim all of the time, but rather it is a systematic process of evaluating the previous messages, videos, images, and updates that generated engagement and reach by resonating with key members of the community. Connecting the data to provide actionable insights for other team members and leadership can make the difference between executing and not executing the content and, in some cases, not getting the project or job. In other words, measuring and reporting content data helps drive future brainstorming sessions, justification for execution, and return on investment for social channels.

- *Setting a consistent brand monitoring and listening ecosystem.* A research plan should specify the protocols for who reports the findings to whom, what is reported, what the deadlines will be, how data will be analyzed and formatted, and how the resulting reports will be shared with clients or senior management.

PLATFORM-BASED METRICS, TOOLS AND SERVICES, AND KPIS

We have discussed a number of universal, platform-independent metrics, but other metrics are uniquely defined and used for specific platforms. Once again, we can evaluate the basic, advanced, channel, and behavioral metrics aligned with each current platform. Like the platforms themselves, the metrics available on each change frequently. Thus, it is important to understand the basic underlying principles of the metrics used and to cultivate a flexible mindset.

Along with collecting the metrics from each individual platform, we also must explore third-party tools that are available to help collect, analyze, and report the insights gathered on each platform. Some platforms (e.g., Twitter) have been open with their application programming interface (API) with third-party tool developers, but others have not.

When evaluating individual platform and third-party tools, ask yourself the following questions:

- *What metrics is the platform already using?* Is it using only basic metrics, or exploring advanced metrics as well?

- *What is the payment model?* Are the tools free? Does the platform have a monthly fee? What different plans does it offer? What features does it offer? Keep in mind that data equal money, and these tools can be somewhat expensive depending on the scope and the amount of data you want to collect.

- *What data is the tool able to collect and report on*? Some tools focus on single platforms, while others are broader and include a variety of platforms. Some platforms provide historical data and different metrics based on location, platform, and key word analysis. Depending on what you are willing to invest in and use, it is important to note where each tool lands in your social media budget and overview.

- *How does the platform measure each metric, and how does it calculate the results in its reports*? If a platform is not willing to share how it comes up with its influence, engagement, and other ratings, this should raise a red flag.

- *Does the platform offer training and educational opportunities*? Examining the clients of each platform, the support it gives to users, and whether or not it is willing to supply training and educational resources are other factors to consider. It's one thing to use a tool, but like all aspects of social media, tools evolve, and it is important to note the longevity of a platform based on this element.

- *How long has the platform been established in the field?* There are a number of monitoring and listening services, and you should note how long they have been part of the community, how many resources they have, what clients they serve, and in which campaigns they have participated.

- *How much does a service cost?* Most social media analytics tools are affordable, but some are designed for enterprise clients, which means they are pretty expensive. When evaluating the cost of these tools, be sure to identify their features, the type of data they are able to collect, and what you will be able to do with the data.

WHAT IS THE BRIDGE BETWEEN MONITORING AND LISTENING?

While there is a difference between listening to social media conversations and measuring the data, the bridge that connects these two areas is strategy. Creating a framework that is able to collect insights from conversations on social media (research) and turn them into applicable action steps (practice) is what strategy can bring to the table. Table 5.3 outlines the key characteristics of monitoring and listening and how strategy connects these two important areas together.

TABLE 5.3 ■ Connection Between Monitoring, Listening, and Strategy		
Monitoring	**Listening**	**Strategy**
• Observing the wave in how it is received (reviewing the reactions people have to the content being created)	• Observing potential landscape for upcoming waves to ride on (story ideas, real-time marketing initiatives, etc.)	• Providing explanation of the wave (story or content impact) that allows it to have shelf life
• Reactive	• Proactive	• Connecting what we are going to do based on what has been collected (research) and explored (application)
• Long-term focus but open to short-term adjustments (e.g., crisis communications)	• Short-term with long-term implications in mind	
• Tied to sustainable goals and objectives for a brand	• Exploring possibilities of creative executions of ideas based on established presence	• Using insights to inform and brainstorm implications, note trends, and identify gaps in the data and what they mean in social media
• Focused more on alignment for data (science)	• Focused more on the creativity and innovativeness of the opportunity (art)	• Tying art and science together

TYING EVERYTHING TOGETHER WITH ANALYSIS

We need to determine the overall impact and significance of our data reports and insights for our day-to-day business and communication activities. These insights can help determine what is working and not working for an organization or business online through various social media protocols. First and foremost, before identifying your key metrics for analysis, you have to align them with the set objectives for your social media channels or campaign. Your goal might be to increase brand awareness, engage in more conversations online, or reduce the level of negative ratings that happen online. The metrics that you focus on have to be interconnected with the objectives you have set forth. Essentially, objectives are what you want to accomplish, and metrics and analysis represent what you actually are able to accomplish. Ideally, you should make sure these objectives follow the key specific, measurable, achievable, realistic, and time-specific (SMART) criteria.

As mentioned and featured in Table 5.4, there are a lot of metrics from which to choose. Ask yourself the following questions to help decide which ones to use (Dawley, 2017):

- How does this metric connect to my objectives?

- Is this metric really applicable to what I want to accomplish?

- What category does this metric represent?

- How will this metric inform me about my social channels and online presence?

- Do I have the right tools (and knowledge) to collect and analyze this metric?

TABLE 5.4 ■ Metrics Available as a Function of Social Channels				
	Basic Metrics	**Advanced Metrics**	**Channel Metrics**	**Behavioral Metrics**	**Tools and Services to Use**
Facebook	• Likes • Reactions • Posts (type, reach, and frequency) • Live video metrics • Messages	• Engagement • Share of voice • Conversation reach • Community • Video metrics (views, time spent on live video, completion of video, etc.) • Advertising revenue	• Likes • Reach • Page views (total views, total people who viewed, sources, etc.) • Shares • Action button • Insights • Polls • Reactions • Posts (type, targeting of audience, reach, engagement, and evaluation of promotion)	• Awareness • Percentage of visits • Page duration • Click-through rates • Impact	• Facebook insights
Twitter	• Followers • Favorites • RTs • Mentions • Number of posts • Direct messages • Polls • Audience (gender/age)	• Activity metrics on platform • Network of the community • Audience/fan base growth • Engagement • Share of voice • Influence • Advocacy • Content • Multimedia content • Advertising revenue	• Twitter Analytics • Video views • Photo views • Profile visits • Impressions • Branded hashtags • Mentions • Tags • Replies • Live views (Periscope)	• Click-through links • Promoted ads	• Twitter Analytics • Keyhole • Tagboard • Hootsuite • Buffer • Sprout Social • Klear • Social Mention • Sysomos
Instagram	• Followers • Favorites • Posts • Reposts • Impressions • Profile views • Posts • Mentions • Saves • Comments	• Engagement • Content performance • Fan base growth • Influence • Views • Audience growth • Advertising revenue	• Views • Comments • Replies • Live views • Tags • Likes • Story views • Story insights • Story screenshots • Story hashtags		• Klear • Keyhole • Tagboard • Brandwatch • Iconosquare • Hootsuite • Instagram Insights • Sysomos

	Basic Metrics	Advanced Metrics	Channel Metrics	Behavioral Metrics	Tools and Services to Use
	• Direct messages		• Story mentions • Story completions • Live video views • Live video view completions • Live video comments		
LinkedIn	• Connections • Community size • Likes • Comments • Visits	• Audience growth • Content publishing metrics	• Views • Audience • Post frequency		• LinkedIn Insights
Snapchat	• Snaps sent • Snaps opened • Snaps received • Total snaps opened • Video views • Followers • Percentage of snaps opened • Chat messages sent/received	• Swipes • Story completions	• Snaps sent • Snaps opened • Snaps received • Total snaps opened • Average views of snaps • Average views of snap stories • Type of content	• Links in chats • Screen shots • Code screen shots • Reposted content	• Delmondo
YouTube	• Views • Shares • Comments • Votes	• Audience growth • Video views	• Views • Comments • Likes • Dislikes • Videos removed from playlist • Average view duration • Average view percentage • Click-through rate • Subscribers • Card impressions • Gross revenue • Playback cost per mille (CPM) • Ad impressions • CPM	• Subscribers	• YouTube Analytics

Source: Keyholeco (2016, 2016-01-19). "Top 25 Social Media Analytics Tools for Marketers - Keyhole." from http://keyhole.co/blog/list-of-the-top-25-social-media-analytics-tools/.

A frequent question that arises in social media is whether or not many calculations need to be done (aka math). The answer is . . . of course. Fortunately, the formulas are straightforward. Some are consistent across platforms, but other services and tools calculate metrics based on their own algorithms. When evaluating and analyzing your data, double-check your data and reports just to make sure they are saying what you think they are saying. Some tools are focused on service-level metrics (e.g., vanity metrics) without diving into the detailed behavioral metrics we may want to add to our social media reports, case studies, and campaigns for clients and brands.

One of the main metrics to report is **social media return on investment (ROI)**. Return on investment is a common metric used to evaluate whether the investment (money) a brand or company put into a campaign accomplished the set goals and objectives. Hootsuite describes social ROI as "the sum of all social media actions that create value" (Dawley, 2017). Essentially, social media ROI can be calculated by multiplying the profit or total investment by 100 (Dawley, 2017). Social ROI is not only a metric that needs to be included to determine the overall success of the campaign you are launching, but it also helps determine

- Overall stance within the industry among your key audiences

- Where you need to invest and drive your resources to in the future

- Both gaps and opportunities for future campaign initiatives

- The impact social media has on your bottom line as well as reputation and community relationships

DOs AND DON'Ts IN SOCIAL MEDIA RESEARCH AND ANALYSIS

Keep the following best practices in mind when it comes to social media monitoring and listening.

First, there *should be a designated person or team for monitoring and listening* to the conversations on social media. With proper training (Google Analytics, Hootsuite, HubSpot, etc.), team members will be prepared to not only help identify the key metrics and KPIs to track, but also to understand how to apply these findings to actionable steps and relate this information and how it is connected to strategy to senior management.

Second, in order to do the best work, social media professionals must *invest in the right tools*, especially social media management tools. Social media management tools come in different sizes, focus areas, metrics and data collection capabilities, and prices. The more data, filtering and historical capabilities, and reporting measures you want to have, the more expensive your tools are going to be. Hootsuite, Buffer, Talkwalker, Sprout Social, Spredfast, HubSpot, Sprinklr, Radian6, Nuvi, Zoomph, and MavSocial are just a few providers to review. Each system has different features, prices, and capabilities, and the social media professional in charge of monitoring and listening has to take all of these items into consideration. Presenting a request for proposal (RFP) to each provider and seeing which one has the best package deal for a company's social media management capabilities and needs may be the best approach.

Third, social media monitoring and listening is just the beginning. It all comes down to how social media professionals *apply these insights to strategies*. Just collecting data in spreadsheets without acting on the results will collect digital dust. Look at the insights and see if any specific strategic or creative applications can be implemented. This could result in creating more content focusing on certain themes or trends, or even posting content at certain times on specific channels.

Fourth, monitoring and listening need to be connected to evaluating the behaviors and actions you want your audiences to take. If you want to achieve certain goals for your organization or business (e.g., engagement and word-of-mouth), you have to *engage and talk with your audiences*. Establish a set policy and engagement protocol, though, that specifies how your team members should properly engage to best reflect your brand voice and community. This means that team members do not go off script and cause a crisis for the team and for the brand. It is very tempting to express emotion or try to be snarky, for example, because it is trendy and people respond to it. This could cause serious issues and drive metrics and trends about your brand in unwanted directions. Or the social media manager could fail to consider all of the different interpretations that a message might have, resulting in miscommunication.

A case in point occurred with the Pepsi brand in April 2017 in its Kendall Jenner campaign. The campaign featured Jenner giving a Pepsi to a policeman when she was part of a protest, which sparked a lot of outrage from Pepsi's audiences. In response, Pepsi apologized to Jenner, but not to Pepsi's audiences. Failing to consider the conversations and sentiment expressed by audiences when constructing its statement resulted in a bigger crisis for Pepsi.

Pushing content you feel is valuable is one thing, but see what happens when you listen to how your audience members respond and send them a relevant response. Whether it is a thank-you, an emoji, or a question to help drive the conversation a bit more, this helps spark a conversation with your audience, which results in engagement. Wendy's, Taco Bell, and The Rock have found that if they not only share content but also engage with their audiences on social media, the result is even more traffic and reach than if they just pushed content alone.

Last but not least, do not let vanity metrics (e.g., number of comments) be clouded by spammers. A lot of bots are designated to like (e.g., like farms), share, or comment on content (e.g., bots on Instagram). While increasing their numbers may be appealing, social media professionals have to look deeper and see if an account is real or not. Filtering out fake accounts can be time consuming, but it's necessary to see what's really going on. Some social media management platforms and services do this automatically, but it is up to the human professional to avoid inflating or misleading others with numbers.

Source: Twitter/@pepsi

Pepsi's Response Regarding Commercial With Kendall Jenner

CHAPTER SUMMARY

Monitoring and listening practices on social media have to be approached from a strategic yet creative angle to balance both the scientific process and the art of taking data and creating innovative ideas and messages. Numbers and data are not going to walk over and integrate themselves into a report by themselves. They have to be analyzed, discussed, and formatted in a way that tells a comprehensive story of where we are, where we are going, what we need to keep our eyes out for, and what we need to do on social media. Like all aspects of social media, the metrics and ways we collect, analyze, and report research findings from social media continue to evolve and change. Social media measurement and analytics make up one of the fastest-growing specializations within the field.

THOUGHT QUESTIONS

1. What is the difference between social monitoring and social listening? When is it appropriate to use each practice?

2. Discuss the key best practices for monitoring and listening on social media.

3. What are the differences among basic, channel, audience, and behavioral metrics?

EXERCISES

1. You are working on the social media team for Marvel's *Guardians of the Galaxy* brand account, and the question comes up whether or not to invest in social media monitoring and social media listening. Do you invest in both, or just one? Provide your recommendation and rationale for your decision with three points.

2. Find an example of a brand or nonprofit of your choice. Evaluate the vanity metrics on its social media sites (Facebook, Instagram, Twitter, and YouTube) and discuss three ways the brand could improve these metrics. Suggest one advanced metric, channel metric, and behavioral metric it would want to track for each platform.

3. During a job interview with the Golden State Warriors, a question comes up about the importance of understanding metrics and KPIs related to social media. Outline three reasons why social media insights can help an organization like the Golden State Warriors. Tie in two business objectives the team would want to have (increase awareness, increase engagement, etc.) and what metrics and proposed tools you would recommend using to measure these.

REFERENCES

Brunnerworks. (2017). 84 Lumber case study: Building a brand in 90 seconds. Retrieved from https://www.brunnerworks.com/brunner/case-studies/84-lumber/.

Dawley, S. (2017, May 16). A comprehensive guide to social media ROI. *Hootsuite*. Retrieved from https://blog.hootsuite.com/measure-social-media-roi-business/.

Keyhole. (2016, January 19). A list of the top 25 social media analytics tools. Retrieved from http://keyhole.co/blog/list-of-the-top-25-social-media-analytics-tools/.

Peterson, T. (2017, February 6). Super Bowl's politically charged ads, like 84 Lumber's, spark social buzz. *Marketing Land*. Retrieved from https://marketingland.com/super-bowl-politically-charged-ads-like-84-lumber-spark-social-buzz-205748.

Shorty Awards. (2017a). Foodtripping: 50 states in 50 days. Retrieved from http://shortyawards.com/9th/foodtripping.

Shorty Awards. (2017b). Stand with Malala. Retrieved from http://shortyawards.com/9th/stand-with-malala.

Ward, D. (2017, February 9). How a Superbowl spot helped 84 Lumber boost brand awareness and talent recruiting. *Spredfast*. Retrived from https://www.spredfast.com/social-marketing-blog/how-superbowl-spot-helped-84-lumber-boost-brand-awareness-and-talent.

UNDERSTANDING SOCIAL MEDIA STRATEGY (CREATIVE AND SCIENTIFIC APPROACHES)

6 STRATEGIC PLANNING FOR SOCIAL MEDIA

Learning Objectives
Humans of Social Media
Introduction
What Is a Strategic Plan?
Components of a Strategic Plan
    Background Information
    Brand Voice
    Vision and Mission
    Environmental Scan Analysis
    Client or Company in Focus
    Social Media Communication Audit
    Situational Analysis
    SWOT
    Goals
    Objectives
    Key Audience Members
    Strategies and Tactics
    Evaluation
    Budget
    Calendar
Final Words of Wisdom and Recommendations
Chapter Summary
Thought Questions
Exercises
References

LEARNING OBJECTIVES

After reading this chapter, you will be able to

- Identify the key components of a strategic plan
- Explain the importance and significance of conducting a thorough background evaluation, situational analysis, competitive analysis, and social media communication audit
- Construct a data- and research-driven SWOT analysis
- Learn the differences between a goal, an objective, a strategy, and a tactic statement for a social media plan
- Understand the framework of each of these elements and how they are interconnected in the strategic plan

HUMANS OF SOCIAL MEDIA
JEFF KALLIN, ASSOCIATE DIRECTOR OF CREATIVE MEDIA FOR CLEMSON ATHLETICS

Introduction

I am in my eighth full-time year with the Clemson University Athletic Department, now serving in the role of associate director of creative media.

My wife, Jill, and I have a son, Mason, and live in Easley, South Carolina. I attended Clemson, earning a bachelor of arts in parks, recreation, and tourism management with a minor in business in 2007 and a master's in human resource

(Continued)

(Continued)

Jeff Kallin

development in 2009. In my current role, I oversee the production of thousands of deliverables, from print and social to motion and digital assets, as well as the brand standards and graphical consistency for Clemson Athletics. I also teach a class in the Department of Graphic Communications in the College of Business, Digital Media Design.

How did you get your start in social media?

I got my start in social media during the Jurassic period, when a .edu email address was required for Facebook. Of course, that's just the beginning of what we think of now as social media. We were doing all of these same things before—talking on the phone, using AOL Instant Messenger, and setting "away" messages to subtly let our ex-girlfriends know we still loved them. In all seriousness, the rise in popularity of social media coincided with my time in college. Twitter started while I was still in undergrad, and Instagram launched a year after I earned a graduate degree. As a young professional, I was one of the early native speakers of the language, which gave me the opportunity to start experimenting with new forms of communication right as I was entering the primitive years of my career.

What is your favorite part of working in your social media area of expertise?

My favorite part of my area of social media, which I claim as anything involving visual content, is being a resource for my students, mentoring them, and teaching my class. I take a great deal

of pride in seeing my work around our program, but it gives me great delight to see the students with whom I work find jobs and succeed. I love coming to work every day. My bosses are great, my coworkers are my friends, and my students keep me young by reminding me every day how old I am. I am extraordinarily fortunate to work in an environment where creativity is fostered so actively, and where I can be included on the front end of discussions as a key piece of communication plans. It has been fascinating to see the industry and profession as a whole evolve—I find that I am as excited to see the next wave of talent infuse new energy as I am to be able to help shape that. I would also be remiss if I didn't mention how much I enjoy teaching in my emphasis area. My students are hungry to learn, ask fabulous questions, and open me to new ideas in every single class.

What is one thing you can't live without while working in social media?

One thing I must have at all times is clarity of purpose. People do what they do for many reasons, sometimes with more selfish motives. I must constantly remind myself who pays my check and what my true goal is—to promote Clemson University. I try to be aware of my surroundings without falling in line and trying to do things just because others are.

What is your favorite social media account (person/brand/etc.) to follow, and why?

My favorite social media accounts to follow are my students'. I love to see what they come up with and witness their outlook developing in real time. If you're pegging me to one account, though, it's probably Bleacher Report, across several channels. The platform aligns with many of my personal interests, and I share some of the same beliefs. Bleacher Report tends to be on the front end of content creation, and aggregates sports news in a way that I prefer to consume. I'd also give honorable mention to Mashable, Gizmodo, ESPN, and, of course, my son's Instagram.

What is the most challenging part of working in social media?

The most challenging part of working in social media is how truly important timing is. You can have the best content, idea, photo, graphic, or otherwise, but choosing the right moment and reaching the right audience can be really tricky. At Clemson, we've spent tons of time on projects that we thought would be big hits but weren't, and on others that brought huge returns despite being spur-of-the-moment or reactionary. We work so hard to plan—and you can do great things this way!—but there is no substitute for capitalizing on a big moment, contextually, for whatever is important to your organization.

What is your take on your area of expertise and the social media industry?

One of the most rewarding experiences I have had came in my absence. In 2015, I missed a football game—one of our biggest social events of the year—due to the wedding of a close friend. My student assistant, now an Adobe employee, stepped in seamlessly. Similarly, when I took time off during football season to be with my newborn son for a few weeks, my student team was incredible, handling requests and really stepping up. For some, the fear of being replaced consumes them. I consider it a compliment. We work very hard to prepare our students for life after Clemson, and for them to be able to seize big moments and perform on a big stage is every bit as powerful as what our student athletes do on the field. Just as they train and prepare to perform when the lights are brightest, we work to prepare our talented students to do the same. It's sometimes easy to

forget that they are the same age, pushing for careers, looking for their big break.

What do you wish you had known when you were starting out?

When I was starting out, I wish that I had been better about reaching out to those in my field and initiating more conversations. So many people I encountered have been so generous with their time. When I started, due to the timing, there were many "industry leaders"—everyone was still figuring it out. Thought leaders began to emerge, and people flocked. This leads me to the second thing I wish I had known—that everyone has different resources and limitations. Sometimes people flock to an approach, an idea, or a philosophy because it sounds good. But will it work for a particular organization? What are the limitations in place? What does the leadership allow? No two circumstances are alike, and it's easy to get caught up in the "everyone's doing it" wave—and I don't mean things like Ice Bucket or Mannequin Challenges; I mean philosophically. Be true to your university and program, and have the gratitude to know when someone is helping out.

Also, I wish I had been better about brand standards. I used a lot of bad fonts.

Jeff Kallin can be followed on Twitter at @CUJeffKallin. To see the work his team implements for the Clemson University Athletic Department, make sure to check out its accounts on social media at @ClemsonTigers.

INTRODUCTION

Social media is at the center of many conversations today. While it provides many personal opportunities to catch up with friends, check in at various locations, and share exclusive experiences with your own personal network, social media is also a powerful tool to be used strategically and applied in professional settings.

The surface level of what we see online is the outcome of the strategizing and hard work that takes place before content is shared with others. Updates, videos, and events tailored for certain communities are based on thorough analyses of data, insights, and research. Research, first defined in Chapter 5, is the systematic gathering of information in a scientific and objective manner to help answer questions. As we observed in the previous chapter, research helps guide strategists and businesses into actionable steps to generate awareness, increase sales, share stories to spark an emotional chord with audiences, and motivate others to take a course of action.

The industry has seen many strategic plans being creatively executed and launched over the years. NBC Sports created significant buzz around its coverage of the 2018 Winter Olympic Games with integrated digital marketing approaches that unified its brand voice across the global stage. Cinnabon realized the shift of attention toward social media among its customers, so the company invested more in its community management and content creation initiatives to help build a sustainable community through real-time engagement initiatives and Twitter chats (#SweetTalk). Social Media Examiner, one of the largest media outlets and communities in the industry, creates a complete strategic plan for its annual conference event called Social Media Marketing World. adidas embraced its influencer audience of creators to spark the #HereToCreate movement. All of these brands have a strategy behind every post, update, and piece of content they share. There are certain goals and objectives they all want to accomplish. In addition, every social media professional has to provide sustainable value, evidence, and impact on how this investment was worthwhile from a communication, business, and reputation standpoint. This chapter will cover the key elements that make up a strategic plan, which will tie in both the creative concepts and strategies and the real research-based applications needed to justify each of these points.

WHAT IS A STRATEGIC PLAN?

Many steps make up the creative and systematic approach of taking an idea from research into reality, otherwise known as a **strategic plan**. A strategic plan is a systematic, thorough, and aligned document that outlines from start to finish what a brand, individual, or organization wants to accomplish to address a problem, take advantage of an opportunity, or explore potential new possibilities through experimentation. This helps the social media professional follow a set of guidelines (like in *Pirates of the Caribbean*—you've got to stick to the code), but also be able to apply these guidelines to various areas, industries, and situations. A strategic plan allows the social media planner not to reinvent the wheel, but to use it as a road map and tailor it for each client and campaign.

Most strategic plans in marketing, business, public relations, and journalism have research as the starting point, and strategic social media plans are no different. However, before beginning the research, the brand, business, or individual needs to identify an overall purpose for the strategic plan. Are you addressing a problem (e.g., crisis) or an opportunity? What are some overall factors of the marketplace you need to consider? Do you have an opportunity to lead the way with a new platform or feature that would differentiate your brand from others (exploring and experimenting)? Do you have the support (financial and emotional) from leadership and your team to make this happen? These questions need to be addressed even before you create a strategic plan.

Such plans can serve a variety of purposes for social media campaigns. They can be created and launched to address an ongoing issue or problem facing a brand. For example, brands involved in crises such as Wells Fargo, Chipotle, and Volkswagen must have a specific plan in place to reduce the negative perceptions, interactions, and engagement on their platforms. However, strategic plans are also established to create buzz about a new initiative, raise awareness of a new product, or announce a venture on a new platform.

In today's job market, employers are looking for social media professionals who are able to think strategically and creatively while linking their proposed action steps with data. Honing these skills will help you differentiate yourself from other "social media marketers" or "social media gurus." Social media professionals create, post, and share tactical or technical elements for the social media space. Like individual trees in the forest, these actions grow, evolve, and sometimes die due to lack of investment (e.g., water is necessary for trees' survival, as are building a community and interactivity for these platforms). A strategic plan provides a road map so that the life span and direction of content is not left to chance.

Technical View of Social Media	**Strategic View of Social Media**

Source: By Frank de Kleine, https://www.flickr.com/photos/frankdekleine/286896094, licensed under CC BY 2.0 https://creativecommons.org/licenses/by/2.0/

Source: Pixabay/StockSnap

A social media strategic plan doesn't just look at all of the trees in the forest, but rather looks at how the forest is connected to the mountains, lakes, and other surrounding areas. The strategic plan spans time, looking for similarities and differences compared to the past, current, and future forest. We have to be aware of the individual, unique features of each community, platform, tool, or trend—but we also have to look at the bigger picture of organizational goals and objectives at all times.

COMPONENTS OF A STRATEGIC PLAN

The main components of strategic social media plans include the following categories and steps. Keep in mind that within each of these steps are specific and very focused areas that need to be addressed, which will be discussed in this chapter:

- Background Information
- Brand Voice
- Vision and Mission
- Environmental Scan Analysis
- Client or Company in Focus
- Social Media Communication Audit
- Situational Analysis
- SWOT
- Goals
- Objectives

- Key Audience Members
- Strategies and Tactics
- Evaluation
- Budget
- Calendar

Taking a drone-like scan of the environment allows social media professionals to identify and explain insights, as well as apply them to actionable steps that combine both research (science) and creativity (art) in a structured plan for implementation.

Background Information

This is where the research (and fun) comes in. Research has to be taken into consideration not only before a campaign has started, but as an ongoing part of the process. A background research section helps the social media strategist get an idea of what has happened in the past, the main issues and challenges, and any gaps that provide opportunities and advantages. There can be creativity (along with science) in this section. Collecting the information to paint the picture of what is going on for an organization or brand in a systematic way is a big task, but by seeing what is happening and identifying the "so what" factor, you are able to use this part of the process as a spark for innovative and impactful ideas.

Brand Voice

Brand voice, the overall tone, personality, and entity that you want to present online, is probably one of the most important elements to consider when looking at either establishing a brand from scratch or enhancing an established brand on social media. Will you be funny and engaging? Or will you have more of a professional or authoritative tone? Interns and professionals need to get into the **strategic mindset** of communicating in the brand voice rather than their own personal voice.

Vision and Mission

Two similar concepts, vision and mission, serve important roles within the strategic social media plan. **Vision** is the guiding principle that describes the overall goals and dreams of the organization, business, or individual for current and future activities. **Mission** describes the key elements of the overall purpose of an organization, brand, or person.

A vision statement for a social media strategic plan includes key personality characteristics a brand, organization, or media outlet is inspired to communicate. These guiding principles and behaviors unify the brand, organization, or media outlet as its own community and help make it unique and purposeful.

Vision statements capture characteristics and principles that organizations or individuals value, which will guide their overall actions and make an impact in the community. Bridging various components in a cohesive statement, the vision of an organization or individual must tie in brand personality, key attributes, core values, and present and future behavioral intentions.

Social media professionals identify clients' unique characteristics, attributes, and future intentions, and make an assessment to determine whether these organizations and individuals are living up to the expectations and goals outlined in their vision statements. A vision should be consistent across all social media communication channels used by the client, and the social media professional determines whether relevant communities are aware of goals and aspirations in the vision statement.

Table 6.1 provides sample vision statements from several companies and organizations.

TABLE 6.1 ■ Sample Vision Statements	
Company/Brand	Vision Statement
BuzzFeed	• We strive to connect deeply with our audience, and give them news and entertainment worth sharing with their friends, family, and the people who matter in their lives. • We have the innovation obsessed culture and structure of a venture-backed tech company with an engineering team focused on building the media platform for today's world, and the future.
adidas	• Our vision is . . . to enhance social and environmental performance in the supply chain, thereby improving the lives of the people making our products.
Mashable	• [We are] a global, multi-platform media and entertainment company . . . [and] the go-to source for tech, digital culture and entertainment content for [our] dedicated and influential audience around the globe.
Warby Parker	• [Our objective is] to offer designer eyewear at a revolutionary price, while leading the way for socially conscious businesses.

Source: Buzzfeed, adidas, Mashable, and Starbucks.

The big difference between the vision statement and the mission statement is timing. While vision statements list inspiring ideals and values held presently and sustained into the future, mission statements focus on what is happening at the present moment. Mission statements characterize the fundamental level of what you are trying to be as a brand, organization, or business.

Let's look at some mission examples. Under Armour's mission is to make all athletes better through passion, design, and relentless pursuit of innovation (Under Armour, 2018). Facebook's mission is to "give people the power to build community and bring the world closer together" (Facebook, 2018). Hootsuite's motto is "Social is in our DNA," and its mission statement describes how the global social media dashboard company is "not just a social relationship platform. We are not just a tech company. We are creators, innovators, and builders dedicated to revolutionizing the way you communicate" (Hootsuite, 2018). Starbucks' (2018) mission is "to inspire and nurture the human spirit—one person, one cup and one neighborhood at a time."

These memorable statements focus on the present. They are short and to the point, which is characteristic of an effective mission statement. Mission statements should not be longer than one sentence.

To prepare a mission statement for your strategic plan, ask yourself the following questions:

- Who are we?
- Who are our customers?
- What are our goals presently?
- What is our voice as a brand, and what is the voice of our community?

- What is our leadership style like?

- What is our operating philosophy (basic beliefs, values, ethics, etc.)?

- What are our core competencies or competitive advantages?

- What are our responsibilities with respect to being a good steward of our human, financial, and environmental resources?

Both vision and mission statements are important components of a social media strategic plan. Without knowing core attributes, intentions for the future, and present goals, it will be difficult to identify an overall place within online and offline communities. In addition, vision and mission statements guide communication strategies, such as tone, brand voice, and which channels to use.

Environmental Scan Analysis

An **environmental scan** helps the social media professional evaluate the current landscape within which a client or an organization operates. A number of factors contribute to this overall view of the environment:

- *Political Factors* (regulators, activism, and social issues). Political elections, social activism cases, bills and regulations from governing bodies and agencies (e.g., the Federal Trade Commission), and other governmental acts can impact a client or organization. These influences operate at the local level, the national level, and even the global level.

- *Legal Factors.* As discussed in Chapter 2 on legal implications in social media, the strategic social media plan should show awareness of key legal challenges, cases, and situations that need to be addressed or may have a future impact on the daily activities of a client or organization. Some entities are more highly regulated (military, government, etc.) than others. New laws and bills may impact how consumers interact with brands, employee hirings, citizen privacy and data collection, or the way advertisers must note whether or not posted content is promoted or sponsored.

- *Economic Factors* (e.g., cost of entry or to participate online). This section evaluates the current financial landscape affecting an entity, which can include spending habits on technology, information, and content creation; key trends happening in the workplace; industry hiring or layoff trends; employee satisfaction or employment trends; and financial barriers of entry.

- *Community Factors* (generational factors, social media factors, and culture). Outlining the key activities for relevant communities will form an essential part of the strategic plan. The social media professional will explore the health, presence, and engagement of a community and predict where it is going in the future. The plan should outline shifts in platform use and identify where people are getting their news. For example, as this textbook goes to press, users are gravitating to Instagram Stories and spending less time on Snapchat. Exploring the overall factors that impact the health of a community is an added component needed in the strategic plan.

- *Technology Factors* (advances, established versus rising technologies, etc.). Evaluate the current trends, fads, platforms, and strategic practices being accepted, used, and discussed in the industry. Note the current landscape and which platforms and tools people are using to share, create, and disseminate content. Consider the overall rankings of each platform per location, community, and audience. Outline the connection between technical trends and consumer behavioral trends.

- *Social and Consumer Factors* (consumer behavior trends, new uses, etc.). An understanding of key audience and generational trends should be incorporated into the strategic plan. The uses, perceptions, behaviors, and views of platforms and channels as a function of relevant audiences will need to be explored in detail.

Client or Company in Focus

The history of the organization. The history of a client organization includes the major events and key points that helped define it and shape it into what it is today. Outlining these accomplishments, and perhaps challenges, presents an opportunity to better understand where the client is today and how it reached this point. While it is important to trace the historical timeline of the client in a traditional sense, it is also necessary to outline the history of the client's social media use. Was it an early adapter on social media? Is it considered an innovator? Are its senior leaders (CEO, COO, etc.) on social media? If so, how active are they? Does the organization have a strong community focus on social media? Or is it always the very last to join a trend or platform?

Brand voice, story, reputation, and industry. Understanding the brand voice will help the social media strategist in the long term. Being able to identify the overall tone, personality, image, and unique attributes embedded within the content shared by the organization is a critical skill. For example, the voice that Four Roses Bourbon expresses on social media is quite different from the voice of Disney. Each brand has a distinct personality, allowing it to share various unique attributes and characteristics. Individuals and media outlets also have their own brand voice and characteristic ways of sharing their stories, updates, and content.

Key players and organizational structure. The strategic plan should outline the organizational structure of key players involved in social media, as well as where social media as a specialization is housed within the organization. Although social media has been established within certain companies as its own department, other organizations add social media responsibilities to the wheelhouse of skills and offerings in existing departments. Social media might be outsourced to a consultant, agency, or group of professionals. These insights will tell you a lot about the overall internal culture and whether social media is valued (or not) within the organization in question. It is useful to understand the background and experience of the social media team. Where did key players receive their education, what social media trainings and certifications have they received, and what is the overall landscape like for leadership and continued education within the organization? The strategic plan should note the likelihood of future social media education investment, and whether the level of commitment to ongoing education is a strength or weakness for the organization.

Products, services, and educational thought leadership. This factor is shared with traditional strategic plans. What main elements are being offered by the client? This is not just about goods and services, but also about what the client is doing to provide educational resources or thought leadership for the community. What webinars, infographics, white papers, resource blog posts, research reports, and presentations is the client providing? All forms of promotional content can create thought leadership opportunities and educational connections with different communities.

Analysis of media channels (PESO).   For social media to be successful, it has to be aligned with the overall mission of the brand as well as the goals and objectives (and voice) of associated departments. These departments also have the opportunity to create and distribute media content on relevant channels. The **PESO model** outlines the associated channels that can be used in social media. *Paid* media focuses on content for which an organization has paid for placement at a certain time, on a certain platform, and in front of a certain audience (Facebook ads, Instagram Stories ads, etc.). *Earned* media occurs when the content an organization shares, creates, or pitches arrives on another platform without charge (e.g., a feature on a blog post). *Shared* media is the essence of social media and how your content is distributed to others (e.g., reposted content or shared videos on Facebook and retweets on Twitter). *Owned* media is the type of content you personally own and control. Your website, blog, and internal assets are examples. For these items, you are able to control the message, updates, and the media design. Social media strategists need to outline what companies (or clients) are currently doing on each of these channels, how much they are spending, what content is going out, and how frequently they are using these channels, and conduct an analysis of their returns in terms of both financial and reputational assets. (See Chapter 9 for a more detailed discussion of the PESO model.)

Previous campaigns and initiatives with social media.   This sometimes is referred to as previous promotions or past campaigns in fields such as marketing, public relations, and strategic communications. As a social media professional, you will want to know what has been done already as far as social media campaigns and plans go.

Different campaign initiatives can be divided into three categories: technical, managerial, and thought leadership, shown as a pyramid in Figure 6.1. Ideally, you want to have the complete picture at the bottom by adapting the technical tools first. The *technical* view of social media focuses on the specific tools that can be used immediately and is short-term focused. These campaigns look at "how we are using this new tool even though we just heard about it 15 minutes ago on TechCrunch or Mashable." These are very short-term blips on the radar for brands, and while you do want to use them to experiment and explore possible new tools, features, and programs, this should not be your only focus. Think about your long-term strategy here. It is important to experiment and be creative in testing the waters for new tools and techniques, but this should not be the foundation for what you want to accomplish in social media.

Managerial roles and views of social media are the mid-level investment. The managerial roles and views of social media focus on building teams to work specifically on separate client accounts and projects, but the focus is tying in more strategy, higher-level brand management, and consultation on specific tools and services that will help accomplish the set business and communication objectives.

The main target for many clients and professionals, which few actually achieve, is *thought leadership.* Thought leaders share strategy, storytelling, and perspectives of the bigger picture not only of what is happening now, but what might be the case in a few years. They look at the interworkings of society, the environment, and industries that might influence what social media is doing internally and externally. Thought leaders actively contribute to the community with their insights, strategies, and experiences.

Thought Leadership

- Innovative ideas and executions
- Content creation and amplification
- Educational leadership across the company
- Relationship building and sustaining teamwork
- Strategically aligned leading campaigns
- Data and creative integration
- Not afraid to take risks
- Long-term strategy

Managerial

- Internal teams
- Branch of social care and conversation creation and management
- Small campaigns
- Focused more on strategy + creative execution
- Push and pull message strategies encouraged
- Connecting expectations and messages
- Building networks of influencers

Technical

- Tactics and tools of communication focused
- Trend focused content pushed
- Jumping on trends to make the quick sale or mention
- Short-term strategy
- Meet and greet influencers (speed dating)

In summary, strategy and a strong foundation in the bigger picture need to come first. Tools, trends, and platforms will continue to change. Flip the pyramid model and create a sound foundation for strategy where each part is interconnected with the others and allowed to collaborate: the community, story, and voice of the client at the center of the Venn diagram in Figure 6.2.

Many brands and accounts gravitate toward social media marketers and other influencers as part of their campaigns. Evaluate the influencers used by your client in the past. Be aware of which influencers are the real deal and which have a lot of window dressing and show-stopping antics but little substance in terms of expertise. Which brands and companies has an influencer worked with in the past on social media? Who is an influencer's agency of record? Who lists the influencer as a client or person they have worked with online? What formal or informal partnerships has the influencer formed with clients? Some of this information will be hard to obtain, but by doing the extra research into who these individuals are and what they have done with a brand, you can determine their level of knowledge, their skill level, and any gaps that may need to be addressed.

Social Media Communication Audit

Conducting a social media communication audit is one of the most important things to do before implementing a strategic plan on social media. Analyze all communication elements, content, channels, and personnel within the client organization. This should be a comprehensive evaluation of the social media tools, campaigns, influencers, online relationships, network analyses, influence and presence on platforms, voice, personnel, and players that are part of each team.

Conducting communication audits is not uncommon in marketing, public relations, and related communication disciplines. This allows us to evaluate what has been done, as well as the opportunities and challenges the organization or key personnel have failed to consider. What campaigns have and have not worked? Why? It is helpful to take a global bird's eye view of the overall social media position of the organization. While completing this task, we will interview personnel and determine internal levels of training, organizational structure, and education relevant to social media.

When doing a social media communication audit, you need to evaluate the client's social media both internally and externally. As a social media strategist, you have to be aware of the internal culture and perhaps politics emerging within the company

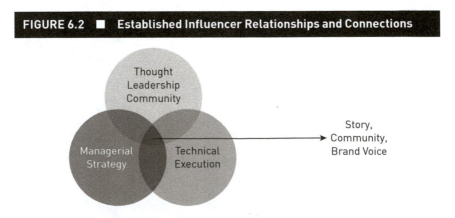

FIGURE 6.2 ■ Established Influencer Relationships and Connections

Thought Leadership Community

Managerial Strategy

Technical Execution

Story, Community, Brand Voice

or brand (e.g., who has ownership of the creative assets used in social media, and who is in charge of the cost and advertising for social media?). In addition to these internal questions, social media professionals need to be aware of external factors of what the company has done, what has worked and what has not worked, and conduct a comprehensive evaluation of each platform at the technical, managerial, and thought leadership level. This will provide a comprehensive view of where the company or brand is, and where it needs to go, on social media. Both short-term challenges and opportunities can emerge from the findings. Completing a social media audit will inform action steps and recommendations for the future.

A social media communication audit has three parts: internal social media analysis, external social media analysis, and competitor analysis. These three parts will help you determine the client's overall standing in regard to what is being created on social media and how the client compares to external audiences and others in the same market. The internal social media analysis evaluates all social media content policies, procedures, and overall interpretation elements within the organization. It covers the responsibility of the social media management and leadership culture, the level of credibility and trust toward social media within the organization, and social media education and mentorship. Some of these items will be readily available to you, but others are likely to require permission. Some relevant documents contain proprietary points of information the organization may be reluctant to share. However, the more information you receive, the stronger your strategic plan will be.

An internal analysis should outline the main leadership, including the CEO/president and other key personnel. Is the CEO on social media? How active are the company's leaders online? What platforms do they use, and do they encourage their employees to use the same ones? The investment necessary for a strong social media presence comes from the top. Your strategic plan should outline present use and attitudes regarding social media as well as reactions from internal and external audiences.

The structure of the client organization will also impact its social media presence. Evaluate how social media is incorporated inside the organization, brand, media outlet, or entity in question. Where are social media functions housed within the organization? Does the organization have its own social media department like Team USA and many other organizations have? If so, to whom do the social media professionals report? Alternatively, is social media part of an established department like marketing, with the chief marketing officer reporting to senior management? For example, General Motors distributes social media functions across various departments, which all ultimately report to the CEO. Jeremiah Owyang (2010) has outlined a number of different organizational structures relevant to social media functions, such as decentralized, centralized, hub and spoke, multiple hub and spoke, and holistic (or honeycomb). An organization's social media functions can be centralized or decentralized, have multiple hubs and spokes, or be coordinated and aligned together or not:

- *Decentralized*: There is no clear organization of where social media is placed and who is in charge.

- *Centralized*: All business reports and social media efforts are dictated by one source and passed down to others (e.g., government accounts for social media).

- *Hub and Spoke*: This function focuses on a cross-functional team, but is a centralized area that helps various business departments have a consistent social media presence. This is where most of the corporate brand accounts fall. Examples include athletic departments (e.g., Clemson Athletics) and brand accounts (e.g., Southwest Airlines).

- *Multiple Hub and Spoke*: This is the same as Hub and Spoke, but on a global stage (e.g., General Motors).

- *Holistic or Honeycomb*: Every brand, department, and person has an opportunity to collaborate on and implement social media. Social media actions are all linear and equal. Examples include Zappos and Dell.

By understanding the leadership viewpoint and the organizational structure for social media, you will be able to identify many opportunities and roadblocks facing an organization in its social activities. Tables 6.2 and 6.3 will help you evaluate the internal and external presence for a brand and determine what actions need to be taken and what areas need improvement.

The next step in the social media communication audit is the external analysis of the social media presence. Now you are being asked to survey trends, issues, situations, and events impacting the daily activities of the client externally with relevant audiences. External communications include everything that the client sends out to its external audiences. These components include marketing, public relations, advertising, and related communication content, campaigns, and relationships. This section focuses on how an organization manages the relationships and communication channels, rather than content and strategies, externally within social media.

The external analysis begins with identifying the platforms on which the organization has a presence—anywhere from a few accounts to hundreds depending on the size of the organization. Listing previous campaigns on social media is also important. These campaigns could have been implemented for no apparent reason based on the research and analysis conducted, or they could have a specific focus like a social selling campaign or an influencer marketing initiative. By identifying the range of campaigns that have been launched for the organization online, you will be able to evaluate whether the campaigns represent the best options for the organization or if there is room for improvement. You can determine whether the organization is making good use of the tools at its disposal, and how key audiences (media, opinion leaders, influencers, etc.) have responded.

Speaking of influencers, the external analysis piece of the strategic plan should identify the primary individuals interacting with the client. Influencers comprise a

TABLE 6.2 ■ Internal Analysis of Social Media Presence Template				
	Background	**Content + Rationale**	**Strengths + Weaknesses**	**Action Steps and Recommendations**
Internal Communication				
Personnel + Team Analysis				
Education + Mentorship				
Employee Social Media Policy/Advocacy Program				
Leadership				
Brand Voice				
Analytics				

TABLE 6.3 ■ External Analysis of Social Media Presence Template						
	Background	Brand Voice	Relationship/ Rationale	Content + Rationale	Strengths + Weaknesses	Action Steps and Recommendations
Platform						
Campaigns						
Influencers						
Community Analysis						
Content Creation/ Message Analysis						
Analytics + Data						

key audience segment that engages with or is the target of online content. We will discuss influencers in more detail in Chapter 8. For the purposes of the strategic plan, we should look at links between the main influencers, motivational factors for engaging with specific influencers, defining characteristics of influencers (tone of voice, personal brand, history on platform, list of personality traits, types of relationships and network connections they have, etc.), and the influencers' current relationship with the content.

The overall state and health of the client's community should be assessed. Identifying the various platforms on which a brand has a presence is critical, but so is discussing the overall nature and unique characteristics of the community on each platform. Each community has its own views, attributes, and motivational factors that make its members an important target for engagement by a specific client. Social media strategists also need to evaluate the community's share of voice in the industry, which essentially means how large a position the client plays in the overall conversation within the community. In Table 6.4, you will be able to see the analysis of the social media content and some key components to take into account when evaluating all of the social media platforms a brand or client has used. Within this analysis, you will need to list each place the client has an established presence; analyze the client's overall content, voice, and community; classify the type of organizational structure it is in; and determine who are its major influencers, its share of voice (percentage of the client's voice compared to the total number of competitors in the market), and what analytics can be collected to tell how engaged it is within the industry and community. With this information, the positives (successes) as well as any short-term or even long-term obstacles (challenges) need to be addressed here. Recommendations based on these points can be provided. These steps give the social media manager a comprehensive view of what is going on with competitors, in order to identify any gaps that can be (1) the focus of the campaign, (2) the key point of messages and creation of content to be strategically executed, or even (3) a jumping-off point to brainstorm creative ideas to integrate into the social media plan.

The last part of the social media communication audit is the competitor analysis, probably one of the most important background elements in a social media strategic plan. By understanding where your competitors stand, you can determine what areas you need to address, but also what factors, assets, and characteristics really define you and your client on social media.

TABLE 6.4 ■ Analysis of Social Media Template

Company	Platforms	Content Voice Community	Org. Structure	Campaign	Influencers	Share of Voice	Analytics	Successes + Challenges	Action Steps
GAP to Address									

Several steps need to be taken into consideration for this part of the process. First, make sure you are able to identify which brands, individuals, or organizations to keep your eyes out for when it comes to the strategic plan. It is important to note not only who is already established in the same space, but also who is rising and emerging as formidable competition. Distinguishing between who is established and who is emerging is absolutely critical. Audiences evolve and change, and we have to evaluate how we can sustain our current relationships, and which groups we need to reach out to. We have to be aware of who is rising in our particular industry and market and making a name for themselves on social media. If we do not take advantage of opportunities to reach these individuals, our competitors will. Attention is the currency we are driving for in the social media industry, and without a relationship connection, this will be lost.

A thorough competitive review takes place platform by platform. The main social media platforms need to be noted here, but we also need to look in new and innovative spaces. Watch for the places where competitors are experimenting, which provides us with an idea of their overall strategy and position in the marketplace. While it is important to note which platforms competing companies are on and to observe their vanity metrics (followers, who they are following, etc.), it is more important to think about how and why they use each platform. For example, what is the company's voice on each of these platforms? What is the overall health and stability of each community the company is a part of online? Are key members of the company team engaging with others and sharing their expertise with fellow professionals (Twitter chats, guests on podcasts, speaking engagements at high-profile events, etc.)? Has the company featured its award-winning or most notable campaigns in the last few years? Were any of its campaigns noticed for all the wrong reasons? We need to be aware of our clients' overall relationship with their community based on what has worked for them in previous campaigns and what has not.

To the best of your ability, identify competitors' overall organizational structure using the same guidelines we followed for the internal audit. Where does social media fit for them? Are they placing social media at the same level as the rest of the companies? What do their leaders do online, or how do they view social media? Identifying these extra steps can paint a picture for competing groups of how they practice, view, and use social media as an organization.

Analytics, covered in Chapter 5, are not only useful for an internal audit, but also provide considerable insight as part of the competitive analysis. Most organizations work on their own or with a third-party vendor (e.g., Sysomos, Sprinklr, or Salesforce) to collect and analyze listening and monitoring data. There is no reason you can't analyze publicly available data about your competitors, too. It is one thing to identify key competitors, but collecting and evaluating data demonstrating their online successes and failures adds further depth to your competitive analysis. Evaluate brand mentions, overall influence, relationships with key influencers, individuals who are advocating for and talking about the brand the most, and how the brand content is doing compared to other brands across other metrics (share of voice, engagement, interactions, influence, etc.). For each of the sections outlined in Table 6.4, data should have a strong role in showcasing evidence of the points being made. Data, especially social media data, can serve as supporting evidence to help make a point and nudge a decision from one direction to a better one.

Collecting this type of background research is a lot of work, but the payoff in the form of your strategic plan will be well worth the time and effort expended at this stage. There are no shortcuts to this step if you wish to produce a fully informed strategic plan.

Situational Analysis

The situational analysis will help you organize all the data you have collected so far, setting up the overall picture of what is going on for a brand, organization, or person on social media. This section allows the social media strategist to combine the findings and takeaways discovered during the external scanning, background research, and communication audit phases. We combine all of the information, data, and insights we have collected into organized columns of information. This thorough approach plays a significant role in determining the steps that need to be taken for this strategic plan. Research is only as good as your ability to identify what is happening, why things are happening, and how you can apply findings to construct sound strategies. Organizing your research efforts can help you see the whole picture at once.

Core Problem or Opportunity. Most strategic plans outline a single main problem that needs to be addressed in a campaign. In the case of social media, this single problem might be trying to determine how social media could help address an ongoing issue for an organization. Challenges might take the form of restoring trust within a particular community after a crisis (e.g., Uber and #DeleteUber or PewDiePie and Disney's breakup) or tying it into a larger case (e.g., Chipotle and the *E. coli* food scare). Often overlooked is the need for social media plans to address new opportunities rather than just solve existing problems. A social media strategic plan might include ways to use social media to take advantage of positive relationships with a community or increase sales and exposure.

SWOT

Four main categories are involved in a SWOT analysis: strengths, weaknesses, opportunities, and threats. SWOT analyses are a traditional part of the communication and marketing campaign process, but essential to the social media strategic plan as well. A SWOT analysis can be used to explore and identify solutions to problems, take advantage of new opportunities and ventures, decide which steps to take to help rejuvenate a community or brand online, or brainstorm new ways of engaging online through social media. The four primary aspects of SWOT, shown in Figure 6.3, are important, but we have to form bridges between these components in a fifth, strategic implications section of the plan.

Strengths: This is where you outline in detail the strengths observed in current social media practices within an organization or for a person. For example, strengths might take the form of an established presence on certain platforms, systematic training for employees so they stay on top of the latest trends, and a collaborative environment throughout which social media is not only used but embraced.

Strengths can be divided into categories to make them easier to keep organized. For example, you could group internal resources by people, financial, or creative. Consider the overall standing of the organization's culture. A positive corporate or agency culture can lead to an environment in which employees feel comfortable sharing ideas or taking leadership roles. Culture is a strength in some cases, but may be classified as a weakness if it holds the organization back.

Each strength must be supported by the data you have collected, which come from your social media communication audit. Construct a rationale, or a summary of each strength relative to the organization's overall mission.

FIGURE 6.3 ■ SWOT Analysis Diagram

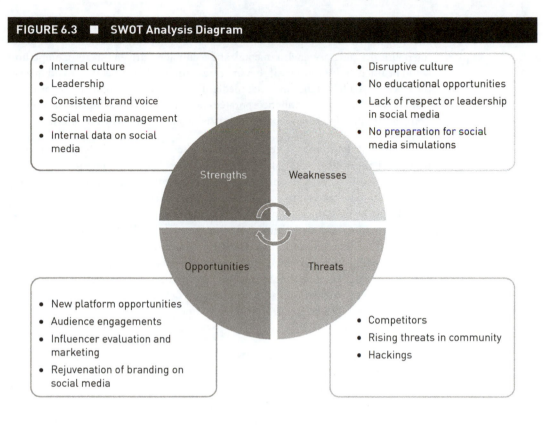

- Internal culture
- Leadership
- Consistent brand voice
- Social media management
- Internal data on social media

- Disruptive culture
- No educational opportunities
- Lack of respect or leadership in social media
- No preparation for social media simulations

Strengths   Weaknesses

Opportunities   Threats

- New platform opportunities
- Audience engagements
- Influencer evaluation and marketing
- Rejuvenation of branding on social media

- Competitors
- Rising threats in community
- Hackings

Weaknesses: Weaknesses hinder or challenge the organization's ability to accomplish its objectives, and are often the complete opposite of the items mentioned in the previous section on strengths. For example, one challenge could be a hostile leadership environment where social media is not valued. In this type of situation, employees would find it very difficult to be creative in their use of social media. Another weakness could be a lack of mentorship and educational training allowing employees to keep up with the changes in social media. As was the case with strengths, you must provide evidence to support your points regarding weaknesses. The communication audit might be sufficient for these purposes, but it might also be helpful to use focus groups or your own observations of the organization's process. Analytics can also support your analysis.

Opportunities: An opportunity is a set of ideas or circumstances external to the client that can lead to new approaches and behaviors. This part of the analysis should include a list of creative ideas to promote brainstorming and to jump-start new initiatives. These ideas can take different forms. Examples include evaluating new social media strategy campaigns and trends, experimenting with new platforms or tools, reaching new audiences that have not been explored yet, and looking for new communities with which to engage. Opportunities combine the strategic insights gathered during research and the creative execution of content and stories. These insights, like the previous sections, should be supported by data, research, and observations collected during the social media communication audit and background research processes.

Threats: Threats are another classic external factor, arising from negative events affecting individuals or organizations. This part of your analysis should explore ongoing political, regulatory, environmental, and technology-driven threats. Competitors could be listed in this category if they are threatening your well-being or taking away aspects that you have built on social media. For example, Facebook has copied several of Snapchat's features and incorporated them into Instagram Stories. If you were doing a threat analysis for Snapchat, this issue would definitely be included.

Strategic Implications: The strategic implications section is a fifth component of the SWOT analysis that looks at the "so what" factor, or why the information in the SWOT analysis is important to consider and which driving factors should be taken into consideration as the client moves forward. This section should be no more than one or two sentences long, and precisely synthesize the information gathered throughout the process of the background research and social media communication audit into a bold, clear statement summarizing the findings, what to do about it, and why it is important. This step is not always presented in other communication- or marketing-related disciplines, and including this information can differentiate you in a positive way from many other aspiring social media professionals.

Goals

Once you identify the main areas to address based on your research analysis, you are prepared to offer a broad statement that captures the overall focus of your social media initiative. You might address a rising opportunity or a significant need or issue for the client. This statement, which should be in the form of a single sentence, is the **goal statement**.

Objectives

After determining the overall focus of your social media plan, you have to set **objectives** that clearly state what you plan to accomplish. Creating good objectives is probably one of the toughest things to do when constructing a social media strategic plan or campaign. Many professionals struggle with this task, so don't be discouraged if you also find it challenging. In addition, there are many classifications of objectives to focus on depending on the discipline. For example, marketing objectives serve the purpose of increasing profit, reaching a higher yield of customers, improving volume of sales, and gaining percentage points in market shares, among others. Others focus on engaging awareness and understanding key issues and initiatives (e.g., journalism and public relations). Social media professionals need to be aware of these and how they are tied to the social media goals for each client.

All of an organization's functions must revolve around its mission, goals, and objectives, which in turn are assessed with measurements that are definitive and quantifiable. To be effective, goals and objectives should be simple and easy to understand for everyone and linked with measurable achievements. Goals and objectives must also be updated at each planning period to ensure they are continually serving the organization's needs and purpose.

Objectives can take many different forms. For example, marketing objectives might look to increase sales, whereas public relations objectives might be to increase awareness about a campaign and restore or rejuvenate established relationships with key audience members. Social media plans can be especially challenging, because we have to consider where this plan will be housed, which professionals will be part of the team creating and launching the plan, and how we will evaluate and measure whether we have achieved our objectives.

All objectives must fulfill certain criteria, referred to as the **SMART criteria**, to be effective. Using the SMART criteria is an established way to categorize effective objectives into five different categories: specific, measurable, achievable, realistic, and time-specific. First, all objectives must be specific. This means we have to be very clear about our objectives for the social media plan. For example, we might say we are looking to increase our community on Facebook. Measurements must be aligned with what we want to accomplish, so we need specific guidance from our objectives about how much we want to increase or decrease a certain element. Measurement is helpful here and will come into play again when we look at evaluation later in this chapter.

The second criterion for objectives is that they are measurable. Objectives have to be practical in nature both in expectations and in time and resources without any issues. Social media professionals do not want to promise the world to a client or organization without fully investing in the necessary tools and resources. Setting forth objectives with a clear mindset of what an individual (or team) can handle is fair to the client and organization, as well as to those who are creating and executing the strategic plan.

Third, objectives must be achievable. This means we must be able to actually accomplish what we set out to do in the social media plan. If a client asks us to increase her followers by a million people in the span of a week, this is unrealistic, and we cannot achieve her objective.

Fourth, objectives must be realistic. Sometimes we need to have a heart-to-heart conversation with a client about this. The client may want to change the world in a day. However, it may not be realistic in the time scope for this social media plan. Having honest conversations with your clients about what is and is not realistic leads to better expectations. This is not always perceived as good news, so a certain amount of authority and poise is required for you to share these insights in a confident way.

Finally, objectives should be precise in their timing. It is only fair that the people with whom you're working on a social media plan know when they can expect objectives to be achieved.

There is no magic number of objectives needed for a specific social media plan. The number depends on the scope of the campaign and the overall goal of the client or organization you are representing.

Key Audience Members

An essential part of a social media strategic plan is how to communicate with our audiences. Understanding the underlying characteristics, motivational factors, perceptions, social media platforms used, and how audiences use each platform are just a few of the factors that come into play. Audiences want to be talked to in a way that is personable, not promotional.

Two types of audience will be outlined in your strategic plan. **Primary audiences** are those you want to target directly and that have a meaningful relationship and connection to the client. **Secondary audiences** are supportive and potentially viewed as influencers by the primary audience members. With both types, outlining emerging audience members—or those who are not necessarily on the client's radar yet, but could and perhaps should be—is very useful.

Understanding audiences means painting a picture of these groups of individuals. **Demographics** are a basic way to categorize a group of individuals and involve the basic population data that are easily collected, such as age, education level, ethnicity, and location. In social media, the description of audiences needs to be expanded much further. The more information we have about our key audiences, the easier it will be to craft effective and personalized messages to fit their motivational needs and expectations.

This is where **psychographics** come into play, where we are able to categorize audiences based on their attitudes, opinions, and values. This higher-level approach to categorization narrows down the groups into specific audiences based on psychological characteristics and attributes.

Human-to-human communication is what distinguishes successful brands in social media from those still struggling to build their community. Ignoring this principle is one thing social marketers are beyond guilty of. Instead of pushing content or playing the "pay for play" game, social media strategists need to think of people as people. Effective key messages can help captivate the brand voice as well as extend reach to the community by providing an opportunity to participate in the conversation.

Understanding your audiences plays a significant role in your ability to write key messages. Messages take time, research, and a dash of creativity to make them effective. This is probably one of the hardest tasks you'll have in social media. Each platform has its own community and brand voice, but this does not mean you should sway at all from your traditional and fundamental brand voice. Instead, you must craft the messages to align with your identity as a brand, and channel this persona and voice to the appropriate audience. The magic comes alive when you provide the right voice in the right channel to the right audience at the right time.

There are two types of key messages: primary and secondary. **Primary messages** are broad statements that you want to communicate to your key audience members. Each primary message should be simple, concise, and to the point. This is not the time to elaborate. Just one sentence long, the primary message must capture what you want to accomplish and communicate to your audiences in a limited amount of time. For example, Under Armour's "Protect This House" is a key message, and the tag line emphasizes building community.

If you want to expand and elaborate on key messages, the secondary message comes into play. **Secondary messages** provide additional evidence to support the primary message. Using facts, statistics, and additional information to build on the point outlined in the primary message, these messages can incorporate evidence of what the client has already done on social media. There is no magic number of secondary messages needed to support your primary message, but you should be thorough in your explanation of these points to avoid audience confusion. A rule of thumb is the more information you can provide to guide your audience members regarding actions they should take, the better off you will be.

Strategies and Tactics

Strategy is obviously the heart of a strategic plan. However, you can have the best ideas for a social media strategic plan, but without proper execution of your strategies, nothing is gained.

Tactics are the tools and applications within social media that you will use to accomplish your objectives and fulfill your strategies. Tactics are the nuts and bolts of your social media plan. For example, using a branded hashtag is a type of tactic. A Facebook Live video showcasing a Q&A with a senior-level manager discussing a new initiative or promoting a giveaway of an exclusive opportunity is another example of a tactic. As you can see, tactics are very specific and very focused. Each tactic needs to be aligned with the strategy.

Managing tactics well is a way to impress employers and clients and use your creativity to stand out among your peers. Tactics allow you to experiment with new trends, tools, and platforms. At the same time, tactics must be used strategically and systematically, not just for fun. Make sure that you can support your choice of specific new tools and platforms with data.

Evaluation

This is truly the part of the strategic plan that is either overlooked or viewed as intimidating. Evaluation is the section of the strategic plan that brings in the value for social media strategies, but also the opportunity to showcase the evidence to support the overall impact the creative and research-based strategies have accomplished in a campaign. Yes, this means there are some calculations to do. If you thought you wouldn't use any math in a social media career, you were very wrong. Measurement skills are an essential area of social media expertise. A growing specialization in social media, as discussed elsewhere in this textbook, measurement involves math, which we use to evaluate whether we have been successful in our campaigns. This does not mean a simple check in a box of "yes" or "no." Instead, we need numbers and specifics. In some cases, we can use traditional research methods, such as focus groups and interviews, to determine whether or not we have achieved our objectives. In the case of social media, we can rely on other tools and services to help answer these questions.

To determine whether or not we have achieved our objectives, we need to establish a set of **key performance indicators (KPIs)**. Key KPIs should be determined *before* the social media strategic plan is implemented. KPIs not only determine what has been accomplished, but inform next steps and measurements for future campaigns.

Here are some typical KPIs for social media plans. We will discuss them in more detail in the listening and monitoring chapter of this book:

- Awareness (share of voice, tone, sentiment)

- Audience (retention rate, lifetime value, audience share of voice, influencer share of voice)

- Conversion (costs per lead, sales, conversation rate of sales and leads)

We will discuss available tools and measurement methods in Chapter 10. For the purposes of the strategic plan, however, we need to outline how we will collect and interpret the data. Senior management will rely heavily on this information to determine whether or not investing in the social media plan was worthwhile. Data collection must always be transparent, and takeaways must be clearly stated. This part of the process can be challenging on a variety of levels because we have to integrate multiple sources of information into a cohesive message.

Budget

Social media campaigns can be quite affordable or quite expensive depending on the services, tools, and programs you decide to include in the strategic plan. You must be able to account for all the resources needed for a social media plan to take place, and these resources must be itemized based on strategy. Items might include the cost of tools and services, the cost of production in creating content, data analytics tools and downloading of data, the amount spent on paid advertising and media postings on various platforms, and the costs of personnel. You might need additional freelancers, consultants, and interns on your team.

TABLE 6.5 ■ Content Calendar Examples

Hootsuite

Time	Type	Topic	Post	Link
BLOG POST			**Day 1 - Monday**	
8:00 AM	NEW BLOG		Top 5 Vegan Paleo Dishes You Have To Try (You Too, Carnivores)	
TWITTER				
6:15	Club Info	Daily Class Schedule	Monday is for #MuscleMass. Get your kettlebell swing game on point.	PHOTO
11:15	Blog Promo - Paleo	Top 5 Vegan Paleo Dishes You Have To Try (You Too, Carnivores)	Vegan Paleo? It's Possible. Get the recipes here:	ow.ly/sample1
11:45	Promo	#HolidayHealth	Winter is coming - share a photo of your favourite exercise for a chance to win a 10 class pass! Add #HolidayHealth to enter.	PHOTO
17:45	Blog Snippet - Paleo	Proteins	"By combining incomplete proteins, you can get complete proteins"	PHOTO
19:35	Food Tips		Dinner time! Harvest Salad with Chicken:	PHOTO
20:00	Exercise Tips	Strength Training	Moderation is key with leg extensions + Picture	PHOTO
FACEBOOK				
6:00	Club Info	Daily Class Schedule	Monday is for Muscle Mass.	PHOTO
11:15	Blog Promo - Paleo	Top 5 Vegan Paleo Dishes You Have To Try (You Too, Carnivores)	Vegan Paleo? It's Possible. Get the recipes here:	ow.ly/sample1
INSTAGRAM				
6:00	Club Info	Daily Class Schedule	Monday is for Muscle Mass.	PHOTO
14:00	Community	Member of the Month	Extra gold stars for @Casey, our member of the month. She hasn't missed a spin class since she joined!	PHOTO
TWITTER			**Day 2 - Tuesday**	
6:15	Club Info	Daily Class Schedule	The Tuesday fitness menu	PHOTO
8:15	Food Tips	Coffee	Grassfed butter, coconut oil, coffee, blend. Have you tried bulletproof coffee yet? Thoughts?	PHOTO
11:15	Exercise Tips	Strength Training	Have you visited the squat rack lately? + Picture	PHOTO
16:15	Community	#TransformationTuesday	"Half the battle is just showing up when you said you will." Dave is a huge inspiration to us all #TransformationTuesday	PHOTO

Sprout Social

Source: Hootsuite Inc., https://hootsuite.com/education/courses/social-marketing/content/content-calendar. *Source:* "4 Steps for Creating a Social Media Calendar" Sprout Social, 2017 https://sproutsocial.com/insights/social-media-editorial-calendar/.

Calendar

A social media calendar has several different components. The strategies, tactics, social media placements, and evaluation and measurement components that will take place in the span of the campaign must be scheduled. This process is sometimes referred to as the customer journey landscape view. The components to be scheduled might include paid, earned, shared, and owned (PESO) media. The calendar also outlines the overall connections of the social media team with the rest of the duties and disciplines within an organization or agency.

The content calendar aligns all of the pieces of content going out at the same time on a social media platform and how they will be evaluated. Specific tools and services, such as Hootsuite and Sprout Social (see Table 6.5), allow you to create content calendars in a very simple and organized manner. Depending on the overall cost of the campaign and investment in social media, the client or senior leadership will have to determine how much they want to invest in these tools.

FINAL WORDS OF WISDOM AND RECOMMENDATIONS

Conclude your social media strategic plan with a summary of your findings and recommended next steps. Along with the executive summary, which is present in most social media strategic plans, the conclusion is where you provide commentary and key takeaways that you want to highlight for the client. This is an opportunity to provide additional recommendations and note suggestions for the future, allowing the social media plan to come full circle while also providing a stepping stone to the next social media strategy the organization, agency, brand, or person wants to pursue in the future.

CHAPTER SUMMARY

The strategic plan is one of the main documents a social media professional is responsible for creating. Strategic plans serve as a systematic guide to determine what has happened in the past, what needs to be implemented now, and whether or not an organization was successful in meeting its goals and objectives.

The strategic plan can spark further ideas and new possibilities. Constructing a sound plan requires both research and creativity, linking the science and art of social media as a field of study and as an element of practice. Some universal steps and categories found in the social media strategic plan are shared by plans in other fields. Other areas are unique to social media. The approach of a social media strategic plan may evolve with the channels of communication. It is up to the social media professional to determine which items to revisit, adapt, or discard when they are no longer relevant. Along with the tools of communication, social media strategic plans evolve over time and must continue to adapt to the changing expectations and needs of the industry and workplace.

Strategic plans are difficult to create and implement, but with practice and collaborative team efforts, you can learn to craft plans that lead to sound decisions and successful social media campaigns.

THOUGHT QUESTIONS

1. Why is a strategic plan important for social media? Identify three reasons why a strategic plan is necessary for a social media campaign.

2. What is the difference between a goal statement and an objective statement?

3. What are the components of a social media communication audit?

4. Identify the five concepts of a SWOT analysis. Where do strategic implications come into play for a social media campaign?

EXERCISES

1. While interviewing with Airbnb for a social media job, you are asked to do a SWOT analysis of the company's social media efforts. Look at its current campaigns and channels and discuss its strengths, weaknesses, opportunities, and threats as a brand on social media. Then write a sentence outlining the strategic implications the company needs to note for future social media campaigns.

2. Samsung is looking to engage and build brand awareness with Generation Z about its new Samsung Notes product. Write two primary messages and two secondary messages for this audience. You will need to do some research regarding the characteristics of Generation Z. Then, propose one strategy and two tactics you could implement to reach this audience for Samsung. Discuss how you would evaluate the effectiveness of this campaign.

3. You are asked to do a social media communication audit for your university. Identify the internal and external characteristics of its social media presence, and make three recommendations based on your analysis.

REFERENCES

Facebook (2018). Facebook Mission Statement. Retrieved from https://investor.fb.com/resources/default.aspx.

Hootsuite. (2018). About us. Retrieved from http://hootsuite.com/about.

Owyang, J. (2010, November 9). *Research: Most companies organize in "hub and spoke" formation for social business*. Retrieved from http://www.web-strategist .com/blog/2010/11/09/research-most-companies -organize-in-hub-and-spoke-formation/.

Starbucks. (2018). Our mission. Retrieved from https://www.starbucks.com/about-us/company-information/mission-statement.

Under Armour (2018). Our mission. Retrieved from http://www.uabiz.com/company/mission.cfm.

7 STRATEGIC WRITING FOR SOCIAL MEDIA

Learning Objectives
Humans of Social Media
Introduction
Content Creation Versus Content Curation
Understanding the Difference Between Tone
    and Voice
        How Do You Find Your Brand Voice in Your
            Writing Style?
        Types of Writing Styles for Social Media
        Common Writing Mistakes on Social Media
Best Practices for Social Media Writing
Chapter Summary
Thought Questions
Exercises
References

LEARNING OBJECTIVES

After reading this chapter, you will be able to

- Evaluate the importance of writing for social media
- Define storytelling and explain its role in social media writing practices
- Distinguish among content creation, content curation, and content marketing

HUMANS OF SOCIAL MEDIA

JARYD WILSON, SOCIAL CONTENT MANAGER FOR THE BUFFALO WILD WINGS, FORMER DIGITAL CONTENT MANAGER FOR THE ATLANTA HAWKS

Source: Courtesy of Jaryd Wilson

Jaryd Wilson

Introduction

I actually went to journalism school, something I wanted to do since high school. I attended the University of Missouri, and when I got there, I realized the importance of understanding convergence journalism—this was where the industry was going, so I majored in it. While in school, I worked at the NBC affiliate and updated its social media and websites. Social media was just getting started, so it was mostly web work.

How did you get your start in social media?

I got my first job after graduation at the Fox affiliate in Colorado Springs (similar to the position I was in at Missouri) where I managed the websites,

(Continued)

(Continued)

managed the accounts and content, and handled the social media as well. I didn't really know social media was my specific interest. Sports was the industry I wanted to be a part of, but it is hard to break into. Getting some news experience would help me stand out and give me the skills I needed to work in the sports industry. I started the process in 2012 by applying for some sports jobs, the Hawks had an opening, and I have been here for four and a half years.

How has your background in journalism helped you in your role with the Hawks?

Having a journalism background is huge. Bad writing on social media is so detectable. You can tell who runs each account and what their background is. A lot of people make grammar and spelling mistakes; they are not good writers. Having a writing background and being able to write for audiences is critical. It is essential not only to understand the basic tactics of writing like grammar and spelling, but also to understand the importance of having a strong writing style to cater to audiences on social media. My background in journalism and writing has helped me tremendously.

Since emojis are one way Hawks fans communicate, however, we use them as well. We try to keep up to speed on what brands are doing on social media, but we also keep up with the behaviors of users and what media they are using.

What is your favorite part of working in your area of social media expertise?

There are some perks to the job. I like what I do, and obviously, to live cover real-time events during basketball games is a high area of interest for me. That's what fans pay the most attention to. It's exciting to see what type of content fans react to, and which content takes off and goes viral. Being in the arena and participating in the day-in and night-out experience is great for any fan of basketball and of the industry. This is a really, really cool perk to the job.

What is one thing you can't live without while working in social media?

You are not the first person to ask me this. We use a tool to cut highlights from a game, and we do this in real time, which allows us to cut videos into highlights as they happen on the court.

Without that tool, our social media would have a completely different look. We use video highlights to help fuel our social media and post content in real time, because that is what fans are demanding and what they want. Being able to deliver that to them, through an easy and automated highlights tool, has been a game changer for the past two seasons. It's now become second nature for us. We have seen our numbers (on social media) spike up tremendously since we got this tool. It has been cool to watch and extremely helpful.

What is your favorite social media account (person/brand/etc.) to follow, and why?

There are several. In our industry, there are a lot. Team-wise, within the National Basketball Association (NBA), I always look at the Portland Trail Blazers. The Chicago Cubs also do a great job, as do the Sacramento Kings, the New England Patriots, the Atlanta Falcons, and the Atlanta Braves. Major League Baseball (MLB) does a really good job at this as well. Looking at brands from outside, I think SB Nation is really strong in terms of content—not so on social media, but the writing is really good. Other brands for news like Mashable, TechCrunch, and SportTechie are also good at the brand level.

Some brands excel on certain platforms; for example, the Falcons are really good at video—that is what they have established for themselves, and they do this across all channels. The Cubs as well as the Kings are great on Twitter. The Golden State Warriors have expanded their reach and become really good at targeting and reaching different fan bases on Facebook.

What is the most challenging part of working in social media?

League guidelines along with organizational guidelines and other challenges are always things we have to consider. We need to be aware of the lines in the sand. It's better to take chances, and sometimes it is easier to ask for forgiveness than permission in our industry. We have done a good job of figuring out where those lines are, but we always want to do more, and sometimes we would love to post, but we know it is not worth the headache at the end. Manpower is also a challenge. Out of the 30 NBA teams, we have the smallest digital staff. It is a challenge to execute an idea with limited resources, but we are trying to be more effective with what we have.

What do you wish you had known when you were starting out?

One of the things I look for is experience. Have you managed a brand before (for an internship, a part-time job, or a school club)? Writing is also important to me. Can you write? I go back to my background and how many people struggle with that basic skill for social media. Part of this is instinctive—do you have it? Do you understand audiences? Do you understand targeting and how rich media and language play a part in what you write? Do you know what makes good content and what doesn't? Can you tell right from wrong? Some of this can be taught, but some of it is instinctive. It is a natural process, I suppose. That's what I would pass along.

Do you have any tips for emerging social media professionals?

Maintain personality of voice in your content. A fair amount of people use social media that way. At the Hawks, we want to integrate our personality in a way that is a little cheeky and a little snarky. But we do not want to be disrespectful. There are times when we respond in a cheeky or witty way, as long as we do not overdo it or cross the line of disrespect. We have seen a positive correlation between this brand voice and our audience engagement. I definitely plan for this, and part of our brand voice involves interjecting when it is appropriate.

When hiring for social media, I look at applicants' personal accounts to see what they are talking about—what they share and how they write. This is important, and you have to show some of the posts or updates you have done for a brand, including content you have created and posted yourself and links or content associated with it. What are you most proud of? As far as a deal breaker, having a social media account is a must. If you do not have an account on one of the major platforms (Facebook, Instagram, or Twitter), I am probably not going to consider you. Establish an active presence on a platform and set your account to public. It makes no sense to have a private account if you want to work in social media. Plus, what does your personal account say about you? Is it professional or informative? You can still be personal while also being professional at the same time. If you have ever managed social media for a brand, I'll want to see you do it before I hire you. Many companies and organizations don't have someone dedicated to social media and would be happy to have a volunteer to help, and this would be a great way to start working in the field. You can even do this remotely, at any time. A lot of experience you can get without a lot of travel.

When writing for social media, you have to know your target audience. That's obvious, and this is the first step. Know the demographics of your audience members and what content they react to. Use some good sample cases that you know do well analytically to produce some good stuff. If you are just spinning your wheels, thinking your audience will react to certain content without any data to back it up, that's probably not a good idea. A writing background is strong (grammar and creative writing skills are a must), and a defined brand voice is huge. Do not treat your social media channels like PR channels because they are not. They are much bigger than that. Having that brand voice and defined style of writing is really important. For us, for example, we want to be the voice of a Hawks fan. Everything we post and do is from the point of view and framework of a Hawks fan. We strive to represent the Hawks in each and every single post we make. Although the voice is different for every brand, knowing your brand's voice and being able to define it will help you. Plus, it will give you a guideline for any content you create.

Jaryd Wilson can be reached at @JarydWilson on Twitter.

INTRODUCTION

Writing effectively on social media is one of the most challenging responsibilities of public relations professionals. Many job postings emphasize this fundamental skill that all young professionals should have in their wheelhouse and tool kit. We sometimes forget that writing is a way to communicate with our audiences, but in order to be a successful social media manager, you need to have strong writing skills along with an understanding of the six *C*s of effective writing for social media:

- Content

- Community

- Culture

- Conversation

- Creativity

- Connection

Writing for social media, however, is not rocket science. You may be intimidated by social media, but this chapter will walk you through the steps to follow not only for your own social media platforms, but also for those of your client, brand, or business. Writing is the bridge that connects ideas and shares them in a strategic and relevant manner. Successful social media writers create messages that are relevant for their audiences, resonating with them on a personal and emotional level, and that at the same time are professional and aligned with the brand's mission and core attributes. The content created for social media also needs to be entertaining, which will give audiences more opportunities to remember and share what they felt and saw with others. Whether you write an update on Twitter or a long-form blog post depends on the brand, community, situation, and goal in mind.

Content. Many people have a stake in creating and writing **content** for social media. Journalists use it to release breaking news to their readers. Marketing professionals use it to manage the data and metrics from their marketing campaigns. Public relations professionals use it to monitor, listen, and engage with audiences in real time to build on relationships and keep track of conversations. All of these roles have a place within the social media space, and all require creating, curating, and featuring relevant content while evaluating its effectiveness for senior management.

Social media professionals need to make sure that the content they share is relevant to their target audiences. We need to be aware of what truly matters to the audience we are trying to reach. Both primary and secondary research can help. In addition, exploring the segments of your audience (different categories and groups of individuals you want to reach in your social media efforts) might come in handy. User interests, location, type, and time on social media are some factors to review to determine the content that may be most relevant to your intended audiences. People also want to receive content that is useful. Promotional ads and updates are not always the most successful, especially for brands that go for the "hard sell" or abruptly push users to take action when there has been no transition or buildup to the relationship.

Writing skills come in various forms and include duties surrounding the importance of creating good content. You can have the best writing style, but the substance of content and information you are sharing, creating, and engaging with on social media also needs to be high in quality. These duties include editing, copy writing, and creating messages that fit the appropriate channel and audience. The content that a brand publishes and presents on social media is the first impression that audiences get online, so if the copy is filled with grammar errors, spelling mistakes, or unrelated jargon that is inappropriate for the audience and channel, this can significantly impact the overall impression the person or company wants to make. These are just some of the reasons why excellent writing skills are so important and fundamental for today's social media professionals.

Not only must we be aware of having professional and unique content on each platform, but we also must understand the differences to take into consideration when posting on one channel versus another. What works on Instagram may not work on LinkedIn or as a blog post. Each post and platform needs to be evaluated based on the audience, brand, community, situation, and channel. With social media, a lot of channels need to be taken into consideration, as well as the rapid evolution of each channel. New features, algorithm and format changes, and other elements are constantly added on to these platforms, which makes it harder in some cases for social media professionals to adapt their content to fit the needs and framework dictated by these social media companies.

Community. **Community**, or a group of individuals who come together based on common interests, values, and characteristics, is part of the mix when it comes to creating content that resonates with audiences. The overall dynamics of people's interactions on social media is one of the most important factors to consider. Do people want to receive content? When do they want to receive content? Do they want engagement, or just to consume content? What are the appropriate times and places to share content and messages with them? These are a few questions we all have to ask ourselves when looking at a community. In Chapter 5, we determined some of the monitoring and listening techniques that can be used to create and foster new ideas for messages, content, and engagement. Sometimes community is also aligned with the overall **culture** (common practices, work-life ethics and practices, professional experiences, and beliefs of a group of individuals) of the company, brand, or community in question. Etiquette, feelings and significant issues, and historical approaches that characterize how each party interacts and formulates relationships are key factors related to culture that social media writers should consider.

Conversation. **Conversation** is also important in making sure social media content resonates with key audiences. People do not want to be advertised to or promoted to all of the time. They will be more likely to tune out and go on to the next thing if they feel a brand is pushing too hard with its promotional messages. Conversation is not just responding to a post, but rather engaging in a discussion that is meaningful to both parties. This is where understanding the type of brand voice and writing style on social media is important. Your response to a person's inquiry about your product could be either formal or snarky. Responding appropriately in communications that are not official social media marketing messages is an important skill. Sometimes we can anticipate these informal types of scenarios, and other times social media managers have to think on their feet, essentially, in their responses. Conversing may take some training, education, and testing to see how each social media manager would respond to each message and how far or closely aligned the responses are to the brand voice and mission.

Social care, discussed in more detail in Chapter 12, takes place when brands are able to have conversations in real time with audiences to answer questions, address concerns, or even bounce around ideas. The **creativity** involved with how these conversations arise (perhaps thanks to monitoring and listening practices) can help build memorable **connections**. Strong writers on social media should have skills to address each type of communication.

CONTENT CREATION VERSUS CONTENT CURATION

Within the overall social media strategy discussed in Chapter 6, content creation and curation are two parts of essential writing. You do not want to have 100% of one versus the other, but rather you want to provide a mixture of content that is originally created (**content creation**) and content that was published from a different source (**content curation**). Remember, whether you are looking to create content or curate content, the key for successful engagement and interaction on social media is to have good, strong content. Good content needs to be aligned with the goals and objectives set in place for a social media initiative. If the goal is to provide a sense of community and build awareness of the brand, you want to create stories integrated with videos, testimonials, and even blog posts. However, if the goal is to increase share of voice and buzz related to a campaign, you want to create content that drives home a strong call-to-action statement (share this, tweet that, use a certain hashtag, create a video, etc.). For example, the amyotrophic lateral sclerosis (ALS) Ice Bucket Challenge succeeded in creating strong content not just for the campaign in 2014, but also as the campaign continues to build momentum. The ALS Association gave audiences clear, concise, and actionable steps.

On the other hand, curation involves collecting and strategically selecting content from various sources that may be relevant for your key audiences. For example, the University of Southern California (USC) Annenberg School for Communication and Journalism might share content from another source about a fellowship or professional opportunity because this content is relevant for its key audiences on a specific platform (e.g., Twitter). This sharing in turn creates a perception among your audience members that you are not only creating original, valuable content, but also taking the time to make sure they get all of the information needed to make an informed decision about various possibilities and opportunities.

The overall purpose of curation is to provide your audiences with useful information that not only resonates with them, but builds on their perception that your brand online is a valuable resource. That said, there should be a standard approach for deciding which resources, accounts, and outlets you would recommend as possible sources from which to share content. It may not be a common practice for a specific brand (e.g., USC) to share content from a competing school (e.g., UCLA) with its audiences, but it is key to monitor and listen to your competitors on social media, just as it is important to note which brands and accounts you would share information from. Once you have a systematic approach and protocol on how to handle this, include it in the social media writing guide (discussed in the next section) as well as the social media policy maintained within a brand, organization, or agency.

Source: Facebook/@The ALS Association

[INFOGRAPHIC] The ALS Ice Bucket Challenge took us part of the way to finding a treatment and cure for ALS. Learn just how far we've come and find out how you can help take us the rest of the way. #EveryDropAddsUp

Progress Since the Ice Bucket Challenge

ALSA.ORG

ALS Association Infographic on Ice Bucket Challenge

USC Annenberg Retweeted

Public Sphere WB @PublicSphereWB · May 10
You still have time to apply to @WorldBank - Annenberg Summer Institute >>
ow.ly/QbJi30bBYjS @AnnenbergPenn @USCAnnenberg #reform

10 reasons to apply for World Bank-Annenberg Sum..
How can professionals looking to lead reform initiatives
find the best way forward? They can start at the World
Bank-Annenberg Summer Institute in Reform Commun...
blogs.worldbank.org

USC Annenberg Curated Content

UNDERSTANDING THE DIFFERENCE BETWEEN TONE AND VOICE

When creating your **brand voice** (Lee, 2014a), make sure it does not reflect your own perspective, but rather that you embody the personality characteristics that are unique, memorable, and authentic to your brand. This is a challenge that can test you as a person for your personal accounts, but also when you are representing a brand online. All brands have an individual voice, characteristics, and history that make them memorable to their key audiences. The voice projected on social media must be aligned with how others perceive the company, organization, or person. Any disconnect between that perception and how people or brands share content online can result in loss of community members, business, and, in some cases, acknowledgement as a viable member of the industry.

Sometimes **tone** (Lee, 2014a) is confused with brand voice, but in a sense, they are interconnected. Tone is the overall voice characteristics you want to interject within the content you are writing. For example, do you want to sound more professional and formal when you are representing a publicly traded business, or do you want to intertwine some personality into your content by adding humor? The tone of your social media content can be tailored depending on the situation, channel, and audience in question (Buffer, 2018). In addition, the social media tone you convey must be aligned specifically to the characteristics of each area. Understanding the key demographics, psychographics, and location of your community (audience) will influence the overall language (professional, casual, hip, etc.) you use to accomplish your overall objectives (e.g., to create awareness, to entertain, or to educate). All of these factors are interconnected with not only the brand voice, but the overall tone set for the social media brand.

Let's apply these concepts to a foodie example. Voice is the ice cream flavor, and tone serves as the extra toppings and sprinkles. Each voice (like ice cream) has a foundation that makes it unique and different. Vanilla ice cream has certain key ingredients, for example, but each brand (like Ben & Jerry's or McConnell's) has a unique twist and process for creating its products, which is analogous to establishing a brand voice. The unique combination of tone, however, is showcased in the toppings. Some people are cookies-and-cream types, and others love chocolate-covered bacon. Each topping (or, in the case of social media, tone) showcases an additional layer of the brand voice. So many different combinations can be created that no one brand uses the same voice or tone in its message strategies. The most important factor to keep in mind is to be yourself. You do not want to "force" your brand voice and persona in your written social media content if it is not authentic. This is a time not to be like everyone else, but rather to separate yourself from others. Identifying the gaps in others' brand voices and the overall tone of their social media content is the name of the game. We are all unique, and we need to embrace ourselves wholeheartedly on social media without any concern about our differences. Brand voice allows us to establish a human connection online, and allows conversations, relationships, and communities to be established in an authentic and true manner.

Along with maintaining a consistent and authentic voice with the appropriate tone, social media content should reflect the overall personality as well as the language of the brand or individual. What attributes do you want to display and communicate in your messages? How will you create content to show this in a certain and consistent way? What is the overall purpose and rationale for each post? Social media professionals must take all of these questions into consideration for each individual post, update, and video created and shared online.

How Do You Find Your Brand Voice in Your Writing Style?

This is an important step to consider before you start writing for social media. Before even writing up a Facebook ad or creating an Instagram Story, ask yourself the following questions to make sure you are being true in your social media messages to your personal brand or to the brand of a company for whom you work:

- How would you describe your brand (or yourself) in terms of personality attributes?

- What are some attributes that do not reflect your brand?

- How would you describe your relationships with your audiences online based on the content you share?

- How do people feel about your content?

- What is in it for your key audiences? What benefits are they getting from being part of these communities and receiving your messages?

- Who are your key audiences? What are they motivated and inspired by?

- How would you describe your competitors? How do they communicate online? What is their overall tone? How would you describe their brand voice?

- What goals do you have for how your audience feels about you?

- What is the purpose for your content? How would you rate your content right now, and what are your goals for how your audience will respond to your content?

- What do you want your audience to do in response to your content?

Table 7.1 outlines the various types of content message strategies and executions that can be organized and framed within a social media writing guide. The table showcases examples of how social media managers can break down their writing content based on platform, type of content, key audiences, what voice to present and implement, what writing style to utilize, and how the writing style will be approached.

Social media managers can take several actions to engage with their audiences on social media and brainstorm ideas for content that supports the brand mission and

TABLE 7.1 ■ Sample Writing Guide for Social Media					
Platform	**Content**	**Audience**	**Voice**	**Writing Style**	**Approaches**
Facebook	Ad, video	Customers, marketing pros	Engaged and interested in purchases	Professional, product/brand focused, audience focused	Have a call-to-action statement and link to a specific place
Twitter	Tweet, video	Fans, media professionals	Entertainment, informative	Witty, snarky, conversational, informational, engaging	Media with specific hashtag or link to track
Instagram	Album, story, post	Bloggers, influencers, fans	Community	Educational, conversational, audience focused, product/brand focused, inspirational	Short update statement
Snapchat	Story	Generation Z, content creators	Experiential, humorous	Audience focused, entertainment	Visual storyboard approach
LinkedIn	Pulse post	Marketing professionals, business-to-business customers	Informative, approachable, educational	Professional, educational	Update with key hashtags tagging key words, and cross shares on Twitter and Facebook

overall voice online. Kevan Lee (2014b) of Buffer outlined 71 ways for social media managers to create content online. Specifically, he mentioned a few to consider for each platform. Table 7.2 outlines some of these suggestions for building and creating content on social media. In addition, resources like Buffer (2018) allow you to tailor posts to a specific channel and platform, which helps social media managers create the most effective content that is relevant for the audience as well as compatible with the platform format.

You also want to have a set plan to evaluate the message creation steps that already take place within the company or agency. Exploring how team members communicate with each other, with audience members, and outside of the brand is a factor to consider here as well. It is important to conduct a team brand voice audit because writing in another voice (e.g., a social media community manager writing on behalf of a brand on social media) is one of the most challenging tasks for social media professionals to master. This audit can be a way to determine the overall feeling and perception of a brand voice, but you can also address and highlight this by doing research. Exploring the main attributes people associate with a brand through survey questions, focus groups, or even word clouds associated with the brand online based on social media monitoring analysis are just a few ways of identifying some of the attributes tied to a brand voice.

Along with a standard approach for social media conduct and policies, there needs to be a written and digital social media writing style guide for all social media professionals to follow, embrace, and engage in. This guide will help set forth the brand

TABLE 7.2 ■ Platform Characteristics and Content Writing Ideas

Platform	Platform Characteristics	Content Ideas
Facebook	• Max character limit is 63,206, but posts that have 80 characters have the most engagement (Read, 2017).	• Start an update with a question • End an update with a question • Create a list • Add a quote from an article, interview, feature, or event/speaker • Update with emojis • Use an image with text overlay • Attribute and tag other accounts • Provide a customized URL
Twitter	• Character limit is 280 but options are available to add images, videos, and collages, and tag users, now. • You do not always have to use all 280 characters.	• Place comments before headline • Place comments after headline • Include commentary + quote of tweet • Place tweets inside the comments • Integrate multimedia • Conduct polls • Attribute with tag • Create Twitter Moments • Use Twitter threads to elaborate ongoing conversations that are more than 280 characters (use /1, /2, etc., as you see fit to complete the conversation). • Tag accounts in image or video
Instagram		• Give tutorials • Try microvisual blogging • Offer giveaways and contests • Ask a question + probe for engagement • Feature products • Share tips and tricks • Give Q&As • Highlight historical features • Give interviews • Post updates • Go behind the scenes • Provide storyboards (posts + Instagram Stories) • Mix up content for Stories (still images, videos, Instagram-based apps, text only, etc.) • Tag accounts in updates, stories, and albums
LinkedIn		• Post an update • Post an update with a URL • Share a Pulse article • Post an update with a video • Post an update with an image

standard and overall voice online, while also ensuring that the messages attached to social media are consistent across the board. This is considered the brand standard and framework for social media professionals.

Certain consistent sections need to be included in the social media writing guide. Sometimes brands will already have established a set social media writing guide, but other times one has to be set forth from scratch. Looking at the main components as follows is important for either following or perhaps creating a social media writing guide for a client, person, or business.

Content you are passionate about. This is content that you feel focuses on your strengths as a person (if you are managing a personal account) or as a representative of a professional account. If you are passionate about blogs, videos, GIFs, tweets, Instagram posts, or another type of content, discuss what makes it relevant to your cause. Most importantly, remember that it may not take as much time to create and write these pieces of content due to your positive association with them. It is always easier to write content that you like to create rather than content you are "forced" to create.

Content that your audience members are passionate about. This is where you will have to conduct a thorough audit of the type of content that will be well received by your audiences, and what content needs to be revamped for the appropriate platform. This content may be similar to or different from the content you are personally passionate about as discussed in the section above. If the content is the same for both parties (the person or organization and key audiences), then you are in a good position for the moment. However, if these perspectives are different, then an adjustment needs to be made. Keep in mind that these items must be surveyed on a regular basis since audiences evolve over time.

Audience and persona summary. Your audience is one of the first things to define and discuss. To write the best content, you first have to note who you will be reaching, what messages and content they want to hear, and what they are looking for in the online community. This is another way to identify the various channels of communication to focus on. You may assume your audiences will gravitate to other places and channels, but in order to fully write effective content, you have to know where they are going in order to reach them. Keep in mind that language and tone are also big factors here since different audiences will have access to these messages at different times and places, and they may want information presented to them in different ways. Social media professionals have to account for the various ways in which people comprehend messages across the channels. Some audience members may be more likely to respond to video, whereas others may have a preference for long-form content. Tailoring the content for the channel, audience, and situation is crucial for social media professionals to establish a strong connection with their audiences.

Branding. Along with writing great content, social media managers need to make sure that their content is informed by the art of branding. Branding is more than just slapping a logo on an image or using a specific hashtag. Instead, it encompasses the way in which a message comes across in its voice, image, community, and perception. There should be a rationale for creating the content, and it should be aligned with and connected back to the overall mission and purpose of the company, person, or organization. Content that is not aligned with the designated characteristics or perceptions of a brand could mislead audiences. Branding also translates into what

TABLE 7.3 ■ HubSpot Content Template			
Content that is reflected in the brand voice	Content that is not reflected in the brand voice	Connection back to the brand (personal or professional voice)	Purpose and rationale

messages are sent out on behalf of the brand. For example, Coca-Cola does not send out social media messages that are not representative of its overall persona or image. The company stays true to its "Open Happiness" mantra and writes content aligned with this perception. Message branding exercises to determine the types of messages reflected in the brand voice and whether they are (or are not) connected to the brand form an important component of the social media writing guide. Table 7.3 provides a template for the type of content reflected in the brand voice, the type of content *not* reflected in the brand voice, how the content is connected back to the personal or professional voice, and a purpose and rationale.

Types of Writing Styles for Social Media

For every brand and professional, a specific writing style and tone for communication is one of the most important things to solidify before executing written content. Creating a writing style guide will provide a consistent and sustainable format for writing, framing, and executing messages on various channels depending on the situation. The following are examples of the writing style approaches brands have taken to create their content (for more examples of voices on social media, see Seiter, 2012):

- Professional

- Snarky and Spunky

- Product and Brand Focused

- Audience Focused

- Inspirational

- Conversational

- Witty

- Educational

- Personality Focused

Professional (General Motors). Brands that are traditional yet consistent with their online presence treat social media like any other traditional communication channel. General Motors has one of the more professional and traditionally oriented voices on social media. The company's approach focuses on providing clear information to

General Motors Instagram Post

Source: Instagram /@Generalmotors

audience members while giving them an opportunity to interact on the account. This does not necessarily force the audience members to engage, but rather extends an invitation to be part of the conversation.

Most of the professionally oriented messages on social media come from corporate accounts, allowing the individual brand accounts (like Chevrolet) to showcase their personalities on social media a bit more. What is good about the General Motors style is that it is concise and appropriate for the platform, and it has a call to action to engage audiences with a question. This provides a window of opportunity and an invitation for the user to participate in the experience and conversation. The focus is to create content and a message that drives back to the corporate brand mission, but also extends a hand to those who perhaps want to join the conversation.

Snarky and Spunky (Wendy's). One rising trend in writing content for social media comes from brands who want to be "snarky"—or integrate their attitude within the messages on social media to provide entertainment and promote reactions. Wendy's, for example, has done this successfully on Twitter. The company has had an active social media presence on this site for years, but only in 2017 did the Wendy's social media manager take over and engage with audience members in a more informal and conversational way. Wendy's has been praised for this interaction by its fan base, while others trying the same approach have not been as well received. Some organizations have tried to jump on the Wendy's bandwagon, but because the tone was not consistent with their overall portrayal online, this caused some additional challenges. As Jay Baer (2017) points out in *Adweek*, some brands may not get the same reception as Wendy's, and posting

Sources: Twitter/@Wendy's; @SabrinaVivianne; Instagram/@Wendy's; @TheKennyBawlin

Wendy's Twitter Interactions

snarky content could result in negative perceptions for a brand, and even loss of trust, among its key audiences.

Knowing when being snarky will work comes down to understanding the community, culture, and position within the industry for the brand. Plus, getting buy-in from leadership also needs to be accounted for when it comes to taking this approach. Feeling the burn or using the fire emoji may have some short-term success (e.g., it might get a laugh or even a mention from a high-profile account), but this approach may be difficult to maintain in the long run. People move on to the next big thing that comes along, and they will be looking at what else is trending. However, building long-term relationships means focusing on the different steps needed to maintain and sustain the community on each platform. Other brands known for their personality approach include Arby's, Denny's, and the Houston Rockets.

Keep in mind that while it is appropriate to be creative and entertaining for audiences when it comes to message execution on social media, brands have to ask themselves, "What do our customers and audiences really want?" The social media management company Sprout Social found that most consumers and audiences want brands to be honest, friendly, and helpful, and being snarky was rated in last place (Morrison, 2017). Understanding what key audiences expect and want to see is an important driver of the content social media managers share, create, and execute on behalf of a brand.

Product and Brand Focused (Under Armour). Some brands use their writing style to "stay in their lanes." These brands, such as Under Armour, are innovative within their industries and among their competitors, but they stay focused on what they want to say and create that will help their bottom line. This Facebook update, for example, showcases a call to action to take advantage of a running series. This focused approach has a certain goal in mind for the user, such as an opportunity, sale, experience, or connection to the brand.

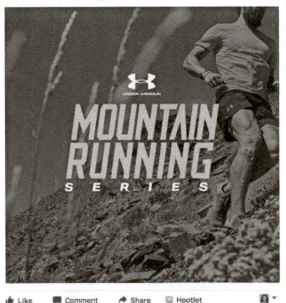

Under Armour
Facebook Post

Audience Focused (Budweiser). One of the best brands for storytelling is Budweiser, and the company has taken a similar approach to social media. When the brand partnered with VaynerMedia for a campaign to celebrate the retirement of Derek Jeter's number (2) for the New York Yankees in May 2017, it integrated the message, content, and execution across all platforms on social media (e.g., Facebook, Twitter, and YouTube). The message was tailored appropriately for the audiences in question, and the focus was creating content that best represented the message. Different video lengths were integrated along with a specific campaign hashtag, #ThisBudsFor2. The hashtag, message, and content all resonated and told the story not just about Derek Jeter, but about the experience Budweiser wanted to share with the rest of the audience, the campaign's primary focus.

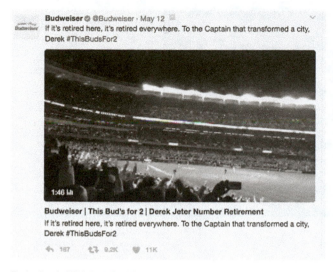

Budweiser's #ThisBudsFor2 Campaign

Source:Twitter/@Budweiser

Inspirational (adidas). There is a time to promote products and services, and there is a time for brands to use their writing style to enhance an idea or feeling. Adidas does this very well for key message strategies on social media. The content from adidas on social media focuses not just on the company's product, but also on the overall psychological emotions it wants to persuade its audiences to feel as part of this community.

Conversational (Dunkin' Donuts). Brands and users alike should note that social media is not always driven by sales. First and foremost, social media is about being *social*—which means striking up conversations. Interaction and two-way communication between brands and others is one way to foster relationships virtually. Several brands do this very well, such as Charmin and Hootsuite. Dunkin' Donuts, as well, not only taps into the interactive nature of social media, but engages with audiences through various appropriate means, including emojis. The overall tone and framework of the content shared by the donut and coffee company is fun and engaging and, for the most part, positive in nature. This inspires people to interact with the content, which then leads to engagement that can be monitored and tracked.

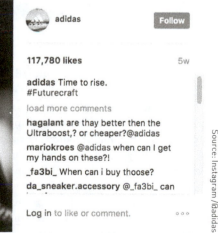

Example of an adidas Instagram Post

Source: Instagram /@Dunkindonuts

Dunkin Donuts Message on Instagram

Source: Twitter/@tacobell; @hayleyjoy96

Taco Bell's Taco Emoji Engine

Witty (Taco Bell). Including humor and cleverness in your brand messages on social media can be both challenging and memorable. Taco Bell as a company has become a leader in the art of being creative yet witty in its strategies and messages, which it executes in a memorable manner aligned with the brand. This approach to crafting messages or adding wittiness to a brand voice may not work for all organizations, but social media managers may want to look at this as an opportunity to branch out to their key audiences. Taco Bell is conversational and fun on social media, but adds a layer of wit to its messages that makes the company a bit different from other brands on social media. The taco emoji campaign (#TacoEmojiEngine) was automated, but the content created to get the word out about this feature was well executed and backed by strategy and insights, which were supported by research and connected back to the brand.

Educational (Sephora). One position people can take on social media is the role of educator. Information, tutorials, resources, and additional articles that may be relevant for key audiences are a few things that brands can contribute. Sharing this type of content will help foster relationships that will extend to others referring their network to the account, which of course builds a stronger community. One brand that has done this very well is Sephora. The beauty company not only promotes its products and campaigns, but creates a content calendar that allows it to schedule messages and content that educate audiences about the latest makeup trends, tutorials, and even how-tos for getting a certain look.

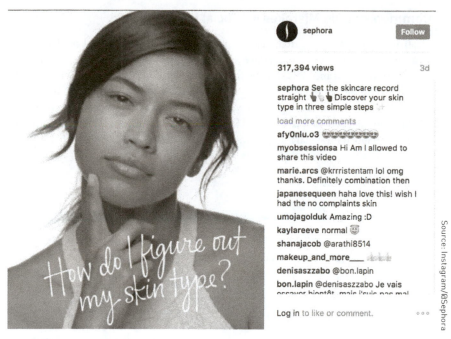

Sephora Skin Care Educational Message

Personality Focused (Charmin). Some brands try to make themselves more "human" in the eyes of their key audiences. Personality-focused accounts can be either loved or despised on social media. It really all depends on how the brand is perceived as a traditional company, and whether or not it has engaged in a way that is authentic, memorable, and entertaining to its key audiences. While earlier in the chapter we discussed the difference in reception to brands that are snarky and brands that are not, brands with a personality voice in their messages focused more on the positive nature of their engagement, rather than trying to make others feel they have been "burned."

One brand that has been very successful in using personality is the toilet paper brand Charmin. The company is engaging and interactive and focuses on a positive tone in all of its conversations on social media. The adjacent message illustrates how Charmin interacted with sports reporter Darren Rovell after the brand sponsored Michigan tight end Jake Butt before the 2017 NFL draft.

Charmin's Interaction Displaying Its Personality on Twitter

Common Writing Mistakes on Social Media

It is possible to make many types of writing mistakes on social media. People write inappropriate content, produce spelling or grammar mistakes, or share false information. Social media is still the first line of communication for a lot of people, and first impressions matter. Making a mistake or taking an approach that is not aligned with how audiences perceive you as an organization or person may lead to further consequences down the line. Here are a few examples of some common mistakes that happen on social media from a writing perspective.

Do not attempt to jump on the bandwagon when it is not appropriate. There is a time and place to interject yourself into a conversation. Ever since Oreo released a tweet during the 2013 Super Bowl ("You can still dunk in the dark"), brands (e.g., United) have tried very hard to interject themselves into a conversation when they have not been invited. Survey the environment and listen to what others are saying. You do not want to start a conversation about how you were "trying too hard" to be relevant on a trending topic or issue. Sometimes, silence is golden.

Source: Twitter/@united

United Jumping Into the #NuggsForCarter Trending Topic

Research all components of your message before posting. Doing your research and double-checking your facts and sources is important. Making sure you use the right image for your message, especially if it is related to a trending event, is key. Otherwise, your mistake will be open for everyone to see and react to, like what happened with Delta when it posted an image for another country rather than Ghana during the World Cup.

Source: Twitter/@Delta

Delta Ghana Tweet

DiGiorno and the #WhyIStayed Crisis

Before engaging in a conversation with a trending hashtag, research the hashtag. In 2014, for example, DiGiorno became a trending topic when it did not research the hashtag #WhyIStayed before creating a message that caused an outrage on Twitter. The #WhyIStayed hashtag was created around the serious issue of domestic violence in light of the NFL cases involving Ray Rice back in 2014. Before speaking, see what people are really talking about.

Nike Twitter Conversation

Check spelling and grammar. Social media is the front door to a brand, and social media managers must be aware that each message and approach to audiences needs to be properly edited before hitting the publish button.

Vera Bradley Instagram Image

Evaluate the possible reactions people might have to your content (good and bad). Before hitting post, ask yourself, "How would people react to this? What are some ways this could be misinterpreted? What are some of the things we would need to address before we send this out?" These extra steps could save brands (like Vera Bradley) a lot of grief and time. People may interpret messages differently, and you may have the right intentions, but if people feel they have been slighted at all on social media, they will come out in full force. Taking the extra time to copy edit and discuss all of these factors will be for the best in the long run.

BEST PRACTICES FOR SOCIAL MEDIA WRITING

Spelling and grammar are still important—and, in fact, are more important than ever—in social media. First impressions matter, and these principles are important in every channel and medium used in communication. While sometimes conversations may be informal online, it is still necessary to use proper grammar and spelling principles. No one wants to see their names misspelled online or to have information presented in a distracted manner. The same principles used in journalism (adherence to a style guide, checking fact errors, etc.) should be not only encouraged in social media writing practices, but enforced. In other words, there is no excuse for spelling mistakes or grammar errors in your updates.

Keep track of the best tools to support your writing. To write the best content, you have to have the right tools and services. While most social media managers use a variety of services for their social media management tools, some are specifically available to help social media managers create the best content possible before hitting the publish button. Here are a few to check out:

- *Grammarly.* This platform allows you to check your grammar and spelling online for a variety of different forms of content. From long-form content to discussion board posts, this tool helps ensure you do not make any grammar or spelling mistakes.

- *Hemingway App.* This tool helps when you are using another program (e.g., Word) to copy and paste content from offline to online.

- *Slick Write.* This online program not only checks grammar and spelling, but helps out with word associations (e.g., thesaurus). It can even check the overall word structure to make sure you are not using the same phrases over and over again, or even writing biased statements you may not have intended to include.

- *Trello.* This is a great tool if you are working on a team (as a social media manager) and want to make sure all of the content going out is synced and aligned with the appropriate message, tone, and content that reflects well on the company. You can have various columns set for ongoing content, completed content, and status of content. This might look similar to a content calendar, but Trello allows the social media team to make everyone aware of the state of the content being created and when it will be executed.

- *Hashtagify.me.* Are you wondering what hashtags to use for your content on social media, specifically Twitter or Instagram? This is a good tool for exploring some of the associated hashtags you might want to use to connect to your key audiences.

- *Ulysses.* Whether you are creating a PDF to upload to SlideShare from a presentation deck or writing content to share on a blog, this tool allows you to download any file, anywhere, which is great for a social media manager on the road.

- *Wordy.* Do you need an editor to review your content? This service allows you to have someone look over your content with another pair of eyes and offer feedback and suggestions.

Brevity is the name of the game. The goal is not to squeeze the highest number of words into a single space. Sometimes, the hardest content to write is the shortest. Your messages should be concise and appropriate for the platform. In some cases, you will be asked to write short-form content (fewer than 140 characters), while in other cases, you will be asked to write long-form content (500–1,000 words). Social media professionals are expected more than ever to embrace multimedia content, or a mixture of short- and long-form content with the addition of multimedia. Whether it is a GIF, video, or infographic attached to an update, all of these elements have to be taken into consideration. Testing these messages based on the platform algorithm (e.g., Facebook versus Twitter) is a very helpful step.

Don't force a certain writing style. Be yourself. While it is tempting to follow in the footsteps of other social media professionals and brands on social media, this may be a temporary fix to addressing key message strategies. Copying others is not viewed as authentic and true to the brand (personal or professional). To build a community and reputation on social media, brands and others have to be true to how they approach their audiences online, and a lot of this depends on how a brand creates content. No one wants to have the same writing style or brand voice on social media—this is almost like the kiss of death. The goal here is to be unique in how you present, share, and create messages using various writing and visual content that is true to who you are. We can always look for inspiration, but we have to ask ourselves, "What are other brands doing that works for them? What can we learn from them as far as how they present their content on social media? What do we have that they do not have? How can we showcase this in a sustainable way across all of our platforms and channels? How does our brand voice on social media impact our mission and vision statement as a brand?" These are just some additional questions we have to continue to ask ourselves and our team members when it comes to our writing style and content.

Put audiences first; write content they not only want to share, but have to. Make sure your content matches what the audience not only needs, but expects to see, from your brand or company on social media.

You want audiences to get the information they need in a quick manner, but also to recognize that they want to experience something in return with the messages and content. **Experiential media** (where audiences feel like they are part of the conversation and community) and content that sparks emotion are more likely to be shared among audience members.

Emphasize embracing messages, not hard-sell messaging. The point of social media is to be social, not to bombard people with paid ads trying to make a quick sell. Social media is about building relationships that could ultimately turn into financial returns, but the steps (whether from a marketing standpoint or a public relations perspective) should never start off with the hard-sell message. Brands have to meet people in a place where they want to actually have a conversation. Not everyone wants to interact with brands on social media—that should be noted and not forced. Understanding the health dynamics of a community (from monitoring and listening protocols) will inform social media professionals about when it is or is not appropriate to enter a conversation with audiences. Evaluating the state of the mood and situation will help determine which messages audiences will embrace, and which messages will be discarded completely or even spark outrage among audiences.

Don't be inconsistent and confuse your audiences. Changes within a company among community managers require a smooth transition to make sure the writing style and brand voice is the same across the channels. You do not want audiences to know there has been a change within the company. Make sure your messages are not full of jargon that is commonly used in the industry but does not translate into other areas. Do not overwhelm your audiences in ways that distract them from the message. It is better to have a clear point and call to action than to distract people with a ton of emojis, visuals, and jargon all communicating different things. Keeping it simple is the name of the game.

Have a balance between your personal and brand voices. Many social media professionals maintain personal and professional accounts. One thing social media professionals struggle with when it comes to writing for their own platforms is the transition between their own personal voice and their professional voice. The purpose of writing on social media is not to make it 100% about you all of the time. You want to have a ratio of four areas when it comes to writing content:

- 25% should focus on your story and personal journey (what you are doing, where you hope to go in the future, what you can offer as a professional and person, etc.).

- 25% should focus on sharing content that may be relevant for your community or industry.

- 25% should focus on engagement (answering questions, giving shout-outs to fellow community members and brands, commenting and sharing your perspectives, etc.).

- 25% should focus on producing value and paying it forward.

Understand the differences in content and writing style based on the platform as well as the audience. Some platforms allow you to communicate visually with not a lot of text, and on other platforms short-form content (fewer than 140 characters) will not be effective or efficient for the intended audiences. For example, updates that are effective on Facebook are a bit longer than those, of course, on Twitter (63,206 compared to 280 characters), but in some cases long-form content will be necessary to explain a concept, idea, or story for an intended audience. Keeping the messages short while writing in an active voice are also elements to consider here, even with the opportunity to write longer pieces on certain platforms.

Be brief and direct. Another goal for writing on social media is not to make it a million pages long. Brevity and concise writing (which sometimes is harder) is the name of the game. Creativity in using each word for a specific purpose is important. However, you do not want to lose your audiences completely by using jargon or emojis they do not understand. We may know what they mean from the social media side of things or even from pop culture, but we have to make sure we edit and tailor our messages to be not only direct, but effective. We are not all mind readers, and you do not want audience members to be confused about what you are trying to communicate on social media. Understanding the call-to-action statements highlighting what you want to do for audiences will be effective in the long term. Tell people what you want them to do based on being exposed to a certain piece of content, but also work toward giving them a direct statement about what to expect once they are exposed to this message.

CHAPTER SUMMARY

Excellent writing for social media is a fundamental task for social media professionals. Writing, like most activities and hobbies, takes time and dedication. Having the right tools and resources to create the best content is extremely important for social media managers. However, in order to become an effective writer, you have to practice writing. Posting content on behalf of a brand, agency, or person requires a strategic framework that identifies the overall brand voice, tone, and writing style to maintain across all of the platforms. Like all aspects of social media, writing style guidelines and expectations for what content should be created on each platform changes, but fundamental skills and best practices remain the same.

THOUGHT QUESTIONS

1. Why is excellent writing for social media important for professionals and brands today?

2. What is the difference between brand voice and tone? How can they be incorporated into social media content?

3. Identify the different writing styles discussed in the chapter. Which ones do you feel are the most effective for brands? Which ones best describe how you approach social media?

4. What are some best practices when it comes to writing for social media? What are some things to avoid doing on social media?

EXERCISES

1. You are a social media manager for a local school system. Some of your colleagues have been watching some larger brands be creative with their writing style, embracing a "snarky" approach. What are some benefits and challenges you would want to identify in this writing style for your client?

2. You are now a social media intern for the Kentucky Derby and Churchill Downs. You have been asked to update a writing style guide for social media for all of their platforms (Facebook, Twitter, Instagram, and Snapchat). What are some things you would want to have in your writing guide? What are a few updates you would suggest they create for Facebook, Instagram, and Twitter?

3. You are programming content to put forth in your content calendar, but you see a trending topic arising in your community. Participating in this trend would be appropriate for you to jump into the conversation. What steps would you want to take before participating in the conversation?

4. You are graduating and about to apply for a job with Droga5, the agency working with Under Armour. If you wanted to showcase your writing skills on social media, what pieces of content would you want to create based on the Under Armour brand voice?

REFERENCES

Baer, J. (2017). Brands need to ditch the social media snark. *Adweek*. Retrieved from http://www.adweek.com/digital/jay-baer-guest-post-brands-need-to-ditch-the-social-media-snark/.

Buffer. (2018). Craft the perfect update for every social platform in one seamless experience. Retrieved from https://buffer.com/tailored-posts?utm_campaign=TP-launch&utm_medium=blog&utm_source=blog-post-cta.

Lee, K. (2014a, April 14). How to find your social media marketing voice: The best examples, questions and guides. *Buffer Social*. Retrieved from https://blog.bufferapp.com/social-media-marketing-voice-and-tone.

Lee, K. (2014b, September 8). 71 ways to write a social media update: Specific tips to engage your followers. *Buffer Social*. Retrieved from from https://blog.bufferapp.com/ways-to-write-social-media-updates.

Morrison, K. (2017, May 16). Brands may think being snarky is cool, but consumers don't (report). *Adweek*. Retrieved from http://www.adweek.com/digital/brands-may-think-being-snarky-is-cool-but-consumers-dont-report/.

Read, A. (2017, May 18). How to craft the perfect post on Facebook, Twitter and Instagram. *Buffer Social*. Retrieved from https://blog.bufferapp.com/how-to-craft-the-perfect-post-on-facebook-twitter-and-instagram.

Seiter, C. (2012, August 13). 20 great social media voices (and how to develop your own). *Marketing Land*. Retrieved from http://marketingland.com/20-great-social-media-voices-and-how-to-develop-your-own-18057.

Wainwright, C. (2017, July 28). How to create a writing style guide built for the web [free template]. *HubSpot*. Retrieved from https://blog.hubspot.com/blog/tabid/6307/bid/31247/The-Simple-Template-for-a-Thorough-Content-Style-Guide.aspx.

8

AUDIENCE SEGMENTATION AND ANALYSIS

Learning Objectives

Humans of Social Media

Introduction

    What Is Audience Segmentation?

Types of Audiences

Communities, Influencers, and Creators

    What Is an Influencer?

    Engaging With Influencers

    Identifying False Influencers

    Creators

    Ambassadors

    Trolls or Haters

Campaigns Using Audience Segmentation

Best Practices

Chapter Summary

Thought Questions

Exercises

References

LEARNING OBJECTIVES

After reading this chapter, you will be able to

- Define audience segmentation and explain why it is important for social media professionals
- Identify audience segmentation categories and how to apply them in a social media context
- Explain the differences between influencers, ambassadors, creators, and trolls/haters

HUMANS OF SOCIAL MEDIA
MICHAEL EHRLICH, VICE PRESIDENT OF MARKETING COMMUNICATIONS FOR INDEPENDENT SPORTS & ENTERTAINMENT

Introduction

I'm a veteran sports communications executive, with global experience working with athletes, entertainers, teams, colleges, brands, leagues, and major sporting events. Currently the vice president of marketing communications for integrated sports, media, entertainment, and management company Independent Sports & Entertainment, I am responsible for building the ISE brand overall and supporting more than 300 MLB, NBA and NFL clients through editorial and social media storytelling and content creation opportunities. I also contribute to frnt-officesport.com, where I explore best practices across the communications and social media industries.

How did you get your start in social media?

I remember first using Twitter in 2009 when I was working at a PR agency and started my own sports blog on the side. At the time, my social media use was solely focused on promoting my site, not really interacting with readers or

(Continued)

(Continued)

Source: Courtesy of Kyle Hannon

Michael Ehrlich

using Twitter as an information source. As social media—Twitter specifically—grew into a go-to news platform, my ways quickly changed. I began leveraging social media as a PR tool for both my business and my personal passions and started to expand my own network at the same time. Meeting new contacts, media personalities, and brand executives became an incredible resource on social media.

What is your favorite part of working in your social media area of expertise?

It's tough to decide on just *one* favorite part, but the fact that social media truly is a network, across the globe—that's what makes the space such a passion for me. The accessibility to industry experts, news sources, athletes, celebrities, and others is invaluable, and the engagement opportunities are endless. Throughout my career, being able to connect with people via social media has been incredibly rewarding— whether that is for my current job or to impart knowledge to the next generation of sports executives. Social media allows you to connect with anyone, anytime.

What is one thing you can't live without while working in social media?

Wi-Fi! (Or at least a strong network connection.) In all seriousness, whenever I watch a live event—whether that's a game, award show, or political debate—I use multiple screens, with at least two of them focused on social media. Beyond the on-air action or analysis, the online commentary and discussion is what entertains me most. Whether it's experts sharing

their thoughts, brands activating in real time, or teams throwing shade, the action on social media is key for my viewing experience. Having slow service puts a major damper on the real-time conversation that I seek.

What is your favorite social media account (person/brand/etc.) to follow, and why?

Person: Shea Serrano, The Ringer. I'm a big fan of Shea's columns and his book *The Rap Year Book*, while his entertaining and hilarious social presence fuses many of my passions in life— basketball, action movies, and hip-hop.

Brand: Beats by Dr. Dre. Not only does Beats partner with a talented and diverse roster of international athletes, musicians, and influencers, but the company is *always* ready with break-through social content the minute one of its ambassadors has success in his or her respective field. Beats is a strong case study on brand marketing in the social space.

What is the most challenging part of working in social media?

The sheer amount of information, content, and conversation on social media is a gift and a curse. It is certainly distracting (for work/life) and challenging as a marketer and brand builder to break through the clutter. If you are planning an announcement or social activation, the competition for eyeballs is now at an all-time high. This trend mirrors the short attention span of today's consumer, making a social media marker's job challenging and putting more pressure on you to create thumb-stopping content.

What is your take on your area of expertise and the social media industry?

I consider myself a storyteller—fusing earned editorial with organic social media—so to be successful today, marketers must adapt to the 24/7 news cycle. The editorial landscape has certainly changed since I started my career, and social media has been at the center of this evolution. PR in particular looks different today than it did only a few years ago, and social media is an invaluable mechanism for brand building, narrative crafting, and breakthrough communication. Moving forward, storytellers must challenge themselves to act faster, communicate quicker, and be more nimble with their strategies and tactics to succeed.

What do you wish you had known when you were starting out?

When I first started using social media professionally and personally, I wish I understood the capabilities of platforms as personal brand-building and networking mechanisms. It took me awhile to figure out the benefits of interacting with folks on social media, picking brains and networking. I now try to answer anyone and everyone who reaches out to me with professional or career inquiries.

Michael Ehrlich is the vice president of marketing communications for ISEWorldwide and the former U.S. director of public relations for adidas. He is also the co-founder of Brand Food, a sports business and marketing think tank. You can connect with Michael on Twitter at @MichaelEhrlich.

INTRODUCTION

What Is Audience Segmentation?

In social media, the goal is not to reach every single person on the planet. Rather, it is more important to focus on the quality of an audience member based on needs, expectations, products and services use, relationship, and engagement. More often than not, social media communities are more **niche** (specifically focused on a particular interest, location, or characteristic) than ever before.

Audience segmentation refers to the process of categorizing people into certain groups based on specific criteria. These criteria can be broad in nature (e.g., demographics and population data) or very specific and focused (niche) on certain characteristics (experiential, visually driven, industry and interest specific, etc.). Audience segmentation is a strategy by which companies, agencies, and brands collect information to create a profile of an audience with which they wish to engage. With insight tools for audience analysis in social media, social media professionals can be very broad in their targeting (prioritizing their audiences and whom they want to reach first) or very specific to the point where they can identify specific people to receive their messages and content. The more you segment your audience, the more focused you will be in narrowing down the people you really want to reach for a social media campaign. You want to reach not everyone, but only those who are relevant for the overall purpose of your social media activities.

Why is it important to be effective in your audience segmentation for a social media campaign? There are several reasons, but a few are especially important:

- *Being more effective in your paid advertisements on social media.* By taking the time to really hone in on the various interests, behaviors, demographics, and channel engagement metrics, social media professionals will reach the right audiences, making the most of their time and financial resources dedicated to social media. Taking the time to gather the data needed to really focus on effective and efficient ads targeted to specific individuals will pay off in the end.

- *Having a clear idea of who you are reaching and what is important to them.* By understanding how audiences think, feel, and behave, social media professionals will have more insight to craft effective pieces of content as assets for their campaign initiatives, promotions, and message strategies.

- *Understanding the range of different touch points for each user.* Users may be engaged with a brand on one channel or on various channels. Audience members should be exposed to the same brand voice and experience across all channels in which they participate. Professionals should provide an **omnichannel approach**, which means a seamless and effortless integration of content, messages, and experiences for the user is linked to multiple communication channels. This is a growing trend for many brands, which realize that their audiences are following and engaging with them on multiple channels. All messages, content assets, and strategies need to be consistent yet tailored appropriately for each audience for each channel.

The first and foremost thing to do before actually implementing ideas for social media is to determine the target audience. Social media professionals sometimes forget that not all audiences gravitate to the same platforms for conversations, news, and information. Understanding each audience will help you develop effective key messages featuring strong points that resonate with each audience member, and help you be more successful in identifying ways to formulate strong connections and relationships.

Certain points of information to include in this analysis go beyond what is typically available in most campaigns. For social media purposes, as described in Chapter 6, we need *demographics* (basic population statistics such as gender, age, location, occupation, and education) and *psychographics* (advanced statistics that focus on the attitudes, opinions, and interests of audience members). For example, we need to know audience views of various news sources and specific motivational factors. Some individuals are motivated by financial or materialistic items (free swag, coupons shared on social media, etc.); however, others are focused on gaining connections and being part of the experience (opportunities for exclusive meetings, sponsored partnerships, VIP treatment for influencers or advocates at events, behind-the-scenes opportunities like at College GameDay, NCAA tournaments, Social Media Marketing World, SXSW, etc.). In addition, different platform channel segments must be considered. While Twitter, Facebook, and Instagram focus on the demographics and psychographics of their audiences, LinkedIn adds specifics about the places people work (industry size, seniority, company, etc.). It is also important to explore the type of user that characterizes an audience. Are the users actively creating content, or are they spectators?

To assist in this type of audience analysis, Forrester created the Forrester Technographics tool in 2011 to outline and divide how people behave online (see go.forrester.com/data/consumer-technographics). Table 8.1 lists different audience categories that might appear in an audience segmentation report.

Several types of audiences are relevant to social media campaigns (see Figure 8.1). As in public relations and marketing, social media professionals consider both internal and external audiences. Internal audiences are individuals who are part of a relevant organization. These could be fellow employees, team leaders, or senior management. Even though most social media activities happen outside of the organization, it is still important to keep the internal audiences well informed. External audiences are those who are outside of the organization, including customers, brand ambassadors, influencers, opinion leaders, and competitors. Each of these audiences will have different motivational factors, attitudes, needs, interests, and social media behaviors to consider. Each audience needs a personalized and tailored approach in the construction of key messages

TABLE 8.1 ■ Outline of Different Audience Segments Relevant to Social Media Campaigns				
Demographics	**Psychographics**	**Platform Specifics**	**Type of Social Media User**	**Social Metrics**
• Age • Gender • Occupation • Race • Location • Language Preference • Relationship status	• Attitudes • Behaviors • Interests • Opinions • Lifestyle • Connections	• Life stage • Company size • Industry • Function/job • Type of user • Influence and presence in the network • Network and place in the community • Loyalty to brand	• Creator • Inactive • Collector • Spectator • Critic • Joiner	• Specific digital behaviors on certain platforms • Likes/follows/interests • Time spent on platforms • Time of day/week most active and responsive • Top word associations (e.g., word cloud) • Top bio word associations (e.g., platform bios) • Content that resonates with audiences on certain platforms • Device used • Other similar interests/brands users follow • Topics they are influential on • Other brands they are connected with • Sentiment toward other brands and accounts on social media

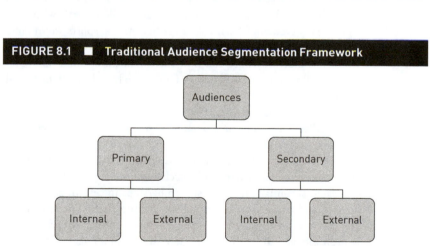

FIGURE 8.1 ■ Traditional Audience Segmentation Framework

as well as the execution of these messages and strategies. One message may not resonate with all audiences, and taking the time to personalize the messages and approaches on social media to each audience will allow you to foster stronger and more stable relationships.

TYPES OF AUDIENCES

Data are a social media professional's best friend when it comes to identifying key audiences and organizing them based on priority and focus. First and foremost, brands and professionals on social media must use the data collected through monitoring and listening techniques to identify the audience they are reaching on social media. Second, these results should be compared to traditional offline reports about these audiences.

The *primary audience* is made up of the individuals you want to target first. *Secondary audiences* are linked to the primary messages, but are not necessarily the key audiences you want to reach at first. (See Chapter 6.) Instead, these could be additional audiences that help persuade and influence the particular audiences you are trying to reach. For example, if you are trying to reach Generation Z, you may want to focus on certain peer groups or influencers these individuals trust and value based on certain interests (sports, fashion and beauty, consumer and design creations, etc.). **Emerging audiences** are those you want to note as individuals, based on the monitoring and listening they do on social media; they could transform into a key primary audience. These audiences are growing in momentum based on their interactivity and engagement with the brand that may be worthy to note for the purpose of social media campaigns and initiatives. For example, brands looking to tap into the Generation Z audience may want to explore high-profile influencers such as Zendaya (as Verizon has done with the #WeNeedMore STEM campaign) and Manny Gutierrez (a male beauty blogger who has signed with Maybelline and Rimmel) (Adweek Staff, 2017).

Opponents, also known as **critics**, are self-explanatory—these audiences are not the biggest fans of the brand or company you represent. Instead, they wish for negative consequences to happen to the brand. They are very active in sharing their views and how they feel about you. Some of these negative opinions could be based on previous experiences, or they could be unprovoked. These voices come from a range of different industries and types of audiences. Looking at a college sports team, for example, such as the USC Trojans, one group that would be listed in this opponent category is UCLA, because the schools are academic and athletic rivals within the city of Los Angeles. However, additional audiences beyond the sports world could include fans, alums, and even other schools outside the area. In any case, it is important to note who these individuals are and how their main motivations and goals might impact the overall success and well-being of your own brand, client, or organization on social media.

Within each of these categories, social media professionals need to construct personas for each audience based on demographics, psychographics, social media behaviors, and channel action characteristics (how individuals use certain channels specifically, like connecting with friends, sharing updates, networking with professionals, etc.). These personas will help describe each audience in a way that outlines key motivational factors, similar experiences, memberships in certain groups, attitudes and behaviors, and trusted sources outside of the campaign. The more information that can be gathered about an audience, the more informed and effective a social media professional will be in crafting key strategic messages. These messages should focus on the connection that needs to be made on a cognitive (sharing information, knowledge, etc.), affective (emotions and feelings that resonate with the audiences), and conative level (calls to action, focusing on encouraging certain audience behaviors). All messages need to be personalized, tailored, and properly tested to make sure the audience in question understands and will act in desirable ways based on these messages.

COMMUNITIES, INFLUENCERS, AND CREATORS

In addition to key audiences to target in social media efforts, other sources of influence must be considered.

Communities, introduced in Chapter 7, can be hosted by individuals, groups, or brands. Online communities encompass a group of people who are invested and interested in a similar issue, brand, or area of expertise. For example, one popular Facebook group for social media professionals is the VIP Mastermind Group, created by Carlos Gil. This community focuses on sharing the latest updates on social media trends, issues, and campaigns, and discusses situations and challenges facing the field. Some communities are open to everyone while others are more exclusive.

Brands can build communities to meet several goals. Some brand communities are designated for loyal customers and fans who want to become ambassadors for the brand. For the most part, they want to create communities where like-minded people can come together to brainstorm, engage, and share knowledge and ideas in a specific space. This space can be hosted within the brand's community (website, etc.) or as an extension of a specific social media site (Twitter with Twitter chats, etc.).

As mentioned before, many channels and platforms can be used to create and maintain a particular community for social media. Each platform is used differently, but what is important is tapping into the motivational factors driving people to specific communities and to each channel. Do they want to be educated about the latest trends in social media? This may be a case for creating videos on YouTube that explore each new trend step-by-step. Or is your audience focusing on building connections in the sports world with fellow industry leaders? If this is the case, getting active and involved on Twitter using the hashtag #SMsports (for those who practice and work in social media and sports) can be effective. Regardless of the purpose, audiences expect certain common features from each community:

- *Exclusivity.* Information and being in the know is powerful. People want to feel like they are getting something that not everyone else is getting. Having the opportunity to get information and updates first is one of the main reasons communities in social media exist. Make sure what you are providing in each community is valuable.

- *Tone.* We are all busy people, and we want to be part of communities created over time that are positive and engaging. However, some members of communities do not follow the rules, so policies for dealing with these individuals must be proactive. Expectations for what is acceptable and what is not, along with clear statements about what will be done if policies are not followed, should be emphasized across all channels and platforms populated by the community. This helps set the overall tone and expectations for the audience and community.

- *Consistency.* People do not want to be part of communities that are all over the place. Communities need a centralized mission, goal, or purpose.

- *Sustainability.* Communities are not formed and immediately abandoned. They are constantly maintained and invested in by the hosts and main administrators. If the members of an audience know a video will be uploaded every day, they will change their behavior to make sure they are there to see it.

Table 8.2 shows some of the ways in which individuals as well as brands can use each specific social media platform to create and maintain a social media community. The third column focuses on tools for evaluating the success of engagement and interactions with each audience based on the platform.

Within each community, some individuals will have a dominant or prominent voice. Communities host a variety of different individuals, who in their own right have created their own brand and media outlet to the point where they are deemed

TABLE 8.2 ■ Platform, Audience Engagement Practices, and Tools to Measure Success Template		
Facebook	• Build a community within Facebook Groups. • Create a public profile page to manage your personal brand with audiences. • Promote your Facebook Group with relevant audience members. • Decide whether or not to make this group open, closed, or secret. • Create a Facebook show to share your ideas in real time. Schedule a time and send out announcements that audience members can save and put into their calendars. • Create branded filters for audiences to demonstrate their membership in a group, conference, or organization (e.g., Facebook frames for Facebook profiles)	• Facebook Audience Insights • Facebook Live (e.g., BlueJeans or BeLive) • Creative Suite for content to use for sponsored and targeted ads
Twitter	• Reach out and communicate with others in Twitter chats. • Possibly host/guest host a Twitter chat. • Create a branded hashtag for your community to share articles, updates, and resources. • Mix content from pushing messages to engaging (answering questions and personalizing each response). • Check in on relevant hashtags for events and professional activities. • Follow and reach out to fellow professionals.	• Hootsuite • Sprout Social • Buffer • Tweet Binder • TweetAnalyzer • Tagboard • Suggested chats: #Hootchat, #SweetTalk, #SocialROI, #AdobeChat, #SMstudentchat, #TwitterSmarter
Instagram	• Post consistently with relevant updates and content. • Focus on emotional content to truly connect with audiences. Content that is entertaining helps the audience grow and be more informed, connect by using emotion, and so on. • Answer questions in Instagram Stories, live video, and comments on your posts. • Save Instagram stories that feature certain interests, expertise areas, experiences, and topics on your Instagram page. Create a branded title cover that is universal for your brand. • Integrate messages with a strong call to action. Tag audience members, comment, follow, share, and so on—all of these actions can help build upon messages.	• Iconosquare • Canva • VSCO • Camera+ • Hype Type • Hyperlapse • Adobe Lightroom and Photoshop • Adobe Spark Post and Video

	• Research potential hashtags to add to your content. • Save comments you like from audiences. • Reach out and comment on other posts and pictures. • Host an Instagram Live session inviting others to participate or focus on a particular issue or topic you'd like to cover.	• Repost • Crowdfire • #ChatGram
Snapchat	• Provide content on a consistent basis that is also exclusive. • Listen and respond to comments and questions. Create stories not only for you, but for your audiences. • Be authentic and true to your audiences. • Experiment to create a personalized lens for events with Snapchat Lens. • Engage in individual and group chats with audiences. • Recognize that Snapchat is not like other platforms, but rather is focused on building upon a story with each new follower. • Have specific points and messages you want to share with audiences. Have a call to action to get them to share content.	• #ChatSnap Twitter chat
LinkedIn	• Reach out to groups to gain access to them to be able to learn, network, and build on your knowledge base. • Create content that resonates with the interests of your audience as well as trending topics. • Acknowledge comments and thank audience members who share your work with others. • Create content relevant to the LinkedIn channels you are interested in and tag them (#) when publishing content on LinkedIn.	• LinkedIn Pulse • Canva (Graphic Post Creator)
YouTube	• Be authentic with your audience and provide consistent content. • Create and share videos about you and your audience. • Have a call to action for your audience members to subscribe to your channel so they do not miss any updates. • Respond to comments and pin top comments at the top of your feed for others to see. • Acknowledge comments. • Reward audiences with exclusivity. • Develop exercises, timelines, and a storyboard framework for your content that resonates with audiences. • Disseminate content across other channels used by your audience.	• YouTube Creator Studio • Canva thumbnails branded for each channel
Digital Media	• Host content in a centralized resource. • Create content and recaps from events and discussions. • Create and launch webinar sessions. • Send out email newsletters for updates and resources. • Provide white papers and presentations that can be downloaded and used in the future.	• MailChimp • Adobe Dreamweaver • Adobe Spark Page • Canva presentations

powerful and persuasive in nature. These influencers are at the focal point of a lot of brands today. Brands and audiences have recognized that many people are gravitating to these influencers rather than to paid spokespeople. However, as discussed later in this chapter, there are challenges and benefits to engaging with influencers.

Types of influencers will be discussed in more detail below. **Creators** are a subset of influencers who focus on creating original content in their own voice for brands rather than just sharing brand-created content. They view their creativity as the most important element of their contribution to their partnership with the brand (Ingalls, 2017). **Ambassadors** are advocates for the brands, but they are perhaps not as influential and focused on reach and numbers as influencers are.

What Is an Influencer?

Influence is defined as "the capacity of power of persons or things to be a compelling force on or produce effects on the actions, behavior, opinions, etc. of others" (Bentwood, 2008, p. 5).

One of the key stakeholders for corporations and agencies presently to target are social media influencers (first defined in Chapter 2), or individuals who are "passionate and skilled professionals who know how to communicate, engage, and create dialogue for all the right reasons" (Solis & Breakenridge, 2009, p. 94). Social media influencers have the power to voice their "thoughts and ideas to be posted online and commented on by millions of users instantly" (Prentice & Huffman, 2008, p. 1). What can influencers do for brands, agencies, and others to benefit their social media campaigns? What are some of their unique characteristics? The specialization involved in researching, engaging, and working with influencers to formulate partnerships with brands and other parties based on their aligned interests and goals is referred to as **influencer marketing**. Influencer marketing is becoming one of the more prominent and fast-paced areas of specialization social media professionals can get into. While most of the time people associate influencer marketing just with targeting audiences on Instagram (Jackson, 2018), every platform has its designated influencers. In fact, there are certain elements social media professionals need to know about influencer marketing, as Jackson (2018) outlines:

- Brands and influencers have to disclose their relationship and partnership to follow Federal Trade Commission guidelines (see Chapter 2 for examples of cases where this did not happen).

- Influencers should be creating relevant content, not just ads, for the brand in their partnerships (e.g., Casey Neistat and Samsung).

- Brands should listen to and partner with the influencers who *actually* love and believe in the products and services they are using (e.g., comedian Tiffany Haddish is now Groupon's official spokesperson after disclosing she uses the company's services constantly).

Social media influencers represent an **online persona**, or an identity constructed by an individual online that may or may not represent who he or she truly is in real life (Zhao, Grasmuck, & Martin, 2008). This type of construction using online technologies creates a new way for individuals to manage how they want to be perceived in terms of their identities and reputations (Zhao et al., 2008). Researchers need more work to conceptualize these individual influencers. For example, are these people perceived as taking the leadership role with their followers? What are some things that others say about them? How much presence do they have online and in the virtual community? Researchers and professionals in public relations and reputation management need to understand how these individuals create these influences, what attributes are assigned to them by their followers, and what makes them appear credible and trustworthy. Understanding how the social media influencer persuades others is important for organizations (Bentwood, 2008).

What do we know about the influencer? An influencer is someone who has built an audience, naturally and over time, and is viewed as an authority figure on a certain subject, area, or perspective in the online space. In addition, an influencer has trust of a community, which allows the influencer to persuade audiences to take a specific action based on what is shared. Influencers bring their experiences, unique perspectives, and brand voice to the table, which makes it difficult to categorize influencers in a consistent way. Some influencers have a strong standing based on their role and profession (entertainment, sports, media, etc.), but for the most part, influencers are regular people with a passion, interest, and dedication to create a name for themselves within their specific industry and community.

Influencers can be compensated in a variety of different ways. Celebrity endorsements, product placements, and statements of support are just some of the traditional ways in which influencers can be used. *Influencers, compared to celebrity endorsers who are paid spokespeople, are more relatable and viewed as a trustworthy source of information.* The primary focus of influencers is to drive conversations and build community around issues and brands that are key to their own interests and investments. This means that they are not going to promote anything that is "off their brand" and unrelated to what they are passionate about. If they do deviate from their brands, they will lose trust within their community. Authenticity and being true to who they are is extremely important. Yet, when it comes to endorsements, influencers are required to acknowledge to their community whether they are getting paid or are sponsored by the brand or another entity for their posts. In general, many audiences feel that posts tagged #sponsored or #ad are not authentic (Minsker, 2017).

Influencers have built their communities over time, not with endorsements, but rather through constant social connections. These conversations emerge across different social media platforms and in different circles. Some influencers have used Snapchat (e.g., Ginicanbreathe) to maintain engagement with their fans, while others have used Instagram (e.g., Shonduras) or YouTube (e.g., Casey Neistat and Roberto Blake).

Influencers know who gave them their influence, and they respect and value this tremendously. All influencers know they would not be where they are without their communities and fans. Both Halsey and Casey Neistat pointed this out during their presentations at the Cannes Lions International Festival of Creativity in 2017. Without the commitment of their fans, Halsey and Neistat would not have risen to the top of their respective professions, music and vlogging. Both of these influencers have been able to get some incredible opportunities for their brands (Neistat is now working with CNN, and Halsey's records are going platinum and she is selling out concerts).

Social media professionals must be somewhat cautious when evaluating influencers. Some individuals acting as

Ryan Seacrest Interviewing Halsey at Cannes Lions Festival

Source: Courtesy of Karen Freberg

Source: Courtesy of Karen Freberg

Casey Neistat
Presenting at
Cannes Lions Festival

influencers may not be presenting true information about who they really are in life, but rather may be projecting the ideal self they strive to be. People construct these online personas to "hide their undesired physical features, and anonymity allows individuals to re-create their biography and personality" (Zhao et al., 2008, p. 1818). In terms of personality characteristics, most research has focused on the "Big Five" factors of personality: extraversion, neuroticism, openness to experience, agreeableness, and conscientiousness (McCrae & John, 1992; Ross et al., 2009). In a research study focusing on Facebook, Ross et al. (2009) suggested that certain personality characteristics can be associated with and attributed to individuals based on how they present themselves on social networking sites. Part of the process of creating an online persona is to determine what personality associations and attributes are being made about you and how to frame them (Gosling, Ko, Mannarelli, & Morris, 2002). People might not appear authentically, but we can still figure out their personality. We need to be able to hone in on our metrics and analytical skills to determine and identify not just those individuals who say they are "influential," but whether or not their actions and the quality of their engagements with audiences show they are truly authentic.

Engaging With Influencers

Not all influencers are willing to engage with their audiences. This is something to expect—some individuals are only interested in promoting their work, while others wish to stay within their close network (think of it as their "circle of trust" like Robert De Niro's character states in the movie *Meet the Parents*). However, once you identify which influencers to reach and start a conversation with, make sure you are engaging with their content. Are you sharing their live videos? Are you commenting on their posts and sharing them with your audiences?

How do brands and social media professionals identify which influencers they want to reach out to and would be relevant for their campaigns? Specific agencies and tools are available for identifying influencers based on specific interests and networks. Others can identify active members of your community, who can then become ambassadors for your brand:

- *Klear.* This tool focuses on identifying influencers on three major networks (Facebook, Instagram, and Twitter) and categorizes them on four different types of influence: celebrities, power users, casual, and novice. This tool also provides an option to hone in on certain skills (sports, blogging, etc.) as well as location.

- *BuzzSumo.* This is a good tool for identifying not only audience members who have influence, but what content they are driving to their networks that is rising in popularity and influence. The reports show not only the audience of the influencer, but the retweet ratio, reply ratio, and average shares on social media. With average shares, you can see how many times on average others are willing to share their content with their own audiences on their respective platforms (e.g., Twitter and Facebook).

- *Followerwonk.* This popular free tool showcases certain accounts based on the key words used in Twitter user bios. The tool sorts audience members based on their level of authority on certain subjects. Another good feature of this tool is its ability to identify members who are following you, your competitors, or others.

- *Onalytica.* This paid service allows brands and others to map, listen, measure, and discover the most relevant social media influencers in their database.

- *Traackr.* This paid service helps identify the current list of influencers in your own network, and also uncovers those who are influencing the influencers. In addition, Traackr provides ways to quantify the relationships, exchanges, and value each influencer has for your brand's campaign.

- *Talkwalker.* This paid service allows audiences to identify key members who are driving the traffic on certain key search terms.

- *Zoomph.* This enterprise platform tool calculates its own metric (Zscores) to determine who is really influencing the behavior and actions of audiences based on the audience's response to their comments.

The fact of the matter is influencers want to see you, as their audience member, value their input and content, and they are willing (or, in some cases, feel it is necessary because the information and content is so relevant to them) to share the same content with their own networks. The first step here is to show active engagement and conversation. Second is to think about ways in which you (as your own media outlet with your respective channels) create content about the influencer. Will you feature the influencer in a blog post or LinkedIn Pulse article? What about interviewing the influencer for a podcast or live show? How will you help the influencer branch out? Many influencers are looking to expand their own reach and audience, and these are ways to accomplish both your goals and the influencer's. Another way to interact with influencers is to see if you can take the conversations from online to offline. Go to events, conferences, or speaking engagements where influencers are featured. See if you can meet up with them in person.

Other ways to engage with influencers include the following:

- *Cite them in research and professional publications.* Do you have a white paper to do for a social media client? Make sure to cite influencers' work and showcase examples of what they have done for their clients. Many influencers have search engines and programs notify them when someone has mentioned them online (Google Alerts, Mention, Talkwalker, BuzzSumo, etc.), so they will note and share this content with others.

- *Give them shout-outs during Twitter chats.* Many times, one question that comes up during professional Twitter chats is "Which influencers would you recommend that the community follow?" Share their user handles and give them a shout-out. Do this on a reoccurring basis to help establish a trustworthy relationship with the influencers.

- *Initiate conversations.* These should be natural and authentic. Reach out to influencers not just for the sake of reaching out to them, but with a specific purpose in mind. State why you are contacting them and why this relationship is important. Influencers will not reach out to you directly, so you will have to take the first step to start the conversation. But, make sure you have a purpose and game plan for not only how you are going to do it, but why.

- *Offer them feedback from a new perspective.* Influencers, like celebrities occasionally, may hear the same thing over and over again from people in their circles. They may also have "yes people"—people who agree with them on everything no matter what. But you can create posts and share insights from a different perspective. Think about what you can offer these influencers that is unique and has not yet been addressed. This will allow you to separate yourself in their eyes by offering something new and different. Attention is the current currency in social media in many ways, but creativity is the foundation to which people respond.

Keep in mind that some influencers are exactly how they present themselves online. These influencers truly understand the complete picture of communities and their role as influencers. Do not be surprised, however, to see some influencers behave differently in person. Some people are much more comfortable communicating with a barrier (computer screen, mobile phone, etc.) between themselves and their audience. Or, they forget how they act online and behave differently anyway.

When approaching an influencer, brands, organizations, and professionals need to ask themselves some additional questions about influencers. Campaign US interviewed WHOSAY CEO Paul Kontonis (2017) about these questions, which include the following:

- Who is following the influencer? Is the influencer engaged with his or her audiences, and what are the characteristics of the audience community?

- Does the audience of the influencer align with your audience? How will you determine this based on your research using audience segmentation strategies?

- What's the influencer's history? Is the influencer professional? How long has he or she been on social media? Which brands has the influencer worked with previously on campaigns and initiatives?

- Can you afford the influencer? Is he or she a celebrity influencer or a micro-influencer (an individual who is highly focused on a particular issue or area)?

- What are your overall goals? Is this partnership just an add-on, or will the partnership help achieve the key performance indicators you have set forth in your campaign?

Identifying False Influencers

Before attempting to identify false influencers, it's important to understand what real influencers are like. There are two influencer groups. The members of one group focus on promoting themselves and presenting a certain image and lifestyle for others to aim for with their large following, while the members of the other group focus on providing value, and everything they share and create is about contributing to their communities and real business (Yu, 2017).

You can identify false influencers at an initial, superficial level just by looking at their publicly available metrics. For example, if individuals have 100,000 followers on Twitter, why do they only have one or two likes or favorites on their tweets? In addition, you can always look at the followers and those who comment on their work on Instagram and YouTube. There are ways to identify the bots (automated programs that do certain actions) on each of these sites. Their profiles are usually all the same, have basic information, and often comment "Like this!" or make another generic request. An ethical issue that comes up with influencers is "buying" followers. This is a no-no for social media professionals, because it is very easy to detect the fake profiles and who has and who has not bought an audience. Yes, it is important to grow your network and gain exposure for your expertise within the community, but buying followers is a short-term solution with long-term negative reputation consequences. Quality in followers and community is always better than quantity.

False influencers also focus on the refollow–unfollow technique. The follow–follower ratio is constantly debated in the area of influencers and social media professionals. Some are more likely to follow their engaged audiences, but others will follow a large number of people, see who follows them back, and then immediately unfollow these same people. This helps create the illusion they have a large audience, but in reality, it upsets people when they are viewed only as a follower number to boost false influencers' ego with the size of their community. This practice is indeed looked down upon. Another emerging trend is the increased use of bots. Affordable for the most part, these bots are programmed to like, comment, and help create followers for certain accounts (Chen, 2017). While this may result in a short-term gain from a vanity metrics perspective (lots of followers equals influence in some people's minds), it is not recommended as a long-term focus for influencers and brands. Some people fear that having an insufficient number of followers on social media will not afford them some of the professional opportunities offered to others, but this does not paint a good picture for the potential influencer. While bots may boost followership and the illusion of influence, if an account has a large following on Instagram (100,000 or more, for example) with no real likes or comments, it is easy to tell the influencer either paid for followers or used bots to create a false presentation.

Dennis Yu (2017), the chief technology officer for BlitzMetrics, outlined how to detect "real influencers" by asking relevant questions:

- Are they actually publishing their knowledge openly rather than just getting paid endorsements?

- Does their network include fellow colleagues or other influencers who help create a mutually beneficial relationship?

- Are they focused on their numbers rather than the connections and health of their communities?

- Have they let their numbers/partnerships/internet fame get to their head and make them forget the real purpose of social media?

- Do they have the experience, and are they able to show the evidence of their work through measureable results based on what they are preaching?

- Are they creating, curating, and engaging with content related to their business, or promoting just themselves?

These factors are relevant not only when exploring potential influencers with whom to partner on campaigns, but also when thinking about your own personal brand. All of us are influential or famous to someone, so we have to be true to who we are (personal brand), and also look at our own actions within our community. A personal brand is defined by a person's actions (not numbers).

Creators

It is easy to confuse creators (people who are useful because of their creative insights and strategy) with influencers (people who have the talent to create a large audience and community) (Bernazzani, 2017). Many influencers claim to be creators because they produce videos, images, or other content that can be consumed on blogs and other online locations. In the current social media environment, creators are perceived more positively than influencers.

Ambassadors

Another type of audience to consider for social media are those who advocate for and promote your work based on their own personal interests and investment with the brand, agency, organization, or person in question. Individuals who leverage their own loyalty as a currency are known as ambassadors. They could be loyal customers, proud alumni and students, or engaged fans, to name a few. To create a successful ambassador program or initiative takes dedication and investment on the part of an organization, brand, or agency because these relationships must be fostered over time. Having a strong internal culture can be helpful in recruiting and engaging external audiences to be part of the community.

Hootsuite has an ambassador program that focuses on engaging professionals who not only use Hootsuite products in their work, but are actively supportive of and loyal to the company. Amplify is a specific tool used to share resources and updates, allowing Hootsuite to disseminate messages, spark ideas, and share content generated

Source: Hootsuite Inc., https://hootsuite.com/community

Hootsuite Amplify Ambassador Program

What Type of Yelp Elite Are You?

Introducing Michael F. as **The Writer**

Introducing Christy A. as **The Photographer**

Introducing Chris W. as **The Adventurer**

The Writer

Sure, some people review everything, but it's not just about how many opinions you can pound out! Whether you review in haiku, max out the review character count, or detail everything, words are your thing. Do you live to write? Is Yelp your blog? Do you love sharing your experiences?

You're The Writer.

The Photographer

Sometimes it's about shooting from the hip, sometimes it's about getting the whole picture, and sometimes... it's just about the food porn. Do you capture every moment? Do you take 10 minutes to line up each shot? Do you live life through the lens?

You're The Photographer.

The Adventurer

There are reviews, there are photos, and then there's just being a total explorer. From hidden forests to brand new local hot spots, you're all about discovery. Do you love that First To Review badge? Do you barely go a week without finding new adventures? Do you come alive outside 9–5?

You're The Adventurer.

Source: www.yelp.com/elite

Yelp Elite Ambassador (YES!) Program

by its ambassadors. The role of ambassador is often voluntary, but sometimes the title of ambassador is applied to employees. Ambassadors can be both internal and external audience members, depending on the scope and overall goal for the brand.

Yelp (2018) also has a consistent and valued ambassador program. The Yelp Elite Squad (YES!) rewards active and engaged Yelp users. To be part of this program, Yelp users must have submitted a range of well-written reviews, participate in active polling and ranking of various brands and places on the site, and have a history of engaging positively with others. Once in the program, users are part of an exclusive community where they can share their stories from their own perspective, but also connect with others in the Yelp community. Along with these benefits, the currency exchanged here between the brand and its ambassadors is the authenticity of true users who believe in the mission and purpose of Yelp; exclusivity in hearing new developments, events, and openings; and ability to list themselves as ambassadors with a prominent brand recognizable by others.

Maker's Mark, which works with Doe Anderson and Taylor Cochran as the social media lead for the brand voice and strategy, is another company with an ambassador program for active and enthusiastic fans. As part of the program, specific industry perks are available, such as the chance to have your name on a Maker's Mark barrel, advance notice of special released bottles, and swag from the brand. This more traditional ambassador program is not dependent on social media, possibly due to the nature of the product (bourbon) and government regulations that limit the company's marketing and advertising to certain audiences.

These are examples of established ambassador programs, but anyone can create an ambassador program for his or her audiences. Mack Collier (2017) provided some good points to keep in mind when thinking about creating an ambassador program and how to launch it for social media strategy purposes:

Research. Use the data you are collecting to recognize the most engaged and active members of your community and what they share. Are they an authoritative voice in the community with others? When did they start engaging with the brand, and what is their overall sentiment toward you online? Identifying these individuals and evaluating whether their characteristics and personae match with your brand is an important step.

Have exclusivity. Your group should meet certain criteria and requirements for participation. This way, you can determine the audience members who are truly passionate and committed to the program versus those who are not. Similar to what Charlie experienced with Willy Wonka and the Chocolate Factory, you want to provide tests, scenarios, and potential obstacles for people to complete to determine who gets into the group and who doesn't.

Offer perks and connections to the brand directly. Sometimes brand ambassadors (like influencers) are paid, but the compensation may not be financial. These ambassadors may get other perks like exclusives on new ideas and product launches, or even swag. The perk in many cases is the opportunity to connect with people within a brand about which you are passionate. These connections are exclusive and can be more valuable to ambassadors than financial incentives. This all comes down to what you feel ambassadors are looking for and what they value most, which can be addressed and explored through research.

Give them power to create and share content. Ambassadors are as creative as creators themselves, and you want (as a brand) to give them the opportunity to showcase this content with their networks. They may be even more effective since they are passionate and invested in the subject and brand.

Start small and grow big. You may start your group with just a few people, but as word spreads, your numbers may increase and you can start creating a group of passionate and energetic audience members who will be loyal to you.

Focus on building a lifestyle, not a product. Some ambassador programs focus primarily on the product (e.g., Maker's Mark), but there is also the need for emphasizing a certain lifestyle within the community that is relevant to the brand. Red Bull, for example, has a college ambassador program, which allows the company to build its product by partnering with fans of the product in a specific market. Red Bull has focused not just on the product, but also on what the product means and represents through experiences, fun activities, and interactions with the brand directly in various settings on college campuses.

Trolls or Haters

Jay Baer wrote a book called *Hug Your Haters* (2016) focusing on how to deal with people who are not the biggest fans of your work. These individuals are sometimes referred to as trolls or haters. They are usually the accounts that comment, tag, and share your work and do not have the most positive things to say about you. Some are merely negative, but others are abusive.

Brands must ensure that they set a policy that prevents these individuals from disrupting or influencing the overall tone or dynamics of the community. Some trolls may not like certain people or brands because of what they stand for, but there could be other reasons as well. These "haters" may have had a negative experience as a customer that turned their view of the company in a negative direction. This is why social care (e.g., customer service, discussed in detail in Chapter 12) is so important on social media. Making sure you address and handle each exchange in a consistent manner could prevent relationships from turning sour. Most of the time, if people have a negative experience with a brand, the deciding factor that determines their future support of a brand is communication (or lack of it) with the brand.

Every brand has followers and audiences who do not like it for some reason, but problems result not simply from having these individuals among your audience, but rather from completely ignoring them. Be aware of your trolls and what they may or may not do, but deleting or ignoring them completely will cause damage in the long run. One way to deal with these individuals is to make sure you have audience members who are supportive and loyal to what you have been doing on social media and as a brand, and who will thus come to your defense.

As you can see from reviewing the previous sections outlining influencers, creators, ambassadors, and trolls or haters, each group is categorized based on what it is leveraging with brands and the social media community. Each audience has distinct characteristics and goals in mind when it comes to interactions and expectations from brands. Table 8.3 outlines the key differences among each of these audiences.

CAMPAIGNS USING AUDIENCE SEGMENTATION

The soda brand Mountain Dew has approached its influencer program slightly differently than other brands (Shields, 2017). Most of the time, influencers are engaged outside of the brand community and are brought in to formulate creative and formal partnerships with the brand.

Mountain Dew took a different direction, creating its own digital media influencers (Shields, 2017), for several reasons. First, influencer marketing has skyrocketed both in popularity and in cost, and many influencers are demanding more and more from brands for their endorsements. Second, Mountain Dew wanted to have a bit more control and say in the content being created by these influencers to make

TABLE 8.3 ■ Differences Between Influencers, Creators, Ambassadors, and Trolls/Haters

Influencers	Creators	Ambassadors	Trolls/Haters
• Leverage size of audience	• Leverage opportunities for creativity	• Leverage level of loyalty and commitment	• Leverage level of outrage and anger toward brands and communities
• Paid endorsements	• Paid endorsements	• Paid endorsements and exclusive access	• View their negative engagement with brands on social media as a spectator sport for the world to see
• Access to brand and events	• Partnership	• Ambassadors are in control of amount of participation involved	
• Brands are in control of relationship for brand voice	• Creators are in control of creativity execution	• Two-way commitment/ co-creation	• Always looking for you to respond in a way that validates their views
• One-way commitment	• Two-way commitment/ co-creation	• E.g., Red Bull student ambassadors	• Constant interactions and comments
• E.g., Lilly Singh	• E.g., Casey Neistat, Shonduras, Shaun Ayala	• Disclose identity and connection	• Tag media outlets for recognition of actions
• Disclose identity and connection/ payment (Federal Trade Commission regulations)	• Disclose identity under name or nickname		• Sometimes do not disclose identity (anonymous)

sure the brand voice was consistent and sustainable across all creative assets being implemented on social media. This approach has shifted the focus from reaching out to influencers who may be aligned with the brand voice and message, to cultivating a set of audience members within the established brand culture for the company and to recognizing the brand voice and community from the start. Instead of focusing on large numbers of influencers to tap, Mountain Dew focused on four, shifting the focus again to working with creators and influencers who produce quality engagements that return results tied to the business and bottom line for the brand rather than mass production of many updates from a lot of people (Shields, 2017). The result of this new focused approach has been encouraging for the Mountain Dew brand, which has received more than 326 million video views from the four designated influencers with whom it is working (Shields, 2017).

Another brand integrating influencers within its various social media campaigns is the shoe company adidas. Adidas has been using both influencers and micro-influencers in its campaigns for the last few years, especially on social media (Joseph, 2017). Micro-influencers may not have the reach of the established celebrities we commonly see in brand campaigns like Steph Curry for Under Armour or LeBron James for Nike. Instead, **micro-influencers** have a specific focus, community, and purpose that help brand messages resonate with audiences. These specific types of influencers have a particular focus, niche, or interest they promote specifically on their social media sites (Bernazzani, 2017).

Other benefits of using micro-influencers, based on research by Markerly (n.d.), include more engagement because their communities are hyper-focused and engaged, have more targeted audience bases, and are more affordable. Engaging with audiences who have a decent reach yet whose content is consumed and viewed much more may be a way for brands to effectively target their focused audiences in a campaign. In addition, there are always concerns related to main influencers on the measurement front and whether or not partnering with an influencer will help achieve business goals and the measurement objectives set forth for the campaign. Instead, by using micro-influencers, brands can tie into specific markets aligned with their own views, and work with these individuals to make sure it's a win-win situation and the partnership is grounded on authenticity, not money.

Adidas, following the trends of other brands like La Croix, used micro-influencers in a partnered effort with Glitch to promote a new set of soccer cleats. Adidas reached out to 30 players from football (soccer) academies in London not only to help promote the new product for the company, but to help design and name it. This partnership was a team effort, but it was focused on utilizing the communities and power of word-of-mouth communication from each player in a way that helped create ownership of the content from the brand's side as well as the micro-influencers' side.

So @adidasUS/@adidasrunning just made a lifetime fan out of me! Sent me #freeswag to help me w/ my Couch-To-5k! 😄 #teamadidas #HereToCreate➕

6:46 PM - 18 Jul 2017 from Leesburg, VA

8 Retweets 156 Likes

Geoffrey Blosat and adidas Running

Source: Twitter/@GeoffTBlosat

The skill of adidas in handling its audiences is illustrated by the case of Geoffrey Blosat, a digital analyst for the Washington Redskins and an active member of the sports and social media (#SMsports) group on Twitter. Blosat was training for his first 5K. Before and after each workout, he would take a picture and tag @adidasrunning in his posts to show the company he was using its shoes for his training. During back-and-forth exchanges over the next few weeks, adidas reached out to Geoffrey about sending him a package. The package sent included a handwritten note with a few swag items to help Geoffrey with his 5K journey. This action prompted Geoffrey to share this package from adidas not only with the community, but also with the sports and social media professionals with whom he is connected on Twitter and Instagram. This community is considered very focused, but in this group, Geoffrey is an influencer in the area of social media and sports, and his posts really encouraged the community to react and reach out to adidas.

BEST PRACTICES

In all audience segmentation practices, certain action steps are needed to promote engagement and work with specialized audiences and communities like influencers, ambassadors, and haters/trolls. Keep the following best practices in mind as you craft your audience section and practices for your social media efforts:

Look beyond the numbers and celebrity aspects of what makes an influencer and creator successful (Williamson, 2016). You need ground rules and criteria for evaluating social media influencers. Looking at the numbers (e.g., vanity metrics) is just one area to consider here. There needs to be more emphasis on what the influencers have actually done over time that warrants their payment and influence. Specific metrics, assets, and results from previous campaigns should be included in their media kits. Bloggers and influencers usually have a condensed document (PDF, interactive PDF, etc.) that compiles information they send to the media for consideration for a story. Fact sheets, biographic sheets, and statistics from platforms (followers, engagement, etc.) with key campaign metrics and results are just a few examples of how to report these data. More brands and social media professionals should ask for such reports, but not rely on them 100% to tell the complete story of what an influencer or creator has done.

Grow your social media community and audience with like-minded people. Think about how to engage with your audiences based on their experiences, expectations, and motivational factors. Take the time to invest in the relationships before jumping immediately into the hard sell:

- *Ask yourself, "What is the overall relevance of the creator, influencer, or ambassador for the campaign?"* Is there a direct alignment? Does the content, voice, and contribution to the community resonate with all audiences (internally and externally)?

- *Be prepared to compensate the creator and influencer.* This compensation does not always have to be financial. In many ways, a lot of creators and influencers want experience. This way, they create content, share their stories, and connect with their own audiences, which can then further their reach and influence factor. In addition, having the power to state they are partnering with a well-recognized entity, brand, or event can help creators and influencers in their own quest for more prominence in their respective communities.

- *Allow creative freedom so there is a mutually beneficial relationship.* Influencers and creators especially do not like being forced to promote something that is not directly theirs. If they have a hand in creating the content and story, that's awesome. Putting it completely into their hands is ideal, but of course, this may not always happen or be feasible for the brand or agency in campaigns. Yet, having the conversation and starting out with the fact that this is a team effort will make things go a lot smoother for both parties.

- *Do your research and look at the influencer and creator data.* As mentioned previously, not all influencers are created equal, and their interactions may be augmented through bots, fake accounts, and promoted schemes. Look beyond the data and see the overall quality of what influencers offer their own communities and industries. Rank these accordingly and see which influencers fit the bill not only for the campaign, but for the brand as well. You want to have an influencer built in within the overall campaign and mission for your social media efforts, not just added on at the last minute because it is the present thing to do among all brands. Also, you want to see not only who the influencers are influencing, but also who is influencing them. These second-layer audience members can be a helpful part of the conversation because they are the eyes and ears of the main influencers and can help solidify the partnership. For example, many brands and professionals reach out to Gary Vaynerchuk's videographer David Rock (aka @DRock) for this very reason—he is super-close friends with Gary.

- *Set out your expectations and guidelines for brand voice and community.* For both legal and ethical reasons, this needs to be stressed. On several occasions, influencers have gotten into hot water with brands because they were not doing activities reflective of the brand's voice. This can cause tension as well as a formal partnership breakup between the influencer and the brand. For example, Jake Paul, a popular YouTuber and Disney Channel star, had to cut ties with the company after a news story said he was disruptive toward his neighbors in Los Angeles (Main, 2017). Disney broke off the partnership due to Paul's actions and how they contradicted what the brand stands for among key audiences.

CHAPTER SUMMARY

Along with the changes happening in the social media industry, social media professionals and brands have to keep their eyes on the changes evolving within their key audiences. As each generation and cohort moves along, the members of each group will have a different perception of social media and how it is integrated into their daily lives. We cannot assume each audience is going to use or even perceive the content shared on social media in the same way, so social media professionals need to be both diligent and active in understanding the motivational factors, interests, and expectations of audience members pertaining to the brand's social media presence. In addition, new emerging audiences may come into play as a way to get messages across to other audiences, but while these audiences may still operate in a landscape like the Wild, Wild, West, some challenges, opportunities, and trends certainly need to be integrated within the social media strategy plan for both brands and professionals.

THOUGHT QUESTIONS

1. Define audience segmentation and explain why it is important in social media practices.

2. What are some unique characteristics of powerful influencers that are relevant for social media campaigns?

3. Identify the differences between influencers, creators, ambassadors, and haters/trolls. What main concerns do brands and social media professionals need to be aware of for each type of audience member?

4. What are the best practices for working with influencers and creators? What are the best practices for working with ambassadors?

5. What are three benefits of focusing on micro-influencers for a social media campaign?

EXERCISES

1. You have been asked by your internship to identify three influencers you'd recommend to be part of the campaign for La Croix. Based on your analysis of their previous partnerships, campaigns, followers and audience, and personal brand voice, provide three reasons you would recommend these influencers to La Croix.

2. A brand asks you to be a partner in creating awareness of a new barre/fitness center in your town. The company is interested in generating buzz for the opening among the fitness community locally, but does not know where to go to when it comes to influencers, ambassadors, or creators. Outline your recommendations based on your research and best practices in approaching each of these groups.

3. As an up-and-coming blogger, you are exploring options to partner with brands and nonprofit campaigns on social media. Outline specific metrics and information you would want to present and organize in your influencer partnership and proposal. Discuss the best practices you follow in creating authenticity with your network.

4. As part of your entry exam for consideration for a social media position, you have been asked to critique three influencers and analyze their social media accounts. Identify three things to look for.

5. You have been asked to create an influencer guide to target micro-influencers for a local restaurant. What are some reasons you would suggest the restaurant implement this type of program compared to launching a general influencer campaign?

REFERENCES

Adweek Staff. (2017, June 1). Gen Z power list: Meet the brands, platforms and creators that teens love. *Adweek*. Retrieved from http://www.adweek.com/digital/gen-z-power-list-meet-the-brands-platforms-and-creators-that-teens-love/.

Baer, J. (2016). Hug your haters: How to embrace complaints and keep your customers. New York, NY: Portfolio/Penguin.

Bentwood, J. (2008). Distributed influence: Quantifying the impact of social media. Edelman white paper.

Bernazzani, S. (2017, July 28). Micro-influencer marketing: A comprehensive guide. *HubSpot*. Retrieved from https://blog.hubspot.com/marketing/micro-influencer-marketing.

Chen, Y. (2017, August 1). How wannabe Instagram influencers use bots to appear popular. *Digiday*. Retrieved from https://digiday.com/marketing/wannabe-instagram-influencers-use-bots-appear-popular/.

Collier, M. (2017, October 26). 10 things to remember when creating a brand ambassador program. *MackCollier.com*. Retrieved from http://www.mackcollier.com/10-things-to-remember-when-creating-a-brand-ambassador-program/.

Gosling, S. D., Ko, S. J., Mannarelli, T., & Morris, M. E. (2002). A room with a cue: Personality judgments based on offices and bedrooms. *Journal of Personality and Social Psychology, 82,* 379–398.

Ingalls, J. (2017, May 5). How to differentiate social media influencers and content creators. *Dash Hudson.* Retrieved from http://blog.dashhudson.com/influencer-marketing-content-creator-social-media-strategy-brand-marketing/.

Jackson, D. (2018, January 9). Top 8 influencer marketing trends for 2018. *Sprout Social.* Retrieved from https://sproutsocial.com/insights/influencer-marketing/.

Joseph, S. (2017, July 7). How Adidas is using micro-influencers. *Digiday.* Retrieved from https://digiday.com/marketing/adidas-using-micro-influencers/.

Kontonis, P. (2017, August 2). 5 questions to ask yourself before investing in influencer marketing. *Campaign US.* Retrieved from http://www.campaignlive.com/article/5-questions-askself-investing-influencer-marketing/1441003.

Main, S. (2017, July 24). Disney Channel and influencer Jake Paul part ways as he causes chaos in his L.A. neighborhood. *Adweek.* Retrieved from http://www.adweek.com/tv-video/disney-channel-and-influencer-jake-paul-part-ways-as-he-causes-chaos-in-his-l-a-neighborhood/.

Markerly. (n.d.). Instagram marketing: Does influencer size matter? Retrieved from http://markerly.com/blog/instagram-marketing-does-influencer-size-matter/.

McCrae, R.R., & John, O.P. (1992). An introduction to the five-factor model and its implications. *Journal of Personality, 60*(2), 175-215.

Minsker, M. (2017). How women really feel about influencer marketing. *eMarketer.* Retrieved from https://www.emarketer.com/Article/How-Women-Really-Feel-About-Influencer-Marketing/1014939.

Prentice, S., & Huffman, E. (2008, March). *Social media's new role in emergency management.* Idaho Falls: Idaho National Laboratory.

Ross, C., Orr, E. S., Sisic, M., Areseneault, J. M., Simmering, M. G., & Orr, R. R. (2009). Personality and motivations associated with Facebook use. *Computers in Human Behavior, 25,* 578–586.

Shields, M. (2017, July 24). Mountain Dew developed its own digital-media "influencers"—and that's terrible news for digital ad middlemen. *Business Insider.* Retrieved from http://www.businessinsider.com/mountain-dew-digital-media-influencers-racking-up-views-2017-7.

Solis, B., & Breakenridge, D. (2009). Putting the public back in public relations: How social media is reinventing the aging business of PR. Upper Saddle River, NJ: Financial Times Press.

Williamson, D. A. (2016, March 3). How brands can work with creator-influencers. *AdAge.* Retrieved from http://adage.com/article/digitalnext/brands-work-creator-influencers/302919/.

Yelp. (2018). YES! Yelp Elite Squad. Retrieved from https://www.yelp.com/elite.

Yu, D. (2017, May 5). Why I am not an influencer. *Influencive.* Retrieved from http://www.influencive.com/why-i-am-not-an-influencer/.

Zhao, S., Grasmuck, S., & Martin, J. (2008). Identity construction on Facebook: Digital empowerment in anchored relationships. *Computers in Human Behavior, 24,* 1816–1836.

CREATING, MANAGING, AND CURATING CONTENT

Learning Objectives

Humans of Social Media

Introduction

Overview of Content Marketing

    Definition of Content Marketing

    Alignment of Content

Types of Content Media

Tools to Create Content

Curating Content

Best Practices

Chapter Summary

Thought Questions

Exercises

References

LEARNING OBJECTIVES

After reading this chapter, you will be able to

- Understand the importance of content marketing for social media
- Explain the difference between content creation and content curation
- Discuss the steps necessary to conduct a content audit
- Identify the four different types of media and which pieces of content work for each medium

HUMANS OF SOCIAL MEDIA
ADAM WHITE, FOUNDER OF FRONT OFFICE SPORTS

Introduction

I am a recent graduate of the University of Miami where I studied sports administration with a minor in marketing.

During my time at UM, I worked with the Hurricane Club as well as interned at opendorse and taught high schoolers at Fordham University in the Bronx. I currently run Front Office Sports, a leading multiplatform publication and industry resource that covers the intersection of business and sports.

How did you get your start in social media?

I picked up social media in high school once I got my first phone (I didn't get my first one till sophomore year) and mainly used it for the social side and not much of the professional and networking side of the industry. When I started Front Office Sports after my freshman year of college is when I really started looking at social media as a professional development tool, and ever since then, we have been able to build a great brand and unique following across a few different platforms. I also used it at each of my roles from the Hurricane Club to opendorse and was able to find ways to use my creativity to positively impact the social presence of the entities' partners.

What is your favorite part of working in your social media area of expertise?

I love being able to have some creative freedom and real-time results. Not many professions

(Continued)

(Continued)

Source: Courtesy of Andres Tamayo

Adam White

engaged with Carter Wilkinson, there would have been no chance for it to occur (Cohen, 2017). I also like seeing how other brands such as Amazon and FedEx provide customer service through social media. It has allowed for real-time service that often feels much more personal than talking to 20 different machine recordings on the phone. It is simple, but social customer service is so powerful.

What is the most challenging part of working in social media?

The most challenging part is being true to your brand and staying fresh while providing value to your followers, because after all they are following you for a reason and you want to make sure every day that you are fulfilling that reason for them.

allow you to see results so quickly. These results allow you to double down on what is working and change/improve what isn't doing as well almost immediately. The metrics involved in this industry also allow you to measure and quantify success or failure quickly and efficiently. Plus, if you put together something that is great and really works, seeing it take off is one of the best feelings ever.

What is one thing you can't live without while working in social media?

I can't live without the openness and sharing of knowledge from other professionals in the field. I am still new at most of this and have learned a lot from everyone who has been working in the field and been very successful. One of the best qualities of this industry is that those who work in it are so willing to help boost others up and share knowledge and best practices.

What is your favorite social media account (person/brand/etc.) to follow, and why?

I love seeing how restaurants like Wendy's and Taco Bell can be so engaging on social media and the impact that it has on customers and overall brand value. Just look at the #NuggsForCarter sensation. I'm sure Wendy's didn't expect it to turn out like it did, but if the company had never

What is your take on your area of expertise and the social media industry?

My take is that the social media industry is still in its infancy and that even over the next year we will see big changes on platforms and the way people use them. Instagram will dominate the market and continue to be a treasure trove for not only influencers, but also brands when it comes to return on investment on ad spend. Social media is also an area where, if you have some skill in design, photography, or even copy writing, you can make an impact right away, especially as an 18- to 22-year-old. If you can bring value to a brand in some way, you can create your own business because so many people are still so brash on the capabilities of the platforms.

What do you wish you had known when you were starting out?

I wish I knew that video skills and graphic design skills would be so important. Luckily, there are so many ways you can teach yourself now, but if I could go back, I would take more videography and graphic design classes in school.

You can connect with Adam White on Twitter at @FOSAdam or follow the work he and his team are doing for Front Office Sports at @frntoffice sport or go to www.frntofficesport.com.

INTRODUCTION

While reading this book, you have heard regularly about the growing importance of creating and managing content to be shared on social media. The common phrases heard frequently in the social media space are "content is king" and "context is queen" or a version of the two. The key point is to create content in the format most valued by and relevant for your key audiences. Sometimes you will be creating content designated for a particular audience, and other times you will be very focused on creating items that are very specific. Ultimately, we create content not just to get a higher ranking or have our audiences see something. Content essentially is anything that communicates a specific message to our audience in a designated channel.

In this chapter, we discuss strategies and tactics, the importance of content marketing, and the different types of content we are creating for our social media activities. We also highlight some cases of brands and others that have used social media content effectively in their campaigns.

OVERVIEW OF CONTENT MARKETING

As mentioned in Chapter 6 on strategic planning, strategies are focused on how to accomplish set objectives for a campaign, whereas tactics are the nuts and bolts of a social media plan, the specific tools and pieces of content. For the purpose of content marketing, the strategies portion focuses on how content marketing can help achieve the objectives set forth through specific action steps as well as through content creation, ideation, and promotion activities. The tactics portion of content marketing focuses on the specific pieces of content (otherwise known as assets) that need to be created, distributed, and evaluated for the campaign.

It is important to discuss how strategies and tactics are key and integrated with the overall purpose of content marketing and strategies. For the most part, social media professionals have to ask themselves ahead of time:

- *What communication and business objectives are the most important to consider for this social media initiative?* For every objective you need to have a purpose and goal in mind. What are the overall activities and behaviors you want the content to accomplish—to increase awareness about a new product you are launching, or to build sales leads for your business? Taking the time to outline what you want to accomplish will allow you to determine how to accomplish these goals and make sure they are aligned with the actions you take.

- *What types of content really resonated with our audiences?* You want to share and provide resources on social media that your audience actually wants to see. Brands, companies, and social media professionals are all about the attention economy, and it is important to create relevant content that audiences value and appreciate. Plus, audiences today want to be entertained, which means using boring content with stock photos that are accessible to anyone may not cut it. Evaluating the messages that go along with the content is a key element to consider as well. What do you want to share with the audiences that ties into the content being presented? Evaluating the data to see what content worked before and with which audience will be helpful in brainstorming what can be done for an upcoming social media campaign.

- *Which channels have been our strongest in the past?* Evaluating the performance and growth of your audiences as well as the metrics (as outlined in Chapter 5) will enable you to see which channels are the most effective in connecting your content with the audiences. These channels may change over time, so it is key to monitor them to see if the content execution needs to be changed.

- *How much in terms of resources do we have to spend on this content execution?* This is one thing a lot of social media professionals seem to forget about. The time spent creating, disseminating, and executing content effectively has to be taken into consideration. It's not about sending out a snap or posting a GIF on Twitter, but rather about predicting the amount of planning, strategizing, and brainstorming needed to make sure everything is aligned.

Definition of Content Marketing

Creating content for the sake of creating content is not helpful to anyone in social media. More brands and audience members are looking at new ways to make a connection, start a dialogue, and reinforce certain perceptions of the brand with the use of content creation on social media. The approach used to promote content to the masses is often referred to as **content marketing**. According to the Content Marketing Institute (2017), content marketing is "a strategic marketing approach focused on creating and distributing valuable, relevant, and consistent content to attract and retain a clearly defined audience—and, ultimately, to drive profitable customer action." This concept is not new for the social media industry, but it has become an integrated tool for helping professionals determine what to create, disseminate, and share with others to accomplish certain objectives.

There are several reasons why it is important not only to share (or curate) content from other people, but also to have the ability to create original content to be posted on social media. Each individual and brand has a distinct voice and perspective, and it is important to determine how and why to share these on certain social media platforms.

Other reasons to create content on social media include

- *Having strong brand awareness.* We are in the attention economy, and brands, agencies, and individuals are all trying to establish themselves in a way that separates them from others. One way to accomplish this is to think about each piece of content as an extension of your digital footprint and real estate. You control all of the content you host on your own website, but it is important to explore guest opportunities to further extend your research with other communities, industries, and partnerships. You may not have as much control or flexibility over the content you share on these other sites, but it is essential that you present a strong brand image with the content you do have and that, based on what you share, you attract new audience members to connect with and bring back to your own hosted content.

- *Gaining respect and reputation in the industry as a trusted resource.* The more people see your content as consistent yet personalized for each of the designated platforms, the more they will trust the information presented and be even more motivated to become long-term readers and followers. If the content is relevant and provides helpful tips, resources, and action steps for audiences, this could be the first step in transforming a loyal audience member into an advocate for your work, which could lead to future connections and professional partnerships.

- *Tying into the search engine optimization capabilities.* In order to drive influence and your reputation online, blogs, white papers, and additional long- and short-form content could help drive traffic back to your owned media assets (media you control) as a return on investment for time and resources spent on social media. This is why whenever you post content (a blog post, white paper, update, etc.), you must do your research on the key terms so if someone comes across your content based on a search, they will see value in it and follow you on the designated platform. Using data insights along with creating relevant content is the one-two-punch needed to maintain a loyal community base that consumes your content on a regular basis.

- *Providing assets to a social media campaign.* Pieces of content are often referred to as assets (items owned and created by an organization, agency, or person) to be used strategically for certain key messages and objectives in a campaign. Without these assets, the messages may fall a bit flat and lose the attention of audience members on social media.

Alignment of Content

An ultimate goal for the social media professional is to create great content. Depending on whom you ask, this could mean a variety of different things. However, great content that is successful for social media purposes is usually relevant, personal, **evergreen** (content that stays relevant for a long time and does not have to be updated as regularly as other types of content), engaging, and targeted to a specific audience with which the information and stories resonate. Creating content and putting it out there for the world to see is not the only strategy and action a social media professional should pursue. One must take multiple components into consideration when aligning content with the strategies and messages of a campaign or promotion for a brand.

First, the social media manager needs to conduct a content audit to determine which assets (e.g., creative and written content) worked and the takeaways from these items in the past. Specifically, a content audit can help you determine what should be removed from a website or database of resources for a brand, identify gaps to help brainstorm future content creation opportunities, and review the overall brand voice to see if additional reviews of copy writing to improve brand voice connection and overall quality are needed (Sizemore, 2017). The first step is to collect all of the relevant pieces of content created by the company, business, or professional and analyze them based on the metrics provided.

Table 9.1 provides an overview of the template that Moz (Sizemore, 2017) provided in its recommendations along with a few additions. The social media professional needs to categorize each asset of content based on the platform and note, according to the PESO model, whether or not it was paid (received compensation for placement or was sponsored), earned (shared without payment and done organically), shared (similar to earned, but directly connected with social media), or owned (shared via a controlled platform).

The next step is to provide the context of the asset, or the URL and title, as a record of the published content to review. It is also key to outline the overall purpose of this content for the audit—what was its focus in the first place, and was it part of a specific campaign or execution by the social media manager? Metrics help the social media manager and team decide what to do with the content, and must be tailored based on where the content was posted or hosted. For example, shares of, comments on, and inbound website traffic to a blog post may be a few metrics to consider. However, for a social media post, basic and advanced social media metrics (engagement, interactions, share of voice, reach, etc.) could be used. Each approach has to be adapted to the content and context being evaluated.

Actions focus on the larger picture of what to do with the content. For example, does a blog post need to be updated with the latest statistics, or should it stay the same because the content is still relevant? Also, social media professionals need to ask themselves what they would do with the content being evaluated in the audit. Is it still usable and relevant for the audience? Can it be updated, or should it not be used again? These are just some of the categories needed to sort the content that is still relevant for the campaign in question and the pieces that need to be set aside.

In Table 9.1, the details column focuses on the specifics to be noted and changed based on the actions recommended. The future recommendations column notes what to keep in mind for the future.

Second, once the content audit is complete, the social media manager and team need to discuss the key areas involved with content marketing, particularly the specialized areas and duties that help align the messages and content with the audience for a brand or organization. *Content strategy*, which primarily focuses on how and why content is created, managed, and updated for future use by the organization in question, includes the internal guidelines necessary to keep things consistent and on message (Moz, 2018; see also Chapter 3). These documents and guidelines help the social media manager (and team) ensure that all content going out on social media across the channels is consistent, aligned with the brand voice and vision, and presented in a style with which the audiences are familiar (Moz, 2018). Content marketing includes setting up a schedule for posting brand content (e.g., content calendar), promoting the content, and determining how frequently audiences will receive the content across various channels.

Content Ideation. One of the biggest challenges in social media content creation is having a strong idea. A great idea helps set the foundation for any strong content and social media campaign. The ability to see the whole picture and strategize how an idea could come alive is a necessary skill many brands and organizations look for in potential social media professionals today. Many ideas are available to choose from, but if you overlook a good idea in favor of a bad one, then you'll spend a lot of time and resources not fully capturing the potential of a campaign.

TABLE 9.1 ■ Sample Content Audit Template							
Platform	URL	Title	Purpose/Campaign Execution	Metrics	Action	Details	Future Recommendations
Paid							
Earned							
Shared							
Owned							

Ideas, especially good ones, do not fall from the sky. Instead, there are some ways to generate ideas:

- *Look at what is outside of the social media industry.* Review and explore previous case studies and stories outside of social media for inspiration. Sometimes, the most brilliant idea that can be incorporated into social media was already realized, but in a different industry. Keep this in mind: Applying an idea that worked in another area to a new context and industry might be all you need. New ideas can also come about through the integration of more than one idea. Professionals can watch their competitors as well. As mentioned in Chapter 6, it is important to see what your competitors are (or are not) doing with their content. These extra steps could help generate some further discussions and ideas for creating content for the social media campaign in question.

- *See what the research is saying.* Look at what is trending (on Facebook, Google, Twitter, etc.), what key words or areas are getting a lot of mentions, what the top media outlets and influencers are writing about that may be worth connecting to your brand or company, and what issues, challenges, and gaps in the industry as a whole your content could address. Use data to your advantage to identify opportunities and challenges to address with new content. Identifying these gaps and looking at how to use content created by your team to address them could be very rewarding and profitable. The strategic implications (the "so what" factor for why this is happening) are key in determining which ideas will be successful and what types of content and information to create and execute successfully for a social media campaign.

- *Categorize ideas in terms of whether they accomplish content goals.* Are the ideas helpful in providing value for the audience? Would it be relevant to create content for a particular audience? Are you producing one-of-a-kind resources people can't get anywhere else? Will the content likely motivate them to share? These are just some of the questions to ask yourself when coming up with ideas for content, because this process will not only further the brainstorming sessions, but also provide a framework for how to make content even better.

- *Set up regular brainstorming sessions.* Setting aside time to brainstorm with your team will be helpful for getting different perspectives and ideas to the table. Brainstorming can be done, of course, face-to-face, but bouncing around ideas in an online setting (e.g., on intranet networks or Slack) could also be beneficial. Participants of the brainstorming session can come in prepared with a few ideas, but at the same time, encourage people to have an open mind and no preconceived view of the situation. Of course, all ideas from the brainstorming sessions should be recorded, summarized, and taken into consideration for the team along with next steps to take.

- *Find the "it" and spark.* Identify the attitudes, actions, motivational factors, desires, and interests that can capture an audience's attention. That said, there are no "bad" ideas that should be disregarded. Instead, ideas should be noted, prioritized, and then built upon by the team. Don't spend too much time on content that essentially bores you (and your audience), but rather invest in those pieces that call out to you and fit parameters for your brand (research insights, industry expectations, brand voice and community, etc.).

- *Note the reasons people like or do not like content.* It's important to look not only at why content works, but also at why it does not. It could be something as simple as people having a hard time accessing the information, or presenting your content on the wrong platform. Seeing both successful and not-so-successful posts could help you identify ideas that will work and ideas to momentarily put aside.

Content Strategy. The strategy component for content is simple: What are your overall goals as a brand or company, and how do you want to execute them? Vision, and staying true to your mission and brand voice, is key in making sure each piece of content, message, and asset is aligned and strategically placed on the designated platform. This also takes into account the visual presentation of the content, showcasing the voice and true nature of the brand.

To get started, social media professionals need to take the content and assets they have created, or will be repurposing and updating, and decide how to execute it on social media. As described earlier in the chapter, a thorough content audit identifying the gaps and opportunities among fellow competitors and evaluating current expectations and needs from audiences provides essential background.

Before you even get started with the creation of content, a set brand voice and style guidelines must be in place. All content and assets should share the voice of the brand, person, and account. Here, as discussed in Chapter 7, following a writing style guide is necessary along with set protocols for promoting the content (key words, search engine optimization tips and techniques, etc.). Other dos and don'ts for content creation and strategy execution should be clearly articulated. All members of the collaborative team should be trained on this background material, which should be included in the main social media policy distributed internally among all of the social media team members.

Once you determine the current state of your content, you have to decide, as a group, where to place the content. Will you host the content on your own media platforms (blog posts, landing pages, webinars, etc.) and then share it out on social media, or will you post the content directly on social media (Facebook videos, Twitter GIFs, Instagram Stories, etc.) with a link back to the website? Finalize these issues to make sure your strategy is intact and your execution sound.

However, don't forget—even if you are trying to sell a product, run a fund-raiser, or get fans motivated for an upcoming season, your content strategy has to have substance, and storytelling needs to be intertwined with the content being shared. The different stories that could be created (e.g., emotional journey, current landscape, humor, educational purposes, or addressing a current opportunity or problem) are ideas that could be personalized and tailored to the content, and executed in a way that resonates with the intended audience.

Many social media accounts, such as the following, have developed content that is relevant and impactful for their intended audiences (Lua, 2017):

- *Humans of New York.* The HONY Facebook account focuses on the entire story of a person showcased in an image, tying in the art of creating a story with the image and update.

- *Airbnb.* Airbnb's work on Instagram is all about the photo with a short update. This balance shows the emphasis on the star of the update for the platform, but also the message that the company is trying to convey. While this approach may not be as effective on other platforms such as Twitter, if Airbnb wanted to repurpose this for another platform, it would have to take the parameters of other channels into account.

- *Buffer.* Buffer, along with other social media management tools and platforms, has its own Twitter chat (#BufferChat). Instead of sending out an email with a recap, the company uses Twitter Moments to provide a summary of the discussions and tweets collected during the chat for people to review at a later time. This content is collected and repurposed to provide a useful guide in case people want to see it later, or if someone missed the chat.

- *MoonPie and Cinnabon.* Both MoonPie and Cinnabon provide relevant content, but in different ways. These two brands are able to interject their personalities into their social media updates, to the point where they provide value in the form of entertainment for their audiences. MoonPie delivers witty commentary related to its products, and Cinnabon interjects real-time engagement and conversations with their audiences.

- *adidas.* A popular graphic design technique to use within Snapchat is to create your own filter, which adidas did for its Here to Create campaign. This helps brand the content on the platform, and also provides adidas with the opportunity to measure how many people have seen it, swiped with the filter, and used it for the measurement component of an effective social media strategy. The content accomplished the goal of raising awareness of the new campaign among a specific audience group.

There are many different ways to create content and execute it appropriately for social media channels. Yet more than just tactical items (specific pieces of content or tools to use in order to create and manage these pieces of content) need to be created. Social media professionals must think about both the content that will hit the surface-level goals for a brand (recognition, awareness, etc.) and the content that helps with higher levels of management strategies and goals (achieving thought leadership status, changing attitudes and behaviors, enhancing reputation, etc.). Table 9.2 presents some suggestions for specific types of content that you could create to achieve certain goals and objectives. All of this content can be created and shared on social media, but some (e-books, blog posts, etc.) will need to be hosted on owned media channels.

Humans of New York
January 22 · 🌐

"We have to keep our relationship secret. Our parents would not approve and we're not courageous enough to tell them yet. So we meet in secret three or four times per month. Since the beginning of our relationship, we've shared a diary. We take turns keeping it. Whoever has it will write down our memories. They'll also write down what they want from the other person, and how they feel misunderstood. Then every time we meet—we hand it off."

(Calcutta, India)

👍 Like   💬 Comment   ↗ Share   😊 ▾

Humans of New York Facebook Page

Content Promotion. You can have the best content possible, but if no one sees it and shares it with their own networks, then it is a wasted effort. Content promotion and execution in reaching out to the audience's feeds and accounts is as important as creativity in your key messages and assets.

As discussed in Chapter 8, you can identify key audience members to target regarding a specific campaign or initiative. Using tools such as Klear, Meltwater,

TABLE 9.2 ■ Specific Areas of Content to Create				
Thought Leadership	**Lead Generation**	**Visual Storytelling and Education**	**Brand Awareness**	**Outreach Efforts**
• Webinars • Courses • How-to guides, resources, and lists • Q&As • Research • Blog posts • White papers • Presentations • Video tutorials/vlogs	• Customer service • Media kits • Tutorials • Testimonials • Webinars • Reviews • Email marketing • Social selling updates • White papers	• Infographics • Videos • Podcasts • Presentations • Animations • Storyboards • Infographics • Templates • Vlogs • Short-form videos	• Branded content • Conversations • Interactive media and social care • Twitter chats • Live video segments • Featured guests/interviews • Podcast, Twitter chat, blog feature quotes	• Social media exchanges • Sponsorships • Quotes • Newsletters • Influencer relations • Blogger relations • Ambassador relations

Hootsuite, Talkwalker, Zoomph, Iconosquare, Followerwonk, BuzzSumo, and others can help you determine which audience members to reach out to based on a certain area of focus. Keep in mind, as discussed in the previous chapter, that influencers come in all shapes and sizes, so identifying not only main influencers but also micro-influencers is important. To determine which influencers to potentially partner up with on a content promotion initiative, you have to examine which platforms they

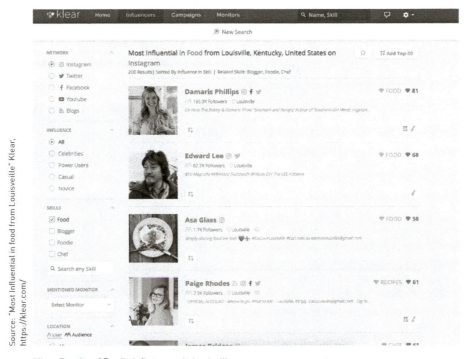

Source: "Most Influential in food from Louisveille" Klear, https://klear.com/

Klear Results of Foodie Influencers in Louisville

are on, what topics they are influential about, and what type of content (or history of content promotion partnerships) they have presented before. The photo below shows the results of a search for influencers who are foodies in Louisville, Kentucky.

For example, the Kentucky State Fair worked with Allison Myers, who manages the Eat Love Louisville account on social media, including the top-followed foodie account on Instagram in the city. To spread the word about upcoming food attractions, the Kentucky State Fair worked with Allison on promotional images. The promotion partnership was a successful venture. Not only was the Kentucky State Fair able to work with an influencer, but the influencer had the chance to create original content that could be shared on the official channel as well. Such cross-promotion efforts focus on getting the content and messages out to key audiences but, at the same time, making it a collaborative effort.

Content Calendar. A content calendar is an important template for keeping the content you share online organized and consistent. This shareable resource is used by social media teams to plan, organize, and coordinate all of the content going out for a brand, organization, or individual on social media.

For social media professionals, the benefits of using a content calendar include the fact that it keeps everything organized in one single document, and also helps you visualize when, where, and at what time each piece of content will be distributed across the social media spaces. According to Convince & Convert (Griffiths, 2018), a content calendar is beneficial for social media professionals because it

- Helps plan out content around key dates and events in a specific industry

- Keeps everything in a single place for everyone to be on board with

- Sets up expectations for when certain content and assets need to be scheduled and/or sent out ahead of schedule (timing is essential for content calendars)

- Sees where you need to add or take out content for your campaign

- Lines up all of the content so everything is coordinated and ready to go

Eat Love Louisville and the Kentucky State Fair

Like Convince & Convert, Hootsuite (Walters, 2017) states that content calendars promote collaboration with other members of your team and save time, which is always good to keep in mind if you are working on multiple social media campaigns and projects at the same time.

To organize your content calendar, you should follow certain steps. First, determine who your audiences are. What groups do you want to reach, and where do they go for their information? Sometimes it is a good idea to create an audience persona, or a description of key audience groups you want to target based on their demographic, psychographic, and motivational factors (Walters, 2017). This will help determine what the audience members are looking for, and what content they would feel most connected with. Essentially, the more you know about your audience, the more successful you will be in discovering what they will and will not want to see come across their social media feeds.

Determining what channels your audiences are on will help inform the assets to create and distribute for the calendar. Once you look at the assets from previous campaigns and see how they have done overall, these insights will help guide the team to determine whether content should be repurposed for certain platforms, updated, or deleted. In addition, this could help the team brainstorm ideas for original content to create specifically for a campaign or initiative. So, ask yourself these questions (Walters, 2017):

- What content got the most comments, likes, and shares?

- What content got the most views and traffic?

- What content got the highest engagement?

- What content was linked and referenced by others (influencers, other blogs, news, etc.)?

The content calendar should keep you on track with important dates, channel updates, and timing/expectations for how many posts, updates, and pieces of content to create for each social media platform. Particular dates (holidays, product launches, campaigns, annual events, etc.; Walters, 2017) need to be taken into account when outlining your schedule.

The frequency of posting for one platform may not work for another. For example, if brands or social media professionals used Facebook like they did Twitter, the frequency would be too high. Also, taking 30 snaps on Snapchat may be okay for a takeover, but not for Instagram. Experimenting and seeing what works and what doesn't work is often helpful.

After developing the content, the next step is scheduling the content to go out on certain platforms. Determining the right timing for your content requires evaluating and examining your own data. Guidelines exist for which time and day certain

FIGURE 9.1 ■ Hootsuite Sample Content Calendar

Title	Author	Topic	Deadline	Publish	Time	Notes
		WEEK 1				
How [New Product] Can Save You Hours of Time	Amelia Pond	product launch promotion	6/15/2017	6/19/2017	6 a.m.	
		WEEK 2				
		WEEK 3				
		WEEK 4				

Source: Hootsuite Inc., https://hootsuite.com/community

posts work on each platform, but ultimately, you want to (1) analyze your own data to determine what works for your community and (2) tweak it if necessary to get better results. It sometimes comes down to experimenting and trial and error. Either way, you will gain lessons and insights for future campaign initiatives.

Sample content calendars are available from various resources like Hootsuite, Sprout Social, and Buffer. In Chapter 6, Table 6.5 (page 134) presents sample calendars created by Hootsuite and Sprout Social to demonstrate how to organize and schedule out content.

The content calendar should also indicate when to stop a scheduled post. For example, when a natural disaster or crisis situation happens, no one wants to see a promoted post or update from a company. Some brands have learned this lesson the hard way. For example, Gap got into trouble on social media when it had a Hurricane Sandy sale during the storm that impacted the New York and New Jersey areas in 2013. Epicurious promoted its Boston recipes during the 2013 Boston Marathon bombing. Most brands have received the message to turn off their scheduled posts during such events, but at the same time, content managers must exercise diligence and be aware of the situation on social media.

TYPES OF CONTENT MEDIA

Some basic definitions of content need to be reviewed. Short-form content is the content you usually see presented on social media. These short snippets of information can be consumed very quickly and effectively. A 280-character tweet with an image is just one example of short-form content. Based on the audience and the platform, this type of content is effective for expressing key messages in a short amount of time. In addition, the attention span for audiences today is much shorter than in the past.

Long-form content expands on a topic in greater detail, which helps showcase the expertise, insights, and education opportunities from the brand or person writing the content. Long-form content can range from blog posts (500–1,000 words) to e-books, webinars, research reports, and online guides, to name a few even longer forms of content. These items are posted on websites for reference and educational purposes. Long-form content also delves into much more detail with additional research (interviews with professionals, survey results, insights shared by experts, etc.) to inform future campaigns and education. However, long-form content is very time-consuming to read and produce compared to short-form content. The resources and time needed to be effective and thorough with long-form content is one reason why not many brands or organizations present a lot of it. Yet effective organizations with a reputation for detailed and thorough resources are known in the industry for their insights, which helps them drive sales and customer bases.

Another type of content that can be shared over and over again because it remains relevant in social media is evergreen content. This content does not focus on the latest tools or gadgets, but rather concentrates on the foundational strategies and behaviors to apply and use depending on the situation.

One model that is frequently used in social media to determine types of content to be created and managed is the PESO model, introduced in Chapter 6. The PESO model, as Gini Dietrich (2018) describes it, merges four media types (paid, earned, shared, and owned) to create an integrated media model for social media professionals to utilize in their campaigns.

Paid media is social media advertising, or a "pay-to-play" model. The company (or advertiser/agency) is paying for the content to appear in a timeline for a certain amount of money. Examples of paid media include the following social media assets:

- Sponsored ads on Instagram Stories

- Sponsored posts on Facebook

- Promoted tweets on Twitter

- Snapchat ads on Snapchat

- Sponsored lenses on Snapchat

- Paid influencers

On the other hand, **earned media** is often connected with public relations. Earned media is *not* controlled by brands, which in many ways makes it more trustworthy and less biased compared to other types of content. Publicity or promotion of content without paying for the content characterizes this type of media. Having strong relationships with key audiences in the media as well as influencers will help drive your messages and content out to other targeted audiences. This can be integrated with paid media, especially if influencers are compensated for their efforts, yet the overall purpose of this type of media is to disseminate the content to people with a large reach and trust level among key audiences.

Some examples of content usually presented in earned media include the following:

- Media relations

- Influencer relations

- Ambassador endorsements

Shared media is often associated with social media, but it is more of an interactive medium where conversations and dialogue emerge as the result of the content being shared (usually linked), which is different from earned media. Some examples of this are as follows:

- Facebook group shares

- Twitter retweets and comments

- LinkedIn shares and linking the content in a LinkedIn update or post

- Slack community conversations

- Instagram pod discussions and shared endorsements

- Influencer promotions and advocacy efforts

- Advocates and ambassadors sharing content with communities

The last type of media discussed in the PESO model, **owned media**, focuses on content and the platform you control as a brand, organization, or person. This content is hosted on your own controlled media platforms such as websites, blogs, branded communities, or email newsletters. Some of the owned media content that can be created includes the following:

- Employee advocacy stories

- Testimonials

- Blog posts and resources

- White papers

- Podcasts and video tutorials

- Reviews

- E-books

TOOLS TO CREATE CONTENT

Many tools are available to help you create some amazing pieces of content (see Table 9.3). Graphic design and videography are some of the fastest-growing areas of need in the social media industry, but they are not the only considerations. Writing skills are also important but sometimes get overlooked in social media content conversations. Keep in mind, like all aspects of social media, tools to not only create content, but curate it (discussed in the next section), will constantly change. Some will be open to use for free, but others will range from a "freemium" model (allowing you to download and use the service for free) to more of a paid structure. Yet, because content always needs to be created for social media purposes, it is sometimes worth it to have the right tools for the job:

- *Written.* Writing tools are helpful in not only creating content, but also checking for mistakes in the content. Using Grammarly and the Hemingway App helps ensure you do not make mistakes in your writing. First impressions count, so investing in such tools will help you make everything publish-ready. In addition, other tools can help you connect on other social media channels. An email newsletter, for example, can help connect audiences back to social media and vice versa, so using MailChimp for this could be useful. Also, Trello is a good tool to help you write down ideas, brainstorm with your team, and coordinate efforts regarding what needs to be accomplished by when. Osana is similar to Trello, but it comes with a different cost and additional features.

- *Audio.* Audio is a powerful tool to use to create content, including podcasts. Several audio tools are available, and it all comes down to which one makes you feel most comfortable. A lot of podcasts are on iTunes and other app-based platforms, but SoundCloud is another platform used to host podcasts for brands and professionals. Anchor allows you to create content with audio. One way to repurpose audio content is to transcribe interviews and post them, as Social Media Examiner has done with its weekly show. The company records the show and then posts a summary outlining the key takeaways from the show to be shared on its blog and then redistributed to its social media channels.

- *Visual.* SlideShare helps transform reports, analytics, and papers into visual presentations. These are used for sharing information from conferences and workshops or providing simple tutorials on how to navigate or do certain activities on a platform (best tips for creating content on Snapchat, etc.). Visual tools help you create content that taps into thought leadership. Canva is great, for example, because it has templates for all types of content that can be formatted in any shape or size. Adobe Spark also uses various templates for its Post products, so if you are crafting updates to go out on specific social media platforms, this will be another valuable addition to your tool kit.

TABLE 9.3 ■ Tools to Create Content				
Written	**Audio**	**Visual**	**Graphic**	**Video**
• Blogging tools (WordPress, Medium, Blogger) • Anchor • Evernote • Google Drive • Grammarly • Hemingway App • MailChimp • Constant Contact	• Anchor • Audacity • SoundCloud • GarageBand • Evernote (generating ideas) • Scripts (WriterDuet)	• SlideShare • Prezi • Haiku Deck • Canva • Adobe Spark Post • Giphy	• Adobe Spark Page • Canva • Piktochart • Infogram • Alive • Camera+ • Enlight	• YouTube • Adobe Premiere • Vimeo • Animoto • BeLive • Zoom • BlueJeans • Adobe Spark Video • Plotagraph

- *Video and Graphic.* Having graphic design skills will make you a very marketable social media professional and content creator. However, you still must be aware of the complete picture, which means you need to have the necessary written and strategy skills. Several tools exist in this area that will make your job easier. For video, the go-to is Adobe Premiere, and if you are on mobile, Adobe Clip will help you craft short-form videos. Final Cut Pro and iMovie are helpful tools as well. Others can be used to create graphics to share on social media. Some tools (e.g., Hyperlapse and Boomerang for Instagram) are integrated within certain platforms.

CURATING CONTENT

We have discussed the essence of content creation, but another aspect to consider is referred to as content curation (see Chapter 7). *Content curation*, according to Hootsuite, is "the process . . . of sorting through large amounts of content on the web and presenting the best posts in a meaningful and organized way. The process can include sifting, sorting, arranging, and placing found content into specific themes, and then publishing that information" (Cisnero, 2014). This is somewhat different from content creation. With content curation, you are searching for relevant articles, resources, and content from other sources you feel your audience will find relevant and useful to consume.

Some practices to note when it comes to curating the best content include the following:

- *Make it personal.* Don't just share the content on Twitter, Facebook, or LinkedIn. Tell your audience members *why* you are sharing it. This helps build a story for why you (or a brand) think it is relevant for audiences to see this content.

- *People gravitate toward valuable content.* If you can determine areas in which your audience wants more information, then this will help you as you search for and uncover content to share with them.

- *Content curation shouldn't take too much of your time, but it should be a factor in your daily routine.* Searching for, discovering, and sharing relevant content should not be your full-time job. Instead, it should be part of it. Taking a few minutes each day to look for items that may be good for your audiences' well-being is all it takes.

Do not share everything you can possibly get your hands on with your audiences—people do not want to be spammed with material that is not relevant to them or that they do not find useful. Be selective and have a strategic purpose for each piece of content you share, and do this in a transparent manner. This means, if you are sharing a piece of content, tell the members of your audience why you are sharing it and why it is beneficial for them to receive it. You also want to note whether or not you have any direct connection with the content (sponsored content, client work, etc.). Being transparent with what you create and share contributes to the trust the audience member puts in the content. And, as always, when you share other people's content, make sure you give them credit (tag them in the update, use their handle on social media, etc.).

Repurposing the content being shared can take many forms. For example, one way to practice content curation is to produce an email newsletter. Delmondo, a creative analytics agency in New York City, sends a designated email newsletter to all of its subscribers not only with updates on its live video and social analytics platforms, but also with articles, updates, and news that are relevant and useful for subscribers of the email listserv. Front Office Sports (as featured in the Humans of Social Media feature in this chapter) has an email newsletter that hosts a variety of articles from the sports industry as well as job and internship postings. Because most of its audience members are young professionals who are still in school or have graduated, this information is extremely relevant and valuable. Some newsletters are focused on one specific feature. MEOjobs (run and hosted by Marc Oppenheim) provides a newsletter each week highlighting the top jobs and internship opportunities in social media, journalism, digital marketing, and public relations. Other big brands, such as Hootsuite, Buffer, and Sprout Social, have designated newsletters. Professionals like Jay Baer and Gary Vaynerchuk also have their own designated email marketing newsletters. According to Cisnero (2014), email is the second most popular digital media marketing channel, yet it is sometimes overlooked. Integrating a newsletter into your a social media content marketing strategy is an opportunity to (1) collect subscribers to connect with more professionals and build your audiences, (2) collect names into a database to provide subscribers with more updates and information on your services, and (3) provide opportunities to share content subscribers may not have seen from your other channels (blogs, social media updates, webinars, etc.).

The Live List

CNN and Volvo Present the Solar Eclipse in an Unprecedented 360° Virtual Reality Live-Stream
CNN and Volvo Cars USA will present the solar eclipse from multiple locations, coast to coast, in an immersive two-hour 360° live-stream experience starting at 1PM ET on August 21, 2017.

Facebook Is Finally Launching Its Long-Awaited Original Video Tab
The social network today announced it will soon be launching the much-anticipated feature, which could help it siphon video advertising budgets and users away from TV networks, Snapchat, Twitter and YouTube. While there could be dozens of partners added over the coming weeks, Adweek has confirmed initial content partners include NASA, Mashable, Quartz, Hearst, MLS and McClatchy.

This necklace camera livestreams your life so you're not wasting it looking through your phone
As easy as it is to livestream with your smartphone, it also takes us out of the moment. Instead of seeing and experiencing events, we now watch them through a glass screen.

Sample Delmondo
Email Newsletter

Other strategies include private or public groups on Facebook and LinkedIn, secret groups on Facebook, and designated hashtags on Twitter to keep up with relevant content.

As for content creation, certain tools can be used to help social media professionals curate relevant content for their audiences. Some of these tools are free, and others are paid. HubSpot (Armitage, 2017) recommends the following tools for content curation activities:

- *Twitter Lists.* Creating a list for various areas of expertise (social media marketing, social selling, public relations, etc.) is one way to keep track of all of the people you want to follow for resources to share with your audiences.

- *Follows on Facebook and LinkedIn.* You are able to follow prominent brands and people on these two social media sites, so you can bookmark and save the articles and links for future uses.

- *Scoop.it and Feedly.* Both of these tools follow certain publications and provide you with a feed of articles that come from each site. Some free services are available from both tools, but there are some paid options as well.

- *Nuzzel and Flipboard.* These tools have mobile apps and take the feeds you follow on social media and provide an interactive newsletter for you to read, consume, and then share on your networks. Both are free to use.

- *Curata.* This paid service helps companies look at relevant content for their complete marketing capabilities on social media. This may be a tool to invest in if you have the budget.

BEST PRACTICES

After reviewing the importance of content creation, strategies, tactics, and content curation, there are some best practices to follow as you head toward this area of social media. Remember and take note of these guiding principles, since they will help you plan, organize, and discover ideas to create new assets to use in a campaign, or help you find and uncover relevant work to share or use as inspiration for further ideas in your community:

- *Create content worth sharing.* As mentioned previously, you do not want to waste your audience's time. Attention is a priceless currency in social media today, and as more options and resources become available, people will go where the content, messages, and community hold their attention. Focus on quality, not quantity, in your content.

- *Look at the data and see what the numbers tell you about the content you have shared.* Data don't lie, and they can provide both a validation of the work being shared and created for social media, but also be tied to insights that can be used to revamp the content creation aspect for a brand or person on social media. Analyze insights from the data about the reactions and receptiveness of the content shared on social media. Use data as a bouncing-off point for future brainstorming sessions, ideas, and potential strategies.

- *Invest in the time to interact with audiences to find out what they are looking for on social media.* As mentioned in other chapters, do not assume you know what audiences want on social media. It may be good to conduct some research and ask them what they are looking for. This interaction shows not only a level of community with the group, but also a sense of respect for what your audiences think is valuable. Take these insights back to your team and brainstorm ways to accomplish these goals and expectations so it is a win-win situation.

- *Make the extra effort and provide more than audiences expect.* Always go beyond what is expected. If audiences find a white paper with a ton of insights and resources, they will continue to visit and come back for more. Provide more information and detail than others have done in the past to take your content to the next level. Always exceed expectations, but never go below them.

- *Edit, edit, and edit some more.* Content is under a microscope for brands and individuals, so taking the time to edit, revise, review, and edit some more is important. However, be aware of the timing of the content to make sure it is ready to go. Perfection is always great to have, but it doesn't help anyone if the draft of a tweet or e-book is never shared and discovered.

- *Find time to write when you think you don't have any.* Research and outline some ideas and look at your peers to see what they would be interested in reading more about. Build time into your daily routine to search for content to share, but also items to research and explore for inspiration for content creation.

CHAPTER SUMMARY

This chapter covers one of the growing areas of specialization in the social media industry, but also an important area of focus for many young professionals entering the workplace. Content marketing, and the ability to share relevant assets that make a connection with your audiences, combines both scientific and creative approaches. Without the scientific process of analyzing the information collected through monitoring and listening mechanisms in social media, social media professionals will not know which posts, updates, or traditional long-form content has worked for them and helped their community. On the flip side, without the distinct creativity of thinking outside of the box and being open to approaching content in a new way, assets and other content produced could go unnoticed and be ignored by the community. To gain momentum and help build brand awareness, trust, and credibility as a brand or as an individual, having a balanced approach to content marketing takes time, but with the proper tools, guidelines, and teamwork, the result will be a win-win within the community and for future social media efforts by the brand or social media professional.

THOUGHT QUESTIONS

1. How would you describe content marketing? What distinct characteristics of content marketing do social media professionals need to know?

2. Define content creation. How is this relevant for social media professionals?

3. What is content curation and its role within social media?

4. Outline the different media in the PESO model. What are some examples of content that could be created for each?

5. What are three best practices when it comes to creating and curating content for social media?

EXERCISES

1. You have been hired to create content for the Nutella Café in Chicago, but you recognize you need to do a content audit. Outline the key steps and content you will need to review for this audit. Provide three content creation recommendations you would want to propose for this position.

2. As part of your entry exam for a new position, Dunkin' Donuts wants you to create an editorial calendar outlining its celebration coming up for "National Coffee Day." Outline some recommendations for how the company should prepare for this national holiday.

3. You are at a networking social media event at SXSW, and you are asked by a social media strategist about your thoughts on content marketing and why it is important for social media campaigns. Write a 15- to 30-second pitch on the key benefits of content marketing, and propose an example case where it worked.

4. You are a part of a student-run agency, and you have been tasked to outline a content marketing strategy to gain awareness of your group on campus. Propose three items you want to create and three items (or areas) from which you want to create information. Create a sample content calendar outlining when each of these proposed items will go out and on what channels.

REFERENCES

Armitage, P. (2017, November 21). 10 content curation tools every marketer needs. *HubSpot*. Retrieved from https://blog.hubspot.com/marketing/content-curation-tools.

Cisnero, K. (2014, August 13). A beginner's guide to content curation. *Hootsuite*. Retrieved from https://blog.hootsuite.com/beginners-guide-to-content-curation/.

Cohen, D. (2017, May 9). #NuggsForCarter: A plea for Wendy's chicken nuggets becomes the most retweeted tweet ever. *Adweek*. Retrieved from http://www.adweek.com/digital/nuggsforcarter/.

Content Marketing Institute. (2017). What is content marketing? Retrieved from http://contentmarketinginstitute.com/what-is-content-marketing/.

Dietrich, G. (2018, January 4). PR pros must embrace the PESO model. *Spin Sucks*. Retrieved from http://spinsucks.com/communication/pr-pros-must-embrace-the-peso-model/.

Griffiths, J. (2018). How to build a content calendar (plus a free template). *Convince & Convert With Jay Baer*. Retrieved from http://convinceandconvert.com/social-media-strategy/how-to-build-a-content-calendar-plus-a-free-template-for-2014/.

Lua, A. (2017, February 22). 20 creative ways to use social media for storytelling. *Buffer Social*. Retrieved from https://blog.bufferapp.com/social-media-storytelling.

Moz. (2018). Chapter 2: Content strategy. Retrieved from https://moz.com/beginners-guide-to-content-marketing/content-strategy.

Sizemore, E. (2017, March 22). How to do a content audit [updated for 2017]. *Moz*. Retrieved from https://moz.com/blog/content-audit.

Walters, K. (2017, June 27). How to create a social media content calendar: Tips and templates. *Hootsuite*. from https://blog.hootsuite.com/how-to-create-a-social-media-content-calendar/.

10

MEASUREMENT, EVALUATION, BUDGET, AND CALENDAR

Learning Objectives
Humans of Social Media
Introduction
Measurement and Evaluation
    Importance of Measurement and Evaluation
      in Social Media
    Importance of Having a Measurement
      Strategy
    Outcomes
Budget
    Areas to Invest in Your Budget
    Metrics to Consider for Budgets on Social
      Media
Further Considerations for Measurement,
    Evaluation, and Budget
Chapter Summary
Thought Questions
Exercises
References

LEARNING OBJECTIVES

After reading this chapter, you will be able to

- Explain the connections between measurement and evaluation in a social media campaign, initiative, or role

- Discuss and explain the main components of social media measurement outlined by AMEC

- Describe the various techniques, metrics, and tools used for social media measurement and evaluation

- Identify best practices and tips for conducting effective measurement and evaluation practices for social media

HUMANS OF SOCIAL MEDIA
DENNIS YU, CHIEF TECHNOLOGY OFFICER AT BLITZMETRICS

Introduction

I'm an ABC. So I'm an American-born Chinese, born in Dayton, Ohio.

English was not my first language; I learned when I was seven. I got a full ride at Southern Methodist University. School directly didn't help much, as most people will admit.

I chose finance and economics because I had a curiosity for why certain things cost what they cost. I didn't speak much English as a youngster, so I found math to be a way to communicate.

That eventually turned into competing in math contests, learning to build financial models, working with the databases that ran American Airlines, and running the internal analytics team at Yahoo. Finance and economics also naturally led me to programming, econometrics, and working with large, multidimensional data sets.

At American Airlines, I got tired of asking the information technology people to run queries for me. They took too long, and I didn't want to wait in the queue. I learned how to write JCL (Job Control Language) and SQL (Structured Query Language) myself.

(Continued)

(Continued)

Source: Courtesy of Mark A. Lack

Dennis Yu

How did you get your start in social media?

I started out 20 years ago at American Airlines where my mentor Al Casey, the CEO, told me to focus on my learning curve, not my earning curve. I turned down a lucrative career at Goldman Sachs and started building the company's internet presence. I was fascinated by playing with the world's largest data system. The Sabre system, owned by the American Airlines parent company, was the biggest nongovernment system out there.

Yahoo was the largest search engine while I was still at American, so I had the opportunity to analyze some outrageous behavior on the web. Facebook is the modern extension of that. Just consider how much data Facebook collects on users and also makes available to advertisers. We want not to spy on people or be creepy, but to truly understand who the best customers are for a business, what content will cause them to convert, and how to assemble a system that will drive business results.

When I started marketing on Facebook in 2007, there was limited competition. I've been fortunate to have a hand in the development of some of these tools, which has given us an advantage as data-driven marketers. I expect marketers who don't live by the numbers to be stomped on by those who do.

What is your favorite part of working in your area of social media expertise?

I have a passion for observing interesting correlations and making connections. I admit that I am a numbers geek and love data, which is the reason

I ended up in marketing and analytics. I follow a process called MAA, or Metrics, Analysis, Action. This means you look at the data, understand the data, and then form your strategy based on the changes. It's one of the nine triangles we use in business, and it will help you when you are breaking down big chunks of data, or even when examining the numbers behind an ad.

What is one thing you can't live without while working in social media?

A top-notch PR team would normally charge $7,500 a month for a basic retainer, but you get that for $1, for every day you boost. "Dollar a Day" is a simple yet effective technique that we use consistently.

You need these key ingredients:

- A third-party endorsement of your skill in a particular area—not your sales literature or what's on your website

- One dollar a day, but it could be more

- An ongoing commitment to create helpful content on a daily basis, as opposed to only promotional material

- A product or service worth talking about, evidenced by happy clients, online reviews, and so on

- Patience, since generating word of mouth and influencing the press takes months

What is your favorite social media account (person/brand/etc.), to follow and why?

There are too many to count, but if you must follow one person, I am a huge fan of Mari Smith. She earned her unofficial title of the Queen of Facebook for good reason; her knowledge and strategies are rivaled by none. She's also a very down-to-earth person, full of love, and someone you can't help but smile at when interacting with her. But as I said, there are so many other great people to follow who have made great contributions to this industry.

I do my best to keep up with the continuously changing industry and try to learn from as many people as I can, including my colleagues Heather Dopson, Alison Herzog, Paul Sokol, and Jason Miller. Each of them adds a unique perspective to the world of social media, and they are all-around great people.

What is the most challenging part of working in social media?

You'd think it would be building systems, tuning complex ad campaigns, or something glamorous. But actually, the hardest struggle, *by far*, is helping people overcome fear, while the second-biggest challenge is screening clients. It's a people issue in both cases. Disguised in other forms, fear shows up as excuses, defensiveness, sickness, procrastination, and all manner of things that distract you from being successful.

The solution is a combination of three elements:

- *Checklists*—break down the big scary project into small, simple tasks.

- *Encouragement*—as a coach, not a boss, you're more interested in helping, not punishing.

- *Accountability*—measuring success against checklists and providing feedback is holding people accountable.

We also want to stop wasting time talking to unqualified prospects who only dangle the carrot in front of us to lead us along:

- Don't let just any random person book time on your calendar, and don't offer free consultations to people who don't fill out at least an intake form.

- Assemble a few packages that describe what you do in detail.

- Crank up your content marketing efforts so that all your leads are inbound. In other words, talk only to folks who come to you.

- Create a screening process to surface the good clients and filter out the bad ones.

- Have an administrator run the process. He or she can schedule, qualify, collect payments, and share basic documents.

You have been active in mentoring future young professionals in social media. What has been the most rewarding experience or moment you have had in helping students?

Mentorship is important to me because it has influenced my life time and time again. My most important mentor was Al Casey, CEO of American Airlines. I strive to provide my team members the best support I can give, answering their questions and helping them grow as marketers. If you're doing it for the money, that's a sign something is wrong. It took me over a decade to realize that using my skills to teach young adults how to optimize digital traffic, then applied to sports teams, lead generation, and whatever, was far more rewarding. You hear a lot of people say, "Follow your dreams."

It all sounds good, in theory, especially when told by folks who are already successful and talented. "But how does this apply to me?" students say, leading to false hope and inaction. The answer is taking incremental steps in something we call "personal branding." The small steps of setting up your profile on different networks, setting up Google Alerts on things you're interested in, and writing short notes about what you observe are what counts. Perhaps you're self-conscious about your writing skills—then blog for five minutes a day. Sure, your initial blog posts will suck, but I promise you that you'll get way better and faster. Do this for six weeks straight, and you'll be surprised how far you go.

What do you wish you had known when you were starting out?

Al Casey was CEO of American Airlines and even Postmaster General—yes, he had a million employees driving around those little white trucks. He was kind enough to share his best advice with me, a poor college kid looking for a job. I wish I heeded his words more carefully, as it would have saved me a ton of heartache, but that's a story for another time.

Focus on your learning curve, not your earning curve.

Another $10,000 a year at Company A shouldn't be the reason you choose it over Company B. When you get your first real job, what you're really getting is experience and a network. In a few years, you'll be making a lot more if you're doing something you love enough to be knowledgeable about.

You can follow Dennis Yu on social media (Twitter, Facebook, LinkedIn, and Instagram) at @dennisyu. Dennis also publishes his articles and insights on his personal website www.dennis-yu.com.

INTRODUCTION

Social media involves math and numbers. These numbers are used both from a pro-active standpoint, as discussed in Chapter 5, and to tell a story of what happened. This is where measurement and evaluation come into play. Along with the creative execution of content, ideas, and stories from a visual and artistic perspective, data tell a story of how audiences reacted and responded to the data. Did the content resonate with them? Did the key messages we integrated into our updates motivate them to take action like we hoped they would? How much media and audience exposure did we get from our uniform and football team schedule unveiling? How many leads and sales did we accumulate in response to what we did? How many people signed up to our webinar with leading influencers?

Businesses, agencies, and social media professionals sometimes forget about a key step in the strategic social media process. In an eConsultancy report on social media measurement, 41% of the respondents had no idea of the financial impact of social media (Baer, 2018). This is surprising to hear, but provides even more reason why both the surface-level metrics and the attitudinal and behavioral metrics that drive actions, relationships, and financial support are areas to cover for social media measurement and evaluation practices.

This is measurement and evaluation, which holds the key to determining whether or not we were successful in our efforts to engage our audiences, accomplish our set objectives for the short and long term, and provide value (emotionally, financially, and socially) for the intended parties. Without measurement and evaluation, social media practices would not have an end game allowing us to determine what we were able to do and whether we were successful. In addition, since social media is usually part of another department or functions within another discipline, we must provide evidence to others (e.g., senior management, clients, and the industry) to show what we were able to do. Metrics and data that show initial results as well as actionable behaviors taken as a result of social media activities are important contributions to measurement and evaluation practices.

Measurement and evaluation sections are usually glossed over because they deal with numbers, data, and other elements that may not be as dazzling as the creative execution of content and stories. Without the measurement and data to show the impact of these pieces of content, however, future campaigns and resources will not be attributed to social media.

Determining whether or not a campaign initiative, idea, or program was success-ful is one of the most important and crucial tasks of the social media professional. In this chapter, we cover the different components needed in the measurement and evaluation stages for social media strategic practices. In addition, we highlight key areas to note when creating a calendar (e.g., customer journey) and budget (yes, social media costs money and time).

MEASUREMENT AND EVALUATION

Importance of Measurement and Evaluation in Social Media

Measurement and evaluation travel hand in hand in many marketing, strategic communications, and public relations campaigns. Measurement focuses on desig-nating specific amounts that reflect change in specific objectives, whereas evalua-tion focuses on the assessment or value of certain actions in a campaign or strategy.

They are two of the final steps to take before providing recommendations for most social media plans, programs, and campaigns.

Many professional associations (Public Relations Society of America, American Marketing Association, etc.) have presented their views on the importance of measurement and how it is tied directly to social media practices. The International Association for Measurement and Evaluation of Communication (AMEC, 2016a, 2016b) has its own framework for key areas to cover in social media:

- *Objectives.* What do you want to accomplish during the course of the social media campaign while following the requirements of the SMART criteria as discussed in Chapter 6?

- *Inputs.* Who is your target audience, what is the current situation, and what resources are available to understand them? This is discussed in Chapters 5 and 8.

- *Activities.* This is the strategies and tactics portion of your PR plan. What content and messages will you be creating and disseminating out to your audiences?

- *Outputs.* These are the specific metrics collected from likes, comments, reach, impressions, and engagement. How did people respond to the content we shared across all social media platforms and channels?

- *Outtakes.* What reactions and behaviors occurred as a result of the messages, content, and actions taken on social media? What actions did audiences take in response to the updates you shared? How likely were they to recall your content with others?

- *Outcomes.* How well did the audiences receive your messages? Did you change their views or attitudes?

- *Impact.* How has the organization, client, or individual been influenced and/or changed as a result of this social media campaign? These higher-level objectives contribute not just to social media protocols and actions, but to the well-being of the entire organization. Examples include reputation, change in policies, or improved business practices.

This measurement framework helps organizations, businesses, and individuals manage and format the evaluation section of their social media strategic plan to identify all required variables. Table 10.1 outlines the components of the framework, discusses their overall focus, and then provides examples of items that would fit from the data collected and analyzed for a social media plan.

Social media professionals do not just do a campaign and leave (or drop the mic on their way out the door). They must articulate clearly what they accomplished relative to their objectives, provide evidence that their efforts and the efforts of their team made this a successful initiative, and provide guidance on what indicators helped in this effort and what needs to be done in the future. This is where evaluation (gathering intel and providing an assessment explaining what happened in this program or campaign) ties back to the initial proposal in the goals and objectives components (as outlined in Chapter 6) for the social media team.

The measurement component of the SMART objectives (specific, measurable, achievable, realistic, and time-specific) is so important. Without knowing what or

TABLE 10.1 ■ Application and Focus for the AMEC Framework		
AMEC Component	**Focus**	**Application**
Objectives	• Communication objectives • Media objectives • Business objectives	• Strategic planning stage after research, communication audit, and situational analysis
Inputs	• Situational analysis • Audience analysis	• Understanding the core group of people at the heart of a social media campaign and identifying the current situation and landscape
Activities	• Specific strategies and tactics to be implemented in the campaign	• Specific social media updates, assets, and tools used to create and disseminate content
Outputs	• Measuring the impact of the social media content	• Metrics designated for specific channels, platforms, and objectives • Likes, follows, shares, comments, reactions, visitors, and so on
Outtakes	• Effects of content and messages from audiences	• Reactions • Feedback • Coverage • Recall
Outcomes	• Effects of content and messages from audience	• Reactions • Feedback • Coverage • Actions taken • Increased advocacy
Impact	• How business objectives are measured and the contribution of social media	• Reputation measures • Attitude changes • Policy changes

Source: Adapted from Integrated Evaluation Framework by AMEC. Retrieved from https://amecorg.com/amecframework/framework/interactive-framework/.

how much they want to increase (audience size, subscription base, awareness, engagement, etc.), social media professionals will not have clear and actionable variables to present to senior management. In addition, most of the time, senior managers want to see hard numbers that clearly illustrate the growth, impact, and results from social media for PR, marketing, reputation, and sales. In this case, social media professionals have to connect the dots with evidence to support each of their points of insight, and make recommendations and assessments accordingly.

Measurement is more than just collecting and analyzing data. As for creative execution of content, there is an art to analyzing and discovering insights gathered from the data to best tell a story of what happened and what to do for the future. This is a *measurement strategy*, which is missing from many social media campaigns. To fully integrate the importance of data analysis in social media, measurement needs to have a seat at the table along with creative content and storytelling.

To succeed in measurement and evaluation, social media professionals must be familiar with both the traditional methods of measurement (focus groups, surveys, interviews, etc.) and the new tools at their fingertips with channel (or platform) analytics (Facebook Analytics, Twitter Analytics, etc.) and third-party tools (Salesforce, Iconosquare, SocialRank, Simply Measured, etc.). Each of these methods has a specific purpose and function in the measurement and evaluation stage. Channel analytics tools show you content on the designated platform and what worked, what didn't, and how to make future improvements. Social media professionals will be able to identify the key metrics (outlined in Chapter 5) for each platform and download the data, analyze them, and integrate these findings into a social media report. In addition, you will have access to other key components like location of the source (where are the people posting from on each platform?), network (how connected are they, and are they influencers?), context and content (in what situations are they engaged with the content?), and consistency (to what extent are they engaged with the content?).

Importance of Having a Measurement Strategy

As for all aspects of social media, a game plan (or strategy) for certain actions, steps, and duties and how they contribute to the overall goal and program needs to be in place. That's why an effective measurement strategy is essential for all social media programs and campaigns. Having such a strategy will allow social media professionals to

- Be better informed about their key audiences throughout the social media program and campaign journey

- Be able to execute and create effective content

- Align content, stories, and other social media updates to be executed at the right time, place, and platform

- Make each post count and be more effective in coordinating a team effort for social media

- Identify more efficiently with key audiences, influencers, and micro-influencers, and discover new audiences to create relationships with (Jackson, 2016)

As mentioned previously, measurement is as important as great content and relationships with your key audiences on social media. Evaluating social media activities is recommended for a variety of reasons (Dawley, 2017):

- You will have a better understanding of how your social media channels benefit your brand and client.

- You will be able to see the overall performance of the content with and without paid support (e.g., organic versus sponsored posts).

- You will be able to note not only the place of social media channels within the community you are engaged with, but how the content spreads and is received by others (influencers, media, etc.).

- You will be able to discover which pieces of content worked well for you, as well as which did not.

- You will be able to determine any missed opportunities, gaps, or lessons to note for the future when it comes to social media content strategy, execution of key messages and channels, and conversations and perceptions among key audiences.

With measurement and evaluation in social media, you can address each of these points. In Chapter 5, we discussed which key performance indicators and metrics to evaluate and set forth for monitoring and listening. The same principles and metrics need to be considered for the measurement and evaluation section of a social media plan. Ask yourself:

- How do these metrics align with my set objectives?

- How easy will it be to calculate, collect, and analyze the data?

- Are these metrics universally used across different departments (marketing, public relations, strategic communications, etc.) or not?

- Will these metrics be able to help in the decision-making process for future recommendations?

- Which metrics align with the outcomes set forth for the initiative and campaign?

In Chapter 6, we outlined the strategic plan for social media. It is important to evaluate objectives (the ones that you are following and for which you are using SMART criteria) to see what you want to do to achieve them. However, once you set these objectives, you have to determine how and why you will be measuring and evaluating them. Measurement tools, methods, and metrics should always be set forth before a campaign or social media program is implemented. Not taking the time to do this will result in lost time and money and, on some occasions, a job loss for the social media professional.

Outcomes

Certain outcomes should be measured and reported as part of your analysis for social media. The strategic communication literature identifies three areas of outcomes to measure: cognitive, attitudinal, and conative. Although they focus on different elements, all three are key to evaluate and report when it comes to understanding what worked and what did not work in social media campaigns.

Whether or not people were able to comprehend what you were trying to say in your messages (informational, etc.) is referred to as the *cognitive outcome*. One case that illustrates the cognitive component is the Whole Foods response to Hurricane Harvey. Hurricane Harvey made landfall in Texas in August 2017, and the Texas-based brand wanted to pass along information during this natural disaster to its audiences on Facebook. The Whole Foods updates provided information, but the reactions and comprehension of the information in the updates for this intended audience should have been evaluated. Each platform has unique metrics (e.g., Facebook has reactions in addition to comments and shares).

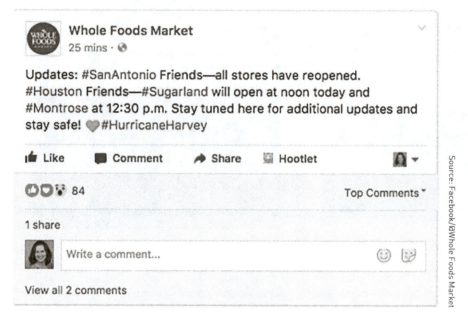

Whole Foods Update in Response to Hurricane Harvey

If you are telling an emotional story as part of inspiring audiences to take action based on a brand voice, outcomes of interest will be attitudinal. *Attitudinal outcomes* focus on measuring the response to the content and audiences' feelings, perceptions, and attitudes about the content in question. For example, was the response positive? Was there a negative perception toward the brand or individual based on what was shared? What is the overall sentiment in response to the piece of content, or even more generally to the campaign? These are just a few questions to consider when exploring how to measure the reaction of audience members to the social media content presented.

Let's see how this could be applied. In August 2017, the San Francisco 49ers posted a video with a tweet showcasing one of their players (Marquise Goodwin) and a young boy named Austin. The video was powerful and emotional and touched the hearts of fans. In addition, the post was extended and went viral, with media outlets including ESPN and Bleacher Report covering the content. The social media team for the 49ers will most likely be able to look at the metrics for the tweet itself (views, shares, impressions, engagements, etc.), but also how the content was integrated and shared or covered in other outlets like the trade and mainstream media. These earned media (media that are not paid for but based on relationships with intended professionals, influencers, or outlets on their designated platforms) will also prove to be valuable for showing the social media team and senior management the amount of coverage earned (and not paid for) and what they received in return.

Conative outcomes focus on behaviors exhibited by audience members after seeing a post on social media. As mentioned before, including a strong call-to-action statement in your post will allow the members of your audience to understand and know what they need to do. Conversions, or how many people were converted from regular audience members to customers or subscribers, are one metric to evaluate here. Many

San Francisco 49ers Tweet With Marquise and   HubSpot Academy Post Announcement of Facebook Webinar
Austin

social media professionals like conative metrics because they show a direct action was taken based on the message shown to a particular audience member. Measuring the direct alignment of the content to the action shows the impact toward a new relationship, sale, or action due to the content shared and created on social media.

For example, HubSpot partnered with Facebook to create a free series, and wanted to let audience members know about this event. Gary Vaynerchuk (who was part of the event) was tagged to give a call-to-action statement focusing on how people could sign up. The URL used was customized, which means that it was personalized for the brand (i.e., HubSpot), and the website is able to keep track of the metrics and traffic on the landing page for the webinar. The content for this website is customized for each platform on social media for HubSpot, which will be able to see

- Which platform generated the most sign-ups

- What time and day was most effective in reaching audiences and getting people to sign up

- What actions audience members took after they signed up (shared the webinar, etc.)

- The number of sign-ups and additional information on each person (name, email, job, industry, etc.)

- The average response time to inquiries across channels (social care, customer relationship management, etc.)

These elements are important to collect and analyze because they will tell us what content, strategies, and channels will be the most effective in reaching our audiences to accomplish our set goals. Without these measurements, social media professionals will not know what worked, what didn't, and what tips to keep in mind for doing

TABLE 10.2 ■ Social Media Measurement Objectives			
Outcome	**Measurement Strategy**	**Measurement Metrics**	**Tools**
Cognitive	The exposure to the message and the overall comprehension of knowledge and information being presented and evaluated by audience members	• Inquiries based on the message and information presented • Comments • Questions • Frequency of comments and responses • Response time to inquiries and responses • Looking at where and when people are coming to your site for what information	SumAll Socialbakers Simply Measured Bitly Google Analytics
Attitudinal	The emotional connection made based on the content, level of awareness, feelings, and perceptions of the content	• Personalized messages in response to content on social media • Sentiment and tone of shares, comments, and word of mouth • Reactions	Sysomos Hootsuite Insights Brandwatch Zoomph
Conative	The digital and offline behavior and actions taken that are a direct result of what was presented on social media	• Specific actions and behaviors taken • Advocacy efforts, ambassador endorsements, and influencer endorsements • Sign-ups • Response time • Consumption of content • Actions taken in response to content • Website and microsite traffic and analytics	Google Analytics Kissmetrics Bitly Ow.ly Likealyzer Spredfast Facebook Analytics Instagram Insights Twitter Analytics

a similar activity in the future. Plus, these measurements and metrics are important when asking for (1) future investment for activities and (2) future investment in social media strategy and creative execution campaigns.

The three outcomes (cognitive, attitudinal, and conative) can be grouped together to formulate a comprehensive social media measurement strategy, a key component to add at the planning stages for a social media campaign or program. Measurement, as stated earlier, should be done not at the very end of the program, but rather throughout the program. Table 10.2 outlines the outcomes, where they fall in the overall measurement strategy, and what measurement metrics are appropriate to measure within these outcomes. Specific tools are also noted as examples of how to capture these points of data.

BUDGET

Numbers are your friend. Showing how your work in social media contributes to the bottom line is also important. Because many professionals outside the field of social media feel that social media is "easy" or can be done for "free," social media professionals need to be up front and educate others that social media can be free, but you get what you pay for. Investing in the right tools, programs, people, and content amplification will get you better results. Social media is part of a "pay-to-play" model with all of the changes emerging on each platform and their algorithms.

In most cases, social media has a budget of about zero. This is not always the case, however, so if you do have the financial support of your employer or client to spend on social media, that is wonderful. Either way, prepare for the cases where you have to do without social media spending.

Areas to Invest in Your Budget

Throwing money at social media will not help anyone. Bad content, no matter how much money you put toward it, will still be bad content. To get the best results, you have to put forth a little bit of investment. Overall, with social media as such a developing and constant field, still some questions remain about what to spend money on and how much you have to work with. Sometimes you will have extensive resources, but other times you will have only a certain amount to spend on each campaign for social media. Choose wisely and invest where you feel you need the most support to get to where you need to be for your client, brand, or agency.

Here are some areas in which to invest:

- *Tools* (content creation, content monitoring, social media measurement, staff time, etc.). You must have the right tools to do the job. For each strategy and tactic you propose for your social media program and campaign, you need a tool to help the social media team accomplish these set objectives. For the most part, some tools (as discussed in Chapter 9) are free for users to use (Canva, Adobe Spark, etc.), but others are not (Adobe Creative Suite, etc.). The same goes for measurement, listening, and monitoring protocols. "Free" tools are available, but they may not be able to collect all of the information needed by the social media professional.

- *People.* To be the best, you must invest in the best professionals as part of your social media team. Investing in strong candidates with great experience means you also want to look at the range of skills, experiences, and perspectives they bring to the table. Which roles do you want to fill, what duties and responsibilities will there be, and what qualifications should be outlined in your job posting and contract agreements? These different roles and teams are outlined in Chapter 4.

- *Consulting fees.* Even if you have a social media team, you may want to set aside some resources for focused projects or seek the help of experts with certain specializations. Videography, crisis communications, ideation, and augmented reality/virtual reality storytelling are just a few areas to consider. However, how many team members you want to bring in really depends on your project and its social media needs.

- *Research.* Yes, research costs money, and resources should be dedicated to both traditional methods (e.g., focus groups, copy testing, interviews, and surveys) and social media methods (e.g., listening, monitoring, and reporting tools) so you can present a comprehensive view of your social media campaign and what you have been able to accomplish. Research, like social media, is not free.

- *Education (books, webinars, and certifications).* Learning does not stop in the classroom, and like the platforms themselves, measurement and content expectations and features change. Investing in education may be a top priority for your social media team. Many brands including Microsoft, Brandwatch, Hootsuite, Meltwater, and HubSpot offer both free and paid certifications and webinars in which to participate. Specific platforms have their own webinars and certifications such as Facebook Blueprint (Facebook advertising, etc.).

- *Promotion and sponsored content.* Because social media is a pay-to-play model, on some occasions (depending on goals and objectives) the social media manager has to boost or even pay for content to appear on someone's timeline to get it noticed. Sponsored tweets, stories, and updates come in all shapes and sizes, but tailoring the ads and posts is important. Taking advantage of Facebook's Creative Hub, for example, to determine the mockups of sponsored ads and posts on Facebook is a worthwhile investment both in time and in money. In addition, setting up ads on the various channels to drive traffic, interactions, followers, and even leads is an important element in which to invest.

As mentioned previously, there are specific ways to budget for each platform's sponsored ads and posts to accomplish set objectives and goals for a campaign. Each platform offers designated trainings, webinars, and workshops to better familiarize social media professionals with the tools and how to create an ad based on their overall goals. For example, Facebook and Instagram outline your overall objective, and then ask you to state your marketing objective. Awareness, consideration, and conversion align for most of the set objectives of social media campaigns. Each ad that is created goes through a series of questions specific to these three categories, and at the end, social media managers have to fine-tune the specifics: who (the audience they want to target), where (the location and platform), when (the frequency and number of times people will see this ad), and how long this ad will run (depending on the amount of investment needed). Do you need to advertise on all of the social media platforms? The answer is no. It all depends on where your audience is talking about your brand and company and what types of content your audience wouldn't mind seeing if it was sponsored or promoted. Table 10.3 outlines the various ad managers for each of the major platforms.

Metrics to Consider for Budgets on Social Media

The push toward paid content in social media also needs to be addressed and discussed. When it comes to paid media and platforms, the channels range in terms of cost for their advertisements and what they charge brands and others. Most of the time, some consistent metrics can be used to evaluate social media advertising.

For example, *cost per click* (CPC) focuses on what the advertiser pays the publisher when an individual clicks on an ad. This is one of the main paid advertising metrics to consider when you are looking at paying for an ad to come up on social media, along with *cost per impression* (CPI) and *cost per action* (CPA). *Click-through rate* (CTR) is another metric commonly used in social media. This web- and digitally focused metric keeps track of the number of people who have seen an ad or post versus those who have taken action in response. So, if 10 people out of 1,000 swiped up on an Instagram post, the CTR would be .10.

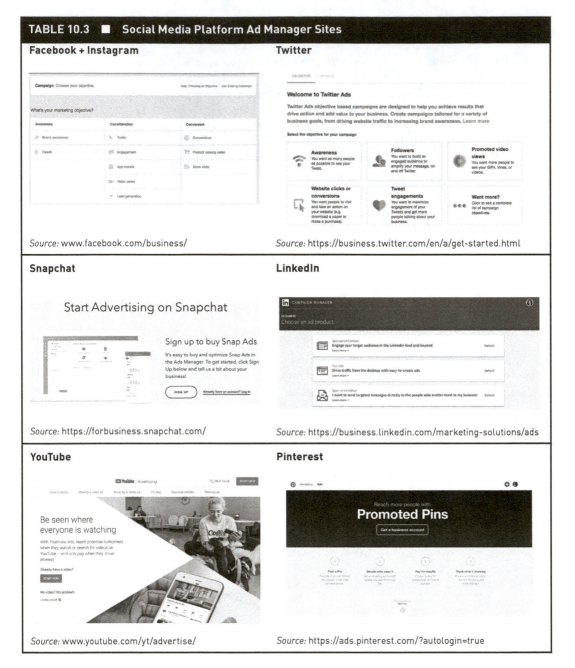

TABLE 10.3   ■   Social Media Platform Ad Manager Sites

Source: www.facebook.com/business/

Source: https://business.twitter.com/en/a/get-started.html

Source: https://forbusiness.snapchat.com/

Source: https://business.linkedin.com/marketing-solutions/ads

Source: www.youtube.com/yt/advertise/

Source: https://ads.pinterest.com/?autologin=true

It is important to outline the overall applications and outcomes aligned with these metrics. For example, CPA aligns more with conative outcomes because it is primarily focused on driving a certain action (or behavior in this case) by the user based on what is presented. The number of times a person likes a Facebook page, follows an account on Instagram, or swipes up on an Instagram Story will be the basis for what the advertiser will be charged for this program. *Cost per conversion* (CPC as well) focuses on the number of conversions made in a campaign, which is a valuable metric for marketers and others in the financial sector of a brand or agency. Showing how many people were converted into subscribers, email listserv joiners, or even new clients based on what was shared on social media, this metric is great because it can be compared across other campaigns on social media, to show the social media professional which ones were most successful in growing the customer and audience base (Paine, 2016). *Cost per engagement* (CPE) focuses on how much people reacted to the content provided for an entire campaign. This is where you divide the cost of the campaign by the total number of engagements. Keep in mind, with this metric, you also have to take into account whether or not you gave it a boost (put some dollars behind a specific post to make it perform better). The top-performing posts for a social media campaign and their associated metrics would also be a good idea to highlight here.

TABLE 10.4 ■ Paid Metrics to Note for Advertising in Social Media Budgets			
Metric	**Description**	**Outcome**	**Application and Implications**
Cost per Click (CPC)	You pay the cost per click from the ad specifically.	Cognitive	• Relatively low costs help drive traffic to your site or microsite for a campaign. • These low costs also provide opportunities to create ads on different platforms. • Everyone is doing this (consider your competition; you don't want to oversaturate the audience member). • Don't just focus on getting people to click your link. Look at how much time they spend on your ad and where they go next. • Avoid large bounce-back rates (people who do not spend time on your site after arriving there).
Cost per Impression (CPI)	You pay the cost every time your ad is viewed.	Cognitive	• Get exposure on an ongoing basis. • This can be costly since you are trying to reach everyone, but conversation is not really the focus. • Impressions are not necessarily evidence that people have actually seen your ad. • This method is good if you want to drive awareness.
Cost per Action (CPA)	You *only* pay for selected items for the audience member to do.	Conative	• Focus on the actions you want the audience member to take.
Cost per Conversion (CPC)	You only pay for the number of people you have converted into customers. Formula: Cost of Campaign / Total # of Conversions	Conative	• Focus on the direct line of how people became customers, based on what was presented on social media.
Cost per Engagement (CPE)	You calculate the cost per engagement for your campaign.	Attitudinal/ Conative	• Focus on the pieces of content that have the most reactions, engagements, and shares within your community. Best-performing pieces of content may need a boost to get even more visibility and exposure for the campaign and program.

Table 10.4 outlines these paid metrics for social media advertising (Copp, 2016) and what to consider when setting up a social media budget.

Consider the following elements when creating a budget for social media. These are some best practices to keep in mind at this stage of implementing a social media campaign or program:

- *Invest wisely.* Yes, like Indiana Jones, you do not want to choose "poorly" when it comes to your budget. Really evaluate the areas you need to invest in, and what tools and services you can get for free. It is better to have the right tools for the job than not be able to effectively implement your ideas in social media.

- *Spend the money on the areas that will take the most time or with which you need the most assistance.* There are only so many hours in a day, so make sure you look at the tasks you have in play, which ones you can do effectively, and in which areas you need a little help.

A budget is part of measurement and evaluation. Most social media platforms, as stated previously, have their own measurement components to collect and analyze. In addition, to see if you have accomplished your goal in a campaign, you have to invest in successful measurement and evaluation, and because they go hand in hand with budgeting, these two areas are interconnected for strategic social media practices. Table 10.5 provides a sample checklist of items a social media professional needs to consider measuring and investing in to make a social media program and campaign successful.

TABLE 10.5 ■ Sample Measurement and Evaluation Checklist		
AMEC Framework	**Measurement**	**Metrics**
Objectives	Business, communication, and social media objectives	• SMART criteria
Inputs	Audience analysis	• Location
		• Demographics
		• Network
		• Interests
		• Behaviors
		• Devices
		• Platforms
		• Event/holiday targeting
		• Key words
		• Influence
		• Activity
		• Engagement
		• Share of voice
		• Sentiment
		• Fans/followers/communities
		• Ambassadors/influencers

AMEC Framework	Measurement	Metrics
Activities	Customer service metrics	• Number of customer responses • Post- or question-to-comment ratio • Average response time • Average number of conversations • Follow-up survey results
Outputs	PESO (paid, earned, shared, owned) media	• Impressions • Engagement • Shares • Influence • Share of voice • Traffic • Referrals • Behaviors • Time spent on site
Outputs	Paid media	• Click-through rate • Cost per click • Cost per conversion • Cost per action • Cost per engagement
Outtakes	Content creation	• Engagement per content • Reactions/feedback • Sentiment • Channel/platform metrics • Advanced and behavioral metrics • Influencers and top key words • Hashtags • Links and shares
Outcomes	Effects on target audience	• Change in attitude • Change in behavior • Increased advocacy and influence for the client
Impact	Organizational and business objectives	• Sales • Donations • Contributions • Change in reputation (%) • Change in attitude (%)

FURTHER CONSIDERATIONS FOR MEASUREMENT, EVALUATION, AND BUDGET

Measurement and evaluation tasks take a large chunk of time and resources for a social media professional. Measurement of data and research should not be scary; instead, you should embrace it with open arms because it can share insights and stories and uncover gaps of opportunities not seen before. This is where the creativity of application comes into play for social media. Without insights and data, we may not have a justification or rationale for our activity on social media.

In order to most effectively implement a social media measurement strategy for a business, company, or individual brand, keep in mind the following tips and best practices:

- *Use plain language that is not full of jargon.* Analytics, measurement, and other forms of evaluation have a lot of jargon. Covering aspects of measurement and analysis is already a bit overwhelming, so make sure you are clear, concise, and able to communicate your insights in a way that allows everyone to understand the metrics and how they contribute to the bottom line for brands both financially and in their relationships and reputation among their audience members.

- *Don't be afraid of numbers with the budget.* As mentioned many times, budgeting for a social media plan is crucial. You get what you pay for, and if your budget consists of a lot of free aspects, you may not get the quality of work and results you are looking for. Budgets are necessary because they (1) provide real actionable measures for the work you put in and what you got out of it, (2) compare spending across different channels, and (3) provide an eagle's eye view of what was spent where, what worked and performed well, what didn't work and needs to be addressed for the future, and what metrics were gained from integrating both paid media and earned media into the social media strategy (DeMers, 2017).

- *Articulate your limitations and note differences in data.* In measurement strategy and evaluation stages, like in research, you have to be up front with the limitations. This will come down to the budget restrictions for your social media efforts. Sometimes you will not be able to afford the enterprise-level measurement tools, and you will have to settle for tools that cannot capture everything. In addition, acknowledging how the data were collected, what was not collected, and whether the algorithm or formula used to calculate certain metrics is different from other tools needs to occur. This is one reason why it is important to have a range of tools for measuring social media efforts so you can see (1) any similarities and (2) missing components or issues for some of these tools. In addition, it is always good to control and bring your data in-house where you can see them firsthand, versus getting the data sent to you by a third-party research tool or program.

- *Check your metrics and methods on a regular basis and do a regular audit of the methods/tools for social media.* Set up a timeline for when you want to collect, report, analyze, and discuss findings. This shouldn't be a once-a-year type of scenario. Setting up a realistic timeline for collecting and analyzing your data also means you have to audit the tools, approaches, and methods you are using for measurement and evaluation. Like all social media platforms, social media measurement tools change. Make sure you have the best tool to do the job, and this means constantly determining which tools and methods will help you accomplish your measurement strategy duties.

- *Invest in measurement training and education.* Measurement expectations constantly change along with the platforms. While many certifications out there are free, it is key to look at workshops, webinars, and other programs that can get you the tools, experiences, and applied insights to be effective and competitive in this area. Your education in measurement and evaluation should be on par with your training and resources attributed to creative execution and content creation.

- *Set forth checklists for measurement strategy and evaluation.* As Dennis Yu mentioned in his Humans of Social Media feature, you want to have a checklist of items to analyze, key words to collect, set objectives and their associated metrics, which tools will be used, and when/how often the data will be collected. Planning these steps relevant to each platform will help not only in the daily measurement activities, but also in educating and preparing for new hires to join the social media measurement and evaluation team.

- *Learn from insights, and adjust when needed.* Once you have evaluated what you accomplished with your objectives and goals for your social media activities, you have to reassess and see what items and measurement tools need to be adjusted, stabilized, or even deleted. Evaluating these insights will help you further advance the measurement strategy for the future, ensuring continued success for the social media program. Measurement and evaluation protocols should not go backward, but advance on the same innovative path as the creative content and brand storytelling on social media.

CHAPTER SUMMARY

Two areas of a social media plan that seem to be intimidating or even forgotten are the measurement and evaluation sections, including the overall budget. Both elements deal with numbers, which a social media professional should not only know, but fully embrace. Insights and applying strategies from data can be extremely rewarding and make a significant difference for a brand in the long run. The same goes for a budget, because without knowing what you can do with a certain amount of resources, you may not fully understand the growing need for social media in your organization or business. Without the numbers and evidence of what has happened on social media, the social media professional can't justify any increased support and spending capacity from senior management.

Without the numbers and evidence to support the impact, the social media campaign will dissolve. Measurement and budget are dependent on each other. Insights telling a story on what happened drives the support financially for social media programs. In order to stand out for future campaigns, social media professionals need to have the right tools to do their jobs, as well as the financial backing and support needed to educate, train, and produce sound pieces of content directly tied to the bottom line.

THOUGHT QUESTIONS

1. What is the overall purpose of measurement in social media programs? Identify three ways measurement can help social media professionals.

2. What are the three types of outcomes to measure for social media?

3. Define the key areas highlighted in the AMEC framework. What are the main components, and what is their overall function in social media evaluation?

4. Describe cost per click, cost per conversion, cost per engagement, and cost per action. In what ways could these be integrated into a social media campaign?

5. What are some best practices when it comes to setting up a budget? What are the main areas to consider when creating a social media budget?

EXERCISES

1. In a job interview meeting, you hear one of the other candidates state, "Measurement is not required" in our social media duties. Provide three reasons why measurement can help, and find a social media case study where measurement was used to explain what happened.

2. You have applied for a social media internship, and you receive a face-to-face interview. You are given a task to create a social media campaign for the upcoming season of NBC's *Saturday Night Live*, but you only have $100 to spend. Discuss your recommendations for the budget, which platforms you would use, and your rationale for approaching the campaign this way on social media.

3. You are working with the campus agency and got a request to create a social media campaign to reach alumni for your university. The impact the agency wants to make is to increase its reputation among this audience group. By using the AMEC interactive framework, identify what objectives you want to set forth (communication), and what inputs, activities, outputs, outtakes, outcomes, and impact you want for your social media campaign.

4. You have been tasked to create a measurement strategy for the Make-A-Wish Foundation, which has given you certain objectives to accomplish (increase donations and awareness of its cause). List the types of outcomes Make-A-Wish may want to measure on social media, and propose an example of the social media content you would create to accomplish these objectives.

REFERENCES

AMEC. (2016a). Integrated evaluation framework. Retrieved from https://amecorg.com/amecframework/framework/interactive-framework/.

AMEC. (2016b). Social media measurement: What AMEC is doing. Retrieved from https://amecorg.com/social-media-measurement/.

Baer, J. (2018). Not tracking social media ROI is your fault. *Convince & Convert With Jay Baer*. Retrieved from http://convinceandconvert.com/social-media-measurement/not-tracking-social-media-roi-is-your-fault/.

Copp, E. (2016, December 12). Are your social ads paying off? 8 metrics you should be tracking. *Hootsuite*. Retrieved from https://blog.hootsuite.com/social-media-ad-metrics/.

Dawley, S. (2017, May 16). A comprehensive guide to social media ROI. *Hootsuite*. Retrieved from https://blog.hootsuite.com/measure-social-media-roi-business/.

DeMers, J. (2017, April 5). 7 reasons social media marketing is still underrated. *Forbes*. Retrieved from https://www.forbes.com/sites/jaysondemers/2017/04/05/7-reasons-social-media-marketing-is-still-underrated/.

Jackson, D. (2016, March 30). 9 ways social media measurement can improve your marketing strategy. *Sprout Social*. Retrieved from https://sproutsocial.com/insights/social-media-measurement/.

Paine, K. (2016, June 20). The best metrics to show off your social media efforts. *The Measurement Advisor*. Retrieved from http://painepublishing.com/best-metrics-show-off-social-media-efforts/.

APPLICATION AND FUTURE CONSIDERATIONS

11 HOW SOCIAL MEDIA IS APPLIED

Exploring Different Specializations, Part I

Learning Objectives
Introduction
    How Social Media Is Applied
Humans of Social Media: *Social Media and Entertainment*
Overview of Social Media and Entertainment
Humans of Social Media: *Social Media and Crisis Communication*
Overview of Social Media and Crisis Communication
Humans of Social Media: *Social Media and Journalism*
Overview of Social Media and Journalism
    Cases Involving Social Media and Journalism
    Best Practices and Recommendations
Humans of Social Media: *Social Media and Sports*
Overview of Social Media and Sports
Chapter Summary
Thought Questions
Exercises
References

LEARNING OBJECTIVES

After reading this chapter, you will be able to

- Identify the areas in which social media can be applied
- Discuss how the sports, entertainment, crisis communication, and journalism fields use social media
- Explain the best practices and guidelines for social media for sports, entertainment, crisis communication, and journalism professionals

INTRODUCTION

How Social Media Is Applied

While exploring this book, you have learned to understand and appreciate social media strategy. We have discussed changes that impact measurement, creative execution, audience analysis, and personal branding. The foundation of strategic planning related to social media has been stressed and emphasized throughout the industry. Yet one thing missing from many cases is a clear visualization of how social media is applied, and in what industries.

Social media, as emphasized in this book, is not owned by one discipline or industry. In fact, that's the beauty of social media. It is a hub form of communication, community building, and relationship management.

In this section of the book, two chapters are dedicated to the specific specializations within social media. This first chapter focusing on how to apply social media provides an overview of the different areas in which social media is applied. Best practices, campaigns, and unique characteristics are discussed and highlighted in each section. One unique attribute characterizing this chapter is that rather than a single *Humans of Social Media* feature, you will find four—one for each specialization within social media. Each specialization will highlight specific expectations, examples of how to use social media for different industries, and best practices. In these sections, we cover how the entertainment, sports, crisis communication, and journalism fields integrate social media into their practices, as well as some challenges, opportunities, and case studies professionals face in their respective industries.

HUMANS OF SOCIAL MEDIA
RUSS WILDE, MARKETING PROFESSIONAL AT THUZIO AND PRESIDENT OF FRONT OFFICE SPORTS

Source: Courtesy of Jess Scott

Russ Wilde

Social Media and Entertainment

Introduction

Hello! My name is Russ Wilde, and I work on the marketing team at Thuzio and am also the president of Front Office Sports. Thuzio hosts an executive client entertainment and networking event series featuring documentary-style interviews with athletes and influencers. Front Office Sports is a digital publication that provides insights about all things at the intersection of sports and business. Previously, I headed strategy and operations for Julius, an end-to-end influencer marketing platform leveraged by brands and agencies to identify creators and manage campaigns.

I grew up in Cranford, New Jersey, and graduated from the University of Miami in 2015 with a degree in sport administration. Fun fact: While at The U, I was a member of the debate team, which finished in the top 10 nationally in 2014!

How did you get your start in social media?

My first *real* introduction to the world of social media started in October 2014 when I joined Front Office Sports. After meeting Adam White for a salad at The Rat on campus at The U (order the no-yes fries if you're ever there!), I jumped at the opportunity to run the social media accounts for FOS.

In just six months, I grew the FOS follower base on Twitter from 200 to 3,000, laying the foundation for the success we have seen over the last few years. The growth of FOS can be attributed to an implemented influencer marketing strategy.

When FOS was first created, we interviewed sports business professionals about their careers with the goal of helping young professionals learn more about the industry. With that, I was able to identify professionals in the social media space with between 1,000 and 5,000 followers and asked them to be interviewed for the site. As time went on and FOS started to become a powerful brand among the #SMsports and #sportsbiz communities, we were able to interview people with 10,000 followers, then 25,000 followers, then 50,000 followers, and so on.

By interviewing these well-known, highly credible "influencers" in the industry, we were associated with them, and over time we became a highly respected publication among executives in the field. Today, we reach over 1 million digital impressions each month.

What is your favorite part of working in your social media area of expertise?

My favorite part about working with influencers is that each individual has such amazing backgrounds and paths to success. Everyone has a story, and through both FOS and Thuzio, I have always tried to showcase the stories of interesting people.

What is one thing you can't live without while working in social media?

The one thing I can't live without has to be my phone. This might be a cop-out answer, but it's 100% true.

What is your favorite social media account (person, brand, etc.) to follow, and why?

Other than FOS, anyone who follows my personal account knows that I am a huge fan of Barstool Sports (not only from a content standpoint, but from a business perspective as well). As with any comedy brand, its stuff isn't for everyone, but I love the content that it produces day in and day out. I think I've become an even bigger fan of Barstool Sports since I started studying the media industry because its growth has been so fun to watch.

What is the most challenging part of working in social media?

The most challenging part for me is finding time to unplug. Even when I'm not "working," I'm constantly reading trade articles or scrolling through Twitter. Sometimes it's hard to take a step back and try to focus on something without thinking about what might be happening in the digital world.

What is your take on your area of expertise and the social media industry?

I'm a huge believer in media companies hiring influencers to work for them. For entities looking to create content for brand partners, it's important to have people on staff who understand how to cultivate large audiences. As display advertising continues to decrease in effectiveness (for a multitude of reasons), native advertising by way of content collaborations is the best way for media companies to monetize.

What do you wish you had known when you were starting out?

One thing that I wish I had known a few years ago is the importance of being on *all* social media platforms. For anyone in the industry, it's important to be active on different social media sites and apps so that you can think about how other people engage on the specific platforms. Whether it's Facebook, Twitter, Snapchat, Musical.ly, or House Party, it's important for people in the industry to stay on top of what's out there and actively learn how to engage on each platform because all of them are so different.

You can follow Russ Wilde on Twitter at @Russ WildeJr and Thuzio at @Thuzio.

OVERVIEW OF SOCIAL MEDIA AND ENTERTAINMENT

As Russ Wilde mentioned, the entertainment world is split up into many different specializations. Thuzio works exclusively with influencers (sports, business, and entertainment celebrities) for its line of work. Entertainment is probably one of the areas where social media is a key component of any strategy for a campaign, from promoting a movie (similar to the entertainment and social media work Rich Calabrese has implemented with Fizziology) to even the work Jeremy Darlow has done with sports (which is highlighted in this chapter).

Within the entertainment spectrum, professionals must understand how to use social media on the brand, agency, and celebrity side, as well as the consumer side. Each area of entertainment (sports, movies, gaming, fashion, etc.) has utilized social media to its advantage by raising awareness of brands (e.g., Zac Posen and his fashion line) and by creating hype for upcoming competitions (e.g., UFC and WWE), television shows and movies (e.g., *Game of Thrones* and *The Wolverine*), events (e.g., SXSW, Cannes Lions, and Comic-Con), creative activations at events (e.g., Westworld at SXSW, adidas at the All-Star Game), individuals (e.g., Gigi Hadid, Beyoncé, and Taylor Swift), and sports figures (e.g., Tom Brady). Each of these brands has become its own direct media outlet where it does not have to go first to the media and then to the customers. Essentially, these brands can go straight to the community and reach followers immediately through a tweet, update, or live video.

There are many cases to explore in the entertainment industry, but when it comes to entertainment social media campaigns, everything has to be tied in to the overall promotional campaign with sound business objectives and measurements. For example, *The Wolverine* won the award for best social media implementation by a movie at the sixth annual Shorty Awards in 2014. The social media professionals behind the *Wolverine* Declassified campaign were able to win this award by strategically utilizing their community (a total of 3.4 million people) and fans to build excitement about exploring the "lost years of Logan" (Shorty Awards, 2018). The movie studio released documents outlining the lost content fans of the film had not seen before, which resulted in the ultimate combination of successes: The campaign created word-of-mouth engagement among the fans and motivated them to share this content with others (essentially driving traffic and engagement metrics), sparking a high level of excitement and brand awareness of the movie before the launch (Shorty Awards, 2018).

As mentioned previously, the entertainment industry wants to use social media strategically to help generate buzz to motivate others to take action in some way on- or offline. Whether it is to download a new song or album or go to the movies or a sporting event, each of these actions can be directly tied to metrics and social media conversations. Another example of an entertainment case study to explore involves Taylor Swift, who deleted items off her social media accounts to create speculation of a new music album (McIntyre, 2017). Once the single from her latest album *Reputation* came out, a massive download of the song and conversation emerged on social media, both positive and negative (Feinberg, 2017). There was intrigue and interest in the album, but a little confusion as to why Swift went dark and silent before launching her new brand and music.

This is somewhat different from other artists who utilize social media for their brand image and music. Some celebrities use social media not to be constantly active and engaged, but to create some mystery while also giving fans and others a chance to see a side they would not have been able to see before. Beyoncé comes into play here with Instagram—she posts regularly, but just enough to create interest, excitement, and occasional viral content (e.g., pregnancy announcements) covered in the mainstream news (Duboff, 2016). Both Swift and Beyoncé use social media to drive attention to their brands and music, but they approach the process in different ways. Each star has her own voice, community, and view of how to use social media, but ultimately, her overall goal is to increase brand recognition for work among the public and her fans, but also drive actions for her music and products.

The entertainment industry has seen a shift not only in how events, individual celebrities, and brands are promoted, but also in how these individuals engage in the space entirely. For example, entertainment professionals have to know how social media affects their work by exploring the following questions (Buchwald, 2016):

- How can social media deliver on the investment put into it?

- How can professionals and teams/brands adapt to the ongoing changes?

- How does the impact of rapid change in format affect the entertainment industry?

Social media is a necessary companion tool for people watching awards shows, sporting events, and high-profile live events (Newman, 2017). Some traditional celebrities rise to the occasion and use social media to amplify their brands (e.g., George Takei from *Star Trek*, Selena Gomez, and Chris Pratt). New celebrities have arisen over the years based on what they have done with YouTube and other social media platforms. Lilly Singh, author of a book called *How to Be a Bawse* (2017), started her career on YouTube with sketches and has since risen to true celebrity status online as a result (O'Connor, 2017). Entertainment professionals working in social media still rely on underlying principles to attach the right celebrity with the right brand and campaign; otherwise, it will not go over very well.

Social media professionals should keep the following best practices in mind when it comes to diving into the entertainment arena:

- *Identify the platforms that can best serve your brand.* Not all celebrities want to be on social media. Some will be active on certain platforms already, but others will be reluctant to join.

- *Have a strategy for all aspects.* There is a time and place for every update, picture, and action taken on social media. You want to be authentic and real for your fans and audiences, but a dash of professional branding should always be attached to the content you share. Think about ways to capture your audience members' attention and make them feel part of the community. Some celebrities, for example, have their own name for their fans (e.g., Lady Gaga's "Little Monsters").

- *Get loyal fans and ambassadors behind your brand on social media.* These people help drive the word-of-mouth communication efforts for the entertainment business. Evaluate these individuals, see what they share and how much it impacts your own brand and network, and create relationships with them.

- *Be aware of trolls and how they can take a toll on the celebrity.* Celebrities and any individuals in high-profile positions are famous and well recognized on social media, but also a target for online trolls. Being aware of the protection they may need online as well as offline is crucial. Celebrities have deleted their accounts entirely due to backlash or because of trolls (Ed Sheeran deleted his Twitter, for example).

For those in the entertainment industry, social media is a key part of engaging with fans and audiences while using the platform to showcase reach and influence. In addition, more opportunities are available for potential sponsorship and partnership deals, all key components to consider for brand marketing. Yes, even with all of these positive elements and opportunities, serious challenges need to be discussed and accounted for. Social media for entertainment professionals is a blessing or a curse, depending on how people view the array of platforms.

Source: Courtesy of Emilie Tournevache

Melissa Agnes

Social Media and Crisis Communication

Introduction

I'm a crisis management consultant and keynote speaker. My goal and passion is helping organizations implement a CRISIS READY™ culture.

My clients include financial organizations, technology companies, health care organizations, government agencies, cities and municipalities, law enforcement agencies, energy companies, global nonprofits, and many others.

Having a CRISIS READY™ culture means that the entire organization is trained and empowered to detect and appropriately respond to incidents, whether issues or crises, instinctively and in real time, rather than being dependent on a crisis management plan that sits on a shelf, collecting dust.

How did you get your start in your field?

My mind always sees risk. It always has. Back in 2010, it struck me one day that no one was evaluating or discussing the risk of social media and real-time communication. This realization ignited a passion within me that I didn't know existed before that moment. At the time, I had never thought about crisis management as a "thing." But that soon changed as my newfound passion fueled my next year of reading anything and everything I could get my hands on, on the topic of crisis management.

One early morning, about a year into my "studies," the vice president of a real estate investment trust, one of our clients, called me in a panic. He told me that the company's president was in his car with a prospective investor, and they were listening to a radio report that one of their buildings was about to explode—which wasn't true. Apparently, the story started on Twitter, and of course the company had no idea what Twitter was! So, the VP called me, the company's web strategist.

I headed to my client's office, and within roughly 30 minutes, we had the media correcting themselves, and we had the company up and running on Twitter—but more importantly, we had Twitter streamlining to its website's homepage as we knew the company's investors would be going to the website, not to Twitter, for news and updates concerning the incident. To make a long story short, the next day I received a call from the president of the company thanking me. Not only had its unit price not gone down since the day before, but it had actually gone up a cent!

So after about a year of studying everything I could on the topic of crisis management, Colt, my husband and business partner, and I had the opportunity to help a client manage a real-time, escalating issue. In those moments, we learned three things:

1. We had a natural aptitude for crisis management;

2. We loved it; and

3. People needed it.

The rest, as they say, is history!

What is your favorite part of working in your area of expertise?

To be honest, I love every part of it. But I suppose if I must choose a favorite, it would be the value that being CRISIS READY™ provides to organizations, every day, not just in times of crisis. For example, implementing a CRISIS READY™ culture helps organizations foster cross-departmental collaborations and relationships, improves internal communication processes, strengthens stakeholder value, and instills a mindset that looks for opportunities in all situations, especially the negative ones.

How does your field integrate social media?

Social media is an inevitable component of all crises in this day and age. On one hand, it amplifies the challenges and obstacles that organizations are forced to face in times of crisis. But on the other hand, it presents unique opportunities to connect, communicate effectively, and, ultimately, strengthen relationships with key stakeholders, while managing those same crises.

What is your favorite social media account (person, brand, etc.) to follow, and why?

It changes all the time. I tend to follow people and organizations that inspire me or teach me something new that I may be looking to learn. Then I move on. However, I can say that, at the moment, my favorite and go-to platform is Instagram.

What is the most challenging part of working in crisis management?

All the work I do is challenging. It constantly challenges me to be at the top of my game, to continue learning and evolving, and to be the best I can possibly be for my clients. But the challenge is one of the things I appreciate the most about what I do. It keeps me on my toes, it keeps me inspired and motivated, and it keeps me excited!

What do you wish you had known when you were starting out?

It would have been nice to know for sure that it would all work out. I always knew I was on to something big—I could feel it in my bones. However, it wasn't always easy. Sometimes, when I look back, I say to Colt that it would have been great to just get a glimpse of where this journey would take us. He then reminds me that we made it here without any glimpses, so we didn't need it. I know he's right, but it still would have been nice!

Melissa Agnes can be contacted via her website (www.agnesday.com) or on Twitter at @melissa_agnes. Melissa is also the author of Crisis Ready, *which is available via Amazon.*

OVERVIEW OF SOCIAL MEDIA AND CRISIS COMMUNICATION

While organizations and individuals experience many positive events and situations, negatively charged events may also distort daily activities and cause financial, emotional, and personal harm to those involved. These situations are conceptualized as crises. Crises come in various forms and can impact an organization or individual at any time. In other words, crises are significant, disruptive events that often feature a rapid onset.

Crises have been defined as events that either cause harm to or have the potential to harm an individual or organization. Whether the harm produces physical, emotional, or environmental damage to individuals and communities involved in the crisis, or damage to the corporate reputation or financial standing of an organization, the range of harm is different in each unique situation. Full understanding of a crisis encompasses not only the actual precipitating event, but also the process or time leading from a precipitating event, including the subsequent perceptions of the crisis by various stakeholders.

While most research has been dedicated to traditional crises, social media crises are quite different due to where they started. Tim Coombs (2013), one of the leading researchers and scholars in crisis communication, classified social media crises as acting somewhat like "zombies" compared to traditional crises. What Coombs means is that a social media crisis is an incident or triggering event (e.g., the actual crisis situation) that

- Happens on social media or on a particular platform

- Rapidly spreads from person to person

- Spreads virally to become a traditional news story

The biggest confusion among social media professionals regarding traditional crises and social media crises is to think they are one and the same. However, they are quite different. Social media crises are caused by certain messages, situations, and responses that emerged on the platforms themselves whereas traditional crises usually happen offline but are discussed on social media. Natural disasters (e.g., Hurricanes Harvey and Irma), workplace or school violence (e.g., Sandy Hook), corporate/political or social scandals (Anthony Weiner), and other traditional crises have all been covered and discussed on social media. The challenges for social media and crisis communication specialists are that (1) the technology and platforms that are used constantly change and adapt, so what can work and what can go wrong become equally important to consider, and (2) you always have to think of outside possibilities and new challenges that could emerge with each new advancement, platform, and use of a tool.

Social media crises have emerged over the years for brands and others. Many brands, agencies, social media professionals, and athletic teams have had their own experience dealing with social media crises, some recognizable. Brands and others, for example, have found themselves in some of the following potential unfortunate situations on social media:

- *Employees (or former employees) going rogue.* As discussed in Chapter 2, HMV, an agency in the United Kingdom, had to lay off a large number of employees due to budget cuts in 2013, and this included its marketing department. Because HMV's marketing employees were the only ones with access to the company's social media accounts, they live tweeted their firings ("HMV Employee Goes Rogue," 2017).

- *Underestimating the impact of crisis history and outrage on social media.* Social media does not forget a brand that has a crisis history, and the result usually ends in more outrage online. In March 2018, United Airlines faced criticism as it was accused of putting a dog in an overhead bin during a flight from Houston to New York City (Gulliver, 2018). This comes nearly a year after the airline's live video passenger crisis from April 2017 (as discussed later in this chapter).

- *Not doing your research on the content or situation.* Trying to interject yourself into a conversation is an art form, and embracing real-time marketing or trendjacking has become quite the competition for brands to showcase relevancy. However, Delta learned the hard way when it shared the wrong photo of Ghana during the 2014 World Cup (DeMers, 2016; see also Chapter 7, page 154). The same goes for DiGiorno. The pizza company interjected itself into a serious Twitter conversation surrounding domestic violence with the hashtag #WhyIStayed. Instead, the company said it stayed "because there was pizza," trying to tie the conversation back to the brand (DeMers, 2016; see also Chapter 7, page 155). This did not go over well for DiGiorno, which had to respond to each tweet with an apology.

- *Not recognizing the tone and concern expressed on social media.* Equifax announced in September 2017 a Category 5 crisis where 143 million customers had their credit impacted by hackers (Temin, 2017). The credit card company was not perceived to respond appropriately to this crisis, and at least from what they shared on their social media accounts, people felt Equifax was not as urgent in addressing this crisis as it should have been.

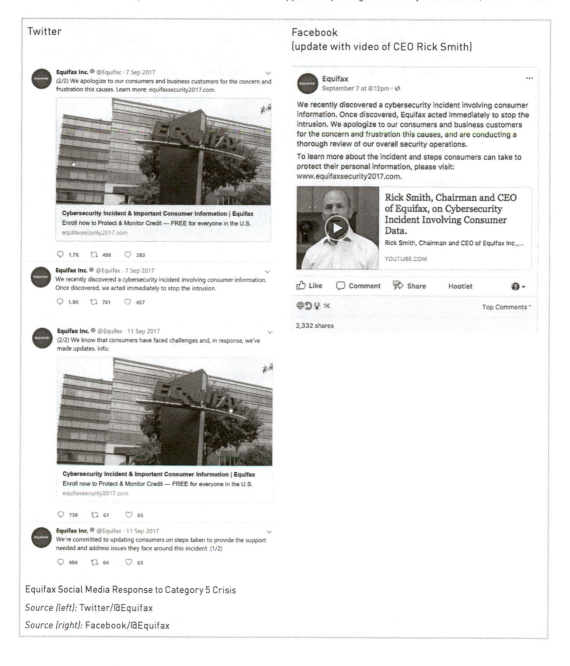

Equifax Social Media Response to Category 5 Crisis

Source (left): Twitter/@Equifax

Source (right): Facebook/@Equifax

- *Not thinking about the impact of a hashtag.* SeaWorld experienced this problem during the height of the *Blackfish* scandal. The theme park wanted to start a conversation with audience members, but others immediately took over, including activists who were not too pleased with SeaWorld (CB Insights, 2017). In addition, McDonald's wanted to do a #McDStories feature, but instead got feedback about all the negative things people experienced with the brand. These were great ideas for engagement, but the brands did not consider all of the potential ways in which people would actually use the hashtags.

In case you have not heard about the following example, it demonstrated the power of social media (specifically live video) to spark a crisis that went viral. In April 2017, a United flight became global news when passenger David Dao was forced out of his seat by Chicago airport security guards and dragged from the plane. The video of the treatment of the passenger on the Chicago to Louisville flight is very disturbing and raised outrage on- and offline. This was the topic of conversation among students and professionals alike. United released a statement from its CEO regarding the situation, which caused even more negative reaction toward and discussion of the brand.

Let's talk about this a bit more. We can evaluate the case in a variety of different ways. The trigger event (or the crisis, as we call this in crisis communications) was the video of the passenger on United Express Flight 3411, but the way United responded with the CEO and the leaked email to United employees did further damage to the brand among its audiences. In addition, as the photo below shows, the initial statement shared on United's Twitter account did not go over well among key audiences and the media. How you respond and act is extremely important when faced with a crisis situation, as demonstrated here with the reputation damage available for the world to see on social media.

The response was not perceived as effective since it was viewed as generic and not displaying empathy to the situation for the audience members. In addition, it is important to look at what metrics and data have to say about things. Understanding the overall sentiment (what people are saying and responding to) about a brand during a crisis is key. For the purpose of the United crisis, data were evaluated through Sysomos to see what topics were covered on Twitter. As Figure 11.1 shows, the results were not that positive. We see the flight number listed second after United, and then we also see the other topics that were organically created (#NewUnitedAirlinesMottos), which brought forth memes and other contributions from the internet—probably not what you want to be trending for your brand.

Another important element to consider is the fact that many people will look not only at the impacted parties during a crisis, but at anyone associated with them. Associated advertisers, donors, and even the media can be called out on social media to address the situation. In fact, this happened with the United crisis. PRWeek (widely known as a trade publication and outlet for the public relations field) recently gave Oscar Munoz its Communication of the Year Award at its annual awards banquet. The publication had a post about the case study on its website, but made no mention of giving this award to United's CEO; nor has it responded to this on social media. Eventually, after facing backlash on this issue, PRWeek had to release a statement as well.

Corporate or reputation crises are not the only crises relevant to social media. In fact, social media can be the means for asking for help and even reaching government authorities to save people's lives.

United ✓
@united

United CEO response to United Express Flight 3411.

This is an upsetting event to all of us here at United. I apologize for having to re-accommodate these customers. Our team is moving with a sense of urgency to work with the authorities and conduct our own detailed review of what happened. We are also reaching out to this passenger to talk directly to him and further address and resolve this situation.

- Oscar Munoz, CEO, United Airlines

United CEO Oscar Munoz's Response on Twitter

FIGURE 11.1   ■   Sysomos Buzz Graph of United Crisis

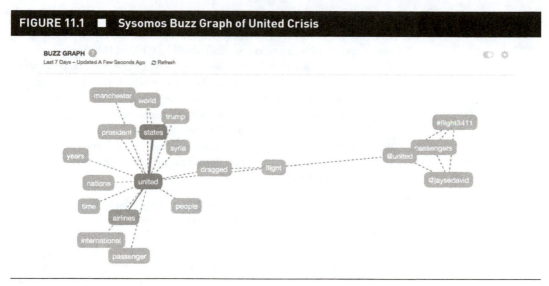

Source: ©Sysomos.

In a natural disaster case, Hurricane Harvey sparked a lot of engagement, discussion, and conversations on social media. While several individuals were able to make a difference in responding to this disaster thanks to social media, others were called out because of their inactivity or initial lack of support. Joel Osteen, the popular pastor in Houston, Texas, has a large church in the city and was called out on social media for not opening his doors to people looking for shelter (Engel, 2017). Conflicting reports about whether his church experienced "major flooding" circulated. Osteen was criticized for how he addressed the situation during interviews and on social media (Phillips, 2017).

Eventually, Osteen opened his doors to those in need in Houston. This case provides another example of the importance of transmitting information using appropriate message strategies, timing, and channels.

Several best practices can guide our responses to a social media crisis situation:

- *Create a social media component for your crisis management plan* (Keys, 2017). Constantly updating a designated section with new trends, tools, best practices, and case studies is crucial in making sure everyone is on board with the social media protocols and practices. This includes making sure a contingency plan is in place in case of certain incidents, such as a disgruntled employee trying to go rogue on the main social media platforms and locking everyone out of the accounts (e.g., HMV).

- *Set up necessary monitoring, listening, and response team strategies.* As discussed in Chapter 5, it is good to see what mentions and discussions come through that may be early warning signs, negative reviews or comments, and rising concerns that are sensitive and need immediate action. For example, Uber had to address the rising trend of people advocating for others to delete its app after reports of unfair surge prices. The trending hashtag #DeleteUber started a negative chain reaction for the brand's reputation and ultimately resulted in several of the company's members (including the CEO) leaving the company (Norton, 2017).

- *Identify where the crisis first started online.* In a case involving Domino's and YouTube in 2009, two employees posted a video of themselves being inappropriate with their food on YouTube. The CEO of Domino's, J. Patrick Doyle, posted a video on YouTube to discuss how the company was going to handle this crisis situation. The brand realized, after seeing the discussion on Twitter (Domino's had to create a Twitter handle to respond to the crisis, and its first tweet was to address this situation), it had to go to the place where the crisis originated to be effective. This practice has been demonstrated across the board in other crises such as the Las Vegas shooting (2017) on Twitter, KFC's chicken shortage crisis (2018) on Twitter, and Logan Paul and YouTube (2018).

- *Write relevant content that is easy to share and easy to understand.* Provide enough clarity in what you want audience members to do in a crisis that they understand it and also realize "This is important for me to follow." Social media is about dialogue, participating in the conversation, and making sure the social media professionals involved are not neglectful of or absent from a crisis. Give your community and audience members a sense of control (or self-efficacy) over the situation.

- *Take a moment and "pause" content during a crisis.* People don't want to see your promoted tweets or updates when they are searching for shelters in a natural disaster. Among brands that have made this mistake are Epicurious (Boston Marathon bombing, 2013), Gap (Hurricane Sandy, 2012; Wasserman, 2012), and DiGiorno (#WhyIStayed hashtag conversation about domestic violence in 2014 after the Ray Rice incident).

- *Make sure to correct any false rumors, information, or news spreading online about you or the situation.* This is an important topic. There are occasions when you have to correct the facts, let others know if images or photos from certain natural disasters or incidents are "fake," and where they can go for trusted news. This situation has occurred in many different crises, such as the Boston Marathon bombing in 2013 and Hurricane Irma in 2017. In the case of Hurricane Irma, the Federal Emergency Management Agency created a designated rumor-control section on its website for people to get confirmed information directly from the source (www.fema.gov/hurricane-irma-rumor-control).

In summary, as for social media in general, crisis communication professionals working in this area are constantly bombarded with new issues, challenges, reputational risks, and opportunities to address in the industry. Keeping up with the trends in social media is one part of the equation for crisis communication professionals, but certain behaviors, message strategies, and crisis communication best practices will still be relevant to note even if the platforms change.

If you are interested in the social media implications of crisis communication, there are certain professionals and groups to follow:

- Melissa Agnes (@melissa_agnes)
- Deirdre Breakenridge (@dbreakenridge)
- Jonathan Bernstein (@bernsteincrisis)
- Tobias Mueller (@TMuellerMUC)

HUMANS OF SOCIAL MEDIA
KERRY FLYNN, BUSINESS REPORTER FOR DIGIDAY

Source: Courtesy of Mike Murphy

Kerry Flynn

Social Media and Journalism

Introduction

I've worked as a business reporter at Mashable since July 2016. Prior, I reported on the business of social media for *International Business Times*. I also interned at *The Huffington Post, Forbes*, and *Money* magazine and freelanced for *The Hartford Courant* and *The Day* in New London, Connecticut. I grew up in western Massachusetts and studied environmental science and economics at Harvard.

How did you get your start in social media?

The first social networks I joined were AOL Instant Messenger (AIM) and Neopets. Those aren't traditional forms of social media from what we hear today, but it was the first time I used the internet to connect with people. I joined Facebook in December 2006 while I was in high school, and I signed up for Twitter in April 2009.

What is your favorite part of working in your area of social media expertise?

My favorite part of reporting on social media is keeping companies accountable. Examples include Facebook's biases with features like the News Feed and Safety Check and Twitter's efforts to curb abuse and terrorism propaganda. I also love connecting with and listening to the larger social media community such as the first influencers on Periscope and sports leagues on Snapchat.

What is one thing you can't live without while working in social media?

My iPhone—simple as that.

What is your favorite social media account (person, brand, etc.) to follow, and why?

The team at @Square and @TryCaviar. The social lead of those accounts is Nick Dimichino. Nick and his team use Twitter as I think it should be used by brands, sharing related content, offering customer support, and also joining in on conversations. Check out this piece as one example: www.adweek.com/creativity/after-slicing-up-a-fart-sandwich-squares-twitter-ninja-says-staying-silent-would-be-deadly/.

What is the most challenging part of working in social media?

Never being unplugged. I have friends in the industry who try to take time away whether they're on vacation or just spending some time each day without their phone. The only times I'm detached from social media is at the gym, in the shower, and when I'm sleeping.

You have been active in mentoring future young professionals in social media. What has been the most rewarding experience or moment you have had in helping students?

A lot of people ask me how to grow their presence on Twitter, which I always respond to with "Be yourself." There's nothing better than authenticity.

What do you wish you had known when you were starting out?

I actually wish I had used social media more during college. I was so focused on studying science and economics and running the print design and metro news sections of *The Harvard Crimson*. But despite being on the platforms, I didn't really take advantage of Facebook and Twitter, for example, when it came to following and sharing news while I was in college.

   Kerry Flynn is a technology and business writer for Digiday, a leading social media technology media outlet. Kerry can be connected on Twitter at @kerrymflynn.

OVERVIEW OF SOCIAL MEDIA AND JOURNALISM

Journalism and social media have become an integrated part of what reporters, news outlets, and feature writers gravitate to for their stories, news, and community building. Social media is one of the major ways people get news today. According to the Pew Research Center, 67% of Americans reported that they get some of their news from social media (Shearer & Gottfried, 2017). In 2017, *The New York Times* released social media guidelines outlining practices its reporters need to follow and adhere to in order to report the news, address questions and comments, and engage with their readership community. In addition, Reuters (n.d.) has a policy with certain requirements for its journalists to follow and be aware of on social media. Some of the overarching guidelines (fairness, asking if the story is a hoax, attribution of sources, no falsehoods, etc.) are general, but they also include specific social media guidelines (Reuters, n.d.):

- Be responsible, fair, and impartial in the stories and conversations on social media.

- Be confidential and refrain from disclosure of insider information.

- Be careful because everything stated on social media is for public viewing, but note social media can be used as a tool to improve your role in the media.

For journalists, social media has become a way to

- *Share breaking news.* Crises and events often break on social media (in many cases, Twitter), followed by news articles on the media's site. The 2009 US Airways Hudson River crash was first reported when a bystander named Janis Krums shared a picture on Twitter (Langer, 2014). This illustrates the rise of citizen journalism, and also puts the traditional media and journalism profession on notice of this rising trend. Now, everyone uses social media to report news first while redirecting audiences to the media's owned platforms (websites, blogs, etc.).

- *Report on stories in real time.* Providing real-time and visual content on the site of the story is one way to use social media for journalism. The media can use Facebook, Twitter, Instagram, and other platforms to play live videos and add on to their stories.

- *Offer exclusives.* To reach new audiences, many media outlets create digital- or mobile-first content, which will allow them to repurpose or even share content on different platforms. For example, *The New York Times* could publish an exclusive interview, but then repurpose teasers of the interview on social media platforms such as Facebook, Twitter, and Instagram in the format of short videos or even pictures.

- *Find stories.* Journalists are looking for inspiration on social media as well as information for their stories. If they see a trending topic, they pursue it to see if there is any particular light to it or if it is something to pass on. However, the days when journalists have to wait around for a source are over. Resources like Help A Reporter Out (HARO) are useful for journalists for connecting with professionals working with brands and clients (e.g., public relations) to connect sources for a story or to discover to whom to reach out via social media.

- *Engage with readers.* Reporters, anchors, writers, and other journalism professionals are encouraged to use social media to be part of the conversation, not always dictating where the conversation needs to go. Journalists engage in conversations via Twitter through direct messages, participating in a trending topic or hashtag, engaging in Twitter chats, or connecting with other professionals in the industry.

Cases Involving Social Media and Journalism

In many incidents, social media is an integrated part of how reporters, mainstream media, news anchors, and bloggers communicate, share, and document their stories. Some worldwide events have captured the media's attention from the journalists' point of view, and social media has become the first stop for getting news for many audience members.

While many events have been documented on social media, several high-profile cases have used social media, from the media's perspective, to capture ongoing events. The 2016 U.S. presidential election with Donald Trump and Hillary Clinton made waves not only on the candidates' own social media accounts, but on accounts used by the traditional media as well. "Brexit," the campaign to get the United Kingdom out of the European Union, saw a huge amount of social media coverage and traffic from the media on the subject around the world. The 2017 Las Vegas shooting at Mandalay Bay was another incident where the media, in some cases, reported news that had not been verified or confirmed. When we live in an age where the media are all about being first and breaking the news first, we need guidelines in place to verify, confirm, and then validate what messages we share on social media. In addition, we must be aware of the rise of uninformed messages that do not come from official sources (aka fake news) and how this affects the trustworthiness, credibility, and impact of the media and journalists within their communities.

Best Practices and Recommendations

Journalists, like all professionals working in social media, have some unique responsibilities and obligations to follow for their profession and the communities they serve. Here are some recommendations and best practices to follow when entering the journalism and social media industry:

- *Have a set ethical code and policy for the newsroom.* As listed in the NPR (2017) social media guidelines, it is crucial to maintain a level of professional conduct that reflects not only the role of the journalist, but the credibility of the news outlet.

- *Be aware of the new responsibilities you have as a journalist.* Not only is it important to write about the content, but journalists (print, broadcast, etc.) have to be active in distributing and promoting their content for others to see. The time and dedication needed to be part of the online conversation today is more important than ever, and the journalists who are active on social media are the more successful ones (Nicholson, 2017).

- *Adopt the professional conduct that reflects your reputation as a media professional.* The New York Times (2017) updated its social media guidelines to reflect this, and spent time outlining not only some key principles for the newspaper to follow, but guidelines for its reporters to follow as well.

- *Confirm and validate all information before hitting the "publish" button.* While it is tempting to be first, being able to rely on your sources and focus on fundamental journalism principles will help not only the reputation of the reporter or journalist, but also the credibility of the news story.

HUMANS OF SOCIAL MEDIA
JEREMY DARLOW, AUTHOR (BRANDS WIN CHAMPIONSHIPS AND ATHLETES ARE BRANDS TOO) AND FOUNDER OF THE BRAND FOOD THINK TANK

Source: Courtesy of Jeremy Darlow

Jeremy Darlow

Social Media and Sports

Introduction

I am the author of a book called *Brands Win Championships*, in which I argue that the most successful NCAA (National Collegiate Athletic Association) programs of the future will be those with the strongest brand, not necessarily the strongest defense or best coach. I recently founded Brand Food, the first and only think tank dedicated to building college sports brands. As well, I'm a graduate of Oregon State University, where I am often an adjunct professor, focused on digital brand management. Finally, I am the former director of marketing for adidas Football and Baseball out of Portland, Oregon, where I helped athletes, entertainers, and programs such as Notre Dame, UCLA, Miami, Aaron

Rodgers, Kanye West, and Kris Bryant promote and build their brands.

How did you get your start in social media?

My career starts and finishes with brand marketing. Along the way, I've either run or managed the social media functions of the departments I've been in charge of. When I started out in brand marketing years ago, social media was just entering the picture. Back then it was Myspace, a platform I used extensively to launch video game products and brands for Ubisoft, headquartered in San Francisco, California. From that point on, every brand I managed utilized social media to tell its story.

What is your favorite part of working in your area of social media expertise?

I'm extremely passionate about brand marketing and brand building. I fell in love with the concept in college and haven't looked back. A reason for that and a key to the brand development process is storytelling, and in today's digital world, there is no better place to tell a story than via social media. I've always compared marketing to a game of chess. The consumer makes a move; the brand makes a move. The consumer makes another move; the brand counters. It's that back-and-forth that has me hooked. That analogy has never been more relevant than today because of social media. A brand can now make changes to a strategy in real time thanks to platforms like Twitter and Instagram.

What is one thing you can't live without while working in social media?

Inserting a brand into culture moments, without a doubt. I've always said, "It's easier to crash a party than throw a party," and these days there's at least one party a month that captures the world's attention. The great thing about a space like Twitter is that when something worth talking about happens, brands and brand managers can instantly become part of the conversation. But there's no time off now. You have to be ready for anything and everything, which keeps you on your toes and keeps your skills sharp. The moment you take your foot off the gas is the moment your competition gets a jump on a story and you're left picking up scraps.

What is your favorite social media account (person, brand, etc.) to follow, and why?

Believe it or not, on a personal level, I stay off of social media. I'm inundated with these spaces every day because of my profession, so when I get home, I like to unplug. For me, social media is strictly business.

What is the most challenging part of working in social media?

The internet doesn't forget. If you say something wrong, people will see it, screen grab it, and share it before you have a chance to take it down. There is very little room for error.

You have been active in mentoring future young professionals in social media. What has been the most rewarding experience or moment you have had in helping students?

Teaching and mentoring are my passion. I'm not a doctor, I'm not curing diseases, and I'm very much aware of that. Self-awareness is important. It's because of that reality that I try to find ways to use my education and experience to help in any way I can. I've found that teaching and mentoring is my way of contributing. When those young men and women who work for me move on to bigger and better things, it makes everything worth it. It truly is a rewarding feeling.

What do you wish you had known when you were starting out?

I wish I had started building my personal brand sooner.

You can connect with Jeremy on Twitter at @JeremyDarlow and get his book and be part of his think tank Brand Food at www.brandswinchampionships .com. Jeremy also released his latest book Athletes Are Brands Too *in 2017.*

OVERVIEW OF SOCIAL MEDIA AND SPORTS

The sports industry and social media have become integrated. When exploring the latest innovative storytelling and scraping techniques professionals could implement into their campaign, some of the best and most creative examples come from the sports industry, at both the collegiate and professional levels.

When exploring how to apply social media, one field that constantly pushes the envelope for innovation and creativity is the sports industry. Social media has transformed the field in a way that can be seen in various sports and arenas. It has transformed not only how people get information, but how people consume information, share and create stories from the team, engage with fans, and use recruiting mechanisms. In addition, sports teams have received more exposure for what they do on social media than for what they do on traditional media channels such as television (Roth & Handley, 2017).

Athletes, as Jeremy Darlow discusses in his book *Brands Win Championships* (2015), can use social media not only for personal branding opportunities, but to make a significant difference and impact on society. Not only are these athletes role models, but they have a level of influence to bring forth awareness of significant issues and causes. Athletes who have a very strong presence on social media include LeBron James (basketball), Cristiano Ronaldo (soccer), and Stephanie Rice (swimming) (Callanan, 2012). ESPN (2017) gives out a regular list of rankings of athletes who are famous but also receive strong endorsements and engagement on social media.

However, it could also be used as opportunities to capitalize on the spotlight by interjecting personality into the mix in a high-profile event. This is what happened to Zach Seidel, the director of multimedia and digital media for the University of Maryland, Baltimore County, during the 2018 national championship tournament in men's basketball. When UMBC, ranked 16, beat the top-ranked team in the country, Virginia, Seidel interjected his personality on UMBC's Twitter feed and went viral (Seidel, 2018). Taking advantage of the right moment on social media for sports teams and professionals can lead to more future opportunities, yet the goal here is to sustain the moment created from the initial post that captured the attention of the mass audience.

In several cases, athletes, thanks to the use of their own platforms, have been able to make a difference and help others. Athletes who compete in CrossFit, for example, have used their own platforms to share workouts, tips, and messages with their fans in a way that has created a true community for them online (Fitzgerald, 2017). In some cases, these athletes also rely heavily on sponsorships. These athletes' ability to use their social media leverage to get sponsorships from brands (Fitzgerald, 2017) shows the shift in athletes becoming their own brands. As opendorse (2018) reported, engaging audiences in traditional ways has not always been the most effective way to reach them, and athletes who are active on social media can provide sponsored content that is more authentic, over the top, and bite-sized to fit the appropriate platform.

A clear example of an athlete using social media not only to bring forth awareness of a strong cause, but to use it effectively in raising funds and gaining awareness for his community, is J. J. Watt of the Houston Texans, currently one of the most recognizable players in the National Football League (NFL). When Hurricane Harvey hit Houston, Watt was quoted as saying, "To see [Houston] going through such a disaster and not be there, not be able to help, it's very difficult to have to watch it from afar and see it on TV, and look at streets that you know and you can barely recognize them under all the water" (Boren, 2017).

Along with other sports figures and stores, Watt reached out to his Twitter community to see if he could raise money to support the Houston community after Harvey came on shore. Watt's initial goal to raise money for those impacted by the hurricane was $200,000 (Rapaport, 2017), but with the power of his camera to take a video asking his online community for support, he raised over $16 million. For each milestone, Watt thanked his community with a short video and a link to how to donate. As of mid-September 2017, Watt had reached over $37 million for his cause to give back to those impacted by Hurricane Harvey.

Watt's success did not go unnoticed by the social media professional community. In fact, many people said that this was one of the social media campaigns of the year. It was authentic and connected to

Source: Twitter/@JJWatt

J. J. Watt's Twitter Account for Hurricane Harvey

a community, and the emotional connection played out on social media to support each other was tremendous. Without social media, this support would not have gone viral. Eric SanInocencio, director of digital and social media for the Houston Texans, made a note of how Watt was able to accomplish this with just a phone and a social media connection. Technology, when used strategically, can change the world.

Director of
Digital Media
for Houston
Texans
Comments on
J. J. Watt

We have talked a bit about the athlete's role in social media, but there is more to athletes when it comes to sports and social media.

For college athletics, Auburn University (2017) and the University of Tennessee (2018) both create real-time rankings for the top teams on social media based on their following on each platform. One college team that excels in innovation and creative storytelling is Clemson Athletics. Under the leadership of Jonathan Gantt, assisted by team members Jeff Kallin and Nik Conklin, Clemson has transformed the area of sports and social media (otherwise known as #SMsports). Whether it is creating viral six-second videos of Coach Swinny dancing after a football game win against Notre Dame or creating long-form stories from a first-person point of view, Gantt and his team present a comprehensive visual story that Clemson Tigers fans can easily consume and share. As Gantt noted in a *SBNation* article,

> we're not as good at being journalists as journalists are. In terms of new coverage of a team, we're not set up that way, in terms of our personnel and the infrastructure that we have. The way we are set up well is more like an advertising agency. Understanding that the target audience, and really all society at this point, everything's visual. They can comprehend visuals a whole lot faster than they can the written words. So you can express a lot more. (Johnson, 2017)

When it comes to sports and social media, we sometimes have to take a moment to breathe. There is constant pressure to be innovative and creative in sports in spite of having limited resources in most cases. It is important to keep a realistic perspective about your role, understand we are all human, and remember that it's okay to not be on social media every single minute of every day. As Jessica Smith (@warjesseagle) shared on her blog in 2017,

> Social media can turn into the wild, wild west for a brand if not careful. A place where gimmicks are awarded and eyeballs viewed as successful. It's a place where brands can lose their soul if the right thought is not given. One of the challenges this industry faces is the pressure to be on, all the time. This pressure means we are constantly doing and not thinking. We push and pray without understanding why. In essence, social media becomes a playground for tactics. And then, everything turns into a sea of sameness. But this pressure, it's created by us. And we need to shake it off. Consumers are not asking us to post and push all the time. The world will continue if you stop and take a couple days for strategic planning. Consumers won't lose their brand affinity if you don't tweet for one day. (Social 'n Sport. "Breathe, Pause, Think," (2017); Retrieved from http://socialnsport.com/breathe-pause-think/.)

Best practices to consider when exploring a career in sports and social media include the following:

- *Network on- and offline.* Volunteer at your local university and with its sports teams, or even a club sport. You will get experience, which is key for sports and social media, and this could lead to future opportunities. Connect with great organizations like Front Office Sports (@frntofficesport) and participate on Twitter with fellow professionals using the #SMsports hashtag. Twitter is the Rolodex for networking and connecting with sports. Follow, reach out, and build these positive connections. Write content, share content, and participate in the community by sharing valuable insights and perspectives.

- *Invest in skills and training.* In many cases, a small team works social media for a sports team. It could be a few professionals, or just you. Invest in all of the skills you can get in order to create, disseminate, and analyze content. You must have a passion, of course, for sports, but you also want to see what other skills you can bring to the table. If you work for a sports team, reach out to local high schools and universities to see if any volunteers and students would like to help out.

- *Don't go for the hard sell with teams for opportunities.* Offer what you can bring to the table when it comes to sports. Reach out to the teams for volunteer work and start small, and work to take your talents to the next level. Don't assume just because you are a fan you will get a job. Instead of telling sports teams why you need them, let them know what you can do with your experience and expertise.

- *Don't fangirl or get distracted by being around high-profile stars, athletes, and coaches.* You have a job to do in social media, and you can't be a distraction to your fellow colleagues, fans, and team by getting a selfie with a celebrity or sports figure. You need to take a moment, collect yourself, and remind yourself of your job. Yes, many aspects of sports are glamorous and exciting, but at the end of the day, certain duties and expectations need to be met, and these can't be done if you are distracted.

In summary, looking at the sports industry for inspiration is one way to brainstorm new ideas, but also continue to build on the creative social media education practices established in other areas. There are certain professionals and teams to review, follow, and engage with online to start a conversation with them about their work, but also follow what they are doing to continue to push the envelope in creative and strategic executions on social media. A list of resources will be provided for this book (see the companion workbook *Portfolio-Building Activities in Social Media*), but here are a few examples of professionals to follow and add to your network in the sports industry:

- Jonathan Gantt (@Jonathan_Gantt) of Clemson Athletics

- Jessica Smith (@warjesseagle) of Yankees Digital and Social Media

- Justin King (@JustinKing) of the University of South Carolina

- Kelly Mosier (@kmosier42), Head of Programming at Hudl

- Russell Houghtaling (@digital_russ), associate athletic director for ideation for Oregon State

- Reva Labbe (@sorevawaslike) of ESPN and College Gameday

- Kyle Benzion (@LantaBenzion) of the Atlanta Falcons

- Adam White (@FOSAdam) of Front Office Sports

- Jeff Kallin (@CUJeffKallin) of Clemson Athletics

- Stuart Drew (@studrew1) of the Miami Dolphins

- Jeff O'Keefe (@jeffokeefe) of Toyota Racing

- Justin Karp (@jskarp), director of social media for NBCSports

- Matt Ziance (@MattZiance), social media for NBCSports and NBC Olympics

- Chris Littmann (@chrislittmann), director of content and platform strategy for NASCAR

- Neeta Sreekanth (@NeetaSreekanth) of IGN

- Nick Marquez (@Quezzymoto) of Facebook and Instagram College Partnerships

- Will Yoder (@WillYoder), sports partnerships at Instagram

CHAPTER SUMMARY

Social media is practiced and integrated in a variety of different ways, as shown in Table 11.1. In many cases, it is used not only as a broadcasting tool, but as one that helps facilitate conversations, dialogue, storytelling, and reputation management. It is important to note that all of the professionals interviewed for the Humans of Social Media features are lifelong learners, are engaged in the community and industry they work in, and have a traditional discipline as a foundation for their work (marketing, journalism, sports administration, etc.). This shows how social media, though established now for several years, is still a relatively new field for degrees or even courses. This field is constantly evolving and changing, and even while taking a social media class, there is a growing expectation that while the platforms and tools may change, human behaviors, attitude and message strategy executions, understanding the community, and other core skills (e.g., research and writing) are always going to be relevant.

While each industry has its own guidelines and best practices, all focus on the tools as a channel to spark a conversation and build a community. In addition, creative education and understanding the growing nature of innovative work continues to be a part of social media professionals' role and job.

THOUGHT QUESTIONS

1. Of the four areas covered in this chapter (sports, entertainment, crisis communication, and journalism), which profession would you want to pursue, and why?

2. What are the core best practices crisis communication professionals need to know about social media?

TABLE 11.1 ■ Social Media Content to Create and Apply in Each Specialization	
Specialization	**Content to Create**
Entertainment	• Social media updates • Strategic briefs • Social media audits • Personal brand audits • Influencer marketing plans • Influencer sponsorship packages • Analytics reports • Graphics and visual assets • Updates and social ads • Guidelines • Press releases
Sports	• Game releases • Game event plans • Social media updates • Content calendars • Analytics reports • Social media audits • Sponsorship packages • Graphics and visual assets • Video (live, shows, long form, short form) • Plans and creative executions • Personal brand audits and strategy plans • Brand marketing kits • Influencer sponsorship packages • Ideation materials • Analytics reports
Crisis Communications	• Crisis plans • Statements for social media • Simulation exercises and training • Workshops • Fact sheets and backgrounders of key professionals involved in crisis • Media monitoring reports • Analytics reports • Social media listening and monitoring reports • Social care protocols (for customer services) • Message maps and strategy statements • Policies • Guidelines • Live video interviews and press conferences

Specialization	Content to Create
Journalism	• Stories
	• Updates (short and long form)
	• Features
	• Articles
	• Exclusives
	• Investigative reports
	• Content editorial calendar
	• Video (live, shows, long form, short form)

3. What are the similarities between sports, entertainment, crisis communication, and journalism when it comes to social media?

4. What ethical and professional guidelines do journalists and media professionals need to follow when it comes to social media?

5. What are some best practices for networking in the sports industry with social media?

EXERCISES

1. You have the choice of applying for a specialized position in social media, but the four positions offered are in sports, entertainment, crisis communication, and journalism. Provide a brief overview of each, and explain their core differences and similarities, and which one you would be most qualified for in social media.

2. You want to produce a great portfolio of work for your summer social media internship application with the Green Bay Packers. Outline some steps to take to make yourself a strong candidate for this position online. Identify three steps you will take in order to accomplish this. Discuss two work samples you will create to include in your portfolio.

3. You are working with a boutique agency specializing in entertainment and social media practices. You have been asked by your vice president to analyze the social media accounts for Mark Hamill, Daisy Ridley, and Adam Driver for Disney and *Star Wars*. Conduct a social media audit for each of these actors, discuss three strategies you would recommend to help them with their social media accounts, and propose an idea to generate buzz for the franchise on social media.

4. You are working for a crisis communication firm, and you find out your client (Kevin Spacey) has become a trending topic on social media due to a significant personal scandal along with the connection to the upcoming season of *House of Cards* on Netflix. This has become global news and created outrage for many people. Your firm has asked you to help address and respond to this crisis on its official social media accounts. Analyze the situation based on what is discussed on social media and in the traditional media, and provide a brief overview of the situation. Outline the strategies you will take to handle this crisis, what social media tools and resources you will use, and how you will evaluate these for the client.

REFERENCES

Auburn University. (2017, September 12). *Social media rankings*. Retrieved from http://www.auburntigers.com/digital/social_media_top_25.html.

Boren, C. (2017, August 28). Houston sports stars leverage social media to help victims of Hurricane Harvey. *The Washington Post*. Retrieved from https://www.washingtonpost.com/news/early-lead/wp/2017/08/28/as-harvey-rages-on-clint-capela-and-j-j-watt-harness-the-power-of-social-media-to-help-houston-residents/.

Buchwald, Y. (2016, September 17). How social media has transformed entertainment marketing. *Social Media Week*. Retrieved from https://socialmediaweek.org/blog/2016/09/social-media-transformed-entertainment-marketing/.

Callanan, S. (2012, May 3). Athletes absolutely killing it on Instagram. *Sports Geek*. Retrieved from http://sportsgeekhq.com/social-media/athletes-killing-it-on-instagram/.

CB Insights. (2017, March 17). *"#Fail: 29 of the biggest corporate brand social media flubs*. Retrieved from https://www.cbinsights.com/research/corporate-social-media-fails/.

Coombs, T. (2013). *Crisis, social media, and zombies*. Presented at NEMO Campus Helsingborg. Retrieved from https://www.youtube.com/watch?v=Sospe3H9oMs.

Darlow, J. (2015). *Brands win championships*. Jack and June Publishing.

DeMers, J. (2016, May 2). The 7 worst (and most amusing) mistakes brands have ever made on social media. *Forbes*. Retrieved from https://www.forbes.com/sites/jaysondemers/2016/05/02/the-7-worst-and-most-amusing-mistakes-brands-have-ever-made-on-social-media/.

Duboff, J. (2016, September 16). Examining Beyoncé's social-media mastery: Less is always more. *Vanity Fair*. Retrieved from https://www.vanityfair.com/style/2016/09/beyonce-social-media-instagram-studies.

Engel, M. (2017, August 28). If J.J. Watt can do it for Houston, so can Joel Osteen. *Star-Telegram*. Retrieved from http://www.star-telegram.com/sports/spt-columns-blogs/mac-engel/article169850902.html.

ESPN. (2017, May 30). *World Fame 100*. Retrieved from http://www.espn.com/espn/feature/story/_/page/worldfame100/espn-world-fame-100-top-ranking-athletes.

Feinberg, A. (2017, August 25). At least conspiracy theorists love Taylor Swift's new single. *Wired*. Retrieved from https://www.wired.com/story/taylor-swift-conspiracy-theories/.

Fitzgerald, K. (2017, August 3). With social media savvy, CrossFit athletes help grow sport. *USA Today*. Retrieved from https://www.usatoday.com/story/sports/2017/08/03/crossfit-games-social-media-savvy-athletes-help-grow-sport/538856001/.

Gulliver. (2018, March 14). United Airlines kills another pet. *The Economist*. Retrieved from https://www.economist.com/blogs/gulliver/2018/03/it-s-dog-s-life.

HMV employee goes rogue, tweets from mass firing. (2017, June 19). *The Globe and Mail*. Retrieved from https://www.theglobeandmail.com/news/world/hmv-employee-goes-rogue-tweets-from-mass-firing/article8047181/.

Johnson, R. (2017). How Clemson became the national champs of social media. *SBNation*. Retrieved from http://www.sbnation.com/a/cfb-preview-2017/clemson-social-media.

Keys, K. (2017, July 17). Are you prepared for a social media crisis? *Forbes*. Retrieved from https://www.forbes.com/sites/forbesagencycouncil/2017/07/17/are-you-prepared-for-a-social-media-crisis/.

Langer, E. (2014, January 15). The five-year anniversary of Twitter's defining moment. *CNBC*. Retrieved from https://www.cnbc.com/2014/01/15/the-five-year-anniversary-of-twitters-defining-moment.html.

McIntyre, H. (2017, August 22). Taylor Swift has returned to social media with these cryptic videos: Is new music imminent? *Forbes*. from https://www.forbes.com/sites/hughmcintyre/2017/08/22/taylor-swift-has-returned-to-social-media-with-these-cryptic-videos-is-new-music-imminent/.

Newman, D. (2017, April 25). Top six digital transformation trends in media and entertainment. *Forbes*. Retrieved from https://www.forbes.com/sites/danielnewman/2017/04/25/top-six-digital-transformation-trends-in-media-and-entertainment/.

Nicholson, A. (2017, September 20). How successful journalists use social media. *Cision*. Retrieved from https://www.cision.com/us/2017/09/how-successful-journalists-use-social-media/.

Norton, C. (2017, July 26). The top 11 social media crises of 2017. *Influence*. Retrieved from http://influence.cipr.co.uk/2017/07/26/top-11-social-media-crises-2017/.

NPR. (2017, July). Social media: The NPR way. *NPR Ethics Handbook*. Retrieved from http://ethics.npr.org/tag/social-media/.

O'Connor, C. (2017, June 20). *Forbes* top influencers: These 30 social media stars rule entertainment, gaming and travel. *Forbes*. Retrieved from https://www.forbes.com/sites/clareoconnor/2017/06/20/forbes-top-influencers-social-media-entertainment-gaming-travel/.

opendorse. (2018). State of sponsored social media: How athletes, teams and leagues stack up. Retrieved from http://opendorse.com/blog/sponsored-tweets/.

Phillips, B. (2017, September 5). How Osteen came under fire for his tardy disaster response. *Ragan's PR Daily*. Retrieved from http://www.prdaily.com/Main/Articles/23186.aspx.

Rapaport, D. (2017, September 2). J.J. Watt has raised more than $17 million for Hurricane Harvey relief. *Sports Illustrated*. Retrieved from https://www.si.com/nfl/2017/09/02/jj-watt-hurricane-harvey-relief-fundraiser.

Reuters. (n.d.). Reporting from the internet and using social media. *Handbook of Journalism*. Retrieved from http://handbook.reuters.com/index.php?title=Reporting_From_the_Internet_And_Using_Social_Media.

Roth, C., & Handley, L. (2017, March 22). Sports teams are getting more exposure on social media than they are on TV: Expert. *CNBC*. Retrieved from https://www.cnbc.com/2017/03/22/sports-teams-are-getting-more-exposure-on-social-media-than-they-are-on-tv-expert.html.

Seidel, Z. (2018, March 19). As the Retrievers stole our hearts, @UMBCAthletics entertained us. Here's the story from the guy behind the Twitter account. *The Athletic*. Retrieved from https://theathletic.com/280189/2018/03/19/as-the-retrievers-stole-our-hearts-umbcathletics-entertained-us-heres-the-story-from-the-guy-behind-the-twitter-account/.

Shearer, E., & Gottfried, J. (2017, September 7). News use across social media platforms 2017. *Pew Research Center Journalism & Media*. Retrieved from http://www.journalism.org/2017/09/07/news-use-across-social-media-platforms-2017/.

Shorty Awards. (2018). *Wolverine* Global Home Entertainment social campaign: Declassified. Retrieved from http://shortyawards.com/6th/wolverine-global-home-entertainment-social-campaign-declassified.

Singh, L. (2017). *How to be a bawse: A guide to conquering life*. New York, NY: Ballantine Books.

Smith, J. (2017, September 7). Breathe, pause, think. *Social 'n' Sport*. Retrieved from http://socialnsport.com/breathe-pause-think/.

Temin, D. (2017, September 9). Equifax: A Category 5 cybersecurity storm. *Forbes*. Retrieved from https://www.forbes.com/sites/daviatemin/2017/09/09/equifax-a-category-5-cybersecurity-crisis-storm/.

The New York Times. (2017, October 13). *The Times* issues social media guidelines for the newsroom. Retrieved from https://www.nytimes.com/2017/10/13/reader-center/social-media-guidelines.html.

University of Tennessee. (2018). Top 25 Twitter accounts: Athletic departments. Retrieved from http://www.utsports.com/sports/2017/6/14/social-top25.aspx

Wasserman, T. (2012, October 31). Gap criticized for insensitive tweet during Hurricane Sandy. *Mashable*. Retrieved from http://mashable.com/2012/10/31/gap-tweet-hurricane-sandy/.

HOW SOCIAL MEDIA IS APPLIED

Exploring Different Specializations, Part II

Learning Objectives

Introduction

Humans of Social Media: *Social Media and Social Care*

Overview of Social Media and Social Care
>   Best Practices for Social Care

Humans of Social Media: *Social Media and Nonprofits*

Overview of Social Media and Nonprofits
>   Best Practices for Nonprofits

Humans of Social Media: *Social Media and Health Care*

Overview of Social Media and Health Care
>   Best Practices for Health Care Professionals

Humans of Social Media: *Social Media and International Campaigns*

Overview of Social Media and International Campaigns
>   Best Practices for International Campaigns

Chapter Summary

Thought Questions

Exercises

References

LEARNING OBJECTIVES

After reading this chapter, you will be able to

- Identify the areas in which social media can be applied

- Discuss the key ways social care, nonprofits, health care, and international campaigns integrate social media into their industries and practices

- Explain the best practices and guidelines for social media to note for social care, nonprofits, health care, and international campaigns

---

INTRODUCTION

As discussed in the previous chapter, there are many different areas to specialize in and focus on within a particular role (e.g., crisis communications and reporting) or industry (e.g., sports and entertainment). Social media is a core duty and area of practice that crosses all disciplines and rules, but each industry and specialization has a unique take on how to approach social media for communication and business practices. It is important to note that more areas of focus can be applied and discussed in regard to social media than can be included in one or two chapters.

This second chapter on applied social media provides an additional overview of several different areas in which social media is applied. In this chapter, we cover how social care, nonprofits, health care, and international organizations and campaigns integrate social media into their practices, as well as some of the challenges, opportunities, and case studies relevant to these respective industries.

HUMANS OF SOCIAL MEDIA
WHITNEY DRAKE, MANAGER AT GENERAL MOTORS

Social Media and Social Care

Introduction

By day I work at General Motors in operational excellence looking for efficiency and cost-savings opportunities, and by night I'm wife to an engineer and mom to twins. I studied communication at Michigan State University and received my master's in integrated marketing communications from West Virginia University. Throughout my career, I have had the opportunity to work with great brands such as Procter & Gamble, 3M, T-Mobile, Children's Place, Budweiser, and Ford. I'm fortunate enough to be bringing my experience to the next generation by teaching both at Wayne State University and online at West Virginia University. I call "Pure Michigan" home, but try not to let the grass grow and enjoy traveling as much as possible.

How did you get your start in social media?

I started my social media journey at Ford when I ran its media and internal communication website.

What is your favorite part of working in your social media area of expertise?

I love the fact that social media is always changing and requires us to use both the art and science parts of our brain.

What is one thing you can't live without while working in social media?

A hunger for knowledge.

What is your favorite social media account (person, brand, etc.) to follow, and why?

On Instagram, @tessthegsp is the story of two German shorthair pointers (GSPs) and a Weimaraner as told by their "hooman." I own a GSP and they are quirky, so there was an immediate connection. But beyond that, these dogs' mom is truthful, funny, and creative. I can always count on this follow to cheer me up and make me laugh.

What is the most challenging part of working in social media?

Showing the return on investment through community management, not just paid.

What is your take on your area of expertise and the social media industry?

I love how customer care has evolved in social care. I can't wait to see how much farther messenger bots take that relationship.

What do you wish you had known when you were starting out?

I wish I had taken a chance and the time to write thought leadership articles.
    You can connect with Whitney Drake on Twitter and Instagram at @goswhit and LinkedIn at www.linkedin.com/in/whitneyedrake/.

OVERVIEW OF SOCIAL MEDIA AND SOCIAL CARE

As Whitney Drake discussed, social care has become an integrated part of contemporary social media duties. It is about not only providing creative executions of campaigns, but also fostering and maintaining existing relationships among members of an online community. At first glance, since customer care is an important relationship-building and communication practice, many assume it is part of the duty and responsibility list for public relations and strategic communications. However, others say it belongs to marketing because it involves reputation management, data, and sales.

Keith Quesenberry (2016) proposed in the *Harvard Business Review* that social care should not be in the hands of a marketing department. Sometimes, it actually needs its own department, which happens to be the case for General Motors. At General Motors, the separate social care department works with marketing, data marketing, public relations, communications, and other associated departments within the brand.

While social care may look like a simple yet overwhelming task for an organization or brand to accomplish, some actions can be taken to create a social care program for an organization of any size. With reputation and relationships on the line, social care must be a top priority for all brands, organizations, and even individual professionals. Quesenberry (2016) offered clear steps for setting up a proactive social care program for businesses and social media professionals, including the following:

- Establish a team of professionals trained in customer relationship management tools to address all aspects of social media information effectively, consistently, and in a timely manner.

- Create designated responsibilities and training protocols for customer service duties for each team member; have protocols in place to make sure the brand voice is consistent among team members and in conversations online, and for how to evaluate and report these conversations.

- Assign specific tasks for certain employees and how they will participate in each conversation online. Have a reporting protocol in place to keep everyone on the team informed with each transaction.

- Establish key performance indicators (KPIs) to determine success or failure for customer service on social media. After measuring these KPIs, draft a report to outline these metrics (e.g., influence of customer, response time, average response time, sentiment of conversation, shares, conversions, and other key relationship and behavioral metrics).

Social care has risen to become one of the most important specializations in the social media industry. As Hyken (2017) mentioned in *Forbes*, social care is the new marketing for professionals, because a great experience with a brand not only impacts the individual interacting with the brand specifically, but also can provide an opportunity for the individual to share this experience with others. Taking the time to respond makes a world of difference to people, and it is an expectation for brands to not only respond to customers, but do so in a timely manner. Individuals can see this firsthand especially on Facebook with brand pages. As Conversocial (Frumkin, 2017) reported, the most important factor of customer loyalty today is the reduction of customer effort. In other words, customers and other members of the online community want to make their lives easier by engaging with a brand online—getting their questions answered or having their situation addressed—in a professional and seamless manner. Investing in the right policies, training, and tools for providing a responsive customer service experience for customers will help brands in many ways.

Strong customer service and a social care program can help brands by

- Making it easy for customers to get on with their business and perhaps spend more money in the process since they had a good customer service experience.

- Understanding it's not only the products people are concerned about, but the experience. A great experience will motivate people to come back and do business or engage with your content more. A negative experience not only will create unhappiness, but could spark outrage in the community, leading to a negative impact online for your reputation.

Brands, individuals, agencies, and other organizations usually post a statement on their website in a social media section (or occasionally under media or press relations) regarding how responsive they are online. In addition, many brands use chat bots (artificial intelligence that is programmed to respond appropriately to certain questions). While brands such as Southwest Airlines use messenger bots to engage with audiences, saving time and streamlining the process, a delicate and human touch is also necessary for engaging with audiences.

Facebook is not the only place where customer service happens. In many cases, customer service occurs on a completely different platform. While all social media platforms have a protocol for handling certain situations, the go-to place (especially in certain markets and industries) for inquiries regarding customer service questions is Twitter. In fact, the amount of customer service requests and interactions on Twitter from 2015 to 2017 increased by 250% (Frumkin, 2017).

The photo below showcases the chat bot that is activated as soon as you open the Southwest Facebook page to start a conversation, and how the airline brand responds instantly.

Several brands have been praised for their strong customer service engagement over the years, including airline brand KLM (which handled a 2010 volcano ash situation extremely well with customers), MoonPie (for engaging customers in an entertaining way related to current events, such as the 2017 eclipse), and Hootsuite (for general inquiries and product mentions). Each social media platform serves as a front door for the brand on social media, so investing in the training and procedures and developing a culture of proactive customer relations measures will reward brands more than just financially—it can be instrumental to increase brand loyalty and advocacy for customers, leading to more endorsements and returns over the long term.

Best Practices for Social Care

Social care is a delicate and strategic area of specialization within the social media field, and as discussed in this section, some brands and organizations have succeeded

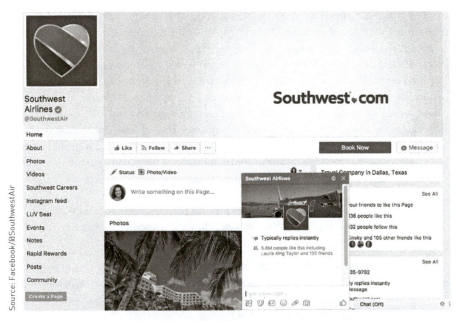

Source: Facebook/@SouthwestAir

Southwest Airlines and Its Facebook Messenger Chat Bot for Customer Service in addressing needs and conversations online. Others have not been as successful. Keep the following best practices in mind when working with brands to implement social care engagement practices:

- *Invest in customer service.* To be the best in social care, this is a must. Investment into social care takes many forms, but tools for monitoring, responding to, and listening to social media are always part of the equation. A robust customer relationship management tool can streamline the conversations and metrics for a brand, which will help in reporting and strategy sessions. In addition, training team members to know not only the social media tools used for customer service, but also how to respond professionally and on brand, is important. These items take both time and money, but what is your brand's reputation worth in the end? It's priceless, and because customer service presently drives business, it is a necessary investment.

- *Be present and engaged on the same channels as your audiences.* This means having a presence on social media platforms and conversing with the individuals who mention you on social media—whether via tagging or @ your handle. You want to have a timely conversation. One update and response back can mean the world to audience members.

- *Have templates in place for responses and inquiries, and try to make these personalized.* Do not use automated responses. Everyone can see through this and would perceive it as not being transparent. As part of the social media team representing the brand, make sure you make a positive first impression and your exchange starts off on the best foot possible, especially if the other party is emotional. While bots may be the way of the future, taking the extra time to tailor the brand's exchange on social media makes a difference. While technology changes, as humans, we still crave human interactions.

- *Recognize that you do not have to be in* every *conversation.* Being on social media and working in the field is a 24/7 job, but this does not mean you have to be actively engaged *all* the time. Be aware of what topics you want to jump on, but also be aware of when it's best to sit back and listen. There is a huge amount of pressure to be active on social media, but constant engagement is not always the best approach. Yes, you may experience a lot of fear of missing out (FOMO), but it's not worth it to update, share, or create something that impacts how others perceive you negatively.

- *Listen and understand the situation and context.* One of the most important elements of social care is understanding the situation the other person (or group of people) is in. Empathy goes a long way in handling this, so make sure you listen to what else is going on. For example, do not take light into a crisis situation or tragedy. Here you have to be responsive and professional, yet aware of the emotions tied to the situation.

- *Don't let your own emotions get the best of you at the risk of the brand's reputation on social media.* We are all human, but a brand's account is not the place to interject your own emotions. Do not create a crisis situation when a problem can be handled in an appropriate way. Take a deep breath and reach out to your fellow social media team members to get their take. Respond in a way that you wouldn't mind seeing in a screen shot. Always take the high road, even if the other member of the conversation does not.

HUMANS OF SOCIAL MEDIA
BELLA PORTARO-KUEBER, FOUNDER
AND CREATIVE DIRECTOR OF BELLA VITA MEDIA

Source: Courtesy of Anna May

Bella Portaro-Kueber

Social Media and Nonprofits

Introduction

My name is Bella Portaro-Kueber. I'm a social media marketer who started a boutique marketing company called Bella Vita Media in 2010. I'm not only creative director but a content creator because of my joy for bringing brands to life through the power of words and images. I'm a freelance writer, a blogger at bellaoflouisville.com, and an entrepreneur with three startup companies that provide my daily life with a beautiful scenery of curiosity for the unknown changes that take place every single day.

How did you get your start in social media?

I started as a community manager for an event company and a design firm. This is when social media started to appeal to businesses to harness its powers into the superhuman force it is today. It's really been an amazing ride to grow with social media as it happens. It evolves every single day, so the field itself never becomes redundant.

What is your favorite part of working in your social media area of expertise?

I enjoy helping nonprofits learn how to use the voice of the organization to cultivate a following for the mission of their interests. An example would be showing nonprofits what their following could be if they used the keys already in front of them. It's amazing to see the light bulb go off in the mind of a CEO or director of marketing. Once it clicks, social media becomes so much easier for them to manage on their own.

What is one thing you can't live without while working in social media?

My phone. If I don't have it with me, I freak out. I'm always afraid that I won't be available to moderate a conversation the way it deserves. Immediately following that, I would say my battery backup charger. I typically carry two with me every minute I don't have my laptop or access to charge my phone while working an event.

What is your favorite social media account (person, brand, etc.) to follow, and why?

The United Nations Children's Fund is my favorite overall. UNICEF is able to story tell in a nonintrusive way to spread the message of its mission while including testimonials with powerful images.

What is the most challenging part of working in social media?

The most challenging part of working in social media is the need I feel to always be available and in marketing mode for a response to public messaging in the different voices of the clients I represent.

You have been active in mentoring future young professionals in social media. What is the most rewarding experience or moment you have had in helping students?

My most rewarding experiences with young professionals I've worked with from the time they're fresh into the field to see them prosper and make strides in social media marketing come from my experiences with your [Karen Freberg's] students at the University of Louisville.

They've worked for me as volunteers for Unbridled Eve Derby Gala and IdeaFestival. I had complete faith knowing I could trust them because I knew I could trust you. Their work delivered impeccably at the level of any other professional I've ever met who isn't fresh out of college. Well done!

What do you wish you had known when you were starting out?

If I could tell my younger self anything about social media, I'd tell myself to grow thicker skin and to not allow negative situations in communications for any company to impact me personally.

I'm still learning this. I put myself into my work, so anytime it doesn't go well, I take it to be my fault when that isn't the case. Letting things roll is easier when moving at a high pace. Remember that and stay focused. Do your best every day and keep your mind open to change as you progress through this field.

Bella Portaro-Kueber can be reached via social media at @bellaportaro. On her website, Bella of Louisville (bellaoflouisville.com), she discusses her social media work, activities, and nonprofit clients.

OVERVIEW OF SOCIAL MEDIA AND NONPROFITS

Nonprofits have used social media very successfully due to its history as an affordable yet effective means to communicate and engage with audiences. Many successful nonprofits are some of the most followed on social media for their creative campaigns, executions of key issues, and innovative uses of new tools and platforms. Some are also effective in creating strong stories across all of the social media platforms. Top-ranked social media accounts for nonprofits include the National Geographic Society, TED Talks, UNICEF, WikiLeaks, and the Museum of Modern Art (Top Nonprofits, 2016).

Sprout Social (Johnston, 2017) listed several goals for nonprofits to note when it comes to integrating social media into their organization:

- Community engagement and education
- Brand building and reputation management
- Program recruitment
- Fund-raising

The shift from a "pay to play" mentality has impacted nonprofits significantly, which means they have had to be a bit more creative in their uses of resources and tools to break through the noise and connect to their key audiences and donors. However, nonprofits must produce creative content that will motivate others to donate and engage with them on social media. According to Sprout Social (Johnston, 2017), nonprofits should think about the following questions:

- *What problems do people have in their own lives when trying to live out the values they share with your organization?* Listen to and monitor what others say on social media, and also conduct your own research by conversing with audience members. What are some problems and challenges facing the community that you could address? What are some areas needing solutions? Think about how these challenges could turn into opportunities for the nonprofit to address and fill gaps.

- *What tips or tools can you give people to make their lives easier?* Nonprofits are not only looked to for support in handling certain key issues and challenges, but also expected to provide resources for education, training, and community building. What pieces of content could be created to help foster a strong culture of education and helping others? What tools could be useful and relevant for audiences relative to their community?

Two ways that nonprofits have actively tried to engage and encourage others to take part in their campaign efforts on social media are crowdsourcing and crowdfunding. **Crowdsourcing** is the process in which groups of individuals come together to provide their insights based on a call to action from an organization, a brand, or even an individual. **Crowdfunding** (using sites like GoFundMe) allows people to come together for a specific cause and raise funds to support an issue or organization. While some third-party tools and sites are dedicated to fund-raising, some of the major platforms (e.g., Twitter and Facebook) give people the power to donate directly online to specific organizations through an update as well as in a live video session.

One of the most successful crowdfunding campaigns happened in 2014, when people participated in the Ice Bucket Challenge to raise funds to support research by the ALS Association. This campaign was started by Pete Frates to raise awareness of amyotrophic lateral sclerosis, or Lou Gehrig's disease. Dumping a bucket of ice over your head and calling out people who needed to take on this challenge next became a viral sensation around the world, and also one of the biggest fund-raising efforts using social media ever. The results were huge, with $220 million to support ALS research raised by over 2 million people participating in this challenge on social media (Chowdhry, 2015).

While the ALS campaign is a few years old, it gained global traction for the disease and brought in many people to share, create, and discuss the disease on social media. The campaign was praised for its strategic implementation of certain social media platforms, including Facebook, which actually led to receiving the 2015 "Facebook for Good" award (Peterson, 2015). Plus, the ALS campaign emphasized the importance of a strong message and opportunities for audience members to feel compelled to take action. Action steps were not just sharing the URL or donation page to support the research but, rather, creating personalized content in a form of a video to share with family, friends, and others in specific platforms.

Ultimately, as a nonprofit, make sure specific messages and content appear on social media that tie back to the communication plan for the nonprofit. Social media integration for nonprofits should be not an add-on, but rather a key part of raising awareness about the efforts of the organization, telling the story of the nonprofit's efforts in its communities, and documenting the return of impact on these communities to create transparency.

Source: "Instagram Profile Page", Movember
https://www.instagram.com/movember/?hl=en

Movember on Instagram

Many great nonprofits have done significant work in addressing the needs, issues, and challenges facing society with social media. A few have used social media not only strategically, but also creatively in various formats and situations to gain traction for their causes. For example, one nonprofit that has used social media especially strategically and effectively is the Movember Foundation. Founded in 2003 to support the issue of men's health, it started in Australia with the overall purpose of encouraging men to grow out their moustaches in the month of November to raise awareness of men's health (Augure, 2017). Many brands have partnered with Movember and its cause, including Harry's and TOMS. Surprisingly, Movember has had success not just in the month of November, but all year long (Anderson, 2017). Movember has not only empowered users to create content on their own social media channels (e.g., the ALS Association), but also integrated influencers (e.g., YouTuber Kian Lawley) into its campaigns to trigger awareness and shares on social media, which ultimately has continued to be a success for the foundation and cause (Anderson, 2017).

Another important element that makes a foundation successful in raising awareness of its issue is a branded hashtag, a searchable term that aligns with the name of the foundation. Nonprofits have either done this with their own hashtag for their own organizations, or tied hashtags into related issues and challenges. Some hashtags that have gained traction for supporting certain issues include the following:

- REI's #OptOutside campaign (promoting outdoor family activities rather than shopping during Black Friday sales)

- The John Wayne Cancer Foundation's #ShowYourGrit campaign (a call to action to support the fight against cancer with courage, strength, and grit)

- T-Mobile's #HR4HR campaign (donating $20,000 per home run at the 2017 World Series event and $2 for every tweet that used the hashtag to support relief efforts for Hurricanes Harvey, Irma, and Maria)

- Metro United Way's #LiveUnited (a yearlong commitment to sharing stories in the community) and #MUW100 (stories about the nonprofit as it celebrated 100 years and support for the community)

- The Salvation Army's partnership with Chris Strub to promote the #FightForGood campaign (raising awareness of the Christmas holidays in November 2017 through social media efforts—Chris used YouTube, Instagram, and Twitter to share his story and videos with the community to try and raise $10,000 for the Salvation Army)

Best Practices for Nonprofits

As for other specializations within social media, there are some universal best practices to be aware of, but others are specifically unique to the environment and challenges facing nonprofits. If entering the field of nonprofit work with social media, keep in mind some of these best practices:

- *Don't rely on either email or social media—they need to be balanced.* Many times, nonprofits want to go all in for nonprofit social media efforts, and other times, email is their golden ticket to donors' contact information. The best of both worlds is to have a balanced approach. You want to have touch points with each of your audiences on social media, but you also want to connect with them on other channels to continue the conversation.

- *Have responsibilities, duties, and a team in place for social media.* Content creation and reporting are just two responsibilities that need to be in place. However, someone who is specialized in paid ads, fund-raising, and sales may also benefit the team by creating messages, content, and a fund-raising sales funnel. This will help the nonprofit to connect the dots to move an audience member from being a new member of the community to a donor.

- *Spend the time to really focus and target your messages, channels, and audiences.* You may not have the resources for all of the tools used in the industry, so be creative in choosing the ones to invest in. Think about where your audiences are going based on the reports and data you collect on each social media channel. You may have to shift your messages and strategies to address these evolving changes. Also, make sure to spend time asking which types of content need to be created and which platforms will be the most effective. For example, the Boys & Girls Clubs of America has been innovative in creating its own content with live video on Facebook, raising awareness about its various locations and hosting interviews and Q&As with attendees and speakers at its National Conference.

- *Allow people the opportunity to share their stories.* If you are able to create stories that allow users to feel comfortable and empowered to share their own stories on social media, then it is a win-win situation for all. Stories that showcase connections, emotions, and personal experiences are more effective (and relatable) for audiences. To accomplish this, you must guide users through how you want them to share these stories, and consider what call-to-action statements you want to communicate with them.

HUMANS OF SOCIAL MEDIA
MARK MURDOCK, DIRECTOR OF SOCIAL MEDIA
FOR KINDRED HEALTHCARE

Source: Courtesy of Charles Wilkerson

Mark Murdock

Social Media and Health Care

Introduction

I grew up in a really small town in middle Tennessee. Sitting with headphones on—in my room, in my closet, in the car—was my escape from feeling isolated.

As a kid, I really wanted to be a DJ. By 14, my mom was driving me to my first job as a DJ on a local station. I eventually branched out into marketing/promotions and got involved with the social media aspect of the job. I've worked on brands including Kindred Healthcare, McDonald's, Big O Tires, the Kentucky Lottery, and CafePress.

How did you get your start in social media?

Before social media was really blowing up, I mentioned in a meeting that no one was taking advantage of the Facebook pages that we had at our company. Sometimes, you don't know what you are volunteering for; it chooses you.

What is your favorite part of working in your social media area of expertise?

Social media changes so often that you have to stay connected to it to be successful. It's like always-on continuing education. I love thinking about how to utilize content pillars, value propositions, and content strategies to express a company's mission. Making connections with people is what I do best.

What is one thing you can't live without while working in social media?

Other than the computer that lives in my pocket and by my bedside, it's my amazing coworkers. Some people have to do this job all by themselves, and I'm really fortunate to have terrific coworkers and friends who enjoy the work just like I do.

What is your favorite social media account (person, brand, etc.) to follow, and why?

I love @jasonfalls not only because he is my friend, but also because he is *hilarious*. I love @generalelectric and everything it does. And I

love @NASA, because it illustrates the amazing work of humankind traveling to the heavens.

What is the most challenging part of working in social media?

Social media being used to divide our society is hard to ignore.

You have been active in mentoring future young professionals in social media. What is the most rewarding experience you have had in helping students?

I hired a student from your [Karen Freberg's] class.

What do you wish you had known when you were starting out?

I wish I had a colleague who brainwashed me into starting a career in social media earlier. I still have a part-time radio shift, but this was the best career move for me.

Mark Murdock is the director of social media for Kindred Healthcare. Before working with Kindred, Mark worked with brands such as CafePress, Four Roses Bourbon, and McDonald's. Mark can be connected with on Twitter at @heyitsmurdock.

OVERVIEW OF SOCIAL MEDIA AND HEALTH CARE

For health care purposes, social media can provide an avenue where patients, customers, and other community members come together. Health care professionals should be aware of several opportunities related to social media. For example, social media offers a lot of benefits for patients to interact with doctors and other patients (participating in virtual support groups, asking questions about doctors, obtaining recommendations for services, etc.) in a virtual community setting (Belbey, 2016a). These conversations could then be shared, repackaged (with patient permission, of course), and used to demonstrate people's stories and experiences with certain health care entities.

The struggle, of course, has been the fact the health care industry is heavily regulated (Mack, 2017) and extremely complex. The industry has to follow strict guidelines outlined by government agencies such as the Food and Drug Administration and the Health Insurance Portability and Accountability Act. Health care professionals must demonstrate that they are supervising the activities of all parties at their organization who have access to patient information as well as other legal issues pertaining to patient privacy and legal cases involving patients, doctors, and hospitals (Belbey, 2015). Another challenge that faces many health care professionals involves state and federal privacy laws, which limit how much interaction and engagement they can have on social media with patients (Belbey, 2015). These organizations and health care providers have to be careful here, because if they are found to have disclosed information about patients online on social media, they could face significant fines (Belbey, 2015).

Some universal concerns face the industry beyond just compliance, but one issue rising in salience is patient privacy. Data protection is the primary focus for many health care professionals, and as new tools and communities are always coming up, social media raises many big issues related to privacy. Privacy could be compromised in many ways for the health care industry—ranging from employees posting pictures of patients and their families during their time at a certain facility, to even broadcasting without permission the information and stories of patients who have come to use the health care facilities. Other important factors to consider when it comes to social media and the health care industry relate to the growing use and prominence of online reviews and ratings. Many different sites are used to curate reviews, including Reputation.com and Facebook check-ins. Other online review sites allow health care professionals to determine what people are saying about the facilities, clinics, doctors, and hospitals they oversee. Reputation management has become a key area of responsibility for social media professionals working in the health care industry. Online reviews can either hinder or enhance the overall reputation and perception by doctors, nurses, patients, and others of the health care system.

Social media has been implemented and incorporated into universal business plans of health care entities in many ways. For example:

> *Hospitals.* Hospitals and clinics have been very successful in implementing various campaigns over the years. St. Jude Children's Research Hospital (2016) partnered with 70 brands for its #GiveThanks campaign to solicit donations and support for research efforts during the holidays. This effort is great because the campaign is aligned with St. Jude's mission of providing services and dedicated cancer research efforts, while also utilizing a unified partnership with brands on their own social media platforms. This then again amplifies the message for the hospital.

> *Clinics.* One of the best examples of social media education and resources for professionals in the industry comes from the Mayo Clinic, one of the best in the industry for its social and digital media efforts. The organization has strong brand recognition and a dedicated social and digital innovation team that helped establish the Mayo Clinic Social Media Network (otherwise known as #MCSMN) for its own team members and others outside of the organization. Social media is embraced at the leadership and mission level, and the Mayo Clinic also promotes innovation within its organizational culture (Pennic, 2014).

> *Insurance Companies.* When you think of insurance companies, you may not be aware of the creative social media partnerships formed within the industry. Insurance companies are also innovative with their partnerships with other brands, such as Aflac. Aflac teamed up with Macy's to create branded emojis and plush toys of the Aflac duck to raise awareness of childhood cancer (Parisi, 2018). This messaging-focused campaign used messenger apps Kik and WhatsApp. The branded emojis for both brands were tied together for Aflac and Macy's, and the campaign was launched before the Macy's Thanksgiving Day Parade. The proceeds from each plush toy sold were donated to support children's cancer research.

Mayo Clinic Social Media Network Webpage

An insurance company that has raised the standards for employee advocacy efforts is Humana. Humana, which partnered with the employee advocacy platform company Dynamic Signal, effectively implemented a brand ambassador and employee advocacy program for its employees on social media (Stein, 2016). The primary focus for Humana was to promote health information, not necessarily sales ("Employee Advocacy," 2017). Employees could help with recruiting (engaging with potential job seekers), social selling (e.g., chatting about the services offered by the insurance company), reputation management (the people behind the logo are in many cases what people look for in a brand besides goods and services), and sharing news about the organization with others (Belbey, 2016b). Humana's goal was to encourage employees to share updates on their internal social networks (which they had been doing), but to also do more posting and engagement on behalf of the company on public platforms like Facebook, LinkedIn, and Twitter (Stein, 2016).

Best Practices for Health Care Professionals

Best practices for working in a social media capacity are especially important in a highly regulated industry such as health care. Again there are some universal characteristics to note, but others are uniquely dedicated and specific to the health care industry:

- *Invest in a legal and public health education.* With the need to understand what federal and state laws and federal agencies say about privacy for patients, anyone working in social media must be aware of these factors and how they impact the role of social media professionals. While you may have a dedicated understanding of social media, you must be aware of the context and industry in which you are working. Education related to legal and public health regulations will help you determine what can and cannot be shared and posted on social media, which will then help in avoiding potential crises.

- *Be aware of what you can and cannot say on social media.* Because the health care industry is so regulated, you must be aware of what you can't say as well as what you can. For example, if someone checks into a hospital and says he has had a terrible experience, the social media manager can't say "We are sorry" because that means the hospital is responsible, and could be sued. The same goes for inquiries about patients, and privacy is a huge issue in the health care industry. Know the industry and government policies and regulations for yourself, but ensure that the entire team of professionals with access to the social media profiles is also up to speed. Training into what to post and what not to post should be a universal educational opportunity for everyone, not just those who work in social media, in the health care industry.

- *Recognize that listening and timing of protocol response is crucial.* Have a template and policy outlined for how to report anything that comes up on social media. Planning, along with legal and professional protocols, will help prevent and prepare for many issues that may arise on social media. Be aware people use social media to vent about patient experiences, document their experiences at a hospital (e.g., live video and online reviews), and even become outraged and try to make a photo, video, or situation go viral. You must have strong crisis communication skills to address, prevent, and react to any situation that may spark online, and understand how this could impact your reputation.

- *Turn your employees into advocates.* As shown with Humana, employees can be encouraged to share their experiences on social media. Stories, information about events, and education about related topics in the industry are just some of the areas that can be covered and shared by employees. Create training sessions, workshops on best practices, polices, and a calendar for content to be shared on social media, and create a leadership board for most active users internally. By building an advocacy culture, the internal environment can become appropriate to share with the rest of the world.

HUMANS OF SOCIAL MEDIA
SIMONA MORAR, PR AWARDS MANAGER AT CANNES LIONS INTERNATIONAL FESTIVAL OF CREATIVITY

Social Media and International Campaigns

Introduction

Based in London, I'm currently working as the public relations awards manager at Cannes Lions International Festival of Creativity. My background is in PR, having worked for a travel and lifestyle agency in the past and as an intern for a music PR agency. Outside of work, I love exploring the city, visiting art galleries, and reading.

How did you get your start in social media?

While I was studying, I cohosted a music show on the University of Nottingham radio station, so it's there that my social media journey began. I set up accounts to promote the show to students and make connections with local musicians. It was great fun! Once I started my music PR internship, I made my personal Twitter account so that I could follow relevant journalists and learn more about the industry, something I carried over to my travel and lifestyle PR role. During this time, I started having to manage client social media accounts and gained an insight into social media strategies—the kind of content to post, when to post it, and how to measure engagement.

What is your favorite part of working in your social media area of expertise?

Now I mainly use my Twitter account to follow PR professionals and agencies as well as journalists of all disciplines that I admire. Chats with hashtags are super useful, and I love reading through them all. Occasionally I'll post about what's going on at Cannes Lions or our regional festivals, but mostly I enjoy tweeting interesting facts or opinions I hear at industry events—plus following the great people that I meet there.

What is one thing you can't live without while working in social media?

For me it's TweetDeck! It's so easy to use, and I can get a good overview of all the different conversations that I'm interested in.

What is your favorite social media account (person, brand, etc.) to follow, and why?

I have a few! For PR news and views it's @WeArePRoofed, the feed for the #FuturePRoof books run by Sarah Hall with links to insightful essays, and I go to Stephen Waddington at @wadds and David Gallagher at @TBoneGallagher for opinions about the industry. My favorite author, Matt Haig at @matthaig1, always has plenty of interesting things to say. Last but not least, @dog_rates never fails to make me smile.

What is the most challenging part of working in social media?

The conversations can move so quickly that it can sometimes feel a bit daunting to join in! From the perspective of running the social media accounts of a client, it's always super important to make sure the tone of voice and type of content you're putting out is relevant to the brand.

What do you wish you had known when you were starting out?

It takes time to build and tailor your accounts for your needs and interests! Equally, it takes time and effort to build a following, but it's not all about the numbers. The quality of your social media activity depends on how and why you use it, so it's important to consider this before you get started.

Simona Morar is the PR Awards Manager for Cannes Lions, which oversees the Cannes Lions International Festival of Creativity, the annual awards show for advertising, public relations, and creative works. Simona can be connected with on Twitter at @s_morar.

OVERVIEW OF SOCIAL MEDIA AND INTERNATIONAL CAMPAIGNS

Social media is a worldwide platform. In many circumstances, the same platforms are universal and consistent across different countries. This is why festivals and conferences such as the Cannes Lions International Festival of Creativity are so important for social media professionals to attend to learn, grow, and understand the different ways to use social media in strategic communications. International awareness also leads to knowledge of additional platforms to explore and possibly incorporate into the social media ecosystem.

Innovative approaches to established practices. Several brands around the world have introduced new ways of implementing social media. For example, in the United Kingdom, fashion designer Marc Jacobs used Twitter as a platform to share stories, insights, and promotions about his products. He was one of the first people and brands to use Twitter as social currency (instead of paying for content with paper or coin currency, a post or update on social media is all that is needed for payment) for customers to use to buy his products (Murphy, 2014). Customers could use their Twitter posts as "currency" to shop at the Twitter popup shop Marc Jacobs had set up in London. This showed the social media industry how to use word-of-mouth in a way that had not been tried before.

Impact of visuals tied to raise awareness. One campaign that generated a lot of interest, shares, and intrigue was Australia's "Meet Graham" campaign, which focused on increasing awareness about road safety in Australia. An artist created Graham to show how he would be the only person who could survive the effects of road trauma. The video introducing Graham went viral, and as a result, the campaign won the Grand Prix prize in the Health category at Cannes Lions in 2017 (Nudd, 2017b).

Raising awareness about serious causes. Social media can be used internationally to raise awareness about issues in specific nations and countries. In some cases, the economic landscape brings forth competitors to address the livelihood of their business, such as what happened with Uber and other ridesharing services in Brazil. These ridesharing companies came together in a joint social media campaign called "Together in Mobility" featuring a viral video warning Brazilians about the dangers of regulating the ridesharing industry (Boadle, 2017). In addition, social media can bring forward a trending topic on the international stage. For example, the world watched as the refugee crisis emerged in Europe and around the world in 2016. Some refugees were athletes who had the ability to compete in the 2016 Rio Olympics. Ogilvy partnered with Amnesty International to create a Refugee Nation flag for these athletes who did not have a country to represent in an integrated campaign that used social media prominently (Nudd, 2017a). To continue building the moment of this issue on social media, Amnesty International created the #TakeAction campaign that allowed refugees to respond in real time in Kenya and Lebanon with videos for audience members and promoted calls to action to sign a petition to support refugee rights that would be presented to the United Nations (Kiefer, 2017).

Brands, with the help of influencers and strategic partnerships, can come together and share stories on social media. Amarula (2017), a South African cream liquor company, partnered in a global campaign with WildlifeDirect on a campaign called "Don't Let Them Disappear" to raise awareness of the declining elephant population. In addition, the company enhanced awareness of this issue by using influencer marketing. Amarula partnered with six Instagram influencers and Dr. Paula Kahumbu in the Amboseli National Park in Kenya to create awareness

Source: Instagram/@Amarula

Amarula Instagram Influencer Post for Elephant Conservation Social Media Campaign

about elephant conservation. Amarula, known worldwide for its logo that features the elephant, one of the Big 5 animals (most prominent yet threatened in southern Africa), used social media to generate more awareness of this cause and presented ways for others to help address the growing crisis among the elephant population in Africa. This campaign integrated influencer marketing with cause-related marketing to address an issue tied with the brand, country, and community on social media on a global stage.

Sharing stories to spark creativity. Personalization (tailoring the content and created messages that truly resonate with intended parties) and allowing audiences to create and share what they have done is a global characteristic of social media. Personalization and opportunities to be unique give audiences the chance to create and share their stories in a way that generates an authentic connection with a brand and its intended audiences. This is illustrated by LEGO and its Kronkiwongi campaign. LEGO wanted to make sure children had plenty of opportunities to be creative without any restrictions. In addition, LEGO encouraged parents to be empowered to help their children embark on their creative journey at an early age to make it part of their lifestyle. These were the overall goals for this campaign (Shorty Awards, 2016).

LEGO sent off a set of LEGO bricks to specific audiences among families in Denmark, and asked them to build their own Kronkiwongi. The company did not disclose what exactly a Kronkiwongi was, but wanted the audience members to create what they felt represented this concept. The results were creative and imaginative, and parents shared the videos they took of their children's creations on the designated Facebook page for the campaign. The result was tremendous for LEGO, reaching 24 million families across 15 countries. The LEGO main Facebook page went up 61% in user traffic during the course of the campaign (Shorty Awards, 2016).

Rising global platforms. When considering international campaigns in social media, professionals have to recognize other channels that are unique and

Source: "Build your Krongkiwongi" LEGO https://www .lego.com/en-us/campaigns/kronkiwongi

LEGO and the Kronkiwongi Campaign

prominently used in other countries. China, for example, uses designated apps more often than traditional social media channels (due to government censorship and blocking of main social media channels such as Facebook). In China, social media sites including Weibo (similar to Twitter) are used more frequently since this is where the community is going. This perspective is universal—go to the platform that the audience is going to, and make sure you understand the similarities and differences in these platforms and integrate these practices strategically in both the content and message strategy for the brand.

The most popular social media sites in China include WeChat and Weibo. WeChat is a messaging app that combines all aspects for users such as games, shopping, and financial services. To illustrate the prominence of message exchanges on WeChat (where there are official accounts for users and brands), over 38 billion messages were sent per day as of November 2017, and use looks like it will continue to rise (Millward, 2017). WeChat is so popular in China and around the world because it is a one-stop shop where users can pay bills, shop, post moments and stories on their walls, get taxis, and engage in many more functions (Thai, 2018).

Weibo, China's answer to Twitter, is a micro-blogging platform. Weibo operates and is formatted like Twitter, and users can update and share visuals (photos, GIFs, videos, etc.). While the Weibo audience is not the same size as WeChat's, a significant amount of users (340 million) do use the platform (Thai, 2018). Several campaigns have used Weibo to engage with audiences, including a number of luxury brands in China such as Louis Vuitton and Chanel. While the audience is bigger on WeChat, many brands and professionals feel the engagement among millennials on Weibo is better (Zheng, 2017). For example, the fashion brand Longchamp wanted to create a campaign targeting millennials for its fashion line by mapping out where audiences on its Weibo account could check in and share pictures with their followers to promote user-generated content (Zheng, 2017).

Best Practices for International Campaigns

Social media provides many opportunities, challenges, and lessons for the global community. Each country has its own designated media, legal, and political landscapes, so it is important to tailor our social media practices to follow these elements. Best practices for operating on the social media global stage include the following:

- *Learn the culture, people, food, and history.* Like being a student of social media, it is important to understand, appreciate, and embrace the culture of the country for which you are designing social media. Be aware of what makes the country unique, and how this uniqueness is showcased on various social media platforms. Conduct research to determine the major media outlets, influencers, brands, companies, and accounts on social media to get a feel for the country's own voice and presence.

- *Choose platforms appropriate for the audiences and goals in mind.* Similar principles discussed so far often apply to international platforms. While there are some dominant global platforms, others are more appropriate. Having a large audience is great, such as in the expanding WeChat, but WeChat is not necessarily the best channel for reaching a certain audience or building more engagement with a community.

- *Open your eyes to new platforms outside of your country.* While we sometimes focus only on what is happening in our own communities and countries, it is key to also look at how social media is being implemented across the world, and what new messaging apps, social media communities, and sites are created each and every day. Be aware also of current social media trends in the country of origin. We Are Social and Hootsuite produce quarterly reports that outline the major trends, platforms, and user data for each country and region around the world (Kemp, 2018).

- *Understand the importance of culture and unique platform characteristics and expectations.* For social media professionals, it is important to understand that while some universal practices are consistent across cultures and communities, other unique characteristics will need to be addressed and acknowledged. Going into a new country and online community with the assumption that what works in your country will work in another will not go over well. Research the current social media landscape, cultures, media expectations, and age cohorts so you understand both the differences and similarities.

- *Sometimes there are universal challenges across all social media platforms.* In all cases, even international ones, social media still raises concerns that are consistent around the world. Privacy, legal issues, political climates, and understanding the implications of data and how data can be applied are just a few examples. Yet, by embracing these challenges across the board and having these universal discussions in the social media community, we will see we are all in the same boat as social media professionals and can solve these challenges together.

CHAPTER SUMMARY

The specialty areas needing social media professionals are diverse, as we have seen in this chapter for nonprofit, social care, health care, and international campaigns. Each of these areas has its own unique challenges and obstacles, whether financial, government regulations, customer expectations, or different media and political landscapes. Each area provides opportunities for social media to do great and wonderful things for relevant communities. While differences exist across these sectors, there are more similarities and opportunities for social media professionals. Social media is a truly global community, channel, and industry, and will continue on this projection. This chapter shows that social media professionals can break down barriers to share stories, insights, and expertise with the rest of the world and community.

THOUGHT QUESTIONS

1. What are the core best practices for social care?

2. Discuss the main social media challenges and opportunities for nonprofits.

3. What are some of the unique elements to note when it comes to social media and health care practices?

4. What are the major similarities and differences in social media practices around the world?

EXERCISES

1. You are the social media care professional for Mattel and just heard the news a recall has happened for one of your main holiday toys. Your Twitter account and Facebook page have become the main places where people express concerns about this news. What action steps will you take to handle this situation?

2. You are volunteering for the Salvation Army, and you have been tasked by your supervisor to create a social media campaign to raise funds during the holidays. However, your supervisor's boss does not feel social media could help out in this area. Write why you feel social media is beneficial for nonprofits and outline a strategic social media plan you could propose for this fund-raising campaign.

3. While working at a hospital in the social media department, you see a rise of check-ins from patients and families rating their experiences. Some of them are positive, and some of them are negative. What course of action will you take?

4. You are about to do a study-abroad internship, and you have the choice of working in social media in either China, Australia, or South Africa. Evaluate the current social media landscape in each country and discuss one campaign using a designated social media platform you like. Evaluate and note the current social media trends highlighted for this country in the We Are Social and Hootsuite global social media report, available at wearesocial.com/blog/2018/01/global-digital-report-2018, in your analysis.

REFERENCES

Amarula. (2017, August 8). Amarula launches new campaign to save African elephants on World Elephant Day. *PR Newswire*. Retrieved from https://www.prnewswire.com/news-releases/amarula-launches-new-campaign-to-save-african-elephants-on-world-elephant-day-300500800.html.

Anderson, M. K. (2017). Welcome back, Movember: Why this viral campaign is still so successful. *HubSpot*. Retrieved from https://blog.hubspot.com/marketing/movember-data-viral-campaign.

Augure. (2017, July 12). *10 communication campaigns about Movember*. Retrieved from https://augure.launchmetrics.com/resources/blog/movember-communication-campaigns.

Belbey, J. (2015, January 21). How healthcare can use social media effectively and compliantly. *Forbes*. Retrieved from https://www.forbes.com/sites/joannabelbey/2015/01/21/how-healthcare-can-use-social-media-effectively-and-compliantly/.

Belbey, J. (2016a, January 31). Is social media the future of healthcare? *Forbes*. Retrieved from https://www.forbes.com/sites/joannabelbey/2016/01/31/is-social-media-the-future-of-healthcare/.

Belbey, J. (2016b, November 17). Is social media and "employee advocacy" possible within regulated industries? *Forbes*. Retrieved from https://www.forbes.com/sites/joannabelbey/2016/11/17/is-social-media-and-employee-advocacy-possible-within-regulated-industries/.

Boadle, A. (2017, November 7). Uber, rival apps join forces in Brazil to stem tide of regulation. *Reuters*. Retrieved from https://www.reuters.com/article/us-uber-brazil/uber-rival-apps-join-forces-in-brazil-to-stem-tide-of-regulation-idUSKBN1D71KE.

Chowdhry, A. (2015, August 26). Remember the Ice Bucket Challenge? Donations from the $220 million campaign enhanced ALS research. *Forbes*. Retrieved from http://www.forbes.com/sites/amitchowdhry/2015/08/26/remember-the-ice-bucket-challenge-donations-from-the-220-million-campaign-advanced-als-research/#6b655460692b.

Employee advocacy drives healthcare social media outreach. (2018). *Ragan's PR Daily*. Retrieved from https://www.prdaily.com/Awards/Special Edition/615.aspx.

Frumkin, T. (2017, January 18). The 6 most important customer service stats for 2017. *Conversocial*. Retrieved from http://www.conversocial.com/blog/the-7-most-important-customer-service-stats-for-2017.

Hyken, S. (2017, April 22). Social customer care is the new marketing. *Forbes*. Retrieved from https://www.forbes.com/sites/shephyken/2017/04/22/social-customer-care-is-the-new-marketing/.

Johnston, A. (2017, July 24). A strategic guide to social media for nonprofits. *Sprout Social*. Retrieved from https://sproutsocial.com/insights/nonprofit-social-media-guide/.

Kemp, S. (2018, January 30). Digital in 2018: World's internet users pass the 4 billion mark. *We Are Social*. Retrieved from https://wearesocial.com/blog/2018/01/global-digital-report-2018.

Kiefer, B. (2017, February 1). Amnesty social campaign lets refugees respond in real time to tweeters. *PR Week*. Retrieved from https://www.prweek.com/article/1422860.

Mack, H. (2017, February 28). How social media can impact healthcare in the right—and wrong—ways. *MobiHealthNews*. Retrieved from http://www.mobihealthnews.com/content/how-social-media-can-impact-healthcare-right—-and-wrong-ways.

Millward, S. (2017, November 9). WeChat users send record 38 billion messages per day. *Tech in Asia*. Retrieved from https://www.techinasia.com/wechat-users-send-38-billion-messages-day.

Murphy, S. (2014, February 6). Marc Jacobs pop-up shop takes tweets, Instagrams for payment. *Mashable*. Retrieved from https://mashable.com/2014/02/06/marc-jacobs-tweet-store/#vzZEVkibngqW.

Nudd, T. (2017a, May 12). Ogilvy's flag for Refugee Nation and its Olympic team wins Best of Show at The One Show. *Adweek*. Retrieved from http://www.adweek.com/creativity/ogilvys-flag-for-refugee-nation-and-its-olympic-team-wins-best-of-show-at-the-one-show/.

Nudd, T. (2017b, June 18). "Meet Graham" wins the first Grand Prix of the 2017 Cannes Lions. *Adweek*. Retrieved from http://www.adweek.com/creativity/meet-graham-wins-the-first-grand-prix-of-the-2017-cannes-lions/.

Parisi, D. (2018). Aflac and Macy's promote holiday campaign with social media and messaging app. *Mobile Marketer*. Retrieved from https://www.mobilemarketer.com/ex/mobilemarketer/cms/news/messaging/23938.html.

Pennic, J. (2014, February 17). 5 reasons why Mayo Clinic dominates social media in healthcare. *HIT Consultant*. Retrieved from http://hitconsultant.net/2014/02/17/5-reasons-mayo-clinic-dominates-social-media-in-healthcare/.

Peterson, T. (2015, June 15). Ice Bucket Challenge, "Like a Girl" take top honors in Facebook Awards. *Ad Age*. Retrieved from http://adage.com/article/digital/ice-bucket-challenge-top-facebook-s-studio-awards/298983/.

Quesenberry, K. A. (2016, April 19). Social media is too important to be left to the marketing department. *Harvard Business Review*. Retrieved from https://hbr.org/2016/04/social-media-is-too-important-to-be-left-to-the-marketing-department.

Shorty Awards. (2016). LEGO Kronkiwongi. Retrieved from http://shortyawards.com/8th/lego-kronkiwongi

St. Jude Children's Research Hospital. (2016, October 25). St. Jude and more than 70 leading brands ask consumers to #GiveThanks while they shop this holiday season during St. Jude Thanks and Giving® campaign. Retrieved from https://www.stjude.org/media-resources/news-releases/2016-fundraising-news/st-jude-thanks-and-giving-thirteenth-year.html.

Stein, L. (2016, August 16). Highly regulated industries try employee advocacy on social. *Ad Age*. Retrieved from http://adage.com/article/agency-news/dynamic-signal-helps-highly-regulated-brands-social/305407/.

Thai, N. (2018). 10 most popular social media sites in China (2018 updated). *Dragon Social*. Retrieved from https://www.dragonsocial.net/blog/social-media-in-china/.

Top Nonprofits. (2016, Spring). *Top nonprofits on social media*. Retrieved from https://topnonprofits.com/lists/top-nonprofits-on-social-media/.

Zheng, R. (2017, October 18). How luxury brands can use user-generated content in China. *Jing Daily*. Retrieved from https://jingdaily.com/tactics-luxury-brands-utilize-user-generated-content-in-china/.

13

WHAT DOES THE SOCIAL MEDIA WORLD HAVE THAT IS NEW?

Learning Objectives
Introduction
Current (So Far) State of Social Media
    Future Trends and Directions
    Students to Students: Advice From the Social
       Media Classroom Seat
Final Words of Wisdom and Recommendations
Chapter Summary
Thought Questions
Exercises
References

LEARNING OBJECTIVES

After reading this chapter, you will be able to

- Summarize the areas covered in previous chapters

- Identify emerging trends to note for the future in social media

- Explain best practices and next steps for continuing to learn about the science and art of social media

INTRODUCTION

Congratulations! You have finished and reviewed all of the chapters of *Social Media for Strategic Communication*! This means you can take the social media world by storm and list yourself as an expert or even guru in the field.

Not quite. In fact, there are no experts.

It is important to note that while many professionals deem themselves experts or specialists in the field, they may be experts only at the particular moment in which Facebook's algorithm is structured in a certain way. Do we have influence over what Mark Zuckerberg decides to do next with the platform? No. Do we have the opportunity to tell Jack Dorsey of Twitter how to make sure false news or information doesn't filter out into everyone's timelines? Wait a second—let me call him up or send him a direct message. Can we tell Instagram we want everything to be in chronological order and not be inundated with promoted ads and posts all the time? We will have to wait and see what happens. Unlike many other channels of communication, social media professionals are at the mercy of what these platforms decided to do (or not do) for their users, which includes both organizations and brands. This is the nature of social media as we are operating in rented space. Rules, formats, expectations, and features will constantly change. We have to be agile, adaptive, and willing to learn on the go when it comes to social media.

While you now have a strong foundation for what it takes to apply and integrate strategy into the mix for social media purposes, learning has not stopped. In the social media field, platforms, algorithms, case studies, and approaches always change. Sometimes this takes a few months, but others can change at a moment's notice.

CURRENT (SO FAR) STATE OF SOCIAL MEDIA

Social media will continue to be a field in which technology, communities, and humans interact with each other in ways based on knowledge sharing, relationship management, and engaging in networks within certain communities and functions. Most of the time, people assume the most popular and current channels being used are social media, but that is not necessarily the case. We can always make assumptions about where people will go next, but in order to make official judgments on this, we have to look at the data and determine where exactly people are. The same goes for when to post on each designated platform as well. Best post timing recommendations may be appropriate in some cases, but not always. Understanding what works for a brand and its designated community on social media has to be approached on a case-by-case basis.

For example, messaging (e.g., SMS and private messages via mobile apps) is number one, followed by social media, email, video chat, and face-to-face (Cohen, 2017). These messaging channels and apps (e.g., WeChat, WhatsApp, Messenger, and QQ) are often referred to as dark social, because these types of media are private and unmonitored or hard to track by social media professionals and brands (Hong, 2017). This raises another issue and challenge for users when brands discover how to automate conversations and program interactions with their audiences using chat bots. Chat bots are programs designed to simulate human conversation with certain actions, and are frequently used to handle customer service inquiries and questions. This, of course, may impact the trustworthiness and authenticity needed to build social media relationships. These programs may be helpful in certain situations, but not others. While the temptation of using a tool for the sake of using the tool is great, understanding the context and being empathic about how others perceive it is even more critical. Authenticity matters most, especially to millennials, when it comes to social content according to a survey conducted by Stackla (Cassidy, 2017).

The definition given in Chapter 1 still applies to what we are currently experiencing in the field of social media, but there will be a time when we must be adaptable (and receptive) to the growing changes in the field as well as how we conceptualize it. Social media professionals today are actively changing the field as we speak, and we have to be fluid and understand this is the way things operate in this field. The first five chapters (from the introduction to ethical and legal foundations, personal and professional branding, industry qualifications, and research) provided a solid foundation for the consistent skills and concepts needed to go into strategic communications and the field of social media. The next set of chapters (covering strategic planning, strategic writing, audience segmentation, creating and curating content, and measurement and evaluation) provided a bit more specialization within the systematic planning and creative execution protocols needed to build on the foundations set for the field. The remaining chapters (exploring the application of social media) showed the different areas of specialization you can go into from a specific role to a particular industry. The opportunities are endless in social media. This is where a lot of the momentum is moving. It is not a question of whether or not to think digital first. We *must* embrace and always think digital is first for what we do in strategic communications.

While the opportunities grow in social media, the future allows us to experience our own challenges. With platforms such as Facebook, Twitter, Snapchat, and others allowing access to their application programming interfaces and metrics, this raises issues not just about whether this is a "pay to play" situation, but more about to what extent. Essentially, social media professionals have to recognize that they still need strong content, but it has to be amplified strategically with a paid media strategy in place (Richard, 2017). The social media platforms that dominate the space will continue to make people and brands invest in targeting their content and making sure it reaches the right people. The days of achieving organic reach are coming to an end (Fontein, 2017).

Other technology- and social media–related trends emerging for social media professionals range from basic content suggestions (e.g., social video) to more advanced tools that encompass the overall digital sphere in society (e.g., voice and automated intelligence, or AI). Talkwalker (Richard, 2017) explored some of these tools in detail:

- *Voice search* (Amazon's Alexa, Apple's Siri, Google, and even Microsoft's Cortana). Our devices are interconnected not just with our platforms, but with every facet of our lives. We can access information directly through these devices just by using our voice. Artificial intelligence can be both proactive and reactive in nature, and we have to think about how this will impact and work in our daily lives. We are seeing more integration of voice in our daily lives, even on social media platforms. We have to be able to integrate mobile, social, and voice together in a seamless and relevant manner for our own purposes, and those for our audiences.

- *Advocacy marketing.* Influencer marketing is one piece of the puzzle for social media. Advocates are audience members who are not only part of the community for a brand on social media, but willing to put forth their name and reputation to endorse brands without the financial compensation an influencer may require. In addition, these audiences gravitate toward sharing more user-generated content on social media, which actually is the type of content most audiences crave (Cassidy, 2017).

- *Ephemeral content.* While social video is becoming more and more prevalent, the content is short lived, mobile first, and only accessible for 24 hours. This content drives high engagement and audiences to relevant platforms (Hutchinson, 2017). If audiences know a video is only available on Snapchat, Instagram, or other similar apps for a certain amount of time, they will come. However, the content and experience still need to create a true comprehensive experience for the audiences.

- *Social media brand protection.* It is important to have an offensive strategy when it comes to social media, but we should also build up protocols to protect the reputation and community for a brand on social media. The rise of rumors, false information, and negative actions taken by threatening parties all have to be acknowledged and planned for in a social media strategy. The threats and risks associated with these actions can directly impact attitudes, behaviors, and communities online. No brand or platform is invincible. Look at what Snapchat has experienced in 2018 with changes in user numbers, or even the outcry of the #DeleteFacebook movement after the Facebook and Cambridge Analytica crisis.

Social media as we see it today is constantly changing, and no one is an expert. Everyone is operating with best guesses on trends and what will be relevant next, and these are just "guidelines," to quote *Pirates of the Caribbean*. The roles, investment, and responsibilities will soon change and of course blur together. The job postings shared for brands, agencies, and organizations are framed much differently compared to others posted earlier in the same year.

With every year that passes, more "influencers" and "keynote speakers" come up to showcase their brands and what they can do for others. Everyone is a media company with a large microphone. However, while social media has been around now for some time, it's not necessarily in its infant stage. It is more along the lines of the teenager stage. Social media professionals are still trying to advocate (and sometimes shout) their relevancy to the world with each of their platforms—trying to one-up each other with how many conferences, clients, and speaking engagements they can take on. This is all fine and good, but those who are trying to make a difference and have new experiences and ideas may be left in the dust. Thus, young professionals not only have to be part of this community, but must bring forth a game plan along with their microphone. This field is still in the Wild West, where everyone wants a piece of the pie or gold mine out there with relationships, influence, and community. The risks associated with misunderstanding audiences and what they are looking for can be detrimental for a brand, and cause additional challenges down the line.

Yet, not all is lost. With each year that passes, the social media space becomes more civilized and structured to the profession's needs. We are seeing a growing need for the congregation of all like minds related to the science and art of social media strategy. The social media industry needs everyone to come together to discuss, brainstorm, and collaborate to make sure all of the research questions, challenges, and opportunities are addressed together in a comprehensive and thorough manner.

Future Trends and Directions

The million-dollar question you will be asked wherever you go in social media is "What does the social media professional have that is *new*?" What next trend do we need to jump on and address? What shiny new tool or platform do we need to put thousands of dollars into?

These questions are not so simple, but they shouldn't be intimidating. New tools and technology platforms will always arise in the business, but it all comes down to this:

- Is this technology sustainable? If so, for how long?

- Is this trend innovative and able to provide value?

- What is the overall case for investing in this tool? What is our rationale for using this tool or platform in addition to the resources we already employ?

- What can we do with this tool to enhance our story and content for our audiences?

- Do we have the investment (financially and in leadership) to move forward with this technology?

These are some of the questions that need to be raised. Buy-in both financially and in leadership is crucial to be aware of and note for the future. Sometimes, it is not the social media professional who makes the call, but the CEO or supervisor. That said, there needs to be a discussion around how to apply new advances. Technology is changing so fast that it is hard to keep up, but some technology advances not only are sustainable, but continue to grow in prominence within the industry.

Two indicators to note when it comes to investing in new tools and platforms for social media purposes are virtual reality and augmented reality. **Virtual reality (VR)** is one of the more guaranteed technology investments not just for professional practices but for understanding how audiences want to interact with the digital and real space, while also creating their own experiences with these new tools. Virtual reality can be defined as "a three-dimensional, computer generated environment which can be explored and interacted with by a person. That person becomes part of this virtual world or is immersed within this environment and whilst there, is able to manipulate objects or perform a series of actions" (Virtual Reality Society, 2017).

Mark Zuckerberg has said he wants to have a billion people on VR, and many brands and professionals are following this shift and direction (Gartenberg, 2017). VR can be used strategically and aligned with the work of social media professionals in several ways:

- Experiential storytelling

- Education

- Impact of cause-related marketing

VR can be used to purposely interject a user into an experience, tapping into more of the emotional cues and responses that may result. This is one of the more prominent and strategic ways social media professionals, along with others, allow users to get inside the story, experience, and moment and walk away feeling impacted in some way. In many cases, brands have led the way in VR, such as NASA providing an opportunity for people to experience a virtual walk around Mars (Good, 2017) or Walmart using VR for employee training to prepare for Black Friday (Robertson, 2017).

Häagen-Dazs launched a VR campaign that raised awareness of bees' impact on the world. The ice cream company created a virtual experience where the user would get the feel of being a honeybee while gaining a growing awareness of bees and their threat of extinction, connecting the campaign back to its brand mission and products (Monllos, 2017). Another brand that has used VR as a way to educate audiences about a topic is General Electric (GE). GE, which has become an innovator in implementing different platforms and tools for brand identity, created a VR series to educate people about different subjects in science (Swant, 2017). Brands are not the only ones incorporating VR into their stories; high-profile events are going in this direction as well. The Breeders' Cup, for example, provides means for fans and others to experience the view of a jockey, whereas the Macy's Thanksgiving Day Parade partnered with Tagboard and Verizon to provide a VR experience of the parade, while showcasing ads with augmented reality technologies for audiences to get the complete experience (Tagboard, 2016).

A related trend, **augmented reality (AR)** sometimes gets confused with virtual reality, but it is slightly different. Essentially, according to Azuma (1997), AR allows programmers to create both real and virtual elements so the individual user is able to interact with both. As Hofmann and Mosemghvdlishvili (2014) stated in their work, AR is different from VR because AR is "a view of physical, real world, but supplements it with layers of digital elements" (Hofmann & Mosemghvdlishvili, 2014, p. 266).

Source: https://lensstudio.snapchat.com/

Snapchat Lens Studio

TOMS is one brand that has used AR to not only tell a story, but also raise awareness of its Virtual Giving Trip campaign (O'Brien, 2017) so people could actually see how their donations are used when they contribute to TOMS. This allows supporters the experience of seeing what they have donated (financially or otherwise) firsthand and the reactions among others. Another brand that has invested a lot into the AR technology is Snapchat. On March 24, 2016, Snapchat bought the app Bitmoji (Primack, 2016), which allows people to create their own personalized avatar based on looks as well as virtual clothing. Snapchat made an update in 2017 allowing people to see their Bitmojis as 3D lenses, which added again to the personal virtual aspect of the app (Newton, 2017).

There are many different ways to create an AR experience for audiences, such as the following:

- *Virtual tours.* A virtual tour allows people to learn about certain locations (e.g., traveling) and see historical notations for significant landmarks.

- *Paid advertisements.* The rise of virtual ads through AR will continue to skyrocket as more people use the technologies. Keep in mind that wherever consumers go, marketers and advertisers will soon follow. If the experience is beneficial and entertaining for the user, then it may be appropriate. If not, it will be all for nothing.

- *Storytelling and personal branding.* Due to updates to platforms like Bitmoji and Snapchat, people can create their own avatars to showcase emotions and their own stories.

These new specializations are "current," and we do not know the longevity of these platforms or how they will evolve. In some cases, a new form of technology (e.g., Google Glass) emerges but is not successful because developers did not anticipate audiences' perceptions, behaviors, and attitudes (e.g., toward wearable technologies). These technologies may be great tools, but some are ahead of their time.

Some rising platforms become dominated by larger ones with powerful brands. Meerkat, a popular live streaming app, faced this challenge when going up against Periscope, the live streaming app Twitter eventually bought. What is important, though, is investing in ongoing education and training for what may emerge, which will tell us why and how a new technology is relevant for an organization and what steps to take to determine whether it is worthy to invest in.

Failure to invest in education and training relevant to emerging tools due to the limited time and resources available for some brands and professionals could cause a "virtual technology desert" for audiences. Like food deserts, **virtual digital technology deserts** provide limited access and opportunities to stand out in the industry, and the resulting community is limited. In addition, future applications and tools have to be analyzed and guided based on where the audiences are going. If your audience is baby boomers, you will need to invest in one subset of tools that might be different from tools used for an audience made up of Generation Z. Each cohort consumes, creates, and shares information differently on social media, and this will have to be monitored, studied, and implemented on a regular basis. Ultimately, where to go next and what content to create has to be a unified decision by everyone involved in strategy and creative execution.

With all of these updates, changes, and advances in the industry happening every day, it may be overwhelming and challenging, to say the least, when it comes to staying up-to-date with every aspect of the industry. Staying relevant and engaged with social media is a challenging task. In a constantly evolving, changing, and shifting field, how does a social media professional continue to stay relevant? Many professionals, students, and professors have asked themselves this question. Instead of worrying about the advancement of tools, look at the advancement of your actions and behaviors to make sure you stay relevant.

Here are some ways to accomplish this task and continue to stay relevant:

- *Treat your understanding of the profession like a sport or hobby.* Olympians do not start training for their sport the day before the trials. They train every day, and invest time and energy to better understand their sport. You need to take the same approach. Do a little bit each day. This means reading up on a few blog posts and white papers, or even reading a new book on the subject. Schedule and watch a webinar or live video show session once every couple of weeks.

- *Follow people as well as media accounts.* The Humans of Social Media professionals are some people you may want to follow and connect with, so this feature gives you a head start on this point. Media accounts will come and go, but those who are actively engaged in the business will not move around as much. Focus on outlining a few online accounts you trust and that provide good content. In addition, follow a few people who are specialists in their field or on a particular platform. For example, Ian Cleary is an expert on various measurement and social media tools, whereas Sue B. Zimmerman focuses on all aspects of Instagram. Follow a few of these professionals to get up-to-date information related to specific niches, so then you have an idea of what is going on, what is relevant, and how to apply this for your role.

- *Be an active participant.* Be present on Twitter chats, live shows, and webinars within the industry. Watch shows created to document and showcase specific journeys (e.g., Gary Vaynerchuk and #DailyVees and Social Media Examiner's "The Journey" with Mike Stelzner). Some Twitter chats that would be helpful for getting connected with the industry include the following:

  - #BlogElevated (all topics related to blogging), Mondays at 10 p.m. EST

  - #BufferChat (all topics related to social media marketing, hosted by Buffer), Wednesdays at 12 p.m. EST

  - #ChatSnap (all topics around Snapchat, hosted by Kristy Gillentine), Wednesdays at 2 p.m. EST

  - #SproutChat (all topics related to social media marketing, hosted by Sprout Social), Wednesdays at 3 pm EST

  - #MarketoChat (all influencers and brands), Thursdays at 1 p.m. EST

  - #TwitterSmarter (all aspects of Twitter, hosted by Madalyn Sklar), Thursdays at 1 p.m. EST

  - #SocialROI (all aspects of social media, hosted by ManageFlitter), Tuesdays at 5 p.m. EST

  - #HootChat (all digital marketing topics and Hootsuite), Thursdays at 3 p.m. EST

  - #PRStudChat (conversations on topics related to students in PR, hosted by Deirdre Breakenridge and Valerie Simon), Thursdays at 12 p.m. (monthly)

  - #SweetTalk (hosted by Cinnabon on all topics, including social media), Tuesdays at 1 p.m. EST

  - #MeasurePR (hosted by Shonali Burke on all topics related to measurement), first Thursday of every month from 12 to 1 p.m. EST

  - #AdobeChat (all digital marketing topics and Adobe-related topics), Wednesdays at 4 p.m. EST

  - #CreateEDU (education-related topics, sponsored and hosted by Education for Adobe), Thursdays at 4 p.m. EST

- *Do an audit of your skills and personal brand every few months.* We are all evolving as professionals, and we want to make sure we set goals for what we want to accomplish and achieve in the industry. Set forth a few professional social media goals you want to achieve (be featured in a guest blog post, be interviewed for a podcast, speak at a conference on social media, be invited to do a keynote, etc.). Analyze what you have done and what you need to do, and list the steps you will take to achieve those goals. With the technology and platforms changing so much, it is necessary to conduct this audit on a regular basis so it is not completely overwhelming.

- *Find a mentor.* Find someone in the industry you want not only to connect with but, more importantly, to learn from. See if people are willing to share their experiences with you, provide guidance and advice, and help you get your start in the industry. As the famous line goes, we all stand on the shoulders of giants, and we all need a little help to get to where we need to go.

Students to Students: Advice
From the Social Media Classroom Seat

When it comes to social media, there are certain things to expect. Professors or professionals can share their own experiences, but when advice comes from peers in a social media class, different insights emerge.

Certain aspects of social media are universal, but students are in the position not only to embrace knowledge and understanding of the tools and concepts, but to apply them in real-life circumstances in and out of the classroom. The students featured in this book are recent and soon-to-be graduates who were enrolled in a social media class and wanted to pass along some of their own perspectives and words of wisdom to the future generation of social media professionals entering the workplace.

Tevin Johnson-Campion graduated with a degree in communications from the University of Louisville and is currently working with Fizziology, a social media entertainment research and analytics company that works with some of the largest movie and entertainment companies in the world. Tevin had extensive experience before graduating in 2017 in event planning (J Wagner Group), entertainment and analytics (Fizziology), and personal branding (Petrino Family Foundation). In addition, he had the chance to be the spokesperson for his family by conducting interviews with MSNBC, the American Civil Liberties Union, MTV, and *The Huffington Post* surrounding the marriage equality rights verdict from the Supreme Court in 2015. Here's Tevin's advice for students:

Source: Courtesy of Philip Truman

Tevin Johnson-Campion

Social media is such a great tool. Literally the world is at your fingertips, and you can connect with anyone in any part of the world at virtually any given time. During my days as a student, it was important to me to learn as much as possible in understanding not only using social media for professional use, but finding the balance of maintaining the personal side to it as well.

Having a presentable social media account is very important, more so than you would think. One of the great things about social media is the ability to connect with people at any time, but with that great advantage comes responsibility. Potential employers and colleagues use social media every day, just like you do. It is important to note that if you are posting content strictly meant for only your close friends to see, that is fine, but be aware that future colleagues and employers can see it too. This does not mean you cannot post personal things on social media, but please be aware of any risks it might pose to your future. Having two social media accounts (one for professional use and one for private use) can be misconstrued because it may look like you have something to hide. Try and find the best of both worlds when maintaining your social media account.

One of the best ways to understand what to post and what not to post is simple. How do you want to be perceived? If the answer is clear to you, then your social media should align with those goals. If the answer is not so clear, then evaluate what it is you want to do and how you want to be perceived.

Getting involved in your desired field can be tricky. What helped me the most was following people on social media, whether it was friends, classmates, or even public figures, who aligned themselves with what I saw as important to my future. Personally, I wanted to be in the entertainment industry working either in music or in film.

(Continued)

(Continued)

I started following people on social media with those same interests and continually tried to reach out to people in the entertainment industry.

A lot of times, your first job comes from someone you know, which means you have to network. Through following people in my industry and learning more about the jobs in social media, I was able to learn what employers were looking for and what I could do to better my skills as both a student and a professional. I suggest reading articles, using LinkedIn, and doing anything you can to soak up as much knowledge as possible in the field that you are interested in. This not only shows dedication, but can also set you apart and put you ahead of the game. Be attentive to any new trends and utilize that when you are either posting to social media or networking with any potential employers.

Lizelle Lauron (@letstellllizelle), the social media coordinator for the Dallas Mavericks, shared her words of wisdom on what to keep in mind when entering the workplace. Lizelle graduated in 2013 with a degree in communications with a sports administration minor from the University of Louisville.

Source: Courtesy of Danny Bollinger

Lizelle Lauron

My advice for future students is to always be in a learning mindset. In my profession, people trust those who put their noses down and grind. So many times we come across interns who have this amazing opportunity to impress us in the NBA, but only want to take selfies on the court.

Present new ideas! Show how the company, organization, or whomever can improve because of your ideas. That's how you make yourself valuable. In social media, anyone can "tweet, Instagram, or post on Facebook." Start conversations with "I saw in the past we've done this, so what do you think about this?" or "I've noticed others doing this, but I think if we did this, it would work better for us!" If you have the drive to show growth, change, engagement, and impressions for your company, people will see you as a team player!

Bell Holder (@TheRebeccaH) has some similar advice for students. Bell, who is graduating with her communications degree in May 2018, has already worked with brands such as the Kentucky Derby and nonprofits like Blessings in a Backpack and Metro United Way in social media, and she shares her experience working in the field:

Know that you will fail and it will be painful. Do it anyway. Failures are the things that teach us, and you are here to learn. Live fearlessly because social media moves too fast to not take chances.

Run your own social media like it is a client. Convert your accounts to business accounts, create content calendars and plans, promote a post on the major platforms (it's not as expensive

Source: Courtesy of Bell Holder

Bell Holder

potential employers, and you have practiced converting likes and shares into actionable data. Volunteering with nonprofits can give you something similar—they usually have smaller staffs, so being a social media "intern" means you have more freedom to learn.

Look at the world differently. If you are taking a picture of an image for Instagram, then think about it from other perspectives. By asking yourself "How can I present this text information visually?" or "How can this text be presented in an image?" you start to see things differently. This is a field that mixes creative with analytic, so make sure you work both sides of your brain. Find other social media professionals and follow them, follow their clients, and follow people they follow. Engage in social media chats on different platforms. Join conversation groups. Talk to people you don't know and learn more information. You can only benefit from it.

Don't be overwhelmed. Social media is a huge job, and learning about it involves an intense amount of information that is constantly changing. Break it down into parts and manage them. Everyone will have a platform they love (Instagram for life) and excel at, but learning about them all will help you understand what each platform's content looks like for your client.

as you think), and use the tools that you want to use with your future clients. Set up 30 posts in Hootsuite and at the end of the month or quarter look at your analytics and write yourself a report like you would for a client, including what worked and what didn't. Practice presenting that information in different ways such as infographics, a Spark page, or a short video. That way, when you graduate, you have a portfolio to show

Emily Hayes (@emceris), a graduate of the University of Louisville with a degree in communication, has some additional suggestions and recommendations. Emily interned with Power, a digital and advertising agency in Louisville, and is currently working as a marketing coordinator for AMD Studios in Austin, Texas.

Source: Courtesy of Emily Hayes

Emily Hayes

My best advice for any student in social media is to never assume you know it all. Social media is an ever-evolving landscape; platforms die out, tools change, and trends fade all the time. But you know how you can navigate this? Be an active participant and student in your field! Try out the latest and greatest, talk to your fellow students, and attend your classes so you know the basics like the back of your hand. Always be on the lookout for the exciting ways social media is evolving around you and how you can become a part of it! Best of luck out there and know we're all rooting for you.

FINAL WORDS OF WISDOM AND RECOMMENDATIONS

As we finalize this chapter and book, there are some parting words of wisdom to share with the future generation of social media professionals. Keep in mind that some things will remain true in spite of ongoing changes. The behaviors, actions, and communities formed are based on human behavior. That said, social media continues to be owned not by one person, but by the community.

The community decides where people make connections and whether they continue online or offline. Social media is more than just taking seflies and sharing updates. As discussed in this textbook, it takes a social media strategic mindset to understand, comprehend, and apply insights from the community to provide the best experience for everyone. The rise of **human interaction marketing (HIM)** is also apparent; it is a strain of relationship management with the strategic purpose of the health and longevity of the relationship being the currency exchanged. It may be tempting to focus on the here and now, but do not forget the long-term implications and benefits. Social media is indeed instantaneous, but always think about the ramifications and connections that can be made in an instant, and how these could transform into roadblocks or opportunities down the line. Social media, with the help of screenshots and Google, does not forget.

In this book, you learned some of the fundamental skills necessary for working in the social media field. However, there are some other aspects to keep in mind as you enter your next phase of working in social media:

- *Be ambitious and embrace what you are passionate about.* Take every opportunity you see in front of you and go for it. These opportunities—whether internships or jobs—will not drop into your lap. They will have to be pursued with passion (the next skill listed here) and thinking outside of the box. There are many, many opportunities to pursue in social media. If you do not like what you are doing, figure out what you do like and pursue that area of interest. There may be some challenging roadblocks, gatekeepers, and obstacles, but if you are willing to put forth the time and investment, you'll eventually meet your goals.

- *Be persistent.* The industry is big enough for everyone to carve out an area of expertise and build a community. Sometimes you may feel certain people (influencers, etc.) dominate the field, or you may say "This discipline owns social media" and try to provide roadblocks to keep it a closed circuit. Ultimately, if you provide great content, excellent resources, and a unique perspective to share with others, you have a place in the social media community. The social media community and industry as a whole is huge, and constantly evolving.

- *Have balance.* Social media will always be there, so it's okay to have a life. Yes, there is a "hustle" mentality, and you do have to invest time and energy—but do it in a smart way. Embrace the digital breaks as a way to brainstorm ideas, gain new perspectives, and actually have a life outside of social media. Certain audiences have the appearance of being online 24/7, but ask yourself, (1) can I sustain this, and (2) even if I can, do I want to? Each person can have different answers to and interpretations of these questions, so do what you feel fits with your overall goals and future directions.

- *Always be a student.* Learning does not stop in the classroom, so you will always need to be a student of the field and learn from others. In addition, you may be called upon to educate others and help them get their start in the field. Embrace the role as an educator and mentor—be a resource for others if they have questions about what the field entails. We are all in the same boat together, and the more we share and help others, the better the field will be.

- *Learn from failures and embrace Plan B.* We sometimes see everyone bask in the light of successes and notable accomplishments, but this is just one side of the coin. To get there, a lot of unsuccessful ventures, ideas, and projects first crash and burn. This happens in all aspects of life, including social media. For every yes, you will hear a lot of nos. Keep in mind that no is just one answer. No, this idea or initiative will not be good for our industry. No, we do not have the time or energy to educate everyone about social media. No, we do not have the resources to get this particular program or tool to do social media this way. No can mean a lot of things, and there are different layers of no to consider. No, this is never going to happen ever in this lifetime. No—as in not yet. Get used to hearing the word *no* a lot, but don't give up and pick up your work. You may have to pursue Plan B. Plan B or even updated versions of your original plan might actually be better in the long run. Sometimes, people say no so you can come back with something better for them to review.

- *Never settle.* Mario Armstrong, TV host and entrepreneur, is a great example of a professional who has never settled on his dream and accomplishments. He wanted to create the first Facebook Live TV talk show, and he did just that, and called it the *Never Settle Show.* The same principles apply here with social media. Never think you have done all that it takes to be successful. Each chapter and experience is a level up, but you have not reached the top of the potential you can bring to the table for your businesses, organization, and individual accomplishments.

CHAPTER SUMMARY

The social media and strategic communications road has come to an end, but the conversation has not. This is just the beginning, and social media is an evolving journey that embraces the entire community together.

The power with which we can use technology to break down barriers in both time and location is unlike anything we have experienced before. For those just entering the workplace—whether it is right after graduating from school or embarking on a new career path—social media has a lot to offer as far as opportunities and challenges. It is important to always have a balanced perspective of the field. It is indeed the giver of pain and delight.

We need to learn to strategically use each of the social media tools to best tell our stories, engage proactively with audiences, use data to inform on what is really happening in the network through scientific measurements, and be inspired to create experiences and memories online that could last a lifetime. Having a strategic mindset that is agile, creative, and scientific is the key to success in all arenas on social media. This is truly one of the most exciting times to be working and learning about social media.

As the author of this textbook, I wish you all the best in the journey you have taken through these chapters. I hope this book has been helpful in guiding you to create a strategic mindset in social media. I hope it serves you well for the future social media endeavors you encounter and face along the way. There will be challenges, but as in all aspects of life, there will also be opportunities. You just have to find them—especially if they are hard to see and hiding from you. This is a time to fully embrace the social media field

with both hands and run with it. Age does not matter; we can all learn from each other and provide insights that could help society, the industry, and our local and global communities. The possibilities are endless, and all it takes is that first step. This first step may be intimidating, but you are not alone.

Let's take the first step together.

THOUGHT QUESTIONS

1. What are some of the benefits of working in social media? What are some of the challenges?

2. After reviewing this textbook, what future trends and applications do you want to learn more about in social media? What steps do you want to take to get there?

3. Some new and old skills will come into play when working in social media. What are some of the core skills a social media professional needs to embrace for the future? Do you agree with these, and would you add anything else to the list?

EXERCISES

1. You are asked to write a post for your local agency about the top five trends that will be relevant for the next year. Research online and see what experts are talking about on the major media outlet networks for social media (Mashable, TechCrunch, The Next Web, etc.) and highlight which ones to watch out for and why.

2. You are advising a high school senior on getting involved in social media. What tips and best practices would you recommend to

the student? Outline three tips while listing three things you will do as the student's mentor to pay it forward to the future generation of social media professionals.

3. Based on your reading of this textbook, what areas within social media would you like to specialize in? This can be a designated role or a particular industry. Outline five steps you will take in order to get a job or internship in this field.

REFERENCES

Azuma, R. T. (1997). A survey of augmented reality. *Presence: Teleoperators and Virtual Environments*, 6(4), 355–385.

Cassidy, P. (2017, November 21). Survey finds consumers crave authenticity—and user-generated content delivers. *Social Media Today*. Retrieved from https://www.socialmediatoday.com/news/survey -finds-consumers-crave-authenticity-and-user -generated-content-deli/511360/.

Cohen, D. (2017, November 20). 330 million people connected with SMBs via Facebook Messenger for the first time in 2017. *Adweek*. Retrieved from http://www.adweek.com/digital/330-million-face

book-messenger-users-connected-with-smbs-for -the-first-time-in-2017/.

Fontein, D. (2017, November 21). Top 5 social media trends in 2018. *Hootsuite*. Retrieved from https://blog.hootsuite.com/top-social-media -trends-2018/.

Gartenberg, C. (2017, October 11). Mark Zuckerberg: "We want to get a billion people in virtual reality." *The Verge*. Retrieved from https://www.theverge .com/2017/10/11/16459636/mark-zuckerberg -oculus-rift-connect.

Good, A. (2017, October 19). Take a walk on Mars— in your own living room. *NASA Jet Propulsion*

Laboratory. Retrieved from https://www.jpl.nasa.gov/news/news.php?feature=6978.

Hofmann, S., & Mosemghvdlishvili, L. (2014). Perceiving spaces through digital augmentation: An exploratory study of navigational augmented reality apps. *Mobile Media & Communication*, 2(3), 265–280.

Hong, J. (2017, November 21). The importance of dark social is rising—here are some tips on how to track it. *Social Media Today*. Retrieved from https://www.socialmediatoday.com/news/the-importance-of-dark-social-is-rising-here-are-some-tips-on-how-to-trac/511358/.

Hutchinson, A. (2017, November 14). Top social media trends that will take over 2018 [Infographic]. *Social Media Today*. Retrieved from https://www.socialmediatoday.com/news/top-social-media-trends-that-will-take-over-2018-infographic/510796/.

Monllos, K. (2017, January 21). Through VR, Häagen-Dazs will let you fly (and sympathize) with imperiled honey bees. *Adweek*. Retrieved from http://www.adweek.com/brand-marketing/through-vr-h-agen-dazs-will-let-you-fly-and-sympathize-imperiled-honey-bees-175686/.

Newton, C. (2017, September 14). Snapchat's Bitmoji avatars are now three-dimensional and animated. *The Verge*. Retrieved from https://www.theverge.com/2017/9/14/16303504/snapchat-bitmoji-world-lenses-animation-gabsee.

O'Brien, D. (2017, April 27). 4 virtual reality campaigns which highlight the brand potential of the medium. *Social Media Today*. Retrieved from https://www.socialmediatoday.com/marketing/4-virtual-reality-campaigns-which-highlight-brand-potential-medium.

Primack, D. (2016, March 24). Exclusive: Snapchat buys Bitmoji maker. *Fortune*. Retrieved from http://fortune.com/2016/03/24/exclusive-snapchat-buys-bitmoji-maker/.

Richard. (2017). 10 social media trends that will shape 2018—the experts' voice. *Talkwalker*. Retrieved from https://www.talkwalker.com/blog/social-media-trends-2018.

Robertson, A. (2017, June 1). Walmart is training employees with a Black Friday VR simulator. *The Verge*. Retrieved from https://www.theverge.com/2017/6/1/15725732/walmart-strivr-vr-training-module.

Swant, M. (2017, January 12). GE just launched a branded virtual reality series about science. *Adweek*. Retrieved from http://www.adweek.com/digital/ge-just-launched-branded-virtual-reality-series-about-science-175521/.

Tagboard. (2016, November 28). "#Verizon360 brings the Macy's Thanksgiving Day Parade to life. Retrieved from https://blog.tagboard.com/verizon360-brings-the-macys-thanksgiving-day-parade-to-life-3971a689f604.

Virtual Reality Society. (2017). What is virtual reality? Retrieved from https://www.vrs.org.uk/virtual-reality/what-is-virtual-reality.html.

GLOSSARY

CHAPTER 1

branded content (BC): content that is created by a business for the purpose of establishing ownership and consistency in brand identity and reputation.

informed decision making: a term coined by Rich Calabrese of Fizziology that focuses on taking creativity, data, and insight into account for social media practices.

online reputation: the collective perception of attributes assigned to an individual or brand based on digital and social media activities, actions, and conversation exchanges.

Return on Relationship (RoR): a term coined by Ted Rubin that focuses on establishing a currency on relationships and human connections between businesses and their audience members.

social media: a personalized, online networked hub of information, dialogue, and relationship management. These new communication technology tools allow individual users and organizations to engage with, reach, persuade, and target key audiences more effectively across multiple platforms. Industry professionals, scholars, and social media users have contributed a number of different definitions and conceptualizations of the concept of social media. Some emphasize the role of social media as a tool kit that allows users to create and share content. Others focus on how social media extend Web 2.0 technologies to bring communities together.

thought leadership: being acknowledged by others in the community for having expertise and experience in the industry and specific skills, insights, and knowledge.

user-generated content (UGC): pieces of content created directly by a user.

virality: rapid dissemination of information from person to person; one of the ways in which news, stories, and updates reach across various networks in a short amount of time.

CHAPTER 2

bot: a social media account that is automated to share and comment on posts.

ethics: a set of moral guidelines and principles that influence our behaviors and interactions.

flame war: an emotional and long argument streamed through a series of online messages that are focused on personal attacks and voicing outrage to a specific person or parties.

going rogue: going against the norm of expectations of society while initiating behaviors that are considered to be out of norm or against social, personal, and professional expectations; going off script on social media without permission and not in an official capacity.

influencer: an individual who is able to persuade audiences to take action; someone who has built an audience, naturally and over time, and is viewed as an authority figure on a certain subject, area, or perspective in the online space.

prosumer: someone who writes reviews, posts comments, and shares content within a network of friends and followers.

reputation dissonance: a disconnect that occurs when audience perceptions of a brand, person, or entity go against its actual behaviors and actions.

trendjacking: when brands try to jump on board with a trending topic, event, or situation on social media to generate buzz about their own brand and interject themselves into the conversation; for example, Oreo in the "Can Still Dunk in the Dark" tweet from 2013, or MoonPie and Hostess Cupcakes during the 2017 Solar Eclipse.

CHAPTER 3

audience strategy: creating content that focuses on the relationships that you have made on specific platforms.

brand voice: the overall tone and format in which you present your updates and other forms of communication.

community: a place where a group of people with similar interests come together online.

content strategy: how you go about sharing specific assets online depending on the audience, platform, and community related to your personal brand.

customized strategy: integrating specific pieces of content to send out related to your personal brand based on the relationships on the platform you are communicating on (audience) while sharing content that is relevant and consistent with your brand image (content strategy).

expertise: having knowledge and authority in a certain area of social media.

finsta: a fake Instagram account where you post "real" (aka "just for your friends") pieces of content for no one else to see.

generalist: someone who knows a lot about a lot of things at the macro level of social media, but does not have expertise in one area.

influence: the ability to shift people to take action or listen to what you have to say on social media.

personal brand: the collection and strategic process of crafting and sustaining a specific image in hopes of establishing a clear advantage in the minds of collective audiences on- and offline.

personal brand association: recognizing specific attributes, events, settings, and interests as going along with your personal brand.

personality: characteristics and attributes that are unique, memorable, and aligned with your personal brand.

specialist: an expert in one specific area of social media at the micro level.

CHAPTER 4

boutique agency or firm: an agency or business that specializes either in one aspect of social media, such as analytics, or in a specific platform channel.

content calendar: a document that outlines, defines, and structures what pieces of content need to be created and disseminated at specific points of time and on which channels for a brand, organization, or individual.

content creator: someone who is well versed in the ability to create pieces of work that resonate with audiences.

consultant: a specialist who provides counsel and advice on social media–specific projects and campaigns.

freelancer: someone who is paid for specific projects, items to create, and products on a project basis.

social media community manager: a professional who can add a personal take on the conversation and engagements with audience members.

social media coordinator: a professional who focuses on the strategic planning and execution of the social media content for a brand or organization.

social media strategist: a professional who ties in the goals and objectives for the company or client in question, and focuses on how to get these measures accomplished.

CHAPTER 5

advanced metrics: calculations that dive into the actions and psychographics (attitudes, behaviors, and opinions of audience members) of specific users (e.g., influencers and advocates).

advocate: someone who shows support, appreciation, and dedication across all digital and social channels publicly.

amplification rate: the average number of shares per post across a specific platform.

analytics: the structured calculation of data and statistics collected from online sources to produce scientific and actionable insights.

basic metrics: metrics that can be collected easily either from the social media channel itself, or by a separate service or program.

behavioral metrics: the measured calculations of the actions users take that are connected to specific strategic initiatives on social media and communication objectives.

channel metrics: specific calculations that are unique to specific channels.

click-through rate: the rate at which people click to navigate to another website from your site.

conversion rate: the percentage of users who initiate a specific behavior based on what is shown and presented to them on social media.

follower: an individual or brand account on social media that is keeping track of your activity on a designated platform.

influencer impact: the percentage of users who actually initiate an action or behavior based on what the influencer has shared.

listening: focused activities on social media to learn, explore, and uncover emerging trends, opportunities, activities, and issues that could impact a company, individual, or brand either positively or negatively.

mention: naming and tagging a brand handle and name on social media.

metrics: data collected by a social media professional in a systematic manner.

microsite: a specific digital page connected to a brand that is utilized for a short-term specific focus to accomplish strategic and communication goals and initiatives for a brand.

monitoring: the systematic process of understanding, analyzing, and reporting insights and conversations on reputation, brand position, community health, and opinion of key audience members virtually.

research: the systematic gathering of information in a scientific and objective manner to help answer questions; one of the primary duties of social media professionals.

social media return on investment (ROI): a common metric used to evaluate whether the investment (money) a brand or company put into a campaign accomplished the set goals and objectives.

vanity metrics: metrics that are pretty to view and report, but do not necessarily impact the business objectives or bottom financial line for organizations and individuals.

CHAPTER 6

brand voice: the overall tone, personality, and entity that you want to present online.

demographics: a basic way to categorize a group of individuals, involving the basic population data that are easily collected, such as age, education level, ethnicity, and location.

environmental scan: an assessment that helps the social media professional evaluate the current landscape within which a client or organization operates.

goal statement: a broad statement that captures the overall focus for your social media initiative.

key performance indicators (KPIs): should be determined *before* the social media strategic plan is implemented; KPIs not only determine what has been accomplished, but inform next steps and measurements for future campaigns.

mission: the key elements of the overall purpose of an organization, brand, or person in the respective spaces.

objective: a clear statement of what you plan to accomplish—probably one of the toughest parts of constructing a social media strategic plan or campaign.

PESO model: a model, created by Gini Dietrich, that focuses on outlining the key components of media for social media such as paid media (P), earned media (E), shared media (S), and owned media (O). (See individual definitions in Chapter 9.)

primary audience: people you want to target directly and who have a meaningful relationship and connection to the client.

primary message: a broad statement that you want to communicate to your key audience members; it should be simple, concise, and to the point.

psychographics: a way to categorize audiences based on their attitudes, opinions, and values.

secondary audience: people who are supportive and potentially viewed as influencers by the primary audience members.

secondary message: a message that provides additional evidence to support the primary message; using facts, statistics, and additional information to build on the point outlined in the primary message, these messages can incorporate evidence and additional information regarding what the client has already done on social media.

SMART criteria: an established way to categorize effective objectives into five different categories: specific, measurable, achievable, realistic, and time-specific.

strategic mindset: communicating in the brand voice rather than one's own personal voice.

strategic plan: a systematic, thorough, and aligned document that outlines from start to finish what a brand, individual, or organization wants to accomplish to address a problem or opportunity or to explore potential new possibilities through experimentation.

strategy: how you will go about accomplishing set objectives and the heart of the social media strategic plan.

tactics: the tools and applications within social media that you will be using to accomplish your objectives and fulfill your strategies; the nuts and bolts of your social media plan.

vision: characteristics and principles that an organization or individual values, which will guide its overall actions and make an impact in the community; vision statements bridge various components together in a cohesive statement, tying in brand personality, key attributes, core values, and present and future behavioral intentions.

CHAPTER 7

brand voice: the strategic position for a brand to express specific attributes through written and visual exchanges interconnecting the brand culture and community.

community: a group of individuals who come together based on common interests, values, experiences, and characteristics.

connection: a valued relationship individuals or brands could have that could link them together based on an experience, similar interest, or other valued activities.

content: anything that is published and presented on social media; pieces of original work that are distributed and consumed by audiences.

content creation: a mixture of content that is originally created.

content curation: a mixture of content that was published from a different source.

conversation: the exchange of words between two individuals or among a group of individuals online.

creativity: approaching situations, ideas, and concepts in a unique and imaginative manner that resonates with audiences.

culture: common practices, work life ethics and practices, professional experiences, and beliefs of a group of individuals.

experiential media: content that immerses audiences in the story and channel.

tone: the overall voice characteristics you want to interject within the content you are writing.

CHAPTER 8

ambassadors: individuals who advocate and promote your work based on their own personal interests and investment with the brand, agency, organization, or person in question.

audience segmentation: the process of categorizing people into certain groups based on specific criteria, which can be broad in nature (e.g., demographics and population data) or very specific and focused (niche) on certain characteristics (e.g., experiential, visually driven, or industry and interest specific).

creators: people who can be useful because of the talent of their creative insights and strategy.

emerging audience: a group that is gaining traction to become a prominent community to reach.

influencer marketing: a specialized area of marketing that focuses on targeting key audience members with strong reach and voice to carry your brand message to the key communities targeted in a campaign.

micro-influencers: similar to influencers, people who have a specific focus, community, and purpose that help resonate with audiences.

niche: a specialized focused area or community surrounding a common interest, location, or characteristic.

omnichannel approach: a seamless and effortless integration of content, messages, and experiences for the user that is linked to multiple communication channels.

online persona: the summation of all of the characteristics and attributes assigned to a person by engaged audiences in online networks; an identity constructed by an individual online that may or may not represent who he or she truly is in real life.

opponent/critic: a person who does not have your best interest at heart and demonstrates this either publicly or secretly online.

CHAPTER 9

content marketing: according to the Content Marketing Institute, a strategic marketing approach focused on creating and distributing valuable, relevant, and consistent content to attract and retain a clearly defined audience—and, ultimately, to drive profitable customer action.

earned media: content that is sometimes connected with public relations, but *not* controlled by brands, which in many ways makes it more trustworthy and less biased compared to other types of content.

evergreen content: information that is created that continues to be relevant regardless of when it was first published.

owned media: content and the platform you control as a brand, organization, or person.

paid media: social media advertising, or a "pay-to-play" model, in which the company (or advertiser/agency) pays for the content to appear in the timeline for a certain amount of money.

shared media: content that is associated with social media, but more of an interactive medium where conversations and dialogue emerge as the result of the content being shared.

CHAPTER 10

No terms defined

CHAPTER 11

No terms defined

CHAPTER 12

crowdfunding: the practice of raising money online with the help of social media community outreach and advocacy efforts in small and large donations.

crowdsourcing: the practice of collecting information, asking for assistance, and reaching out to the community for help to solve a problem or address an opportunity online in a centralized space.

CHAPTER 13

augmented reality (AR): both real and virtual elements created by users and programmers so the individual user is able to interact with both.

human interaction marketing (HIM): a strain of relationship management, with the strategic purpose of the health and longevity of the relationship being the currency exchanged.

virtual digital technology desert: limited access and opportunities to stand out in the industry, putting the resulting community at a disadvantage.

virtual reality (VR): a digital and real space in which users interact, while also creating their own experiences.

INDEX

Abandonment sin, 31
Account access issue, 39
Adidas, 114, 151, 180–181, 193
Adobe Clip tool, 199
Adobe Creative Suite tool, 216
Adobe Dreamweaver tool, 169 (table)
Adobe Lightroom/Photoshop tools, 168 (table)
Adobe Premiere tool, 199, 200 (table)
Adobe Spark tools, 59, 168 (table), 169 (table), 199, 200 (table), 216
Advanced metrics, 93, 94, 99, 100 (table), 104–105 (table)
Advertising activities, 40–41, 217, 218 (table), 280
Advocacy marketing, 277
Advocates, 99, 100 (table), 188–189, 277
Agnes, Melissa, 232–233
    background information on, 232
    challenges of crisis management and, 233
    crisis communication, social media role and, 232–233
    crisis ready culture and, 232
    favorite social media account and, 233
    professional advice from, 233
    social media, start in, 232
Airbnb, 192
Alexa, 277
Alive tool, 200 (table)
Altruist persona, 53
Amarula elephant conservation campaign, 268–269
Ambassador programs, 177–178
Ambassadors, 9–10, 42, 170, 176–178, 179 (table)
American Marketing Association (AMA), 209
Amnesty International campaign, 268
Amplification rate, 7, 99
Analytics, 91, 92
    application programming interface and, 11
    audience/content data, engagement with, 18
    behavioral metrics and, 93
    click-through rates and, 93
    hashtag monitoring/evaluation and, 11
    metrics and, 91, 92, 99, 100 (table)
    online reputation evaluation tools and, 60–61
    research skill and, 57–58
    search engine optimization and, 60
    storytelling approach and, 22
    vanity metrics and, 54, 93–94
    waves in conversations, potential impact of, 92
    See also Measurement/evaluation; Metrics; Social media research; Strategic planning
Anchor tool, 199, 200 (table)
Application programming interface (API), 11, 101
Applications. See Social media applications
Areseneault, J. M., 172

Armstrong, M., 287
Artificial intelligence (AI), 256, 277
Atlanta United FC social media coordinator role, 76–77, 76 (table)
Audacity tool, 200 (table)
Audience segmentation process, 33, 93
    audience categories and, 164–165, 165 (table)
    best practices/recommendations for, 181–182
    community factors and, 167–170, 168–169 (table), 181–182
    definition/description of, 163
    demographics and, 164, 165 (table)
    emerging audiences and, 166
    external audiences and, 164, 165 (figure)
    influencers and, 168, 170–172
    internal audiences and, 164, 165 (figure)
    message relevancy and, 164–165
    micro-influencers and, 180
    niches and, 163, 180
    omnichannel approach and, 164
    opponents/critics and, 166
    personas, construction of, 166
    platform specifics and, 164, 165 (table)
    primary audiences and, 165 (figure), 166
    psychographics and, 164, 165 (table)
    secondary audiences and, 165 (figure), 166
    social media campaigns, segmentation principles and, 163–164, 179–181
    social metrics and, 164, 165 (table)
    strategic messaging and, 166
    target audience, identification of, 163, 164, 221 (table)
    traditional segmentation framework and, 164–165, 165 (figure)
    types of audiences, 165 (figure), 166
    types of social media users and, 164, 165 (table)
    See also Ambassadors; Community; Creators; Haters; Influencers; Trolls
Audience strategy, 56, 163
    See also Audience segmentation process
Audio content tools, 199, 200 (table)
Audits. See Brand voice; Content; Personal brands; Social media communication audit
Augmented reality (AR), 279–280
Authenticity, 23, 43, 143–144, 157, 171–172, 276
Automated direct messages, 34
Avatars, 8, 29, 280
Avery, E. J., 6
Azuma, R. T., 279

Baer, J., 53, 149, 178, 201
Basic metrics, 99, 100 (table), 104–105 (table)
Behavioral metrics, 93, 99, 100 (table), 104–105 (table)
BeLive tool, 200 (table)

Bentwood, J., 170
Beyoncé, 230
Bitly tool, 215 (table)
Bitmoji app, 280
Blake, R., 171
Bleacher Report, 83, 112, 213
Bleacher Report content editing role, 83, 83 (table)
Blogger, 11, 200 (table)
Blogs, 6, 11, 15, 197
   endorsement/advertising activities and, 40–41
   microblogs and, 6, 11, 17, 270
   social media job applicants and, 70
   vlogging and, 22, 171
Blosat, G., 181
BlueJeans tool, 200 (table)
Boomerang persona, 53
Boomerang tool, 199
Bots, 32, 52, 63, 107, 175, 256, 276
Boutique agencies/firms, 72
Box, 11
Brand ambassadors, 9–10, 42, 170
Brand journalism, 9
Brand voice, 55, 116
   brand ambassadors and, 9–10, 42, 170
   consistency in, 55
   content creation and, 17, 192
   key defining questions about, 144
   personal branding and, 17, 22
   platform selection criteria and, 17
   social media campaigns and, 6
   storytelling approach and, 21–22
   strategic mindset and, 116
   team brand voice audit and, 145
   thought leadership and, 17
   tone and, 42, 50, 55, 97, 116, 118, 119, 143–144
   unified brand voice, digital marketing approches
      and, 114
   voice vs. tone and, 143–144
   See also Personal brands; Professional brands
Branded content (BC), 9
Branded hashtags, 11
BrandsEye software, 60
Brandsphere, 8, 8 (figure)
Brandwatch tool, 104 (table), 215 (table), 217
BrandYourself service, 60
Breakenridge, Deirdre, 3–5, 53, 170
   background information on, 3–4
   challenges of social media and, 5
   favorite social media accounts and, 4–5
   instantaneous interaction, potential for, 4
   professional advice from, 5
   public relations practices and, 5
   social media platforms and, 4–5
   social media, power of, 4
   social media, start in, 4
Brexit campaign, 6
Brunnerworks agency, 94
Budgets, 216, 222
   advertising management and, 217, 218 (table)
   best practices/recommendations for, 220, 222
   budget restrictions, articulation of, 222
   consulting fees and, 216

   educational resources and, 217
   investment decisions and, 216–217
   measurement/evaluation activities checklist and,
      220, 220–221 (table), 222, 223
   metrics to consider and, 217–221, 219–221 (tables)
   pay-to-play model and, 216, 217
   professional personnel and, 216
   promotional/sponsored content and, 217
   research activities and, 216–217
   tools and, 216
   See also Measurement/evaluation; Strategic planning
Budweiser, 150–151
Buffer tools, 104 (table), 106, 145, 168 (table), 193,
   196, 201
Bullying, 33
Business networking sites, 11
Buying followers, 32, 54, 175
BuzzFeed, 21, 78, 82, 117
BuzzFeed video producer role, 78, 82 (table)
BuzzSumo tool, 172–173, 194

Calabrese, Rich, 21, 89–91, 229
   actionable marketing strategies and, 90
   background information on, 89–90
   challenge of social media and, 90
   data analytics applications and, 90
   data/audience insights, business decision process
      and, 90
   favorite social media accounts and, 90
   internet connection, essential nature of, 90
   social media, start in, 90
   social messaging, evolution toward, 91
Cambridge Analytica crisis, 277
Camera+ tool, 168 (table), 200 (table)
Canned Lions International Festival of Creativity,
   267, 268
Canva tool, 58–59, 168 (table), 169 (table), 199, 200
   (table), 216
CareerBuilder, 70
Careerist persona, 53
Censorship, 36, 270
Certification programs, 62
Channel metrics, 99, 100 (table), 104–105 (table)
Charmin, 153
Chat, 6, 51
Chat bots, 19, 63, 256, 276
Chief relationship agent (CRA), 3
Cinnabon, 193
Cisnero, K., 200
Clemson Athletics, 245
Click-through rate (CTR), 32, 93, 217, 219 (table)
Codes of ethics, 31
Collier, M., 177
Comm, J., 52
Communication. See Social media communication audit
Community, 50, 54, 141, 167
   brand communities and, 167
   channels/platforms and, 167
   common features of, 167
   consistency in, 167
   digital media community and, 169 (table)
   engagement initiatives and, 114

Facebook community and, 168 (table)
growing community, recommendations for, 181–182
influencers, role of, 168, 170
Instagram community and, 168–169 (table)
LinkedIn community and, 169 (table)
networks of communities and, 7, 8, 9
online communities, description of, 167
personal branding and, 50, 54
Snapchat community and, 169 (table)
social media community manager role and, 74–75, 74–75 (tables)
social media ownership and, 286
sustainability of, 114, 167
tone of, 167
Twitter community and, 168 (table)
YouTube community and, 169 (table)
See also Audience segmentation process; Connection; Influencers; Social media
Connection, 141–142
affective-level connections and, 166
cognitive-level connections and, 166
conative-level connections and, 166
human interaction marketing and, 286
online/offline connections and, 8, 63
storytelling approach and, 21–22
See also Community
Connector persona, 53
Constant Contact, 200 (table)
Consultant role, 83–84
Consumer product/service ratings forums, 6, 264
Consumer-to-consumer conversations, 6, 7
Content calendar, 76, 190, 195–197
Content creation, 101, 140–141, 142–143, 187, 221 (table)
aligned content and, 189–190
audience targeting and, 194–195
audio content tools and, 199, 200 (table)
authentic messaging and, 23
best practices/recommendations for, 202–203
brainstorming sessions and, 191, 196
brand awareness, support of, 188, 194 (table)
brand voice/style guidelines and, 192
branded content/journalism and, 9
content audit and, 189–190, 190 (table)
content creation vs. curation and, 142–143, 200
content creator role and, 77, 81–82 (table)
content ideas, generation of, 190–192
content media, types of, 197–199
content strategy and, 190, 192–193
creative innovation and, 21
digital tools and, 58–60
engaging content and, 23
evergreen content and, 189, 197
graphic content tools and, 199, 200 (table)
influencers, identification of, 194–195
lead generation content and, 194 (table)
long-form content and, 197
outreach effort content and, 194 (table)
ownership issues and, 35–36, 40
PESO model, asset categorization and, 189, 197–199
rationales for, 188–189

relevant/impactful content, development of, 192–193
repurposed/reformatted content and, 17, 33
search engine optimization and, 189
shared content, online networks and, 7
short-form content and, 197
social media campaigns, assets for, 189
storytelling approach and, 21–22, 192, 194 (table)
strategies/tactics and, 193
systematic process of, 101, 142–143
thought leadership content and, 194 (table)
tools for, 199, 200 (table)
trusted information/informants and, 188–189
uniformity sin and, 33
user-generated content and, 7, 9
video content tools and, 199, 200 (table)
virality and, 9
visual content tools and, 199, 200 (table)
visual/snackable forms of, 12, 21
visual storytelling/education content and, 194 (table)
writing/visual content creation skill and, 58–60, 192
written content tools and, 199, 200 (table)
See also Content curation; Content marketing; Strategic writing
Content creator role, 77, 81–82 (table)
Content curation, 188
best practices/recommendations for, 200, 202–203
content creation vs. curation and, 142–143, 200
definition of, 200
newsletter production and, 201
private/public/secret groups and, 201
repurposed/reposted content and, 201
social media content marketing strategy and, 201
strategic sharing, transparency and, 200–201
tools for, 201–202
See also Content creation
Content marketing, 187
assets, provision of, 189
brand awareness, support of, 188
channel evaluation/selection and, 188
communication/business objectives and, 187
content audit and, 189–190, 190 (table)
content calendar and, 190, 195–197
content creation, rationales for, 188–189
content ideas, generation of, 190–192
content strategy and, 190, 192–193
definition of, 188
newsletter production and, 201
overview of, 187–188
relevant content and, 187, 192–193
resource allocation and, 188
search engine optimization and, 189
strategies/tactics and, 187–188
trusted information/informants and, 188–189
See also Content creation
Content Marketing Institute, 188
Content strategy, 56, 190, 192–193
Conversation, 6, 7–8, 10, 15, 43, 92, 171, 193
Conversion rate, 99
Coombs, T., 233
Copp, E., 219
Copyright infringement, 39–40

Corporate social media teams, 73
Cortana, 277
CoSchedule Headline Analyzer took, 59
Cost per action (CPA), 217, 218, 219 (table)
Cost per click (CPC), 217, 219 (table)
Cost per conversion (CPC), 218–219, 219 (table)
Cost per engagement (CPE), 219, 219 (table)
Cost per impression (CPI), 217, 219 (table)
Creative Suite tool, 168 (table)
Creativity, 17, 21–22, 141–142, 245, 259, 269
Creators, 170, 176, 179 (table), 181
Crisis communication, 233
    best practices/recommendations for, 237–238
    content creation for, 238, 248 (table)
    crises, definition/description of, 233
    crises, subsequent perceptions of, 233
    crisis history/outrage, underestimation of, 234
    crisis management plan, social media component
        for, 237
    employees going rogue and, 234
    false rumors/information, correction of, 238
    hashtags, impact of, 235
    Hurricane Harvey, natural disaster case and, 237
    monitoring/listening capability and, 237
    negative interjections into conversations and, 234
    origins of crises, identification of, 238
    pause content and, 238
    research on content/situation, inattention to, 234
    response team strategies and, 237
    social media crises and, 233–234, 237–238
    tone/concern expressed, inadequate recognition
        of, 234–235
    trigger events and, 236
    United Airlines, corporate/reputation crisis and,
        234, 236, 237 (figure)
    See also Social media applications
Critic. See Opponent/critic
Crowdfire tool, 169 (table)
Crowdfunding, 21, 260
Crowdsourcing, 11, 260
Culture, 37, 43, 71, 118, 122, 128, 129 (figure), 141,
    180, 256, 270, 271
Curata tool, 202
Current social media environment, 275–276
    authenticity, importance of, 276
    chat bots, relationship building and, 276
    collaborative practices, necessity of, 278
    dark social, messaging channels/apps and, 276
    emerging professionals, engagement/support of, 278
    evolving social media, adaptability and, 276,
        278, 281
    human interaction marketing and, 286
    human-technology interaction and, 276
    influencers/keynote speakers, growing numbers
        of, 278
    misunderstood audiences, impact of, 278
    organic reach, end of, 277
    pay-to-play model and, 277
    programming interfaces/metrics and, 277
    relevant/engaged professionals, practices of, 278,
        281–282

social media opportunities, expansion in, 277
    strategic communication, digital solutions and,
        276, 277
    student-to-student advice and, 283–285
    targeted audiences/content and, 277
    See also Social media; Trend identification
Customized strategy, 56
Cyberbullying, 36, 37–38
Cybersecurity, 35

#DailyVees, 52
Dao, D., 236
Dark social, 276
Darlow, Jeremy, 229, 242–243
    background information on, 242
    brand building/marketing and, 242
    challenges of social media and, 243
    cultural moments, brand insertion and, 242–243
    favorite social media account and, 243
    mentoring emerging professionals and, 243
    professional advice from, 243
    social media, start in, 242
Dawley, S., 93, 94, 106, 211
Deadspin case, 39–40
#DeleteFacebook movement, 277
Delmondo tool, 72, 105 (table), 201
Demographics, 131–132, 163, 164, 165 (table)
Dialogic theory, 20
Dietrich, G., 53, 197
Digital Millennium Copyright Act (DMCA) of 2000, 39
DigitalGov website, 36
Direct message (DM), 4, 34
Discussion boards, 6
Disick, S., 41
Domino's Pizza case, 41
Dorsey, J., 17, 275
Drake, Whitney, 254
    background information on, 254
    challenges of social media and, 254
    customer care, evolution of, 254
    favorite social media account and, 254
    professional advice from, 254
    search for knowledge and, 254
    social media evolution and, 254
    social media, start in, 254
"DRock" videographer, 22
Dropbox, 11
Dunkin' Donuts, 151–152

Early adopter persona, 53
Earned media (E), 8, 8 (figure), 120, 135, 189, 198, 221
    (table)
Eat Love Louisville, 195
Edelman DC Digital Content Studio content creator
    role, 77, 81–82 (table)
Editing skills, 83, 83 (table)
Ehrlich, Michael, 161–163
    background information on, 161
    challenges of social media and, 162
    editorial landscape, evolution of, 162–163
    favorite social media accounts and, 162

global network, access to, 162
network connectivity, importance of, 162
professional advice from, 163
social media, start in, 161–162
storytelling approach and, 162–163
84 Lumber Company advertisement, 94
Elonis, A., 36
Emerging audience, 166
Endorsements, 40–41
Engagement metrics, 99, 100 (table)
Enlight tool, 200 (table)
Entertainment industry, 229
brand awareness, development of, 230, 231
buzz/audience actions, generation of, 230
content creation for, 248 (table)
mystery/excitement, creation of, 230
promotional campaigns, business objectives/
measurements and, 230
social media best practices and, 231
social media, companion tool of, 231
social media effects and, 230–231
social media, utilization of, 229–230, 231
sponsorships/partnerships, potential for, 231
See also Social media applications
Environmental scan analysis, 118–119
Equifax data breach, 234–235
ESPN, 38, 243
Ethics issues, 29
abandonment sin and, 31
alternative accounts and, 35
automated direct messages and, 34
bullying and, 33
buying followers and, 32
codes of ethics and, 31
credit allocation/misallocation and, 33
employee rebellion and, 34
ethical principles and, 31
ethics, definition of, 31
ethics questions and, 30
excessive/inappropriate sharing and, 33
expectation violations and, 30
flame war outrage and, 33
going rogue and, 34–35
ignorance sin and, 32
manipulation sin and, 31–32
misappropriation sin and, 31
monotony sin and, 32
narcissism sin and, 32
personal information, access to, 31
professional behavior and, 30
relationship development, expectations in, 30, 34
trendjacking and, 31
trust, development of, 30
uniformity sin and, 33
See also Legal fundamentals; Social media policies
Evaluation. *See* Measurement/evaluation
Evergreen content, 189, 197
Evernote tool, 200 (table)
Experiential media, 157
Expertise, 15, 23, 52, 54
External audiences, 164, 165 (figure)

Facebook, 4, 9, 11, 12
advertising management and, 217, 218 (table)
algorithm, changes in, 91
audience demographics/psychographics and, 164
basic facts about, 12 (table)
community creation/sustainability and, 168 (table)
content writing ideas and, 146 (table)
#DeleteFacebook movement, 277
feature innovation and, 17, 19
follows on, 202
Instagram acquisition and, 12
major milestones for, 13 (table)
metrics/tools, types of, 104 (table)
National Geographic Channel partnership and, 97
networking function and, 54
Oculus Rift community manager role and, 75,
75 (table)
pay-to-play model and, 15, 92, 197
personal data, collection of, 16, 36, 277
terms of service and, 35
use data for, 15, 16 (figure)
verification checks and, 35
visual content and, 17
writing guide for, 145 (table)
Facebook Analytics, 211, 215 (table)
Facebook Audience Insights, 168 (table)
Facebook Blueprint, 62, 217
Facebook Creative Hub, 217
Facebook Insights tool, 104 (table)
Facebook Live, 4, 9, 11, 168 (table), 287
Falls, J., 53
Fanzo, B., 57
Faulds, D. J., 7
Fear of missing out (FOMO), 6, 23, 256
Federal Trade Commission (FTC), 32, 39, 40, 41,
118, 170
Feedly tool, 202
Final Cut Pro tool, 199
Finsta, 50
See also Instagram
FiveThirtyEight, 90
Fizziology, 21, 89, 90, 91, 229, 283
Flame war, 33, 42, 61
FleishmanHillard, 72
Flipboard tool, 202
Flynn, Kerry, 239
background information on, 239
challenges of social media and, 239
corporate accountability and, 239
favorite social media account and, 239
mentoring emerging professionals and, 239
professional advice from, 239
smartphone communications and, 239
social media, start in, 239
Focus groups, 211
Followers, 52, 54, 63, 94, 99, 100 (table)
See also Buying followers
Followerwonk tool, 173
#FoodTripping campaign, 94, 95, 194
Forrester Technographics tool and, 164
Freberg, K., 7

Free speech issue, 36
Freelancer role, 83
Front Office Sports (FOS), 201, 228, 229

Gantt, J., 245
GarageBand tool, 200 (table)
General Electric (GE), 280
General Motors, 254–255
Generalist, 61
GIFs, 11, 39, 147
Gil, C., 53, 86, 167
Giphy tool, 200 (table)
Gizmodo, 112
Global society, 6
  brand ambassadorship programs and, 9–10
  global social media management and, 9
  See also International campaigns
Goal statement, 130
GoFundMe, 260
Going rogue, 34–35, 41, 42, 234
Google:
  pay-to-play model and, 15
  reputation management system and, 50, 60
Google Analytics, 60, 62, 106, 215 (table)
Google Drive, 11, 200 (table)
Google Glass, 280
Government entities, 73
Grammarly tool, 156, 199, 200 (table)
Graphic content tools, 199, 200 (table)
Grasmuck, S, 172
Gratification theory, 20

Häagen-Dazs, 280
Hacking, 35, 42, 96, 129 (figure), 234
Haiku Deck, 200 (table)
"Happy" video, 21
Hashtagify.me tool, 156
Hashtags, 11
  application programming interface and, 11
  branded hashtags and, 11, 261
  impact of, 235
  monitoring/evaluation of, 11
  nonprofit organizations/issues and, 261
  promoted posts/sponsored ads, disclosure of, 41
  user-generated hashtags and, 11
Haters, 178–179, 179 (table)
Hayes, E., 285
Healthcare industry, 263
  best practices/recommendations for, 265–266
  clinic settings and, 264
  complex nature of, 263
  data protection, focus on, 264
  employee advocacy efforts and, 265, 266
  healthcare business plans, social media and, 264–265
  hospital settings and, 264
  insurance companies, social media partnerships and, 264, 265
  legal constraints and, 263, 264
  legal/public health education, investment in, 265
  online reviews/ratings and, 264

patient stories/experiences, dissemination of, 263, 264
  posting constraints and, 265–266
  privacy considerations and, 263–264
  regulatory environment of, 263–264, 265, 266
  reputation management and, 264
  response protocol, policy/response templates and, 266
  virtual communities, provider-patient interaction and, 263
  See also Social media applications
Help A Reporter Out (HARO) resource, 240
Hemingway app, 60, 156, 199, 200 (table)
#HereToCreate movement, 114
HMV agency, 34, 234, 237
Hofmann, S., 279
Holder, B., 284–285
Hootsuite Academy, 62
Hootsuite Ambassador Program, 9, 10, 176–177
Hootsuite Insights tool, 215 (table)
Hootsuite tools, 61, 104 (table), 106, 134 (table), 135, 168 (table), 194, 196, 201, 215 (table), 217, 271
Houston Rockets, 38
Howes, P., 6
HubSpot Blog Ideas Generator tool, 59
HubSpot tools, 59, 106, 148 (table), 201, 214, 217
Huffman, E., 170
Hughey, Samantha, 67–70
  background information on, 67–68
  challenge of social media and, 69
  favorite social media accounts and, 68–69
  impossible tasks, accomplishment of, 68
  professional advice from, 69–70
  relationship, essential nature of, 68
  social media, start in, 68
  storytelling approach and, 69
  visual content/user-generated content, success of, 68–69
Human interaction marketing (HIM), 286
Humana, 265
Humans of New York, 192, 193
Hurricane Harvey disaster, 237, 244
Hyken, S., 255
Hype Type tool, 168 (table)
Hyperlapse tool, 168 (table), 199

IBM Watson, 60
Ice Bucket Challenge, 6, 21, 142, 260
Iconosquare tool, 104 (table), 168 (table), 194, 211
Ignorance sin, 32
iMovie tool, 199
Industry qualifications/roles, 70
  adaptive skills/expectations and, 70
  applicant experience/skill requirements and, 70–71
  boutique social media agencies and, 72
  commitment/dedication and, 70
  consultant role and, 83–84
  content creator role and, 77, 81–82 (table)
  continuous learning/growth and, 70, 85
  corporate social media teams and, 72–73

effective professional practices, guidelines for, 286–287

freelancer role and, 83

general guidelines for, 85–86

government/political entities and, 73

job applicants, online information about, 70

job applicants, social media presence and, 70, 71

job market/roles, evolution of, 70

key social media roles and, 73–84

large social media agencies and, 72

large social media companies and, 72

media/journalism, social media presence and, 73

multimedia/video producer role and, 78, 82 (table), 83

network development and, 86

nonprofit sector and, 73

salary statistics, social media jobs and, 84–86, 84–86 (figures)

self-employment and, 72

side hustle, importance of, 86

small business/agency and, 72

social media community manager role and, 74–75, 74–75 (tables), 85

social media coordinator role and, 75–77, 76 (table)

social media director role and, 85, 86 (figure)

social media manager role and, 74, 84, 84 (figure)

social media positions, various demands of, 70

social media specialist role and, 61, 85, 85 (figure)

social media-specific agencies, characteristics of, 71

social media strategist role and, 77, 78–81 (tables)

sports organizations and, 73

work settings, overview of, 71–73

writing/editing roles and, 83, 83 (table)

See also Social media applications

Influence, 50

Influencer impact, 99

Influencer marketing, 170, 277

Influencers, 40, 99, 168, 170

ambassadors and, 9–10, 42, 170, 172, 176–178

authenticity and, 171, 172

buying followers and, 175

characteristics of, 171–172

communities/fans, influencer power and, 171, 172

community development and, 171

compensation packages for, 171, 181

content creation and, 194–195

creators and, 170, 176

definition of, 170

endorsement/advertising activities and, 40–41, 171, 179 (table)

engagement with, 172–174

evaluation of, 122, 171–172

false influencers, identification of, 174–176

follow-follower ratio and, 175

influencer marketing and, 170, 277

micro-influencers and, 180, 194

online personas and, 170–171, 172

personality characteristics of, 172

promoted posts/sponsored ads, disclosure of, 41

quality vs. quantity argument and, 175

real influencers, detection of, 175

refollow-unfollow technique and, 175

social connections/conversations and, 171

social media influencers and, 170

strategic planning and, 124–125

vanity metrics and, 175

See also Influencer impact

Infogram tool, 200 (table)

Informed consent, 36

Informed decision making, 21

Instagram, 4, 9, 11, 12

advertising management and, 217, 218 (table)

audience demographics/psychographics and, 164

basic facts about, 12 (table)

community creation/sustainability and, 168–169 (table)

content writing ideas and, 146 (table)

creative partnering and, 21

endorsement/advertising activities and, 40, 41

Facebook acquisition of, 12

finsta and, 50

follower rate inflation and, 52

major milestones for, 13 (table)

metrics/tools, types of, 104–105 (table)

pay-to-play model and, 92, 197

Royal Caribbean "Intern-ship" contest and, 22

terms of service and, 35

use data for, 15, 16 (figure)

verification checks, 35

visual/snackable content and, 12, 17

writing guide for, 145 (table)

Instagram Insights, 91, 104 (table), 215 (table)

Instagram Live, 11

Instagram Stories, 91

Institutional review boards (IRBs), 36

Internal audiences, 164, 165 (figure)

International Association for Measurement and Evaluation of Communication (AMEC), 209, 210 (table), 220–221 (table)

International campaigns, 267

appropriate platforms, selection of, 270

awareness campaigns, visual elements and, 267–268

best practices/recommendations for, 270–271

brands, strategic partnerships with, 268–269

cause-related marketing and, 268–269

creativity/personalization, opportunities for, 269

cross-national platforms and, 267

established practices, innovative approaches to, 267

global platforms, awareness of, 269–270, 271

influencers, role of, 268–269

local culture/history, understanding of, 270, 271

serious causes, raising awareness of, 268–269

social media ecosystem, expansion of, 267

strategic partnerships, role of, 268–269

unique platform characteristics/expectations and, 271

universal social media challenges and, 271

user-generated content, shared stories and, 269

See also Social media applications

Internet discussion boards/forums, 6

Internships, 61–62

Interviews, 211
iTunes, 199

Jackson, D., 170, 211
Jacobs, M., 267
JESS3, 8, 8 (figure)
Johnson-Campion, T., 283–284
Johnson, D., 49, 53
Journalism industry, 240
    best practices/recommendations and, 241–242
    brand journalism and, 9
    breaking news, sharing of, 240
    citizen journalism practice and, 240
    content creation for, 249 (table)
    digital-/mobile-first content and, 240
    ethics codes and, 241
    Help A Reporter Out resource and, 240
    high-profile events and, 241
    information confirmation/validation and, 242
    newsroom policies and, 241
    professionalism, maintenance of, 241
    readership, engagement with, 241
    real-time reporting and, 240
    repurposed content and, 240
    social media guidelines and, 240
    social media/journalism partnering and, 241
    social media, utility of, 240–241
    story inspiration and, 240
    trending topics, pursuit of, 240
    See also Social media applications
Justine Sacco case study, 37

Kallin, Jeff, 111–113
    background information on, 111–112
    challenge of social media and, 112–113
    clarity of purpose and, 112
    favorite social media accounts and, 112
    professional advice from, 113
    social media, start in, 112
    student expertise, facilitation of, 113
    student social media accounts and, 112
    teaching/mentoring activities and, 112
Kardashian endorsements, 40
Kawasaki, G., 52
Key performance indicators (KPIs), 96, 101, 106, 133
Keyhole tool, 104 (table)
Kissmetrics tool, 215 (table)
Klear analysis tool, 9, 61, 104 (table), 172, 194
KLM Airline, 256
Kontonis, P., 174
Kramer, B., 53

Lariscy, R. W., 6
Lauron, L., 284
Learning opportunities, 61–62, 70
Lee, K., 51, 145, 146
Legal fundamentals, 29, 35
    account access issue and, 39
    consent, disclosure of, 36
    content ownership issues and, 35–36, 40
    copyright infringement and, 39–40
    employee branding mishaps and, 36–38

    endorsements, bloggers/influencers and, 40–41
    free speech issue and, 36
    negative/hateful comments, documentation of, 43
    online threats/cyberbullying and, 36–38
    privacy concerns and, 38–39
    promoted posts/sponsored ads, disclosure of, 41
    prosumer activity and, 39
    reputation dissonance and, 39
    rumor mongering and, 36
    terms of service agreements and, 35–36, 35
        (table), 40
    See also Ethics issues; Social media policies
LEGO, 269
Likealyzer tool, 215 (table)
LinkedIn, 11, 12
    advertising management and, 218 (table)
    audience demographics/psychographics/
        geographics and, 164
    basic facts about, 12 (table)
    community creation/sustainability and, 169 (tabe)
    content writing ideas and, 146 (table)
    follows on, 202
    major milestones for, 14 (table)
    metrics/tools, types of, 105 (table)
    network function of, 54
    terms of service and, 35, 36
    use data for, 15, 16 (figure)
    verification checks and, 35
    writing guide for, 145 (table)
LinkedIn Insights tool, 105 (table)
LinkedIn Pulse tool, 169 (table)
Listening process, 96
    audience behaviors/actions, evaluation of, 107
    benefits of, 97–98
    content creation, systematic process of, 101, 141
    current objectives, integration with, 101
    insights, strategic application of, 107
    items for listening and, 98, 101
    listening ecosystem, guidelines for, 101
    listening/monitoring, bridge between, 102, 103 (table)
    listening plan, implementation of, 100–101
    monitoring vs. listening, differences between,
        96–97, 96 (table)
    training for, 101
    See also Monitoring process; Social
        media research
Live streaming, 11, 48, 57, 281

MailChimp tool, 169 (table), 199, 200 (table)
Make-A-Wish Foundation, 21
Maker's Mark ambassador program, 177, 178
Mangold, W. G., 7
Manipulation sin, 31–32
Martin, J., 172
Mashable, 17, 77, 78, 112, 120, 239
Mashable creative strategist role, 77, 78 (table)
MavSocial tools, 106
Mayo Clinic Social Media Network (MCSMN), 264, 265
McHenry, B., 38
Measurement/evaluation, 208
    accomplishments, articulation of, 209, 210
    actionable variables and, 210

activities measurement and, 209, 210 (table), 211–212, 221 (table)
attributions, placement of, 208
audience analysis and, 220 (table)
best practices/recommendations for, 222–223
channel/platform analytics tools and, 211
checklist for, 220, 220–221 (table), 222, 223
continuous measurement process and, 215
evaluation, focus of, 208, 209
framework for, 209, 210 (table)
impact measurement and, 209, 210, 210 (table), 221 (table)
importance of, 208–211
inputs measurement and, 209, 210 (table), 220 (table)
insights, reassessment and, 223
language of, 222
measurement, focus of, 208, 211–212
measurement strategy, application of, 211–212, 214–215, 215 (table), 222–223
measurement strategy, definition of, 210
methods audit and, 222–223
methods/tools/metrics, selection of, 212, 215 (table)
metrics/performance indicators and, 211, 212, 215 (table), 221 (table)
objectives measurement and, 209, 210 (table), 212, 220 (table)
outcomes measurement and, 208, 209–210, 210 (table), 212–215, 221 (table)
outputs measurement and, 209, 210 (table), 221 (table)
outtakes measurement and, 209, 210 (table), 221 (table)
SMART criteria and, 209–210, 212
social media plans, development of, 209, 211–212
third-party tools and, 211
traditional measurement tools and, 211
training/education for, 223
See also Analytics; Budgets; Metrics; Strategic planning
Media channels, 8
Medium, 11, 200 (table)
Meerkat, 281
"Meet Graham" campaign, 267–268
Meltwater tool, 99, 217
Mention software, 60
Mentions, 94
Mentorships, 282
MEOjobs newsletter, 201
Messaging platforms, 11
Messenger, 11, 276
Metrics, 91, 92
    advanced metrics, 93, 94, 99, 100 (table), 104–105 (table)
    basic metrics, 99, 100 (table), 104–105 (table)
    behavioral metrics, 93, 99, 100 (table), 104–105 (table)
    budget considerations and, 217–221, 219–221 (tables)
    calculation of, 106
    channel metrics, 99, 100 (table), 104–105 (table)
    click-through rates and, 93
    cost per action and, 217, 218, 219 (table)
    cost per click, 217, 219 (table)
    cost per conversion, 218–219, 219 (table)
    cost per engagement, 219, 219 (table)
    cost per impression, 217, 219 (table)
    customer service metrics, 221 (table)
    Facebook metrics/tools and, 104 (table)
    Instagram metrics/tools and, 104–105 (table)
    LinkedIn metrics/tools and, 105 (table)
    platform-based metrics, 101–102
    selection criteria for, 103
    Snapchat metrics/tools and, 105 (table)
    social media return on investment, 106
    Twitter metrics/tools and, 104 (table)
    vanity metrics, 54, 63, 93–94, 107, 175
    YouTube metrics/tools and, 105 (table)
    See also Analytics; Measurement/evaluation; Social media research; Strategic planning
Micro-influencers, 180, 194
Microblogs, 6, 11, 17, 270
Microsites, 94–95
Misappropriation sin, 31
Mission/mission statements, 116, 117–118
Mixed reality, 19
Mobil-based platforms, 11
Monitoring process, 96
    audience behaviors/actions, evaluation of, 107
    benefits of, 97–98
    content creation, systematic process of, 101, 141
    current objectives, integration with, 101
    insights, strategic application of, 107
    items for monitoring and, 98, 101
    monitoring ecosystem, guidelines for, 101
    monitoring/listening, bridge between, 102, 103 (table)
    monitoring plan, implementation of, 100–101
    monitoring vs. listening, differences between, 96–97, 96 (table)
    training for, 101
    See also Listening process; Social media research
Monotony sin, 32
Moody, M., 19
MoonPie, 6, 193, 256
Morar, Simona, 266–267
    background information on, 266
    challenges of social media and, 267
    favorite social media accounts and, 267
    professional advice from, 267
    social media, start in, 266
    tweeting practices and, 266–267
Moreno, A., 19
Mosemghvdlishvili, L., 279
Mountain Dew campaign, 179–180
Movember Foundation, 260, 261
Moz content audit template, 189, 190 (table)
Multimedia/video producer role, 78, 82 (table), 83
Munoz, O., 236
Murdock, Mark, 262–263
    background information on, 262
    challenges of social media and, 263
    favorite social media accounts and, 163

mentoring emerging professionals and, 263
positive collegiality and, 263
professional advice from, 263
social media continuing education and, 263
social media, start in, 262–263
Museum of Modern Art, 259
Myers, A., 195

Narcissism sin, 32
National Football League (NFL), 39–40
National Geographic Channel, 97
National Geographic Society, 259
National Public Radio (NPR), 41
Navarro, C., 19
NBC Sports, 113–114
Neill, M. S., 19
Neistat, C., 171, 172
Nerdy Nummies, 50, 53
Niches, 163, 180
Noise, 21, 92
Nonprofit sector, 73, 259
    action steps, development of, 260
    balanced approach to social media and, 261
    best practices/recommendations for, 261–262
    branded hashtags and, 261
    communication plan, specific messages/content
        alignment and, 260
    crowdfunding capability and, 260
    crowdsourcing process and, 260
    focused campaigns and, 262
    funding mechanisms and, 260
    motivational creative content, questions about, 259
    pay-to-play model, shift from, 259
    personalized content, creation of, 260
    social media integration, goals for, 259, 260
    social media teams, establishment of, 262
    story sharing opportunities and, 262
    strategic social media use and, 260, 261
    successful nonprofits and, 259
    See also Social media applications
Nuvi tools, 106
Nuzzel tool, 202

Objectives, 130–131
Oculus community manager role, 75, 75 (table)
Omnichannel approach, 164
Onalytica tool, 173
Online personas, 8, 53, 64, 170–171, 172
Online portfolio, 71
Online reputation, 8
    evaluation tools for, 60–61
    online conversations/interactions and, 43
    reputation, nature/value of, 51
    social media fails and, 36–38
    See also Personal brands; Reputation
        management
Online threats, 36, 37–38
Oppenheim, M., 201
Opponent/critic, 166
Oreo digital legend, 6, 72, 154
Orr, E. S., 172
Orr, R. R., 172

Osana tool, 199
Osteen, J., 237
Outcomes measurement/evaluation, 208, 209–210,
    210 (table), 212
    attitudinal outcomes and, 213, 214, 215 (table),
        219 (table)
    cognitive outcomes and, 212–213, 215 (table),
        219 (table)
    conative outcomes and, 213–214, 215 (table),
        219 (table)
    social media measurement strategy and, 215
    See also Measurement/evaluation
Ow.ly tool, 215 (table)
Owned media (O), 8, 8 (figure), 120, 135, 189, 198, 221
    (table)
Owyang, J., 123

Paid media (P), 8, 8 (figure), 120, 135, 189, 197,
    221 (table), 277
Pansino, R., 50, 53
Parker, S., 31, 33
Pay-to-play model, 15, 92, 197, 216, 259, 277
Peer-to-peer approach, 4
Pepsi commercial, 107
Periscope, 11, 94–95, 281
Personal brand associations, 55–56
Personal brands, 17, 22
    angle, determination/development of, 56–57
    audience strategy for, 56
    audits, personal identity/goals and, 54–55, 282
    augmented reality and, 280
    benefits/challenges for, 53–54
    brand associations, determination of, 55–56
    brand establishment, process of, 49–50
    branding mishaps and, 36–37
    branding process and, 51
    communities, interactions with, 52, 57
    communities, opinions of, 50
    components of, 51–53
    consistent brand image/voice and, 55, 63
    consistent personality attributes and, 52
    content strategy for, 56
    continuous improvement/expansion of, 57
    continuous learning mindset and, 61–62
    customer service specialists and, 61
    customized strategy for, 56
    data analytics, strategic application of, 60–61
    development/establishment of, 54–57
    digital personal identity and, 50, 54
    digital presence, necessity of, 50–51
    expertise and, 52
    fakery, identification of, 52, 54, 62–63
    finsta, establishment of, 50
    follower rate inflation and, 52, 54, 63
    imitation, avoidance of, 52–53
    networking/interaction potential and, 51, 54
    online/offline personas, alignment of, 63
    online reputation evaluation tools and, 60–61
    personal brand audits and, 55
    personal community, investment in, 57
    personal influence, factors in, 50
    privacy, lack of, 50

professional brand, integration with, 56
quality vs. quantity argument and, 52, 63
recognition/appreciation, development of, 54
reputation management and, 49
reputation, nature/value of, 51
research skill and, 57–58
search engine optimization and, 60
skill set, brand development and, 57–63
social media jobs, preparation/application for, 62
spamming and, 53
strategic approach to, 56, 60–61, 63
trust/credibility, establishment of, 54
types of, 53, 53 (table)
unique qualities, focus on, 56, 57
vanity metrics and, 54
voice, role of, 49, 51, 55
writing/visual content creation skill and, 58–60
See also Industry qualifications/roles; Online reputation; Professional brands; Reputation management; Social media policies
Personality, 51
consistent personality attributes and, 52
influencers, personality characteristics of, 172
personality-focused writing style and, 153
platform selection criteria and, 17
reputation and, 51–52
social media content and, 144
Personality Insights by IBM Watson tool, 60
Personas, 8, 53, 64, 93, 147, 166, 170–171, 172
PESO (paid/earned/shared/owned) media model, 8, 8 (figure), 120, 135, 189, 197–199, 221 (table)
Pesta, A., 38
Peterson, T., 94
Pew Research Center, 240
Pharrell's "Happy" video, 21
Piktochart tool, 200 (table)
Pinterest:
advertising management and, 218 (table)
copyright infringement and, 39
terms of service and, 356
use data for, 15, 16 (figure)
Planned behavior theory, 20
Platforms:
analytics, audience/content data and, 18
audience factors and, 16, 17–18, 18 (table)
blogs and, 6, 11
brandsphere and, 8, 8 (figure)
business networking and, 11
content/marketing, creation of, 7–8, 17
creative innovation and, 17, 21–22
cross-platform presentations and, 17, 22
crowdsourcing sites and, 11
current key platforms and, 12, 12–14 (tables)
first-impression management tools and, 7
live streaming and, 11
media channels and, 8
messaging platforms and, 11
microblogs and, 6, 11, 17
ownership of social media and, 12, 14
personal business voice, representation of, 17
platform decision action steps and, 18, 18 (table)
platform performance evaluation and, 18, 18 (table)
platform use inventory and, 18, 18 (table)
purpose of, 16
relationship development and, 16–17
repurposed/reformatted content and, 17
selection criteria for, 15–18, 16 (figure), 18 (table)
social media ecosystem and, 7–8
social media monitoring platforms and, 11
storytelling approach and, 17, 21–22
strategic use of, 15–19
terms of service agreements and, 35–36, 35 (table)
thought leadership and, 15, 17
trustworthiness factor and, 16
uniformity sin and, 33
visual/snackable forms of, 12
web-/mobile-based platforms and, 9, 11
wikis and, 11
See also Ethics issues; Legal fundamentals; Social media
Plutagraph tool, 200 (table)
Policies. *See* Ethics issues; Legal fundamentals; Social media policies
Portaro-Kueber, Bella, 258–259
background information on, 258
challenges of social media and, 258
favorite social media account and, 258
mentoring emerging professionals and, 258–259
nonprofits, voice of, 258
professional advice from, 259
smartphone communications and, 258
social media, start in, 258
Prentice, S., 170
Prezi tool, 200 (table)
Primary audiences, 131, 165 (figure), 166
Primary message, 132
Privacy concerns, 38–39, 50
Professional brands:
continuous learning mindset and, 61–62
customer service specialists and, 61
data analytics, strategic application of, 60–61
online reputation evaluation tools and, 60–61
personal brand, integration with, 56
reputation management and, 49
research skill and, 57–58
search engine optimization and, 60
skill set, brand development and, 57–63
writing/visual content creation skill and, 58–60
See also Industry qualifications/roles; Personal brands; Social media policies
Professional roles. *See* Industry qualifications/roles
Promoted media, 8, 8 (figure)
Prosumer activity, 39
Psychographics, 132, 164, 165 (table)
Psychological empowerment theory, 20
Public relations practice:
codes of ethics and, 31
skill set for, 19
social media and, 5, 28
Public Relations Society of America (PRSA), 209
Public shaming, 37, 38
Pure Performance, 3

QQ software service, 276
Qualifications. *See* Industry qualifications/roles
Quality vs. quantity argument, 23, 32, 52, 63, 175

Radian6 tools, 106
Rating forums, 6, 264
Refugee Nation flag, 268
Repost tool, 169 (table)
Reputation dissonance, 39
Reputation management, 11, 49
    Google capability and, 50
    healthcare industry and, 264
    platform purpose/trustworthiness and, 16
    reputation, nature/value of, 51
    social media fails and, 36–38
    values, offline/online consistency in, 43
    See also Online reputation
Reputation.com, 264
Request for proposal (RFP), 106
Research, 19–20, 57–58
    actionable marketing strategies and, 90
    budget for, 216–217
    definition of, 91, 113
    See also Analytics; Social media research
Return on Relationship (RoR), 19, 52
Rio Summer Olympics of 2016, 40
"The Rock", 49, 53, 107
Rock, D., 22, 52
Roles, *See* Industry qualifications/roles
Ronson, J., 37
Ross, C., 172
Royal Caribbean "Intern-ship" contest, 22
Rubin, T., 19, 52, 53
Rumors, 36

Sabre system, 206
Sacco. *See* Justine Sacco case study
Salary statistics, 84–86, 84–86 (figures)
Salesforce tool, 211
Scoble, R., 53
Scoop.it tool, 202
Scripts tool, 200 (table)
Search engine optimization (SEO), 60, 189
Secondary audiences, 131, 165 (figure), 166
Secondary message, 132
Selective persona, 53
Self-employment, 72, 83–84
Sentiment metrics, 99, 100 (table)
Sephora, 152–153
Shaming. *See* Public shaming
Shanks, C., 38
Shared media (S), 8, 8 (figure), 120, 135, 189, 198, 221
    (table)
Silver, N., 90
Simmering, M. G., 172
Simply Measured tool, 211, 215 (table)
Singh, L., 231
Siri, 277
Sisic, M., 172
Slick Write tool, 156
SlideShare tool, 199, 200 (table)

SMART (specific/measurable/achievable/realistic/
    time-specific) criteria, 103, 131, 209–210, 220
    (budget)
Snackable content forms, 12, 21
Snap Inc., 6
Snapchat, 4, 6, 9, 11, 12
    advertising management and, 218 (table)
    basic facts about, 12 (table)
    Bitmoji app and, 280
    community creation/sustainability and, 169 (table)
    endorsement/advertising activities and, 40, 41
    innovation and, 17
    major milestones for, 14 (table)
    metrics/tools, types of, 105 (table)
    ownership rights and, 40
    pay-to-play model and, 197
    personal business voice and, 17
    terms of service and, 35
    use data for, 15, 16 (figure)
    visual/snackable content form and, 12
    writing guide for, 145 (table)
Social care practices, 254
    best practices/recommendations for, 256–257
    brands, benefits to, 255, 256
    chat bots, use of, 256
    constant engagement, negative aspects of, 257
    customer loyalty, reduced customer effort and, 255
    customer service, investment in, 255, 257
    emotional responses, avoidance of, 257
    empathy, cultivation of, 257
    General Motors social care department and,
        254–255
    marketing department duties and, 254
    marketing power of, 255
    outstanding brands for, 256
    personalized messaging and, 257
    presence on social media and, 257
    proactive customer relations, culture of, 256
    responses/inquiries, templates for, 257
    responsive customer service experiences and,
        255, 256
    social care program, set-up for, 255
    Twitter customer service and, 256
    See also Social media applications
Social media, 5
    amplification rate and, 7
    applications/opportunities of, 10
    audience factors and, 16, 17–18, 18 (table), 21–22, 23
    authentic messaging and, 23
    avatars and, 8
    brand personalities and, 6
    branded content/branded journalism and, 9
    brandsphere and, 8, 8 (figure)
    consumer-to-consumer conversations and, 7
    content/conversation, creation of, 7–8, 10, 15
    creative innovation and, 17, 21–22
    current state of, 11–12, 12–14 (tables)
    definition/classification of, 6–10
    ecosystem of, 7–8
    engaging content and, 23
    evolving nature of, 10, 11–15, 19

fear of missing out and, 6, 23
first-impression management and, 7, 23
global society, presence in, 6
hashtags and, 11
individual empowerment and, 7
informed decision making and, 21
learning opportunities and, 61–62
media channels and, 8
message communication function of, 6–7, 8
monitoring platforms and, 11
network of communities and, 7, 8
online reputation and, 8
owned vs. shared media and, 15
ownership of, 12, 14, 23
participatory use of, 7, 10, 17, 21, 23
pay-to-play model and, 15
personal branding purposes and, 6, 17
platform selection criteria and, 15–18, 16 (figure),
    18 (table)
platforms, social media ecosystem and, 7–8, 11
power of, 6
practice/creative execution of, 20–21
professional media work, tasks/skills/expectations
    and, 19, 23
public nature of, 9, 11
quality vs. quantity argument and, 23, 32, 52, 63
relationship building function of, 7, 8, 9, 16–17
research/theoretical frameworks of, 19–20
return on relationship and, 19
science/artful practice, convergence of, 20, 22–23
scientific exploration of, 19–20
shared content, online networks and, 7, 8, 9
social networking sites and, 11
storytelling approach and, 17, 21–22
strategic use of, 7, 15–19, 23
trending events/issues, brand insertion into, 6
user-generated content and, 7, 9
virality and, 9
visualization of, 8, 8 (figure)
web-/mobile-based applications and, 9
See also Current social media environment; Ethics
    issues; Industry qualifications/roles; Legal
    fundamentals; Measurement/evaluation;
    Platforms; Social media applications; Social
    media community manager; Social media
    policies; Social media return on investment
    (ROI); Strategic planning; Strategic writing
Social media applications, 227–228, 253
crisis communication and, 233, 237 (figure), 238,
    248 (table)
entertainment industry and, 229–231, 248 (table)
healthcare industry and, 263–266
international campaigns and, 267–271
journalism industry and, 240–242, 249 (table)
nonprofit sector and, 259–262
social care practices and, 254–257
sports industry and, 243–247, 248 (table)
Social media communication audit, 122
action steps/future directions and, 123
client internal/external social media and, 122–123
competitor analysis and, 127

components of, 123–127, 124–126 (tables)
external social media analysis and, 124–125,
    125–126 (tables), 127
internal social media analysis and, 123–124, 124
    (table), 127
organizational structures and, 123–124
See also Strategic planning
Social media community manager role, 74–75, 74–75
    (tables)
Social media coordinator role, 75–77, 76 (table)
Social Media Examiner, 114, 199
Social media policies, 41
audience awareness of, 41–42
authenticity, impact of, 43
employee awareness of, 41
employee conduct/personal identity code and, 42
going rogue/employee misbehavior and, 41, 42
legal/ethical issues, guidelines for, 42
negative/hateful responses to content and, 42–43
news reporting accuracy and, 41
purpose of, introduction to, 42
rationale for, 42
responsibility for content and, 42
revision of, 42
tone/errors/threats, employee action steps and, 42
values, offline/online consistency in, 43
See also Ethics issues; Legal fundamentals; Social
    media; Social media research
Social media research, 91
advanced metrics and, 93, 94, 99, 100 (table),
    104–105 (table)
advocates metric and, 99, 100 (table)
amplification rate and, 99
analytic results, research insights and, 91, 92,
    103, 106
audience personas, marketing campaigns and, 93, 95
audience segmentation and, 93
basic metrics and, 99, 100 (table), 104–105 (table)
behavioral/attitudinal data and, 94, 99, 107
behavioral metrics and, 93, 99, 100 (table),
    104–105 (table)
best practices/guidelines for, 106–107
brand awareness, insight into, 94–95
brand failure, analysis of, 95–96
brand financial standing/reputation and, 95–96
campaign objectives, sponsored messages and, 92
channel metrics and, 99, 100 (table), 104–105
    (table)
content creation, systematic process of, 101
content/message strategies, waves in
    communication and, 92
continuous updating process and, 91
conversion rate and, 99
fake accounts, identification of, 107
first impressions and, 91
followers' actions, social media content/presence
    and, 93, 94, 95, 107
followers, identification of, 94
future content, generation of, 95
humanized brands and, 95
influencer impact and, 99

key performance indicators and, 96, 101, 106
marketing/public relations communication and, 95
metrics, business decisions and, 91, 92, 103
metrics, calculation of, 106
metrics, types of, 99–100, 100 (table), 101–102, 103, 104–105 (table)
microsites, creation of, 94–95
monitoring/listening, benefits of, 98
monitoring/listening, bridge between, 102, 103 (table)
monitoring/listening ecosystem, guidelines for, 101
monitoring/listening, items for, 98, 100, 101
monitoring/listening plans, implementation of, 100–101
monitoring vs. listening, differences between, 96–97, 96 (table)
pay-to-play model, data-driven nature of, 92–93
platform-based metrics and, 101–102
platforms/third-party tools, evaluation of, 102
rationale for, 95–96
social media return on investment and, 106
specialized departments for, 95
strategic communication and, 91–95
strategy, monitoring/listening bridge and, 102, 103 (table)
success indicators and, 99, 103–106, 104–105 (table)
third-party data, checks/balance approach and, 95
trend identification and, 95, 96, 97, 101
vanity metrics and, 93–94, 107
See also Analytics; Measurement/evaluation; Metrics; Strategic planning
Social media return on investment (ROI), 106
Social media strategist role, 77, 78–81 (tables)
Social Mention tool, 104 (table)
Social networking site (SNS), 11
Social video, 277
Socialbakers tool, 215 (table)
SocialRank tool, 211
Solis, B., 8, 50, 170
SoundCloud tool, 199, 200 (table)
Southwest Airlines, 256
Spam, 32, 33, 53, 107, 200
Specialists, 61, 85, 85 (figure)
Spectacles bot, 6
Sports industry, 29, 73, 90, 243
athletes, personal branding and, 243, 244
best practices/recommendations for, 246
college athletics, real-time rankings and, 245
content creation for, 248 (table)
Hurricane Harvey fund raising case and, 244–245
ideas, generation of, 246
individual personality, interjection of, 244
innovation/creative storytelling and, 245
on-/offline networking and, 246
pressure to post and, 245
professionals, listing of, 246–247
"right moment" access, future opportunities and, 244
social media, integration with, 243
social media skills/training, investment in, 246

society, impacts on, 243, 244
sponsorship opportunities and, 244
sports communication, transformation of, 243
See also Social media applications
Spredfast social analytics strategist role, 77, 79 (table)
Spredfast tools, 77, 79 (table), 106, 215 (table)
Sprinklr tools, 106
Sprout Social tool, 61, 104 (table), 106, 134 (figure), 135, 168 (table), 196, 201, 259
St. Jude Children's Research Hospital, 264
Starbucks strategy analyst role, 77, 80–81 (table)
Stelzner, M., 282
Storytelling approach, 17, 21–22, 33, 69, 192, 280
Strategic mindset, 116, 286
Strategic planning, 113–114
audience, communication with, 131–132
background information and, 116
best practices/recommendations for, 135
brand voice/story/reputation and, 116, 119, 122 (figure)
budget planning/documentation and, 133
calendar, components of, 134 (table), 135
campaign initiatives, categories of, 120, 121 (figure)
client organization, focus on, 119–122, 121–122 (figures)
community factors and, 118, 122(figure)
core problem/opportunity and, 128
demographics and, 131–132
economic factors and, 118
environmental scan analysis and, 118–119
evaluation phase and, 133
goals/goal statement and, 130
human-to-human communication and, 132
influencers, evaluation of, 122
influencers, role of, 124–125
key performance indicators and, 133
legal factors and, 118
managerial strategy and, 12, 121–122 (figures)
media channels, analysis of, 120
mission/mission statement and, 116, 117–118
objectives, clarity in, 130–131
organizational history and, 119
organizational structure/key players and, 119
past social media promotions/campaigns and, 120, 121 (figure), 122
PESO media model and, 8, 8 (figure), 120, 135
political factors and, 118
primary audiences and, 131
primary messages and, 132
products/services, offerings of, 119–120
psychographics and, 132
secondary audiences and, 131
secondary messages and, 132
situational analysis and, 128
SMART criteria and, 131
social/consumer factors and, 119
social media communication audit and, 122–127, 124–126 (tables)
strategic mindset and, 116

strategic plan, components of, 115–116
strategic plan, definition/description of, 114–115
strategy/tactics and, 132–133
SWOT analysis and, 128–130, 129 (figure)
technical execution and, 120, 121–122 (figures)
technology factors and, 118–119
thought leadership community and, 119–120,
  121–122 (figures)
vision/vision statement and, 116–117, 117
  (table), 118
written content tools and, 199, 200 (table)
See also Analytics; Budgets; Content marketing;
  Measurement/evaluation; Metrics; Social
  media applications; Social media research
Strategic writing, 139
  audience-focused content/writing style and,
    150–151, 157, 158
  audience interest in content and, 147
  audience/persona summary and, 147
  authenticity and, 143–144, 157
  best practices/recommendations for, 156–158
  brand voice, key defining questions about, 144
  brand voice vs. tone and, 143–144
  branding, art of, 147–148, 148 (table)
  brevity/directness and, 157, 158
  common mistakes and, 154–155
  community and, 141
  connections, formation of, 141–142
  consistency and, 158
  content and, 140–141
  content creation, suggestions for, 145, 146 (table)
  content creations vs. curation and, 142–143
  content strategies/executions, writing guide for,
    144, 145 (table)
  conversation and, 141–142
  conversational writing style and, 151–152
  creativity in conversations and, 141–142
  culture and, 141
  educational writing style and, 152–153
  effective writing, six Cs of, 140
  embracing vs. hard-sell messaging and, 157
  first impressions, importance of, 154
  inspirational writing style and, 151
  message creation steps, evaluation of, 145
  personal/brand voices, balance between, 158
  personality approach and, 150
  personality-focused writing style and, 153
  platform-based content/writing style and, 158
  platforms, selection of, 141
  product-/brand-focused writing style
    and, 150
  professional writing style and, 148–149
  relevant messages, creation of, 140, 141, 150
  skill set/tasks in, 140–141
  snarky/spunky writing style and, 149–150
  style guide, availability of, 145, 147
  styles of writing and, 148
  team brand voice audit and, 145
  witty writing style and, 152
  writer interest in content and, 147
  writing tools for, 156

Strategy, 56, 63, 132, 187, 193
Strub, Chris, 47–48
  background information on, 47
  brands, public perceptions of, 48
  challenges of social media and, 48
  human networks, power of, 48
  live streaming, authentic presence and, 48
  professional advice from, 48
  social media, start in, 48
SumAll tool, 215 (table)
Surveys, 211
Sweetser, K. D., 6
Swift, T., 230
SWOT (strengths/weaknesses/opportunities/threats)
    analysis, 72, 98, 101, 128
  opportunities and, 129, 129 (figure)
  strategic implications and, 130
  strengths and, 128, 129 (figure)
  threats and, 129 (figure), 130
  weaknesses and, 129, 129 (figure)
  See also Strategic planning
Sysomos tool, 104 (table), 215 (table), 237 (figure)

Taco Bell, 152
Tactics, 132–133, 187, 193, 245
Tagboard tool, 104 (table), 168 (table)
Talkwalker software, 60, 106, 173, 194
Tasty videos, 21
TechCrunch, 120
TED Talks, 259
Tench, R., 19
Terms of Service (TOS) agreements, 35–36, 35
    (table), 40
Thought leadership, 15, 17, 119–120, 194 (table)
Threats, 36, 37–38, 42
360-degree immersive experiences, 19
Thuzio, 229
TOMS Virtual Giving Trip campaign, 280
Tone, 42, 50, 55, 97, 116, 118, 119, 143–144, 167
Traackr tool, 173
Trello tool, 156, 199
Trend identification, 58, 61, 95, 96, 97, 191, 277
  advocacy marketing and, 277
  augmented reality and, 279–280
  "best guess" operations and, 278
  brand reputation/community, protections for, 277
  cohort differences, technology use and, 281
  emerging platforms, larger powerful brand
    dominance and, 281
  ephemeral content, social video and, 277
  evolving social media environment and, 281
  influencer marketing and, 277
  longevity issues and, 280–281
  new tools/technology platforms, evaluation/
    applications of, 278–279, 281
  ongoing education/training, investment in, 281
  platform vulnerability and, 277
  relevant/engaged professionals, practices of,
    281–282
  virtual digital technology deserts and, 281
  virtual reality and, 280

voice search capability and, 277
wearable technologies and, 281
See also Current social media environment
Trendjacking, 31, 234
Trolls, 36, 178–179, 179 (table)
Trust, 30, 54, 171, 188–189
Trustworthiness factor, 16, 188–189, 276
Tweet Binder tool, 168 (table)
TweetAnalyzer tool, 168 (table)
TweetDeck tool, 61
Twitter, 4, 5, 9, 11, 12
    advertising management and, 218 (table)
    application programming interface and, 11
    audience demographics/psychographics and, 164
    basic facts about, 12 (table)
    chat list, engaged/connected professionals
        and, 282
    community creation/sustainability and, 168 (table)
    content community manager role and, 74, 74
        (table)
    content writing ideas and, 146 (table)
    creative partnering and, 21
    customer service questions and, 256
    Deadspin case and, 39–40
    endorsement/advertising activities and, 41
    follower rate inflation and, 52
    innovation, audience input and, 17
    major milestones for, 13–14 (table)
    metrics/tools, types of, 104 (table)
    networking function of, 54
    Oreo digital legend and, 6, 72
    pay-to-play model and, 92
    Periscope acquisition and, 281
    terms of service and, 35
    use data for, 15, 16 (figure)
    verification checks and, 35
    writing guide for, 145 (table)
Twitter Analytics tool, 104 (table), 211, 215 (table)
Twitter Lists, 201

Ulysses tool, 156
Under Armour, 49, 117, 136, 150, 159, 180
UNICEF, 259
Uniformity sin, 33
United Airlines crisis case, 234, 236, 237 (figure)
User-generated content (UGC), 7, 9, 68–69, 94,
    269, 277
User-generated hashtags, 11

Vanity metrics, 54, 63, 93–94, 107, 175
Vaynerchuk, G., 22, 52, 55, 56, 201, 214, 282
Verification checks, 35
Video content tools, 199, 200 (table)
Video producer role, 78, 82 (table), 83
Virality, 9
Virtual advertising, 280
Virtual digital technology desert, 281
Virtual dossier, 71
Virtual Reality Society, 280
Virtual reality (VR), 19, 280
Virtual tours, 280
Vision/vision statements, 116–117, 117 (table), 118

Visual content creation, 58–60, 199, 200 (table)
Vlogging, 22, 171
Voice search capability, 277
Volunteer opportunities, 62
VSCO tool, 168 (table)

Walt Disney Company, 21
Watt, J. J., 244, 245
We Are Social reports, 271
WeChat site, 270, 276
Weibo, 11, 270
Wendy's MoonPie, 6, 193, 256
WhatsApp, 9, 11, 16 (figure), 276
White, Adam, 185–186
    background information on, 185
    challenges of social media and, 186
    creative freedom and, 185–186
    favorite social media accounts and, 186
    openness/knowledge sharing and, 186
    professional advice from, 186
    real-time results and, 185–186
    social media industry, continuing evolution of, 186
    social media, start in, 185
Whole Foods Market campaign, 212–213
WikiLeaks, 259
Wikis, 11
Wilde, Russ, 228–229
    background information on, 228
    challenges of social media and, 229
    favorite social media account and, 229
    influencers, hiring of, 229
    native advertising, content collaborations and, 229
    professional advice from, 229
    smartphone communications and, 229
    social media, start in, 228
    storytelling focus and, 229
Wilson, Jaryd, 137–139
    background information on, 137
    challenges of social media and, 138–139
    emerging media professionals, tips for, 139
    favorite social media accounts and, 138
    game highlights video tool and, 138
    journalism background, usefulness of, 138
    professional advice from, 139
    social media, start in, 137–138
    sports events, real-time coverage of, 138
WordPress, 11, 200 (table)
Wordy service, 156
WriterDuet, 200 (table)
Writing skills, 58–60, 83, 83 (table), 140, 199, 200 (table)
    See also Strategic writing

Yandle, Chris, 27–29
    background information on, 27
    buy-in, encouragement of, 28
    challenges of social media and, 29
    creative/planning process and, 28
    favorite social media accounts and, 28
    professional advice from, 29
    social media, start in, 28
    sports digital space and, 29
Yelp Elite Ambassador (YES!) Program, 177

YouTube, 12, 200 (table)
  advertising management and, 218 (table)
  basic facts about, 12 (table)
  community creation/sustainability and, 169 (table)
  endorsement/advertising activities and, 41
  major milestones for, 14 (table)
  metrics/tools, types of, 105 (table)
  personal brands, establishment of, 49–50
  terms of service and, 35
  use data for, 16 (figure)
YouTube Analytics tool, 105 (table)
YouTube Creator Studio tool, 169 (table)
Yu, Dennis, 175, 205–207, 223
  background information on, 205
  challenge of social media and, 207

dollar-a-day technique and, 206
favorite social media account and, 206
learning vs. earning curve and, 206, 207
mentoring emerging professionals and, 207
Metrics/Analysis/Action process and, 206
professional advice from, 207
social media, start in, 206

Zagat, 94
Zerfass, A., 19
Zhao, S., 172
Zimmerman, S. B., 281
Zoom tool, 200 (table)
Zoomph tools, 106, 173, 194, 215 (table)
Zuckerberg, M., 280